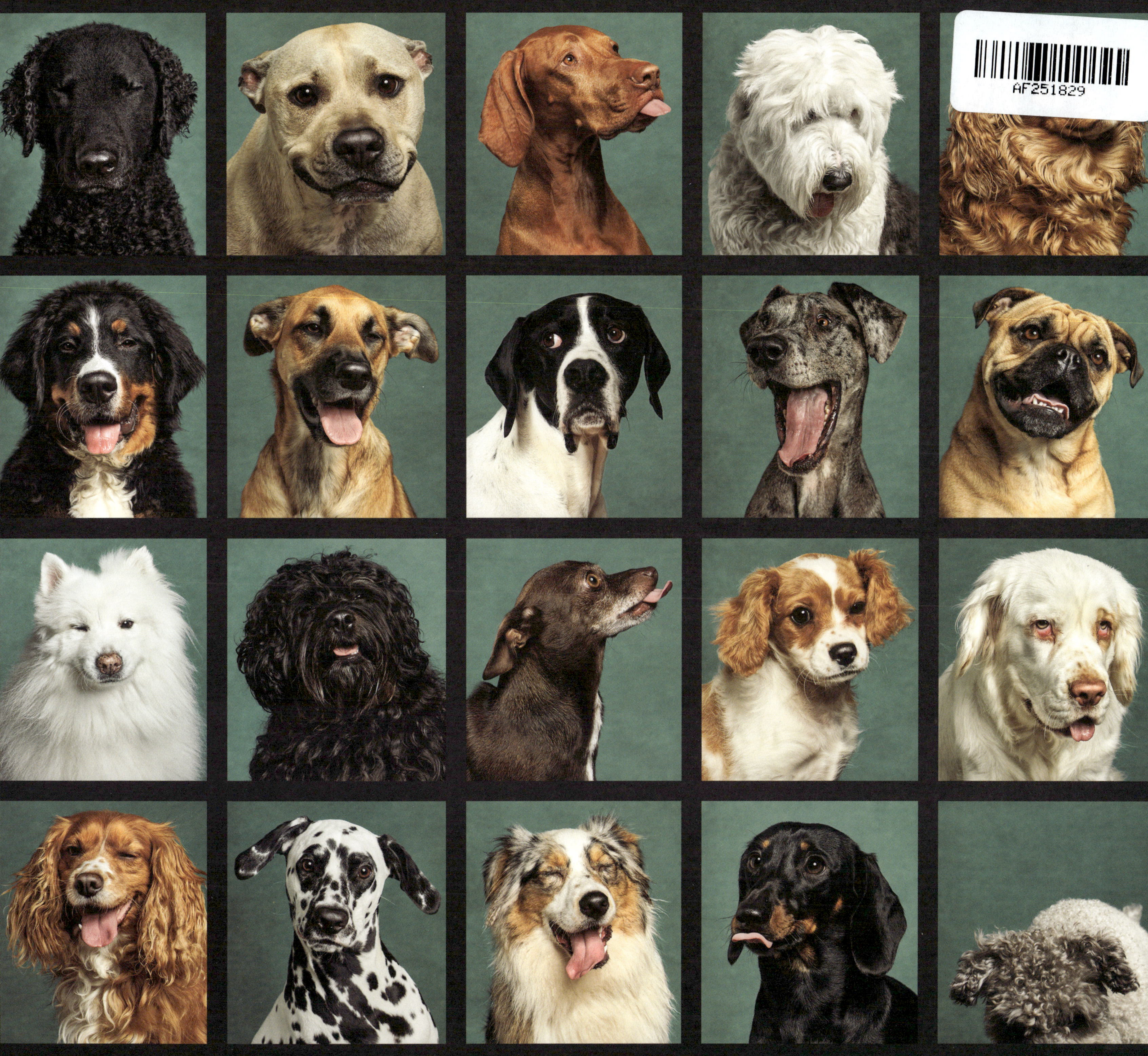
AF251829

This Book Belongs To

....

(Pawprint goes here)

Published by:
Wilkinson Publishing Pty Ltd
ACN 006 042 173
Level 4, 2 Collins Street
Melbourne, Vic 3000
Ph: 03 9654 5446
www.wilkinsonpublishing.com.au

A catalogue record for this
book is available from the
National Library of Australia

A catalogue record for this
book is available from the
National Library of Australia

Planned date of publication: 10-2018
Title: Muttshots
ISBN(s): 9781925642476 : Printed - Paperback

Internal Design by Loz Dalton
Title typography and cover layout design by Darren Henderson
Additional design by Tango Media

Pages 120 and 121 photos by agreement with Luke Pownall

Printed in China

For Harley

2000 – 2017

Always Aloof But Always By My Side.

Good Night Buddy, Sleep Well xx

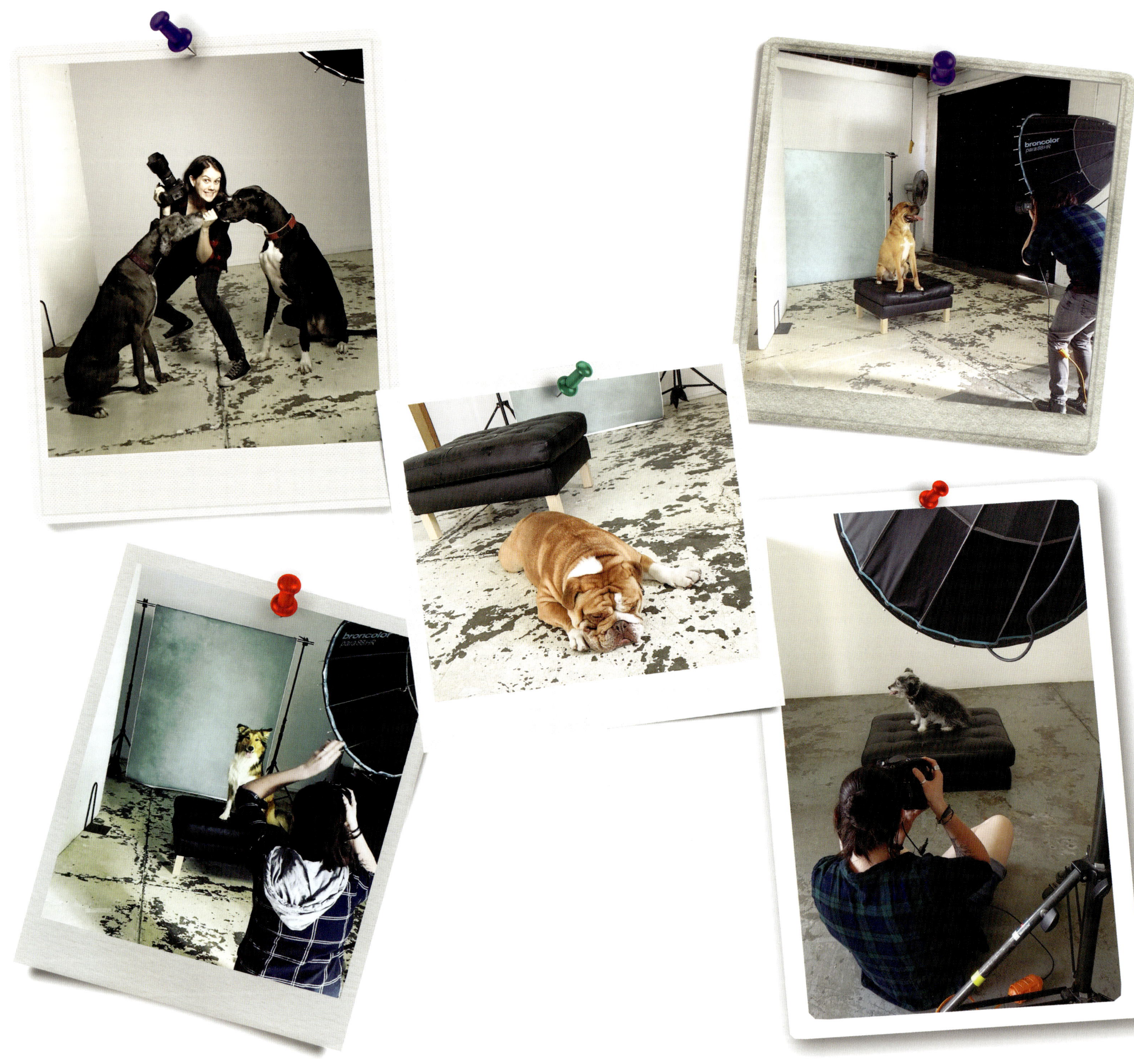

INTRODUCTION

I have loved dogs ever since I can remember — so much so that one of my earliest nicknames from my family was 'Woofer'. Apparently, before I could talk, I would sit up and make 'barking' noises at passers by. This fascination progressed, as did my communication skills, into pestering my parents for a dog every birthday and Christmas until they finally caved and said yes... when I was 16.

My Dad and I were looking for Labrador breeders when we came across a tiny, pot-bellied sleepy Beagle who hadn't yet grown into his ears — needless to say, we didn't get a Labrador.

Muttshots is a culmination of a lifetime passion for canines and the desire to create.

Dogs' faces are all so unique — eyes that can see deep into your soul; noses long and short with textures and colours ranging from the blackest black, to pink and every shade in between; the length of their ears and whether they stand up straight, droop low or perhaps a combination of both; the infinite arrangements of coat markings and hair lengths, curly or straight; wrinkled jowls, wrinkled foreheads, whiskers, teeth, tongues, eyebrows... you get the idea.

My aim was to capture as many of these details, from many breeds, in crisp photographic form. A front, side and back profile against a simple background — to examine these furry faces from different angles. It was a seemingly ordinary concept but as the images themselves were placed side by side *Muttshots* was born.

The evolution of the series became a joyful exploration into the breeds but also uncovered the personalities, quirks and stories that came along with them. The way people lit up when telling these stories highlighted the huge bond we have with our animals and how pure and special their unconditional love for us is — even if they express it in inconvenient (sometimes downright devious) ways — like stealing our food or ripping up our cushions.

Over the course of the series, I have seen dogs who I photographed as young puppies grow into lanky adolescents and teenagers — my newest dog Ludo included. His puppy shots were the first set of images I took in the series and his last shots, taken just under a year later, shows how fast the time goes by.

This truth is heartbreakingly realised through the loss of two of my portrait sitters — Noodles the Great Dane, who passed away in July 2017, and my very first dog Harley, the once tiny pot-bellied Beagle, who did finally grow into his ears, and who had been with me for over half of my life. I am so very grateful to have captured both of these beautiful souls before they left us for the big kennel in the sky.

And so, without further ado, snuggle in with your furamily and enjoy this compilation of canine characters.

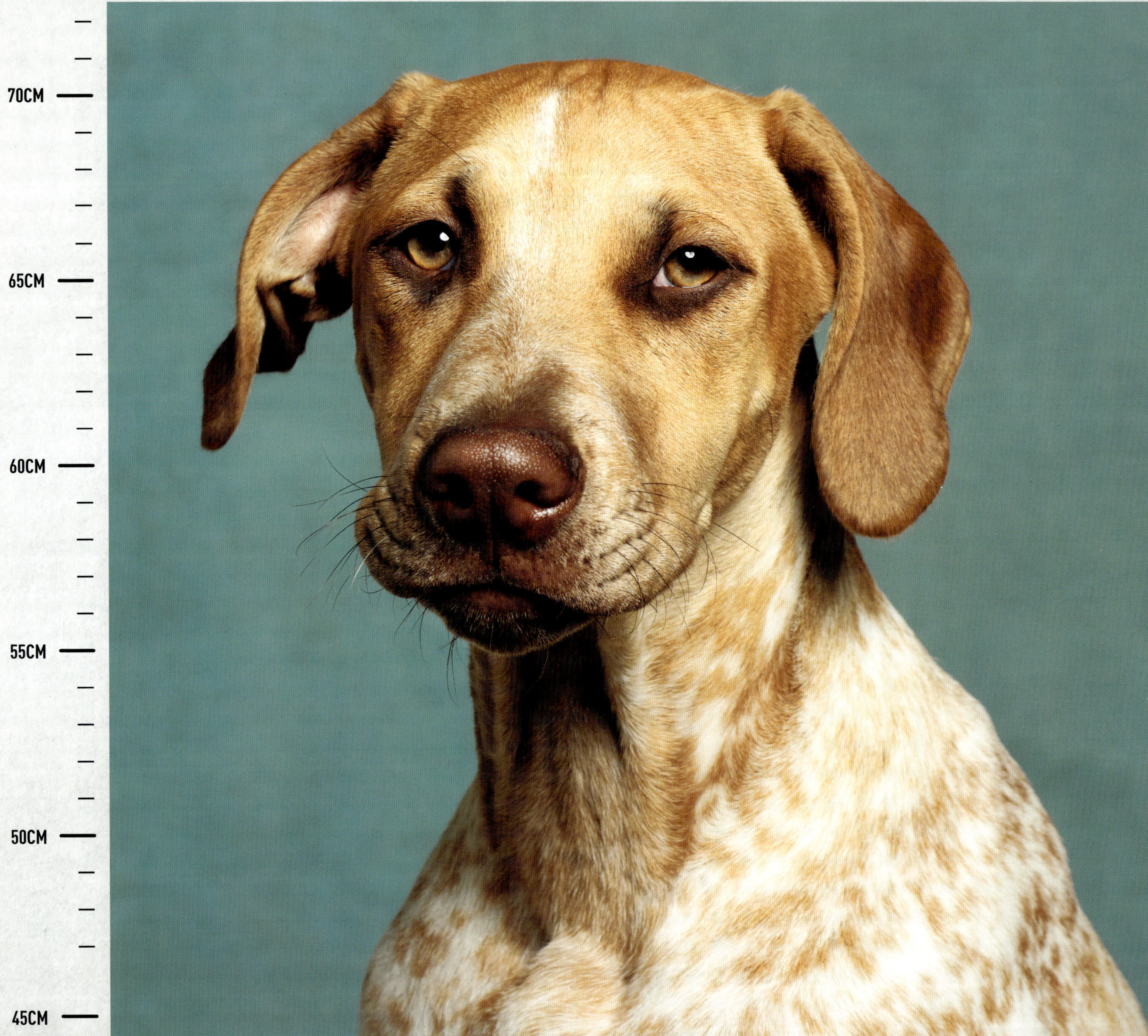
70CM
65CM
60CM
55CM
50CM
45CM

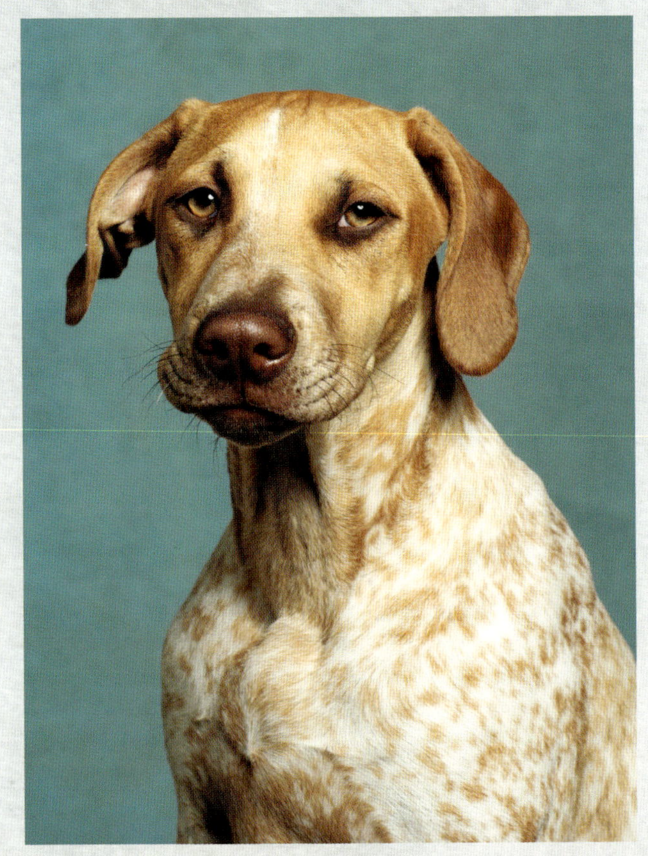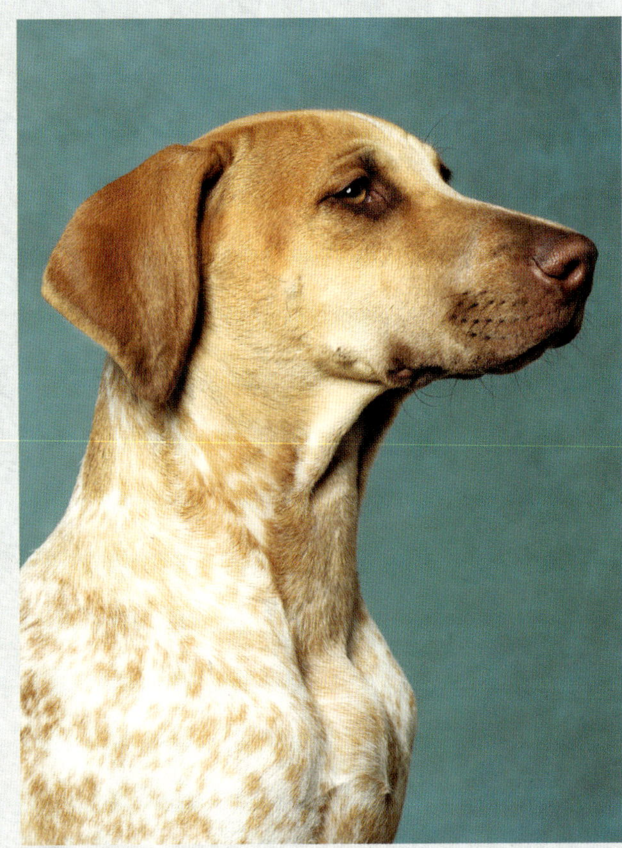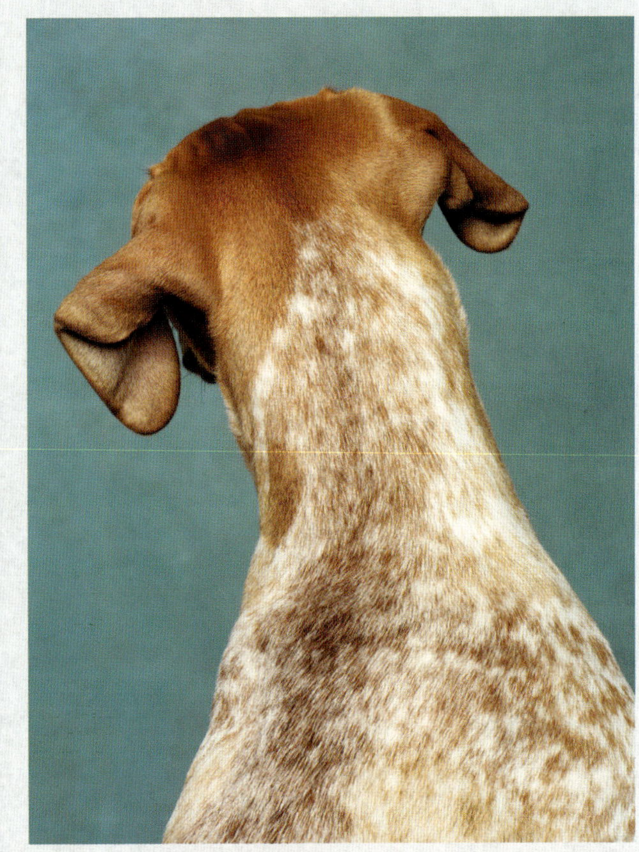

D, LUDO

ALIASES: Ludes / Little Man

BORN: 05/10/2016   **TRADE:** Studio Dog   **BREED:** Pointer Cross

BUILD: Lanky   **EYES:** Copper   **HEIGHT:** 71cm   **HAIR:** Caramel / White

MARKS: Heart Shaped Patch on Rear End

PECULIARITIES: Has extra toe on back legs

M.O: ETC. Stick obsession, occasional sock thief, teasing of fur sister, master of sad eyes, general cheekiness.

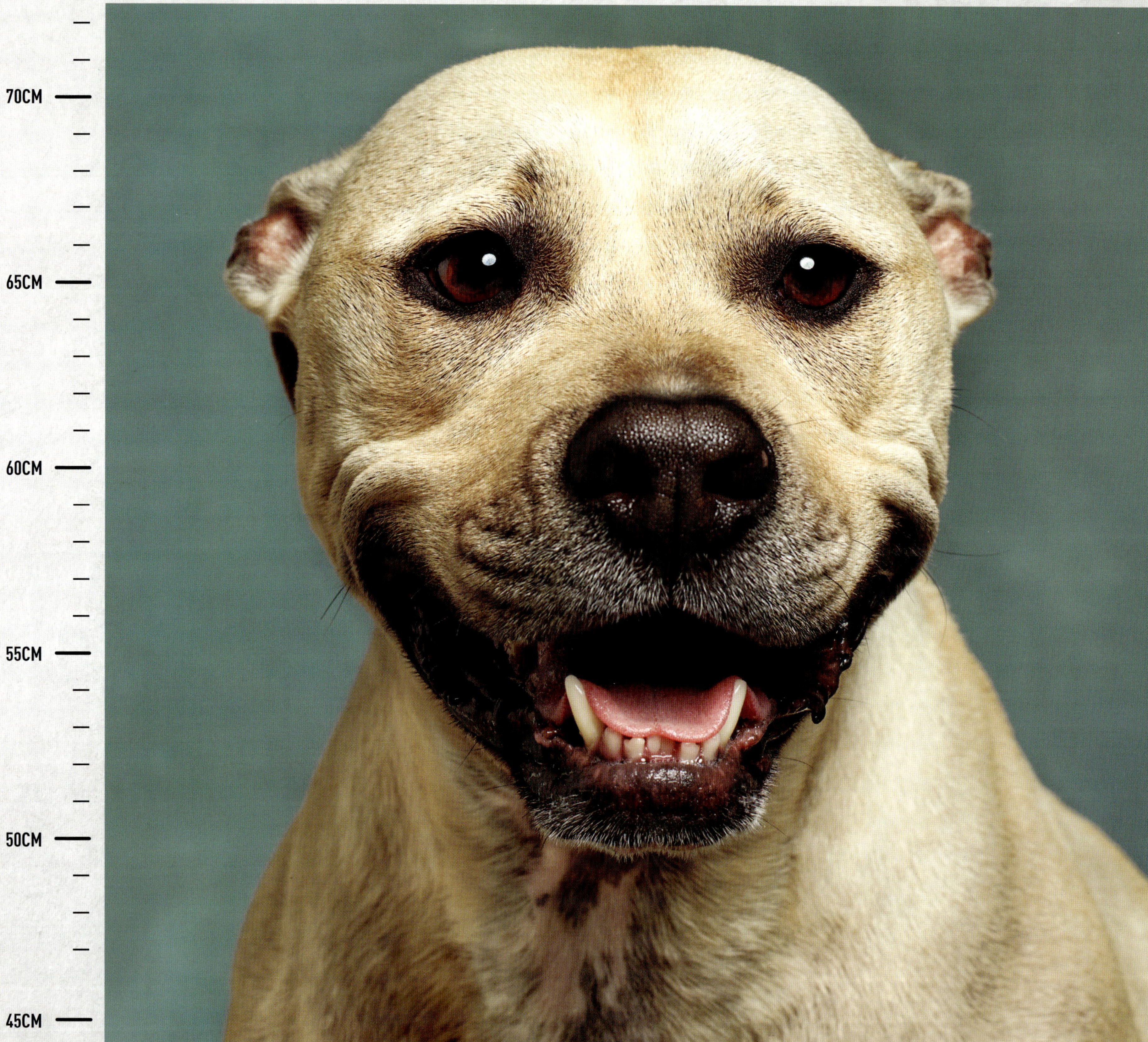
70CM
65CM
60CM
55CM
50CM
45CM

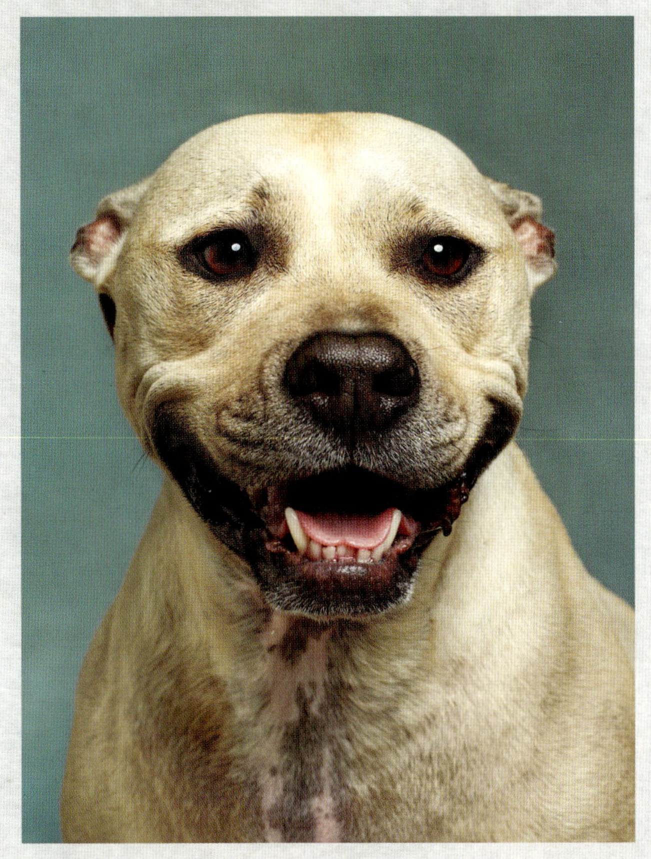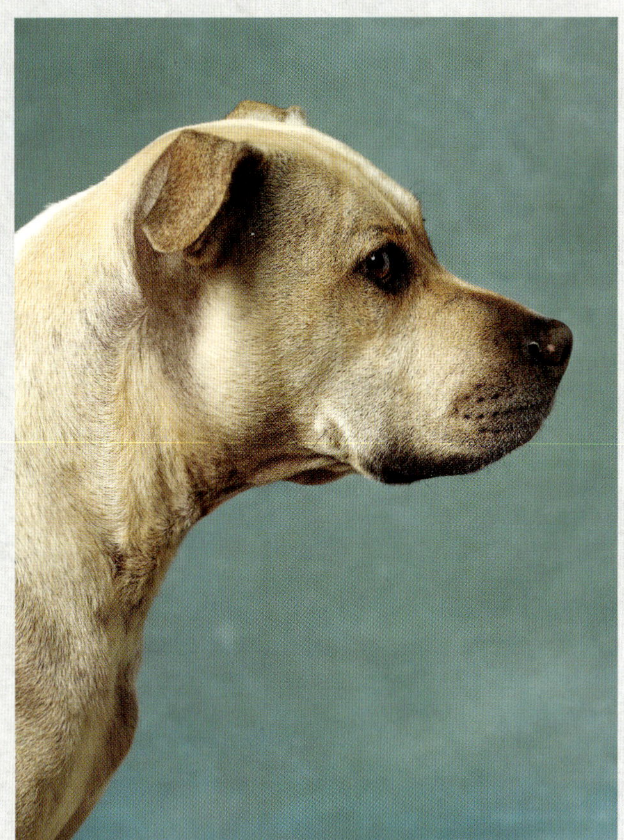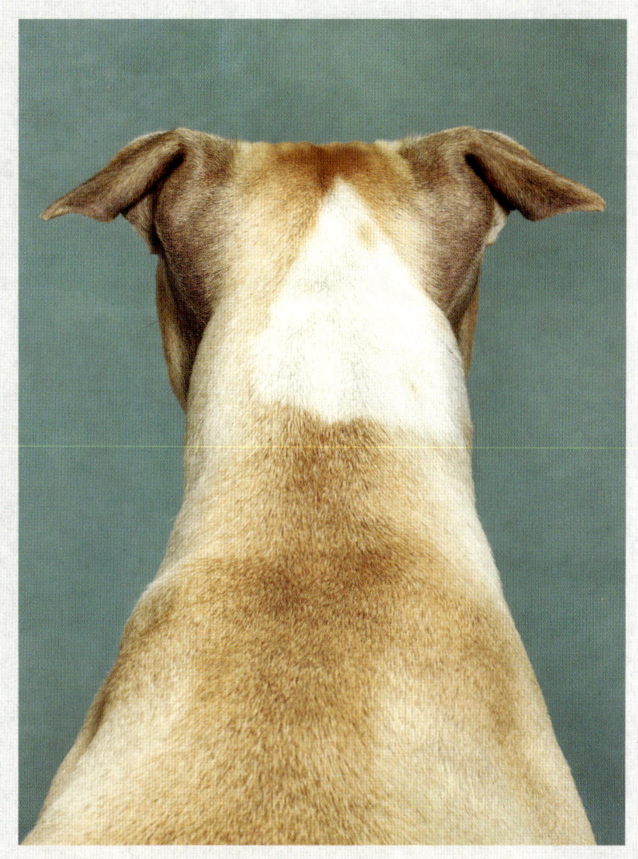

N, Sia

ALIASES:	Wiggle Bum

BORN:	14/02/2010	TRADE:	People Pleaser	BREED:	Staffy Cross

BUILD:	Like a Brick	EYES:	Brown	HEIGHT:	62cm	HAIR:	Blonde / White

MARKS: White triangular patch on back of neck, black spotty belly from sun baking

PECULIARITIES: Can speak human words 'Hello' and 'I Love You'

M.O: ETC. Over excitement at the arrival of any human at any time, has been known to exhibit loud snoring and vocal dreaming.

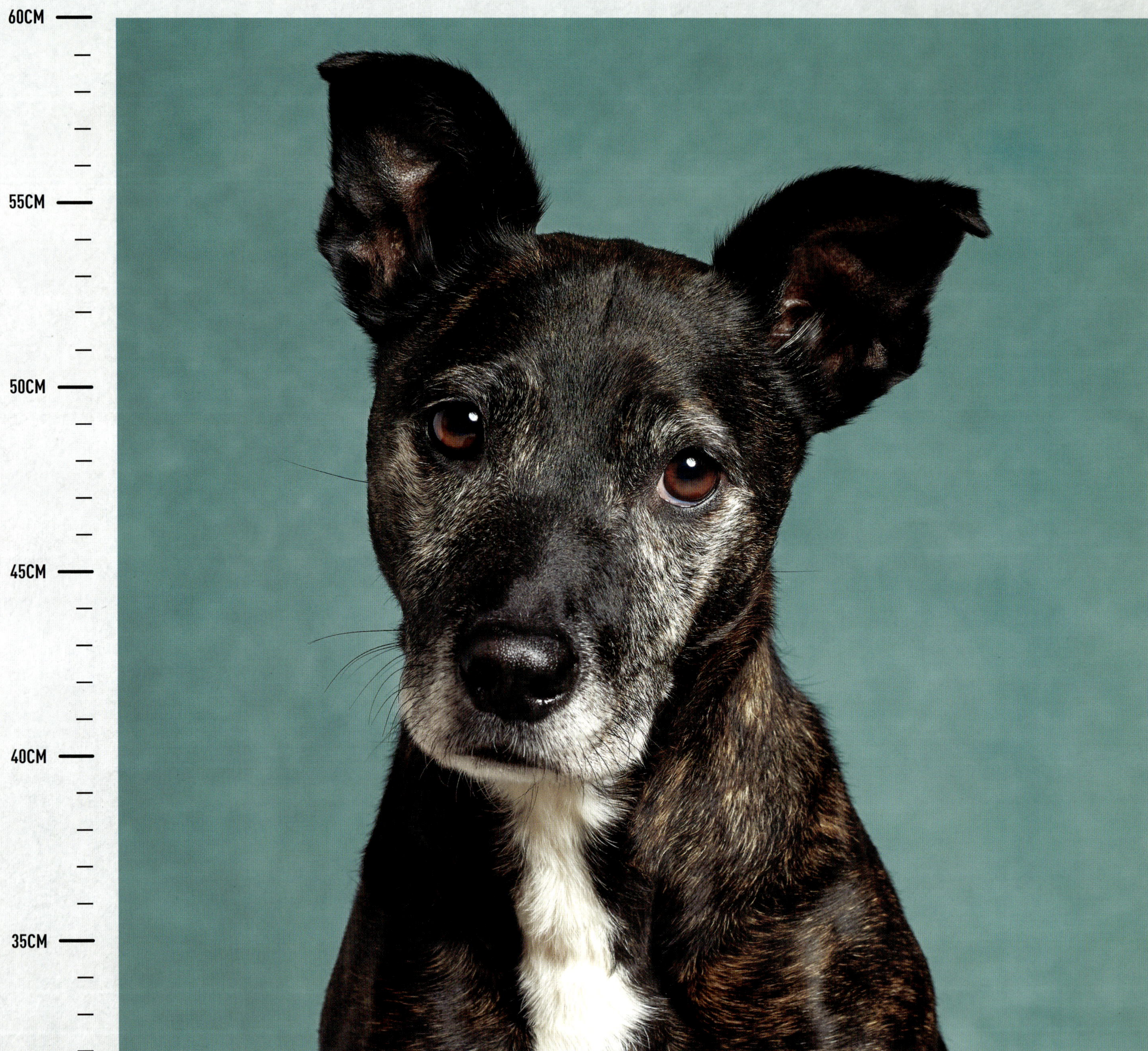

60CM
55CM
50CM
45CM
40CM
35CM

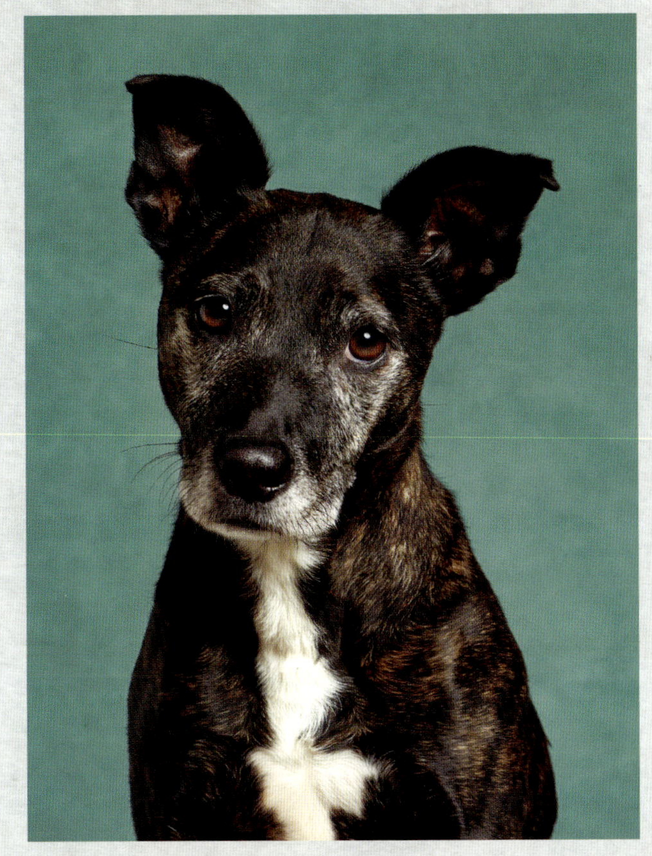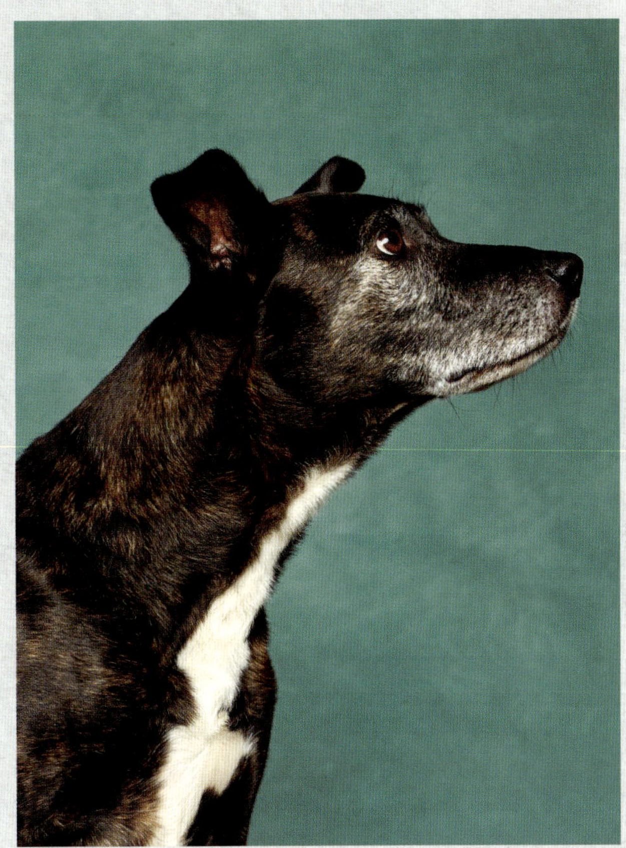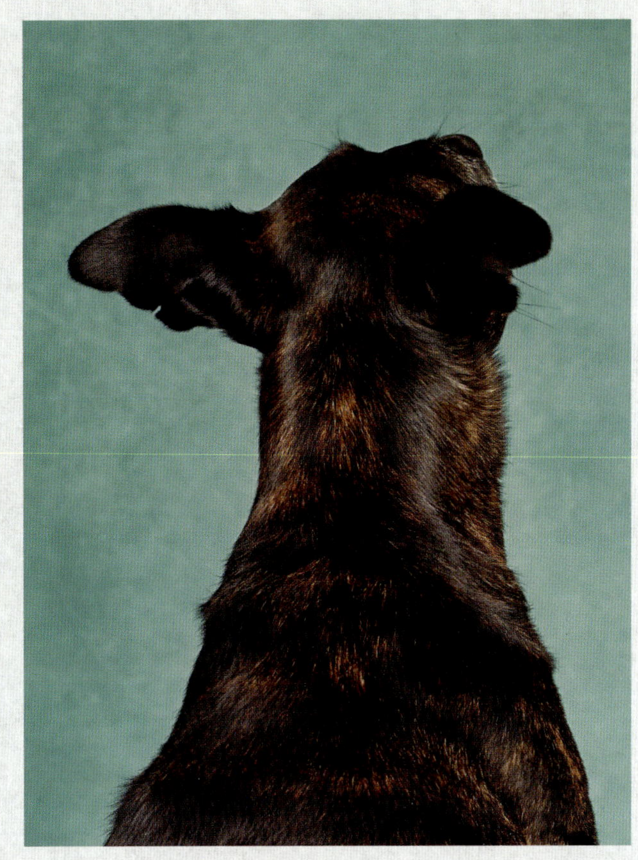

A, Cleo

ALIASES: Cleopatra

BORN: Unknown, 11 yrs approx TRADE: Matriarch BREED: Staffy / Kelpie Cross

BUILD: Compact EYES: Brown HEIGHT: 59cm HAIR: Brindle

MARKS: Greying around the eyes and muzzle

PECULIARITIES: Enjoys being adored unconditionally whilst simultaneously wanting to be left alone

M.O: ETC. Has been known to herd small children in parks, with unconfirmed reports of nipping at ankles to get them in line.

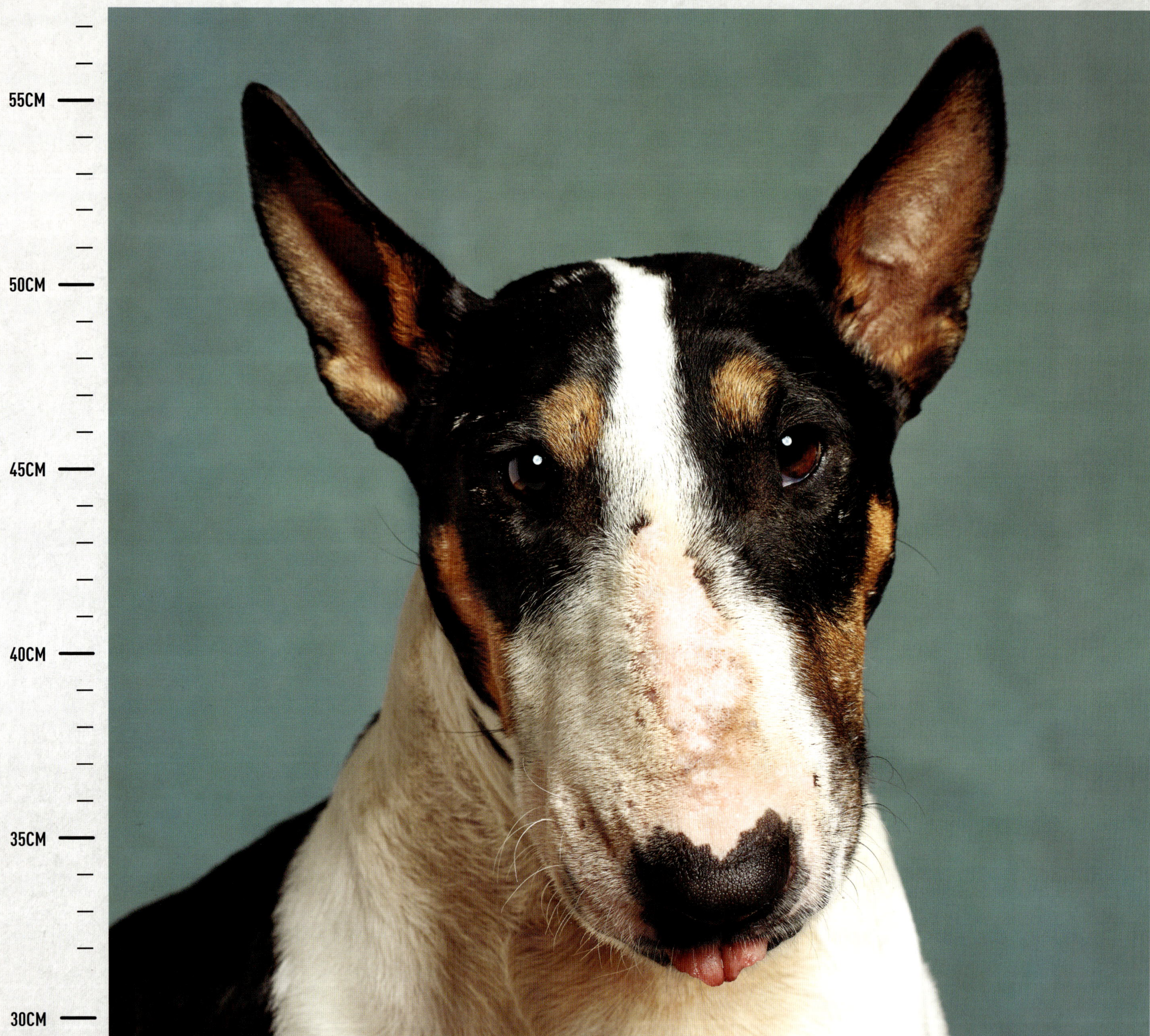

55CM
50CM
45CM
40CM
35CM
30CM

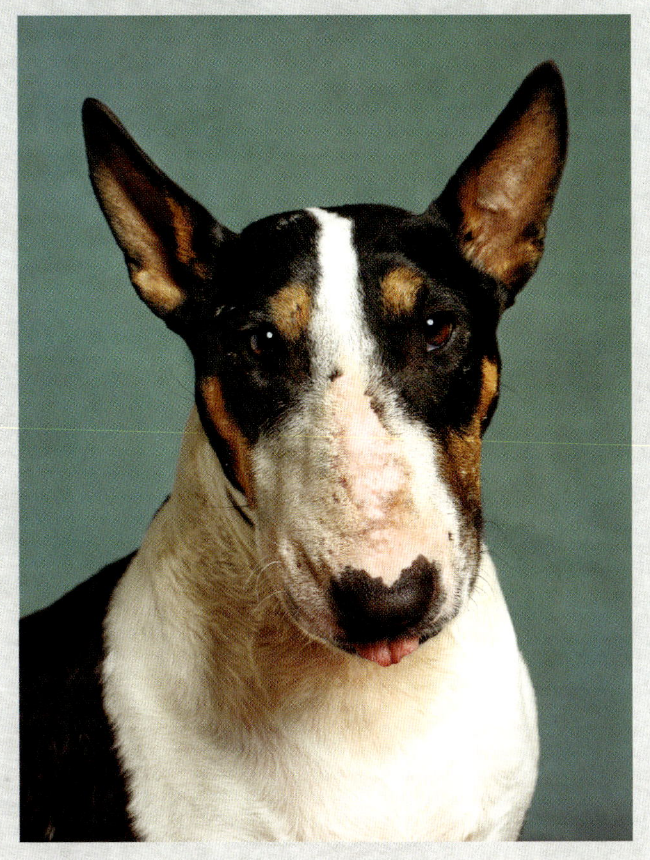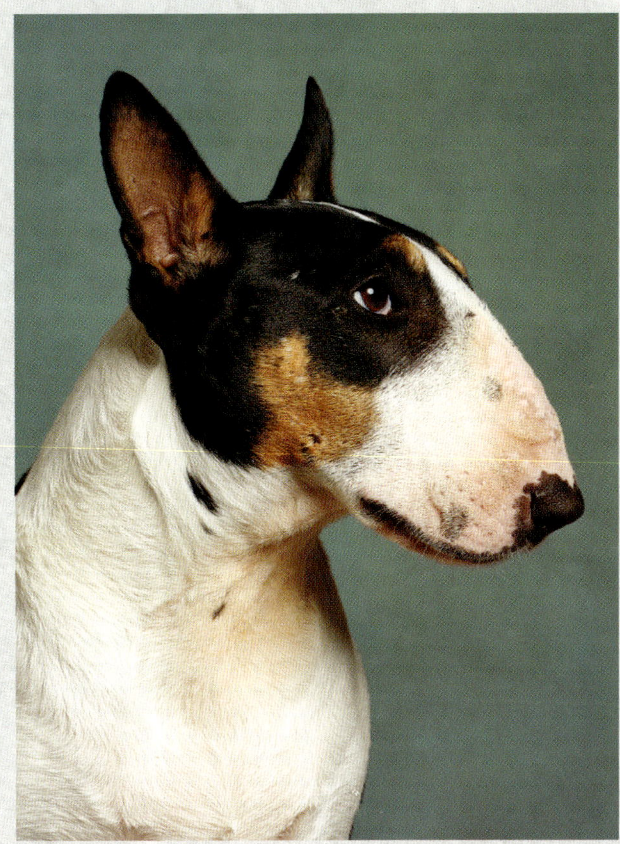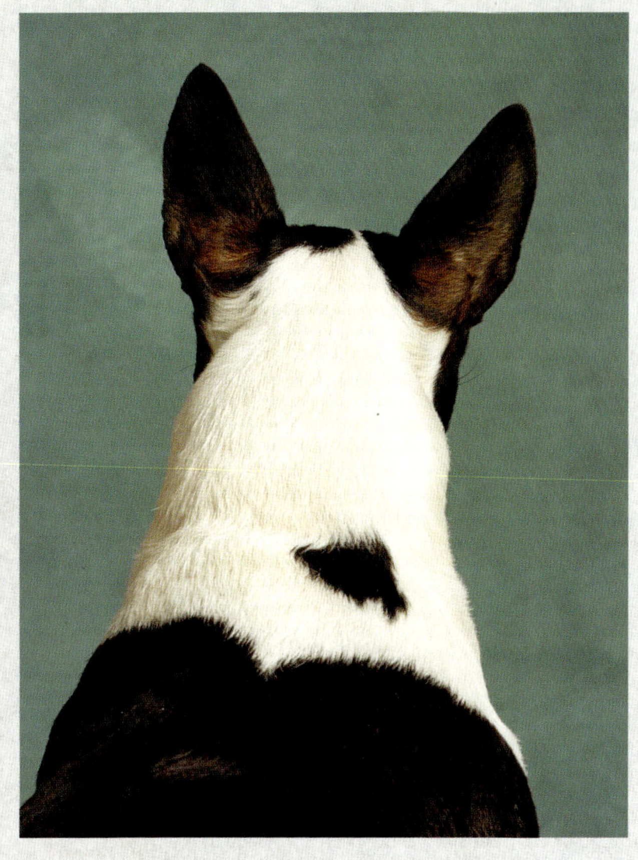

A, Lily

ALIASES: Lil / 'Not the Brightest' / No / Trouble

BORN: Unknown, 2-3 yrs   TRADE: Ramming Rod   BREED: Mini Bull Terrier

BUILD: Stocky   EYES: Brown   HEIGHT: 57cm   HAIR: Black / Tan / White

MARKS: Long, pronounced nose — perfect for door ramming

PECULIARITIES: Enjoys 'Forbidden' Rooms

M.O: ETC. Has been known to continually ram closed doors so she can
plunder/destroy/feast upon the room's contents.

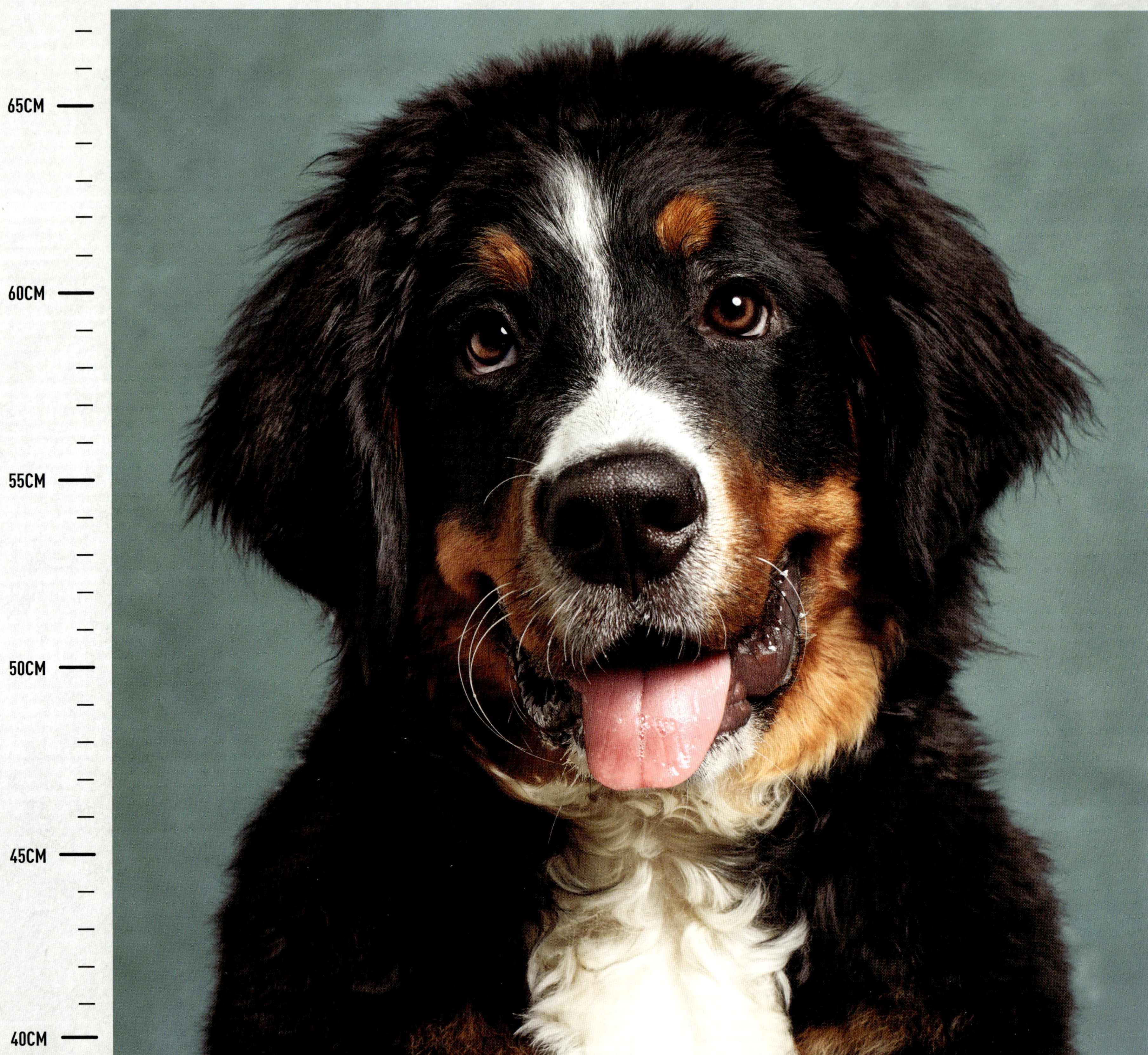

65CM
60CM
55CM
50CM
45CM
40CM

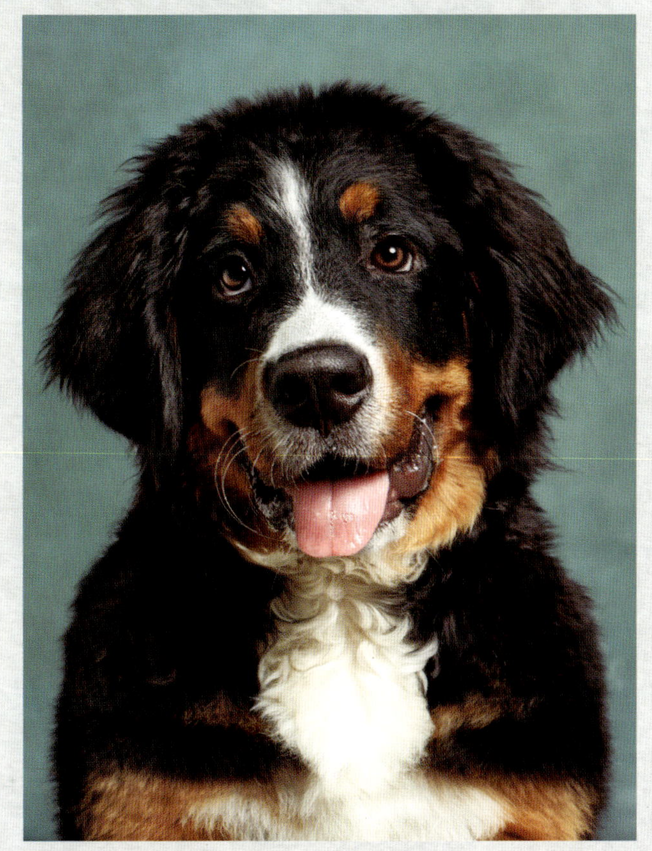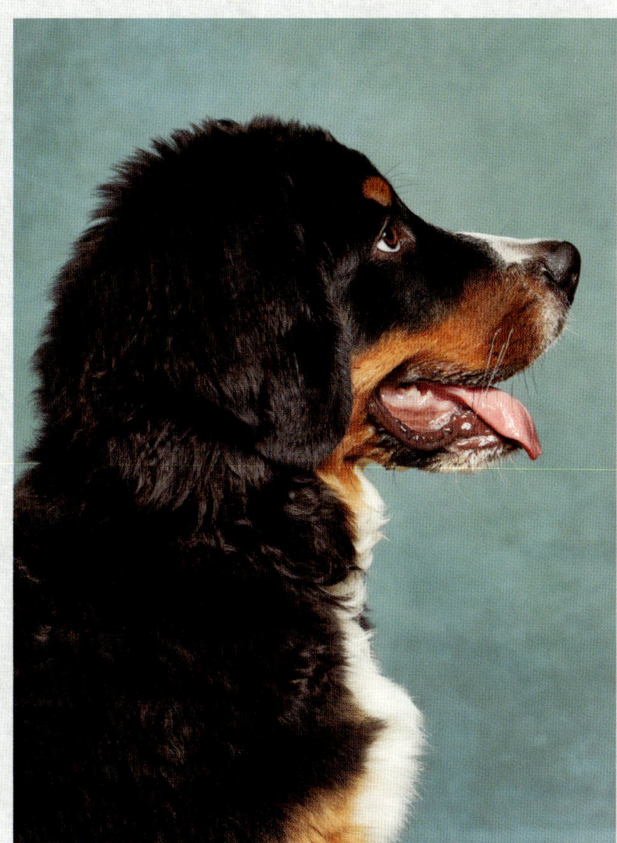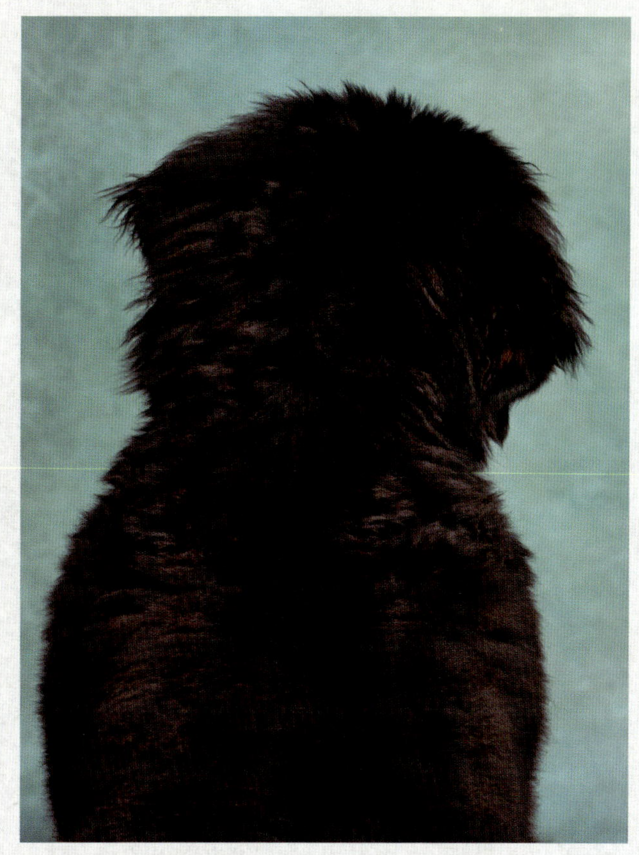

H, Willow

ALIASES:

BORN: 22/11/2016   TRADE: Charmer   BREED: Bernese Mountain Dog

BUILD: Mini Mountain   EYES: Brown   HEIGHT: 67cm   HAIR: Black / Tan / White

MARKS: Slight curl to freshly washed fur

PECULIARITIES: Has a taste for Dad's jocks and socks

M.O: ETC. Has been known to frequent beach areas, trawling for treasures
such as seaweed… and dead birds.

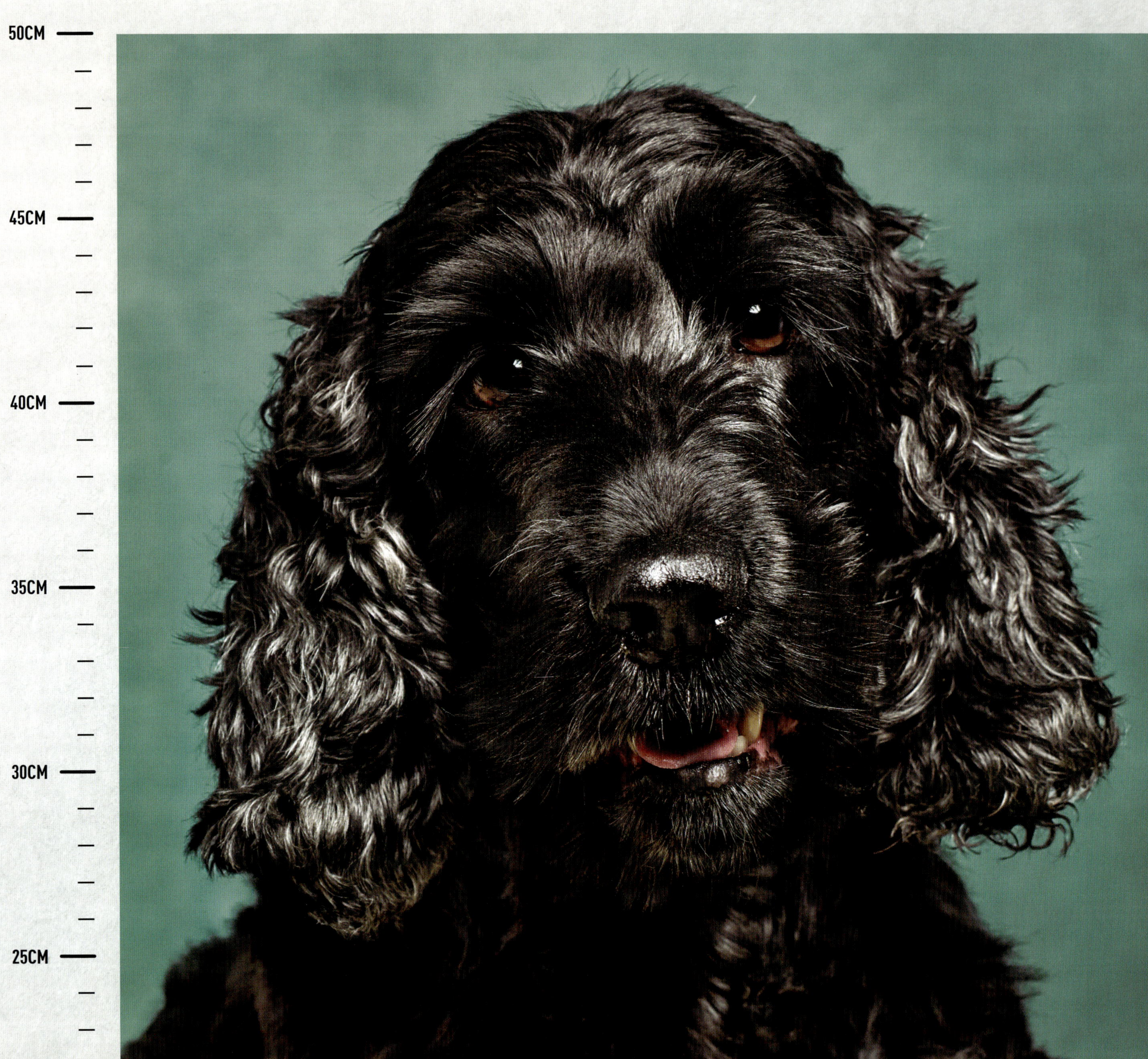

50CM
45CM
40CM
35CM
30CM
25CM

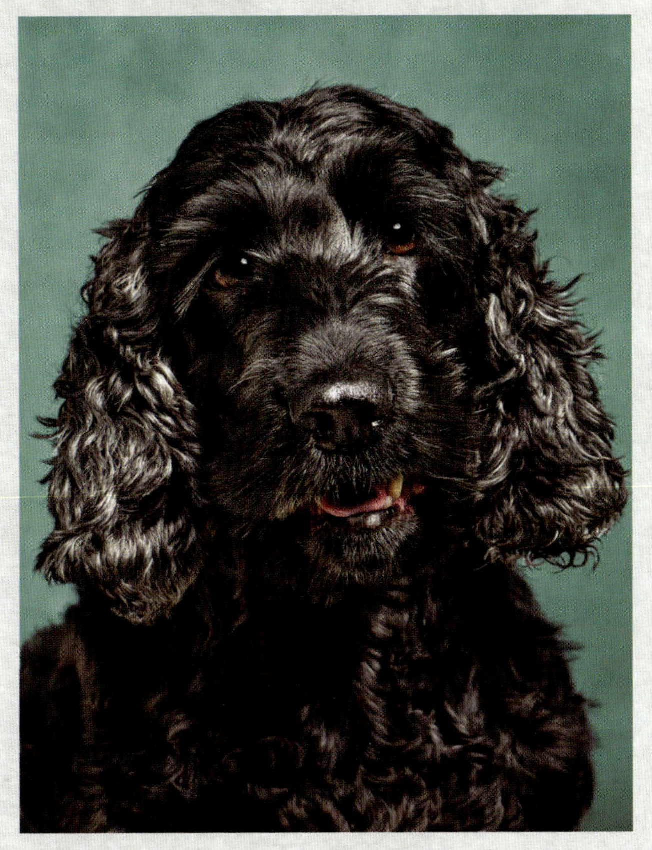 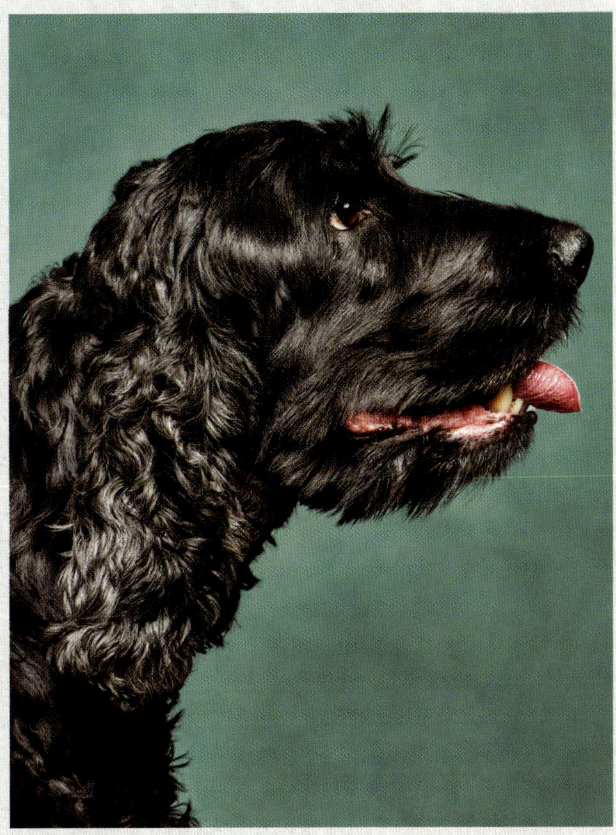 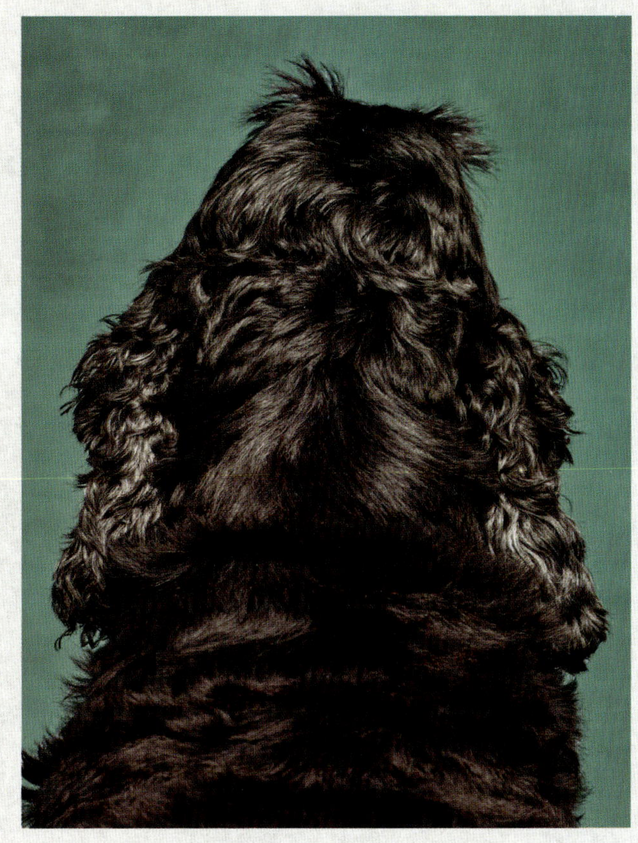

J, Delphinium

ALIASES: Delphi

BORN: October 2008

TRADE: Lady Boss

BREED: Cocker Spaniel

BUILD: Mini

EYES: Brown

HEIGHT: 49cm

HAIR: Black / Silver

MARKS: Starting to get a silver shine to black coat

PECULIARITIES: Has a tongue that turns up into a leaf shape

M.O: ETC. Can often be found looking over her domain from the comfort of a leather couch.
Has been known to cut and run with her prize at the beach.

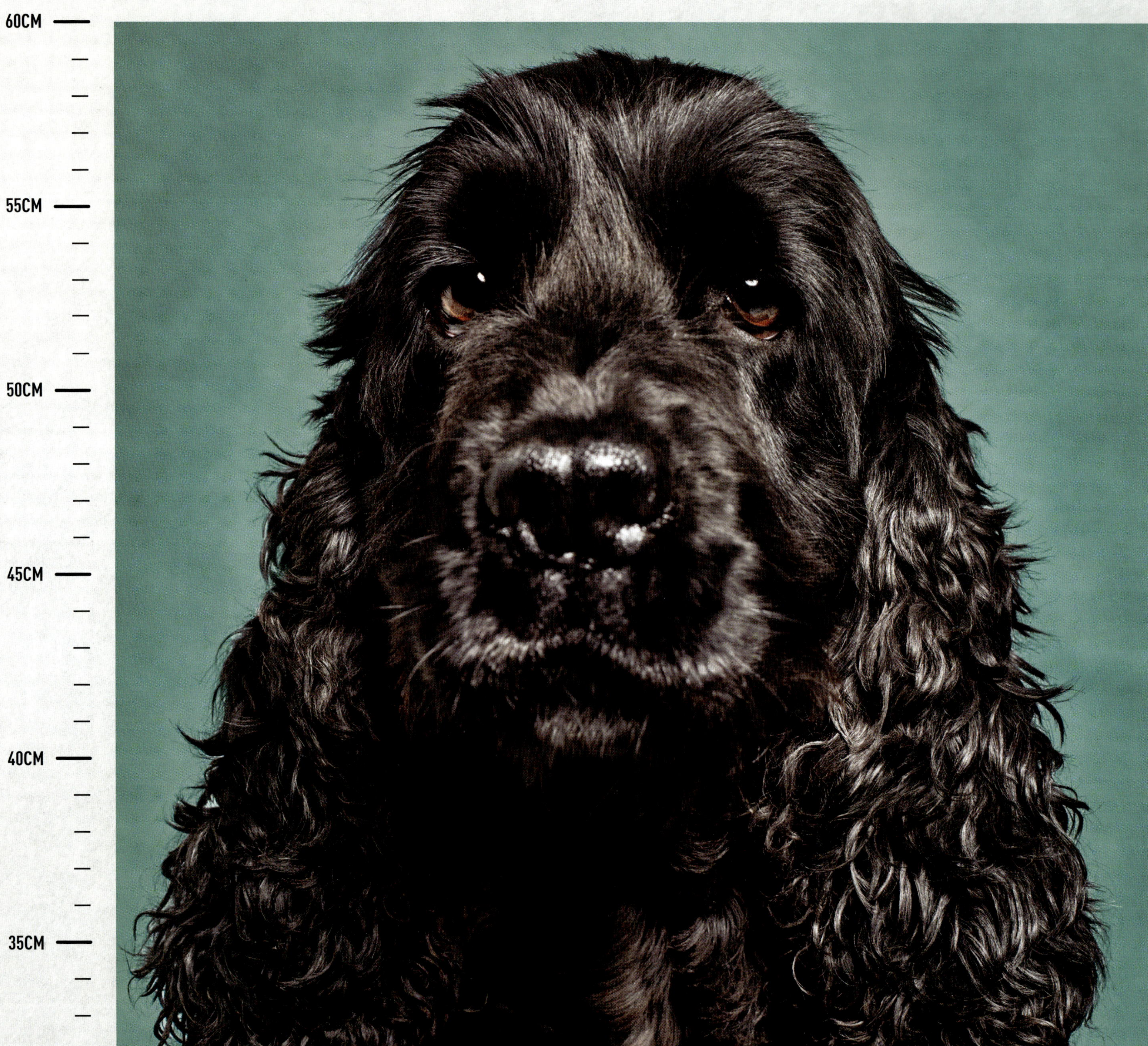

60CM
55CM
50CM
45CM
40CM
35CM

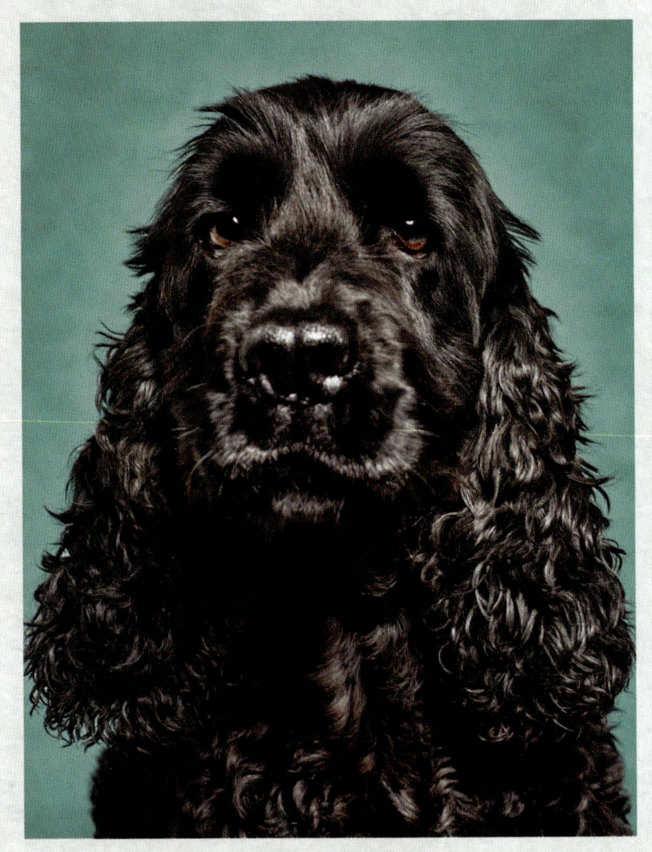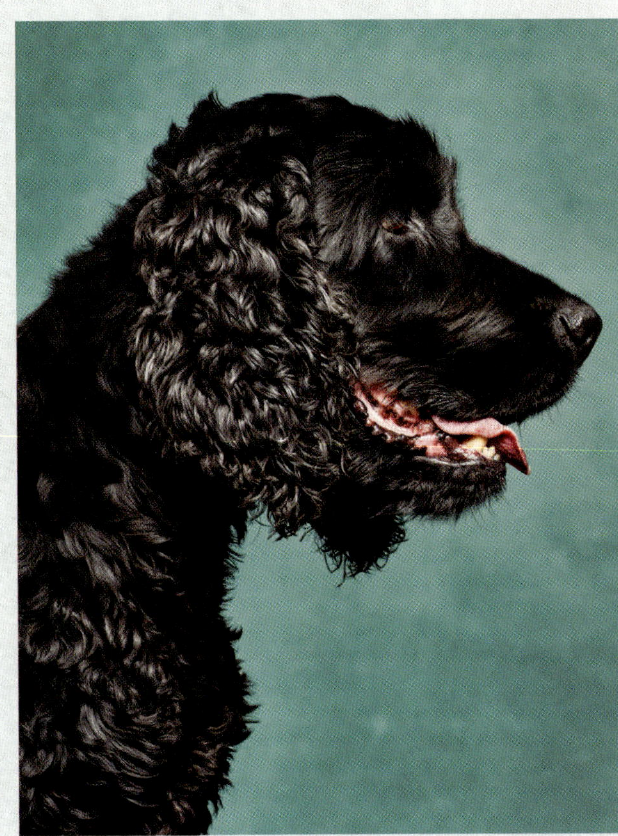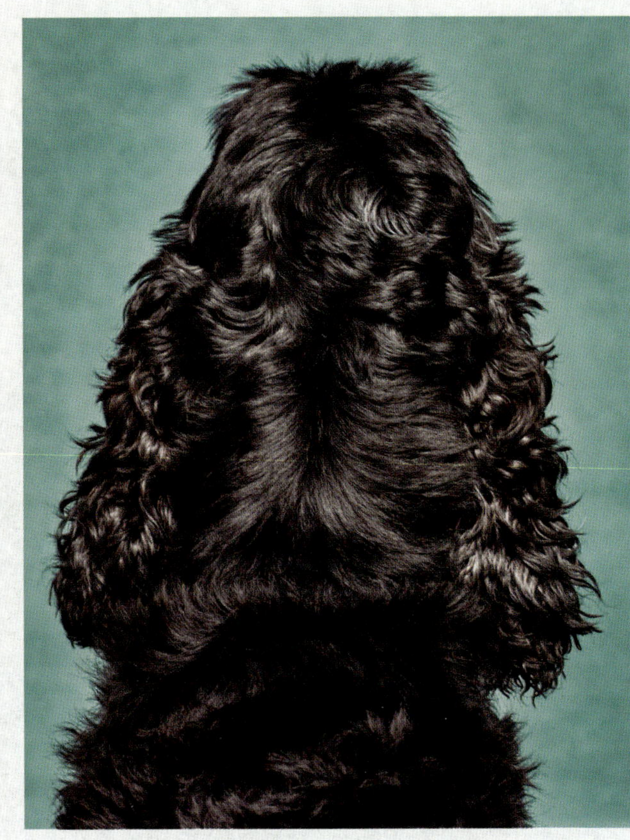

J, Murphy

ALIASES: Murph / Murph the Smurf

BORN: November 2009

TRADE: Scout & Swimmer

BREED: Cocker Spaniel

BUILD: Cuddly

EYES: Brown

HEIGHT: 58cm

HAIR: Black

MARKS: Commonly has dirt on nose

PECULIARITIES: May have been a fish in past life as loves being in the water

M.O: ETC. Has a super sense of hearing — can hear friends and foes well before they arrive. Can bark at intruders while holding a teddy in his mouth.

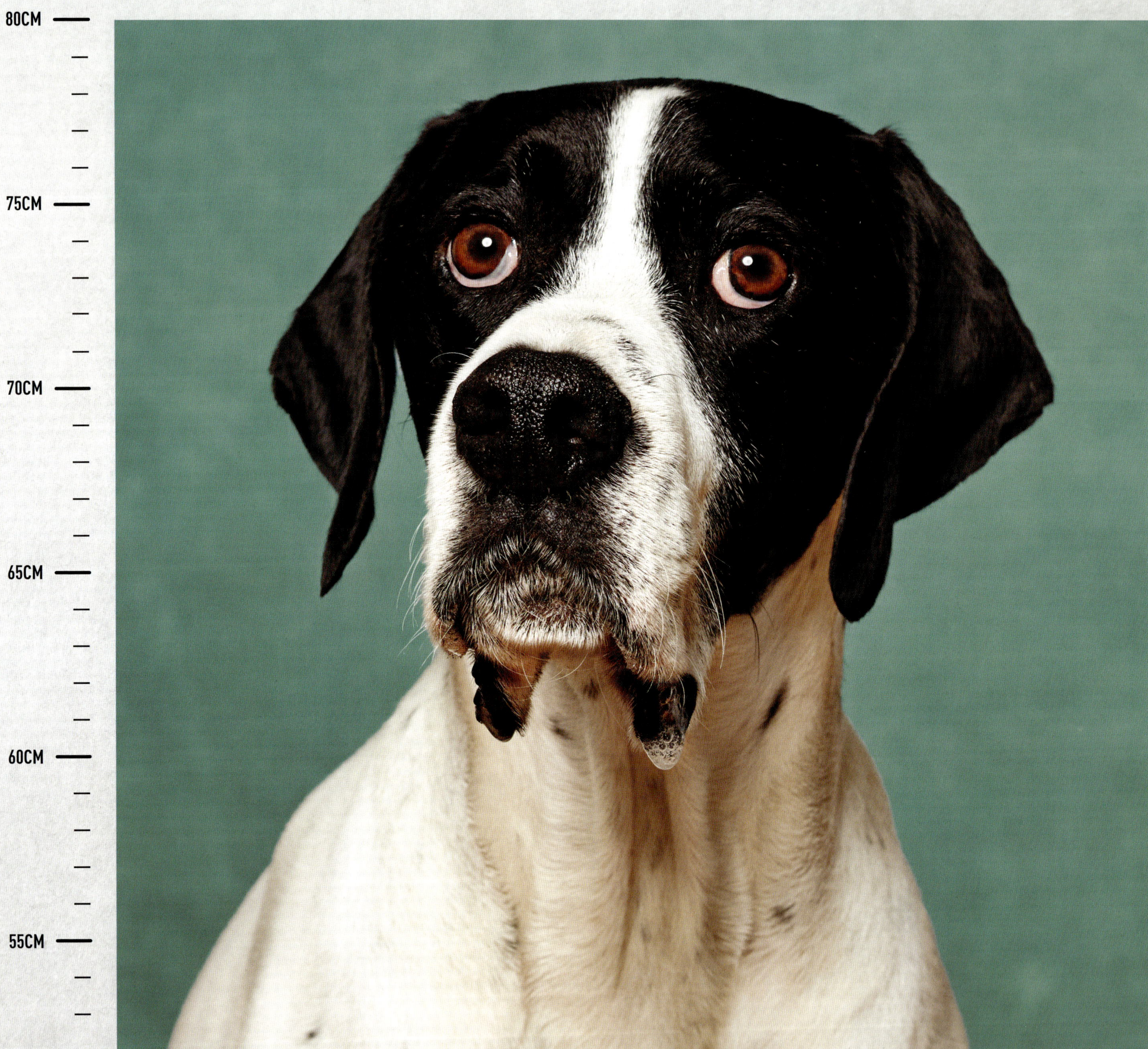
80CM
75CM
70CM
65CM
60CM
55CM

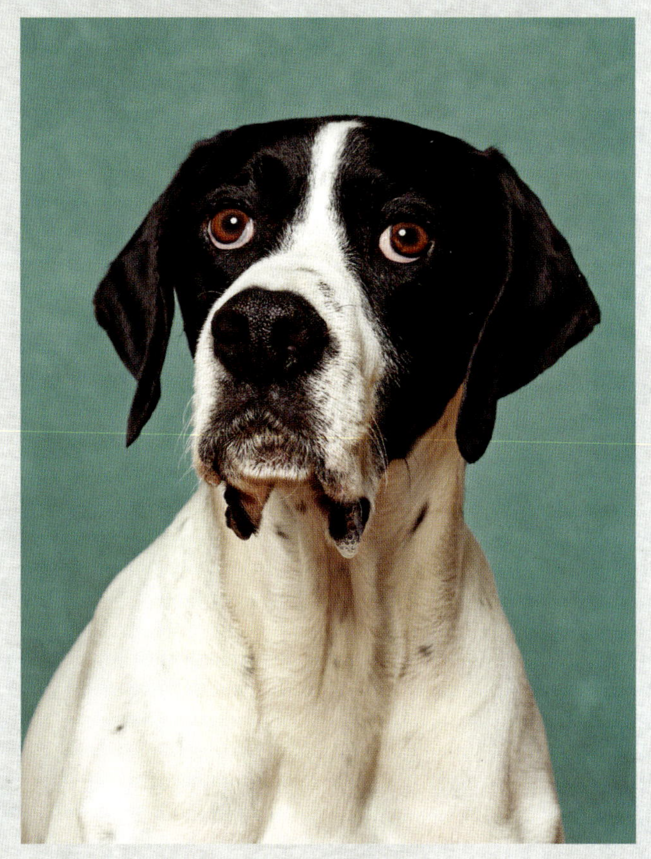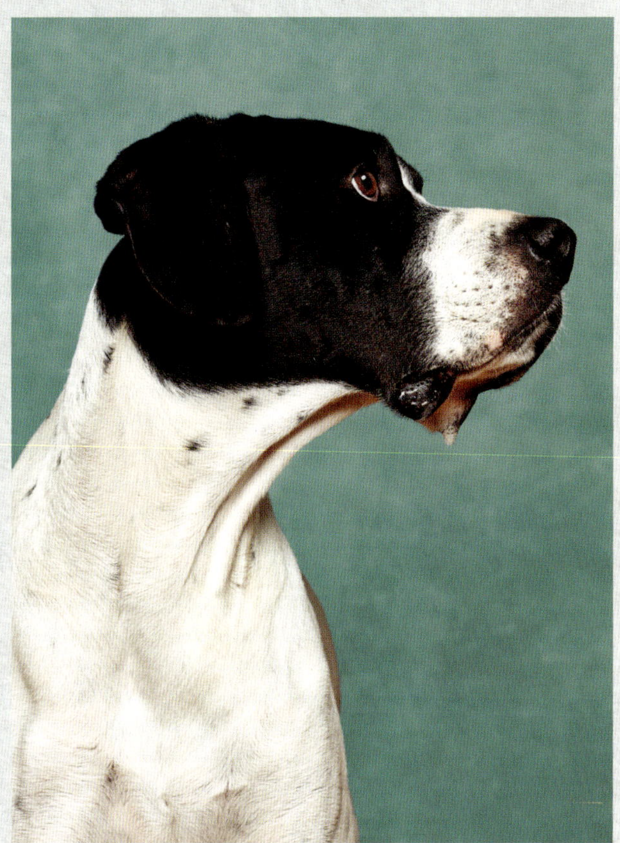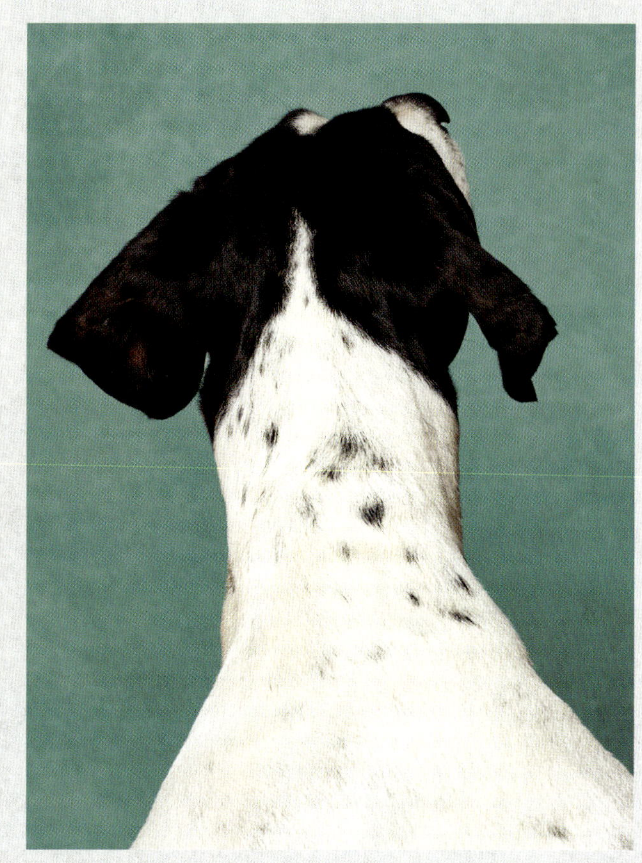

HW, Duke

ALIASES:	Mr Pickles / Dudda Bug

BORN:	Unknown, 11–12ish yrs	**TRADE:** Sensitive Soul	**BREED:** English Pointer
BUILD:	Transformer	**EYES:** Brown	**HEIGHT:** 80cm **HAIR:** Black / White

MARKS: A black spot just above his tail — a marker for his favourite place to be scratched

PECULIARITIES: Has been observed partaking in a rather elaborate dance for a biscuit

M.O: ETC. Has a soft spot for a good café latte and some chill time in a colourful wing-back chair overseeing his domain.

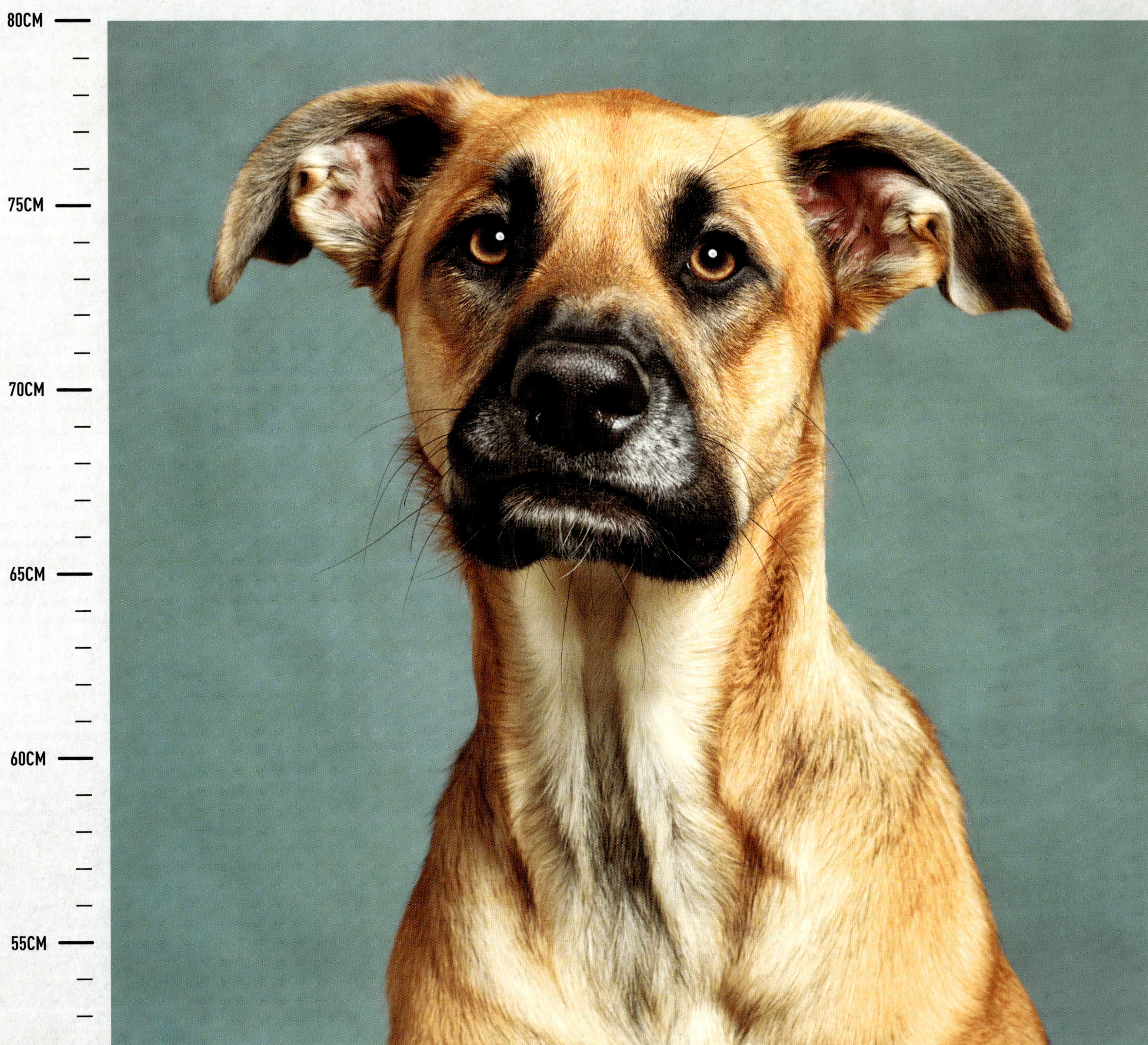
80CM
75CM
70CM
65CM
60CM
55CM

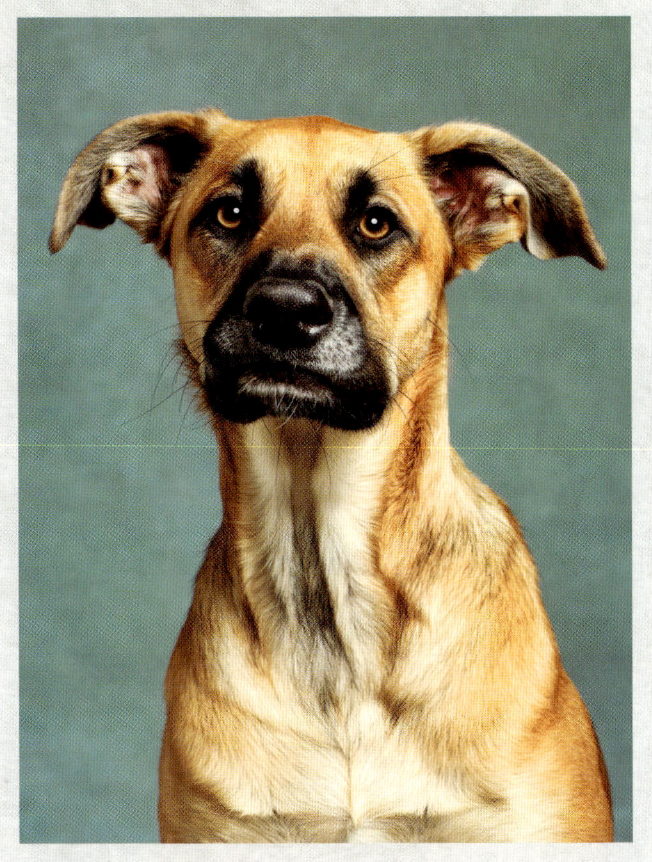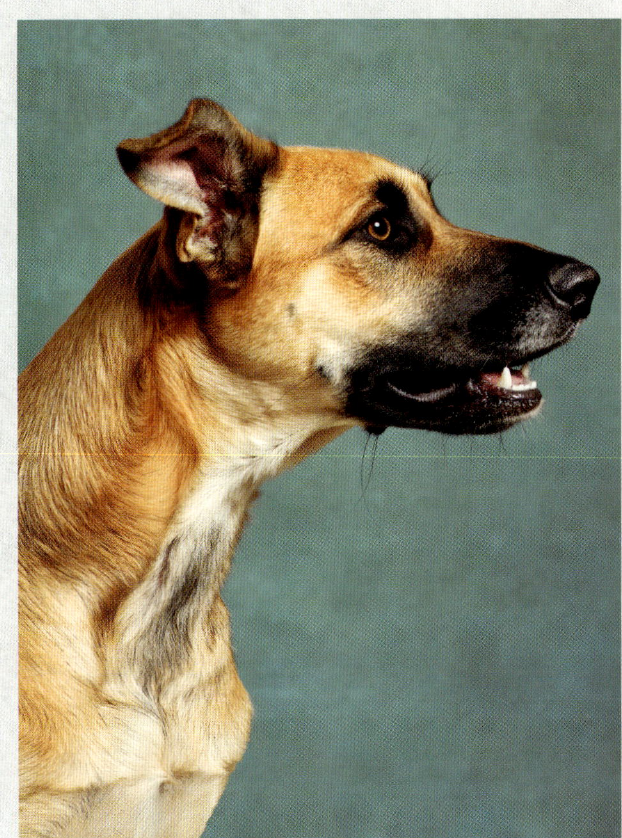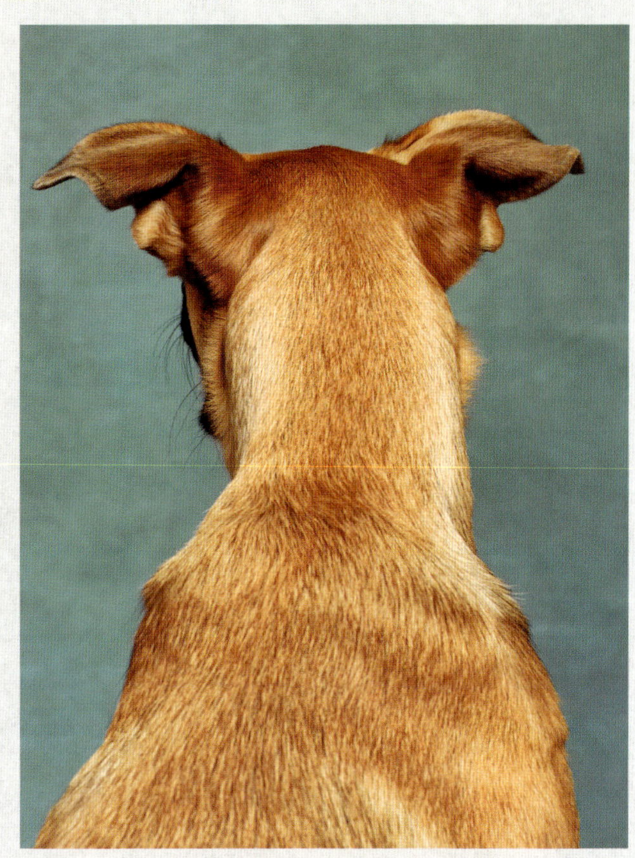

D, Nikki

ALIASES: Nikita

BORN: 16/02/2016   TRADE: Kleptomaniac   BREED: Shepard Mix

BUILD: Lean   EYES: Copper   HEIGHT: 79cm   HAIR: Blonde / Black

MARKS: Eyebrows on Point

PECULIARITIES: Finds it stressful being separated from her partner in crime, Angus

M.O: ETC. Has a history of stealing items within her reach and tends to relocate items, rather than vandalise.

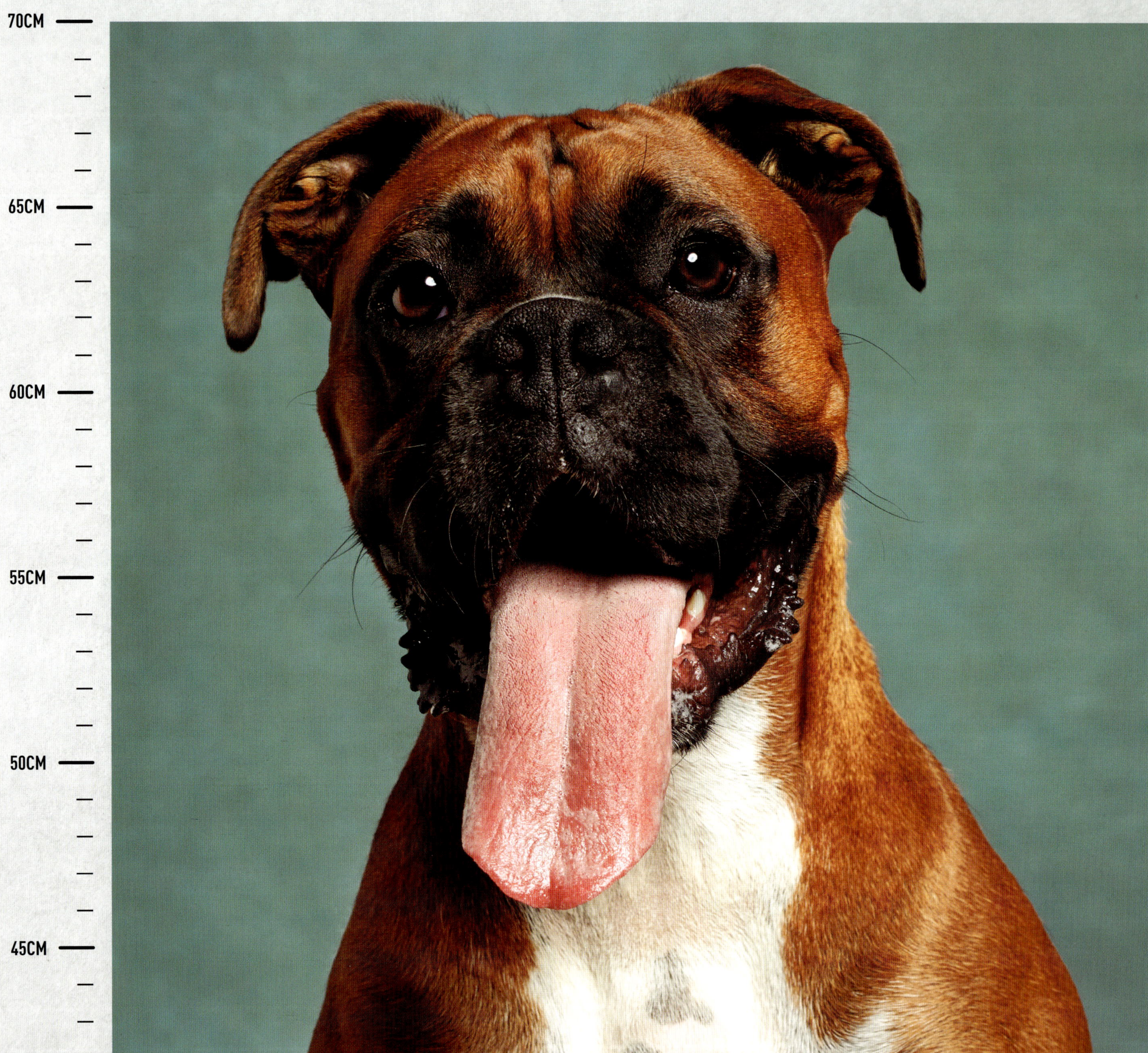

70CM
65CM
60CM
55CM
50CM
45CM

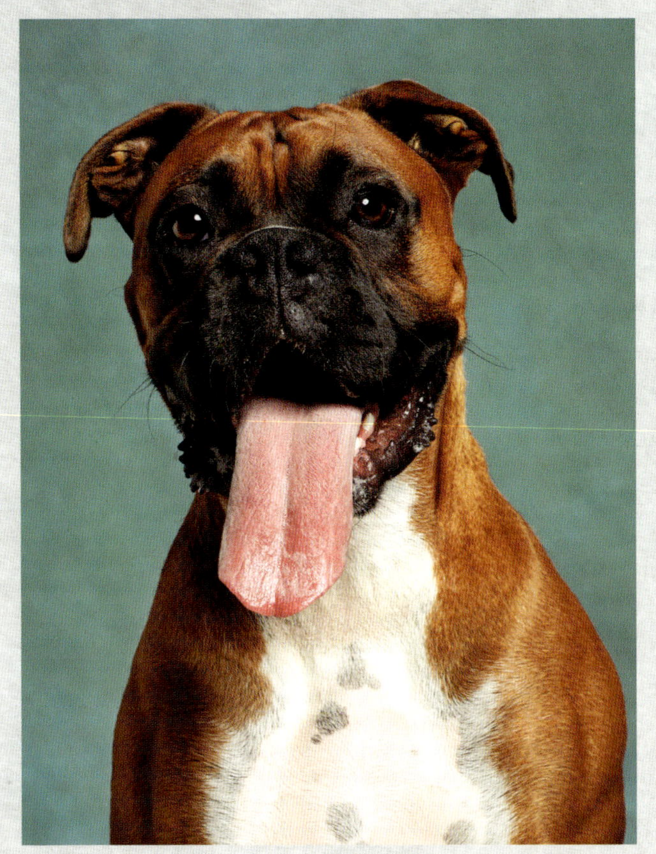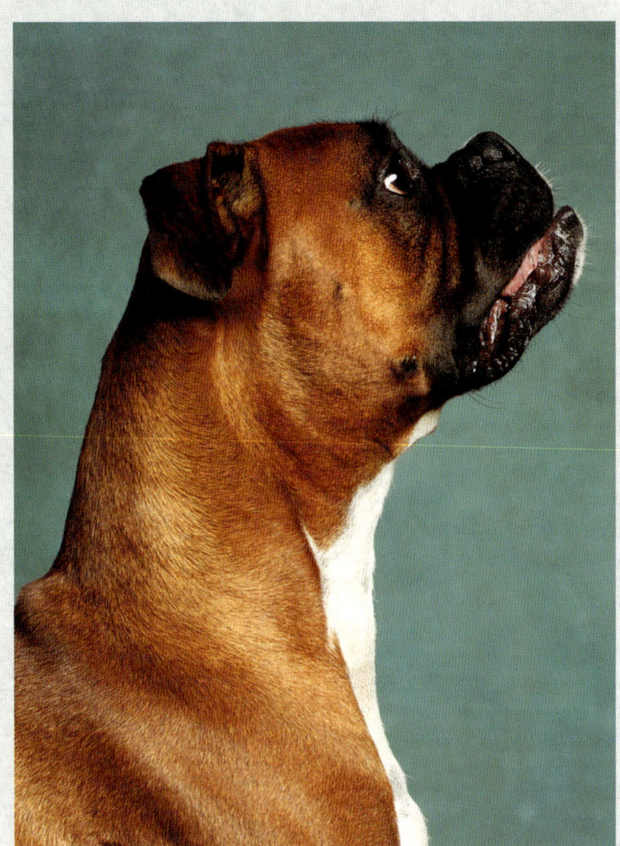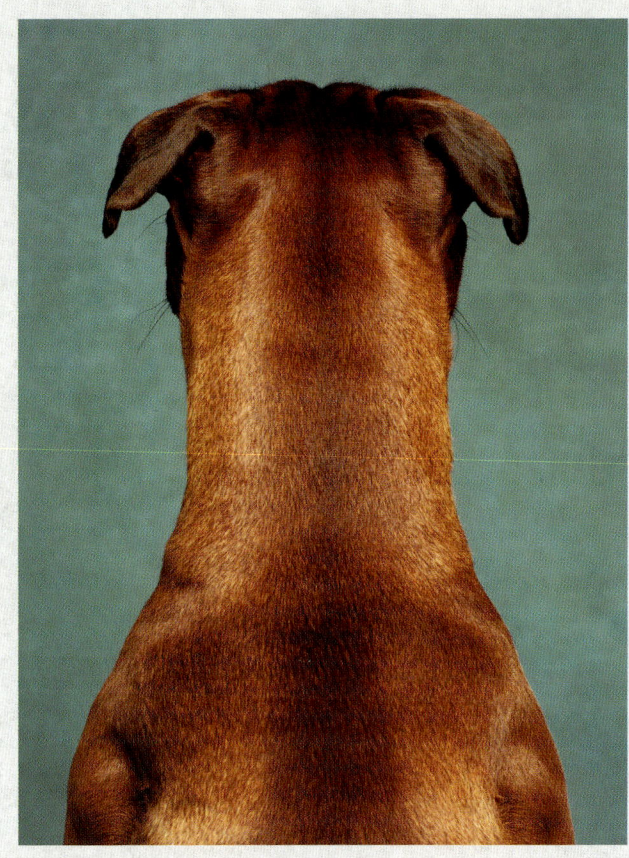

D, Angus

ALIASES:	Ahhnus / Nus / Anustepher / Anustepharian

BORN: 08/01/2015	**TRADE:** Ball Chaser	**BREED:** Boxer

BUILD: Muscular	**EYES:** Brown	**HEIGHT:** 67cm	**HAIR:** Rust / Black / White

MARKS: Squishy Face

PECULIARITIES: Can use wagging tail as propulsion aid, strong mothering instinct

M.O: ETC. Has history of being a canine Houdini but does not handle freedom and prefers the confines of his pack, has a ball obsession.

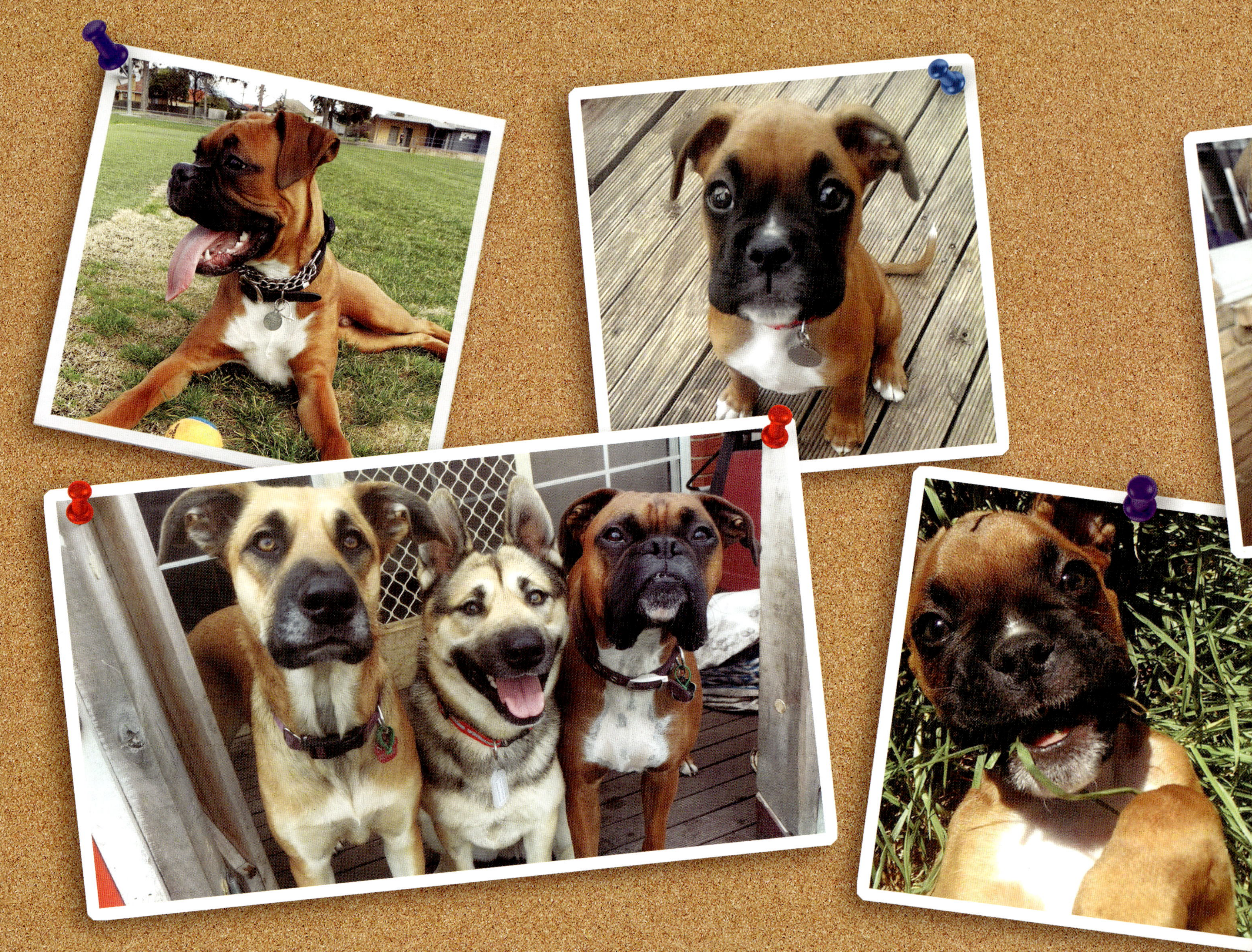

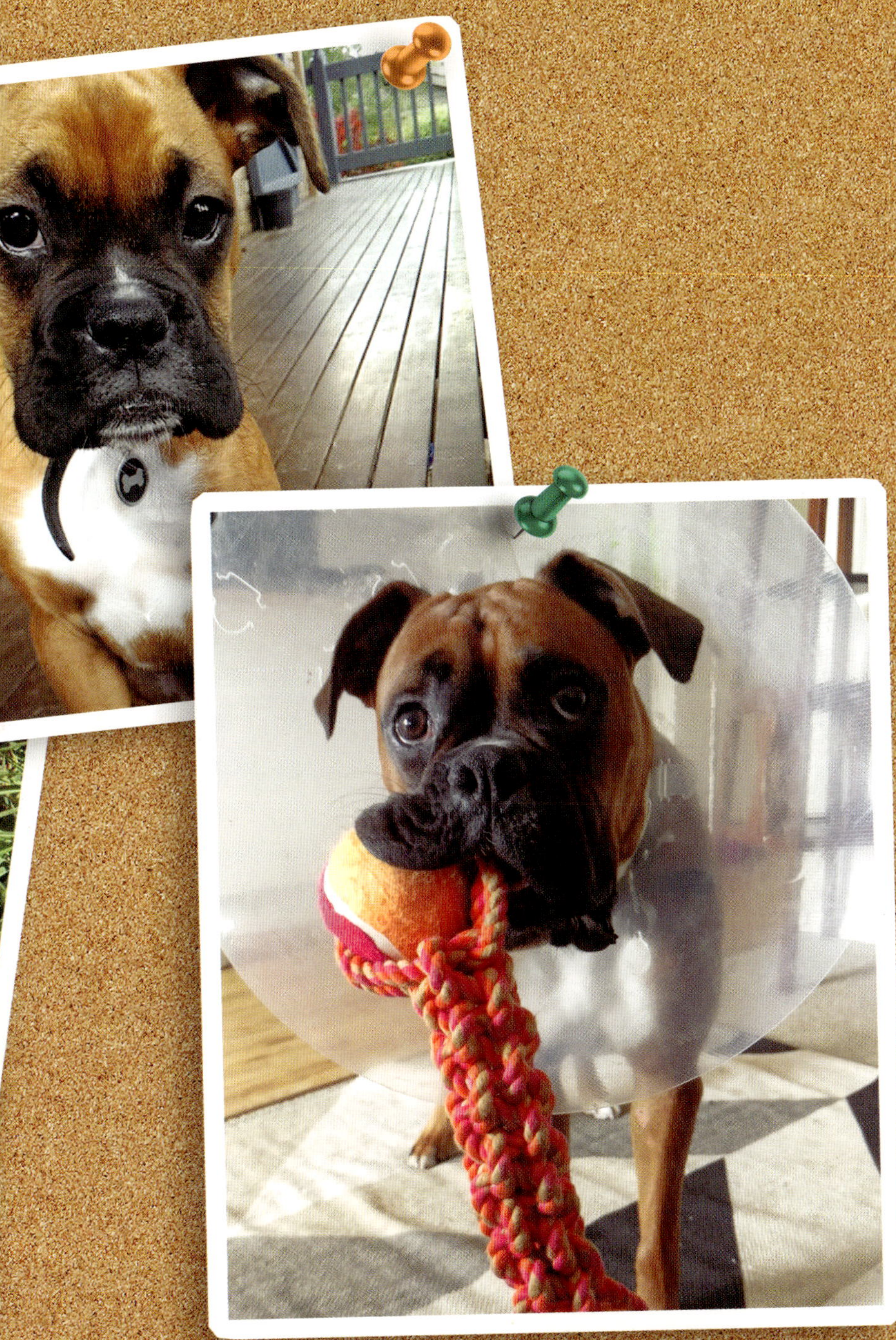

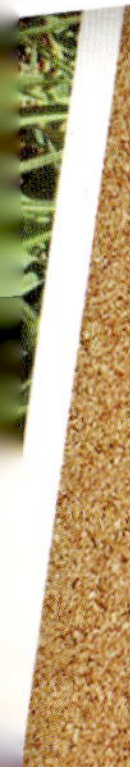

ANGUS
THE FOSTER CARER

Angus fosters dogs through Second Change Animal Rescue.

He is great at getting the dogs to come out of their shell and teaches them essential doggy social skills. One particular foster was a small timid dog who was petrified of other dogs, after a few days she and Angus were firm friends and she left for her forever home a completely different dog.

One foster dog, Nikki, was particularly special. Angus was so smitten, he would sleep in her crate with her even though he had never been crate trained. Angus loved Nikki so much he wouldn't leave her side, so his humans decided to let him keep her. Now together they foster all kinds of pups getting them ready for their forever homes.

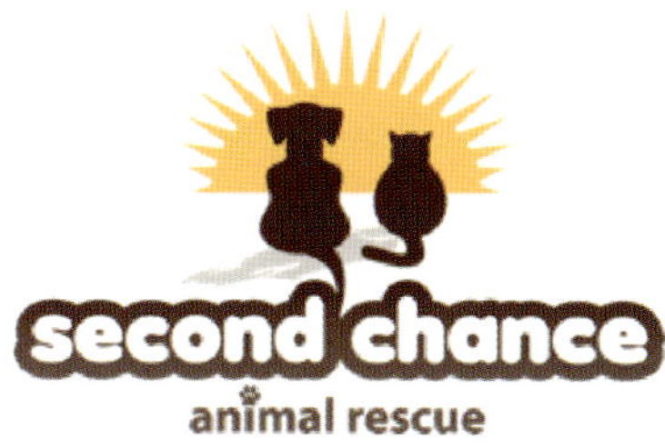

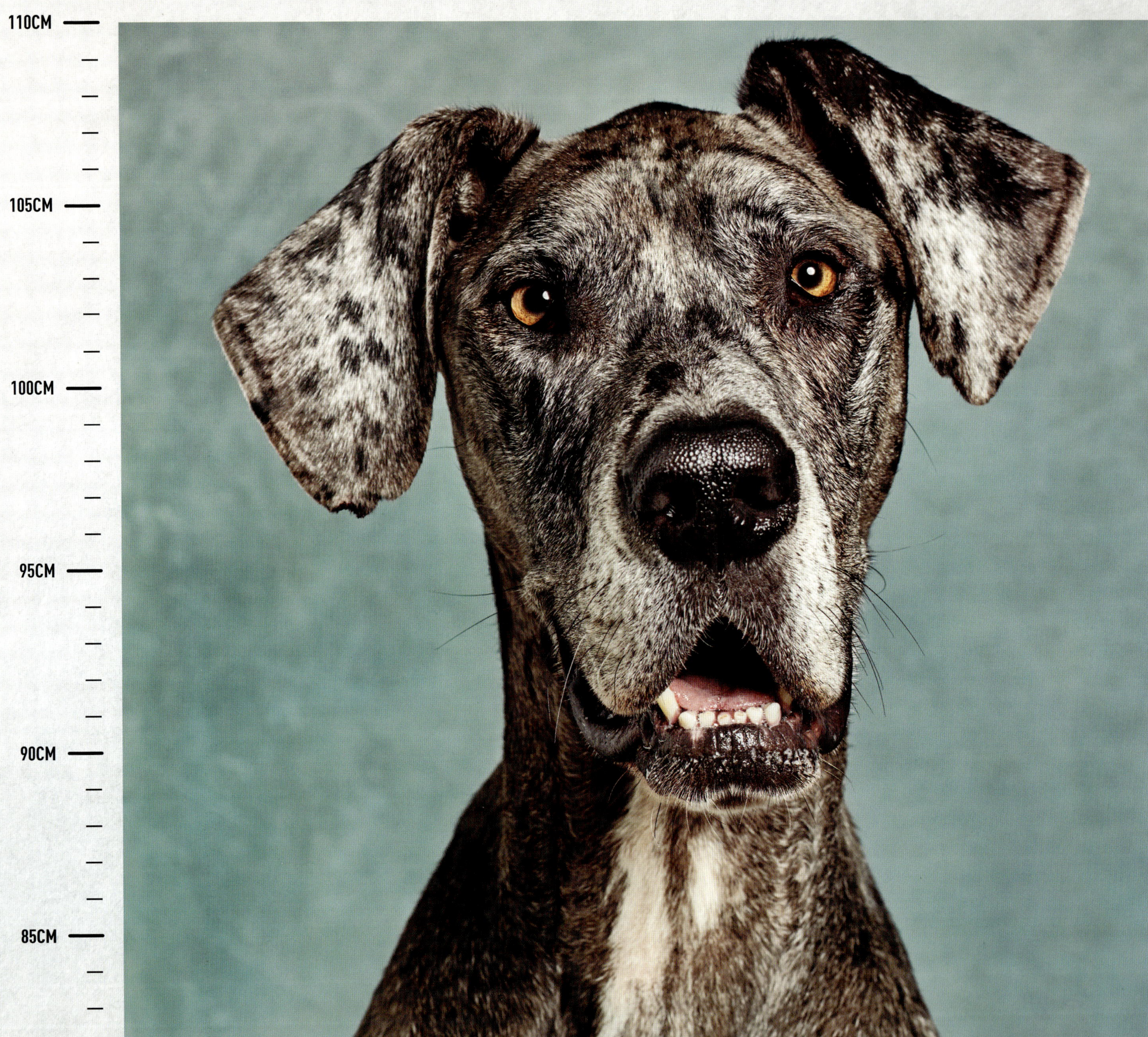
110CM
105CM
100CM
95CM
90CM
85CM

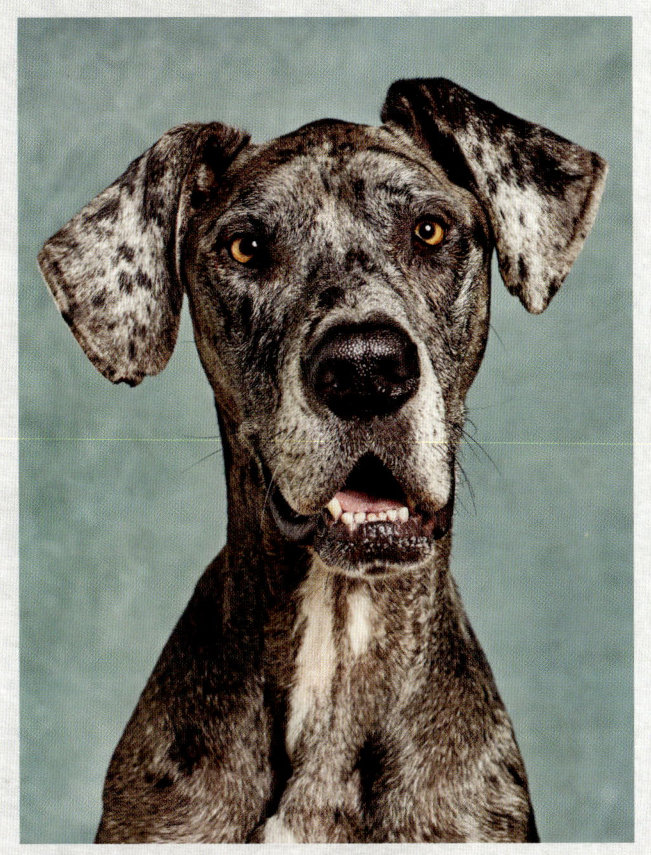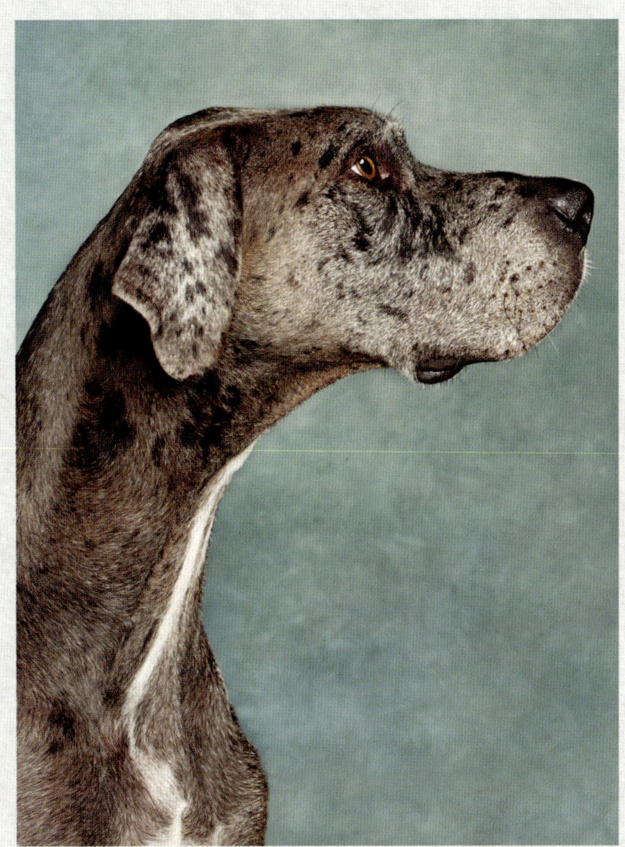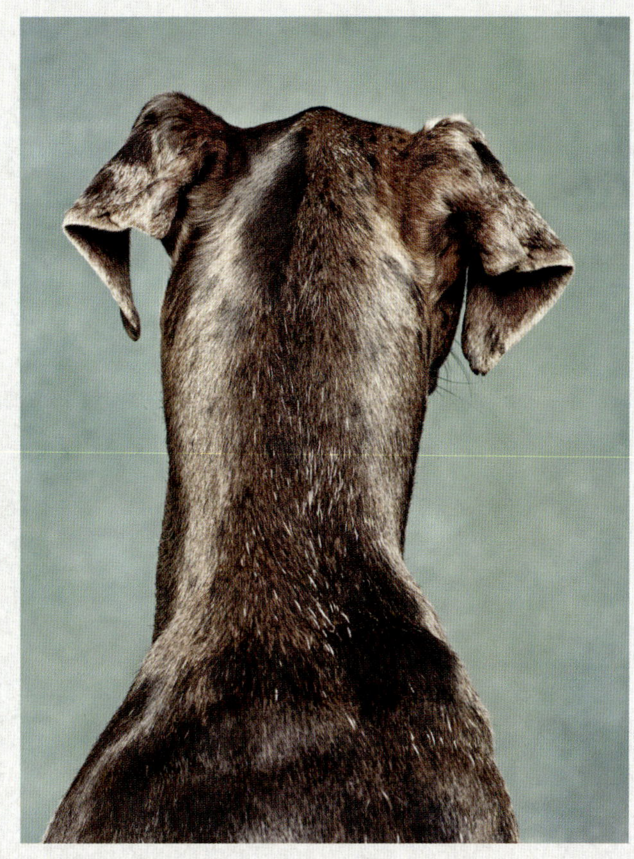

S, Mina

ALIASES: Peanut

BORN: 08/01/2013   TRADE: Opportunist   BREED: Great Dane

BUILD: Extremely Tall   EYES: Brown   HEIGHT: 110cm   HAIR: Blue Merle (Grey)

MARKS: Spots around eyes, nose and ears

PECULIARITIES: Food obsessed

M.O: ETC.   Goes to extraordinary lengths to obtain/steal food. Reported to have pushed a chair to a fridge in order to retrieve food that was hidden on the top.

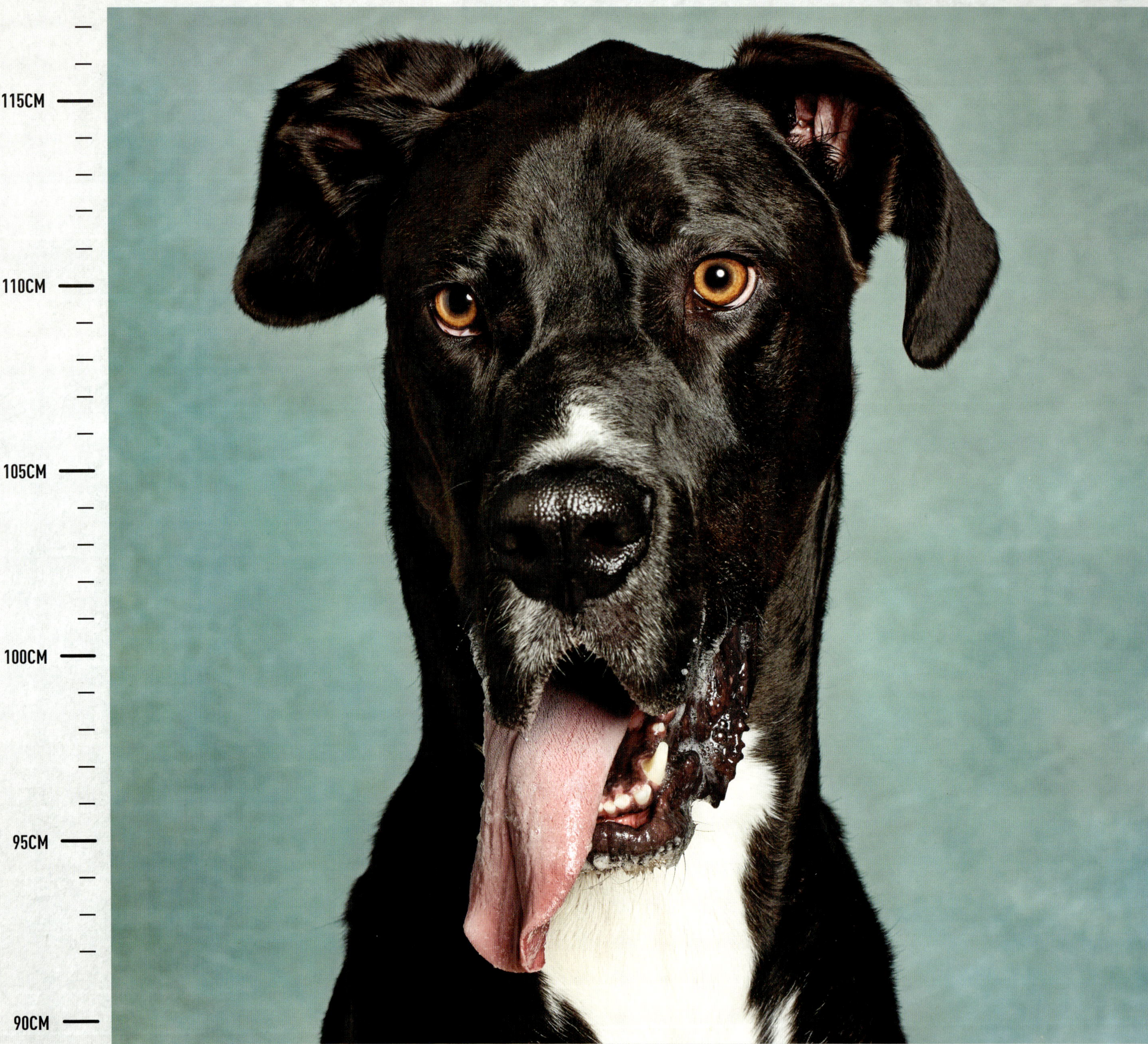
115CM
110CM
105CM
100CM
95CM
90CM

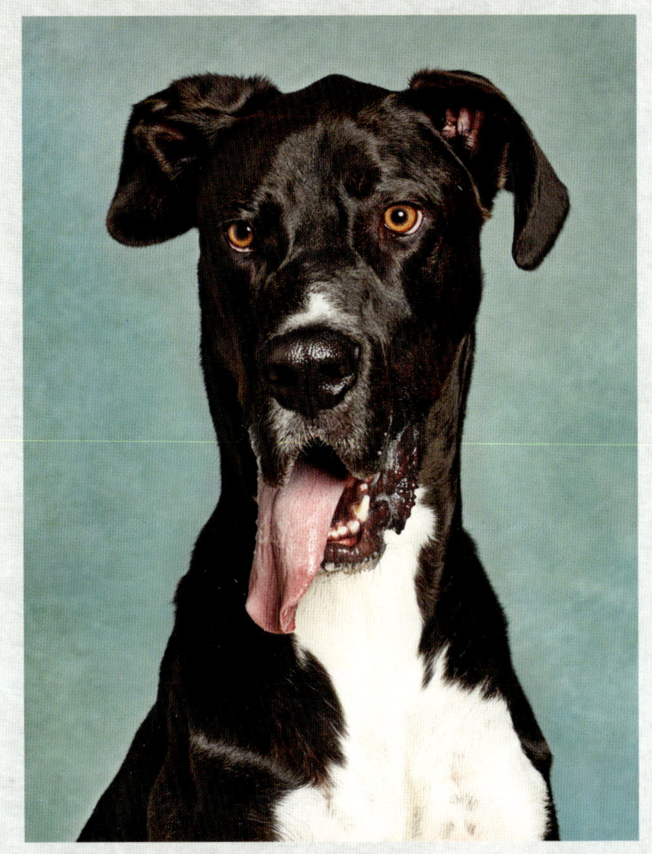 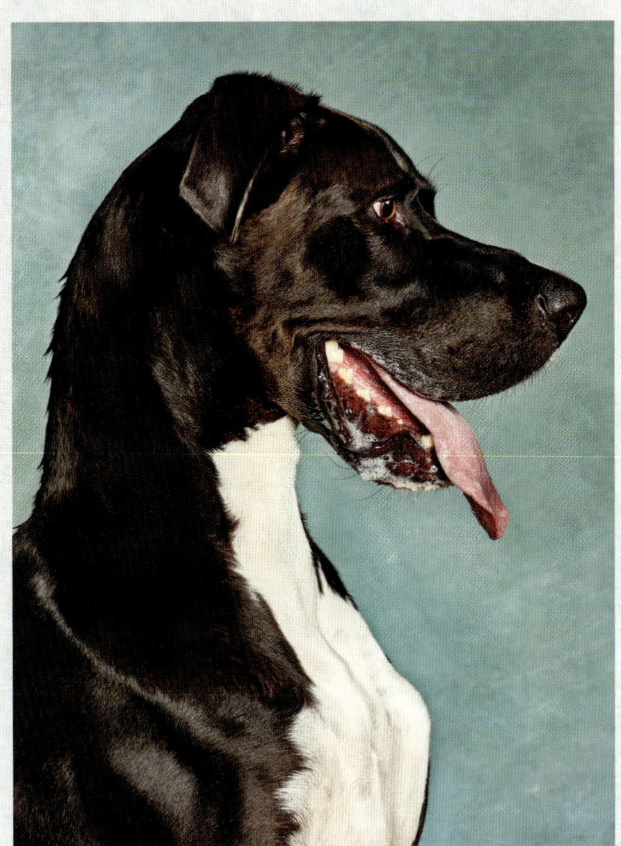 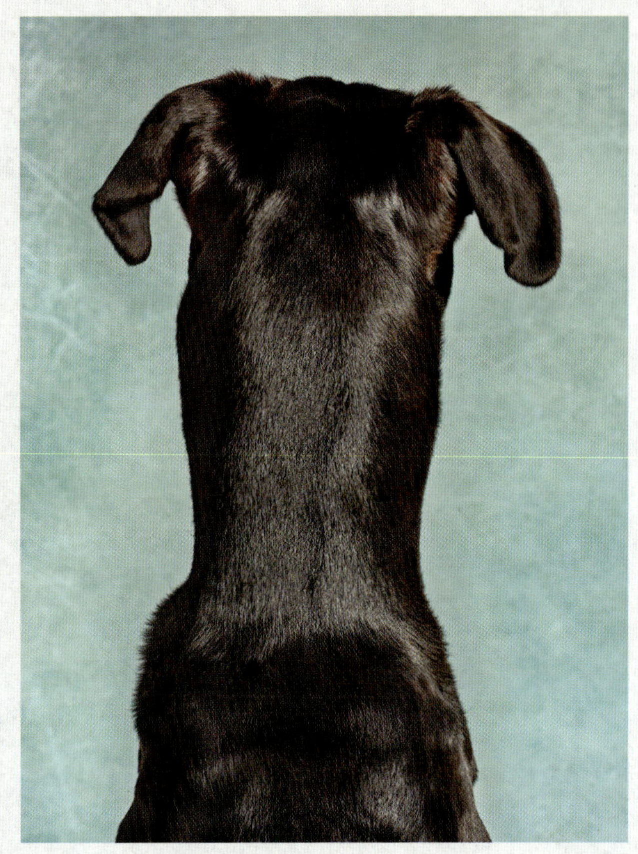

S, Noodles

ALIASES:

BORN: 18/03/2012 **TRADE:** Leaner **BREED:** Great Dane

BUILD: Lanky & Super Tall **EYES:** Copper Brown **HEIGHT:** 117cm **HAIR:** Black / White

MARKS: Has white 'socks'

PECULIARITIES: Has an exceptionally large head, and long tongue

M.O: ETC. Has been reported to bark at unseen enemies. Also known to climb into an occupied bath — not to wash, but to drink the bath water.

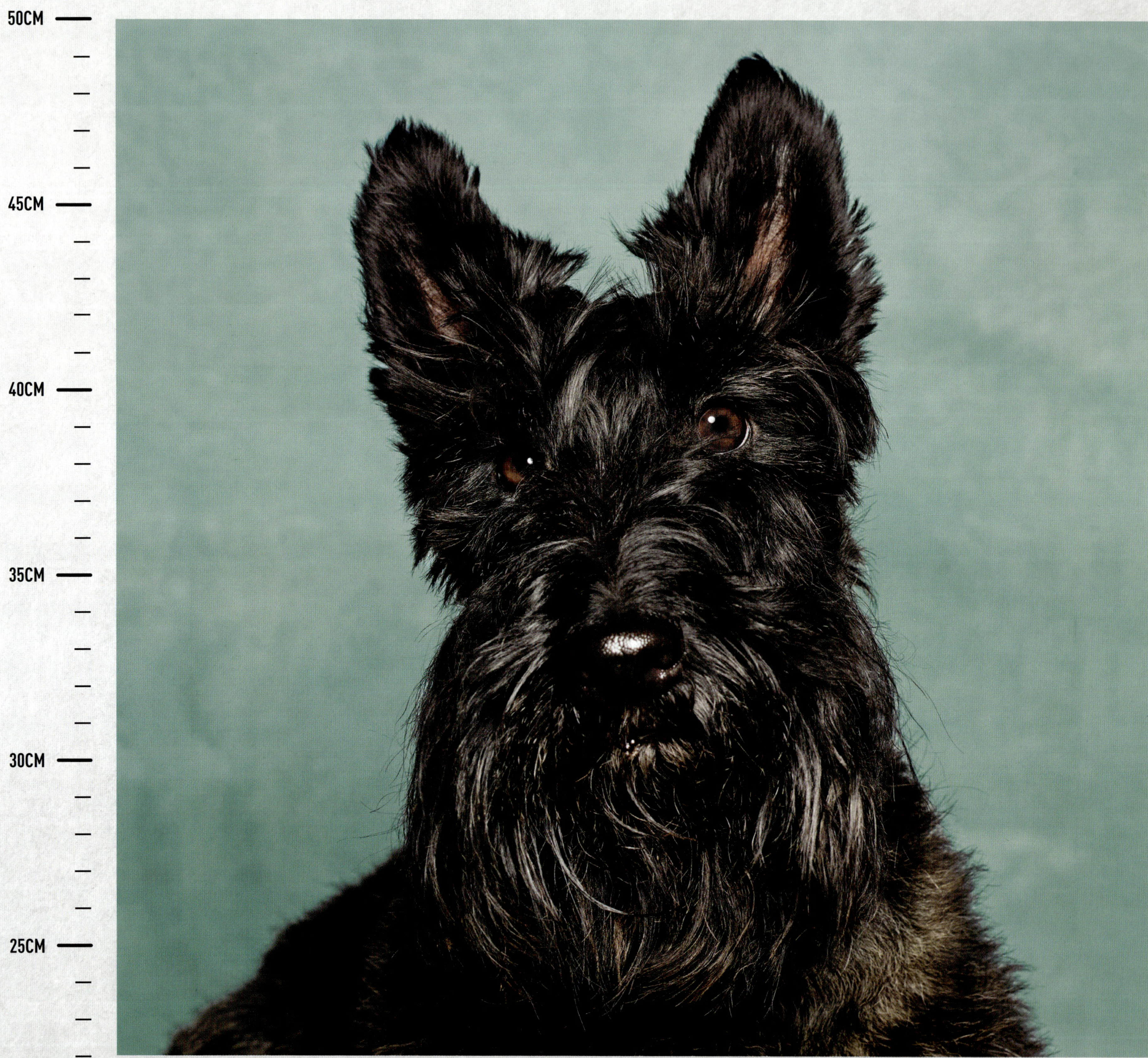

50CM
45CM
40CM
35CM
30CM
25CM

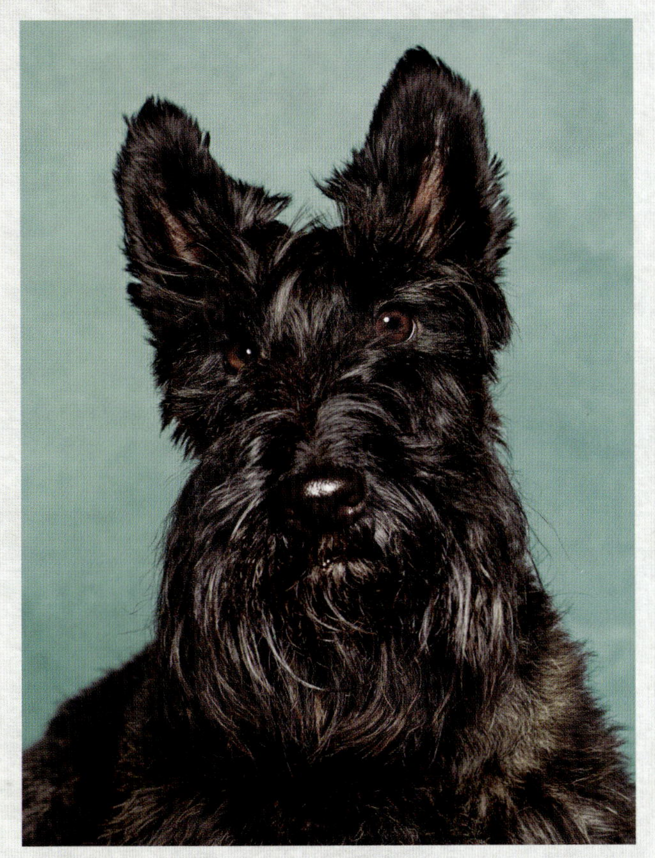 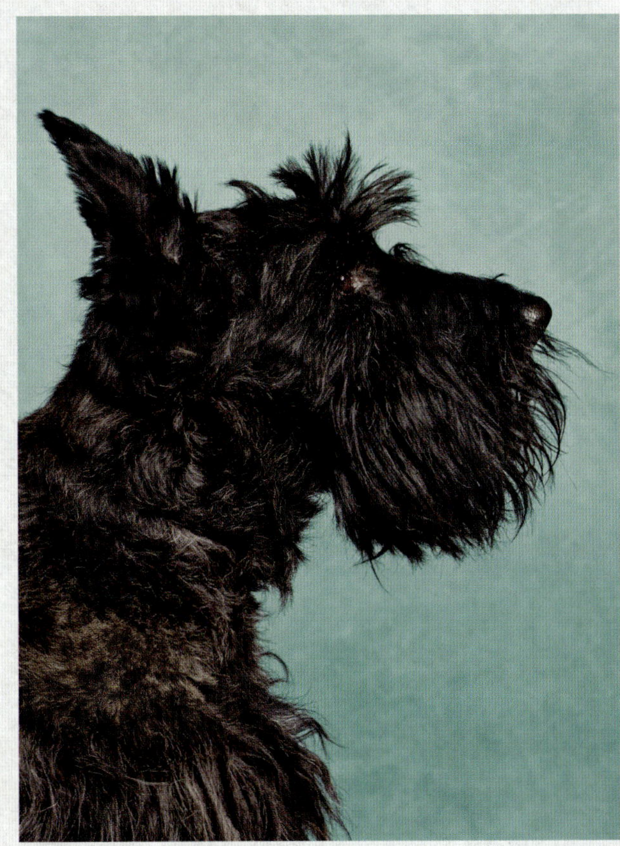 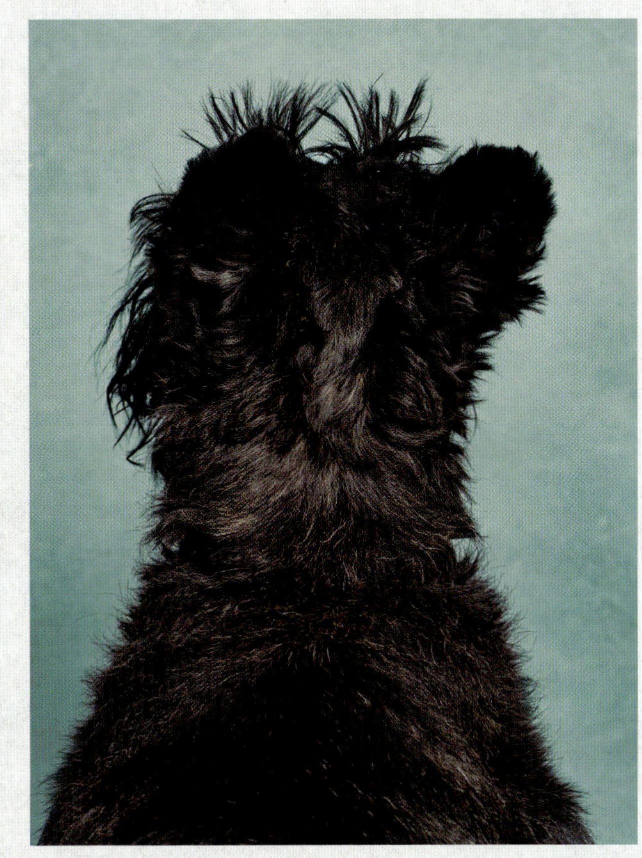

D, Alfie

ALIASES: Baggers / Mimi

BORN: 14/06/2013   TRADE: Worrier   BREED: Scottish Terrier

BUILD: Square   EYES: Brown   HEIGHT: 50cm   HAIR: Black / Brindle

MARKS: Is not actually pure black — has brindle flecks

PECULIARITIES: Requires a clean beard at all times and uses his head as a mop to keep it clean

M.O: ETC. Is a terrible guard and often falls asleep on patrol at the window while staring down his nemesis Mr Snuggles.

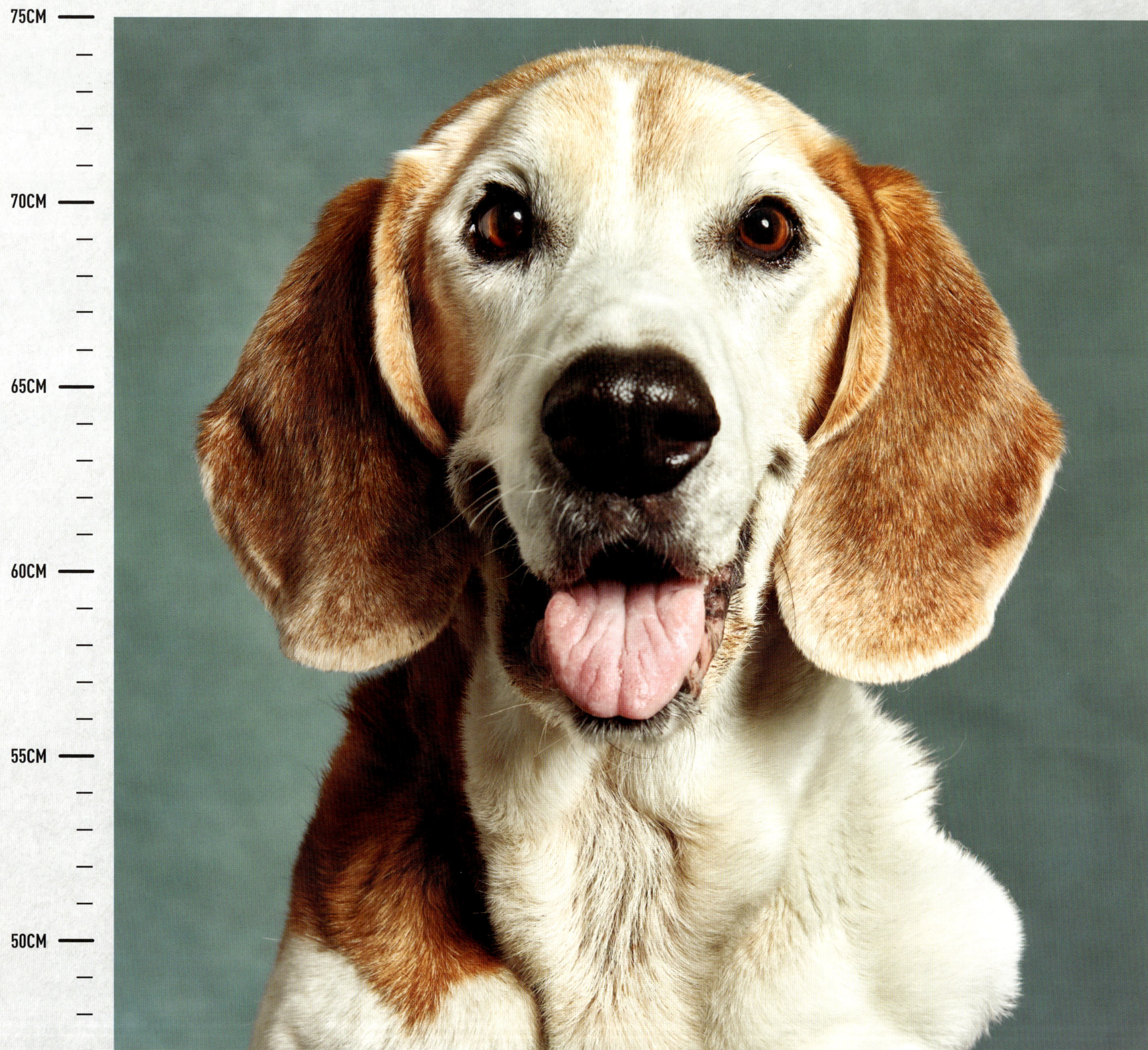
75CM
70CM
65CM
60CM
55CM
50CM

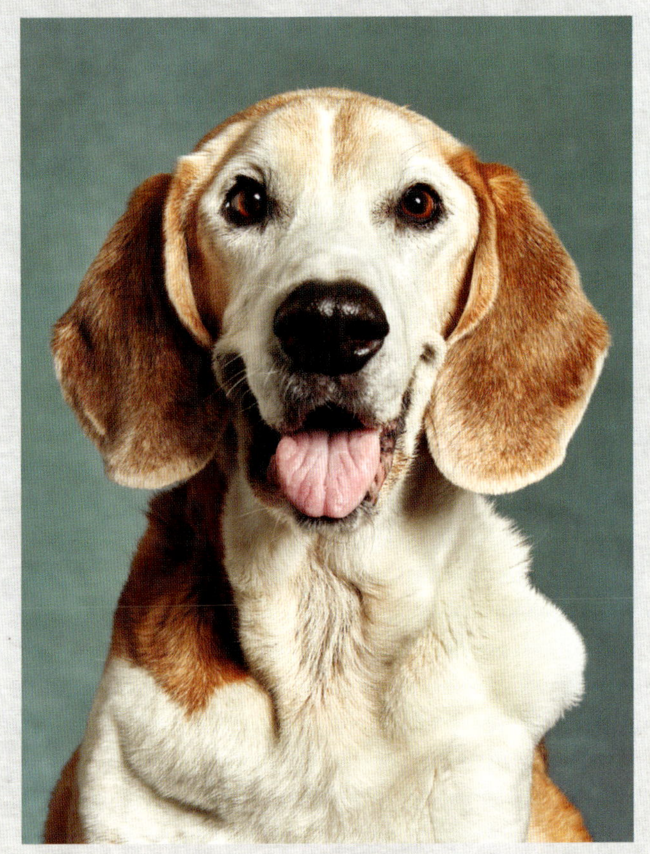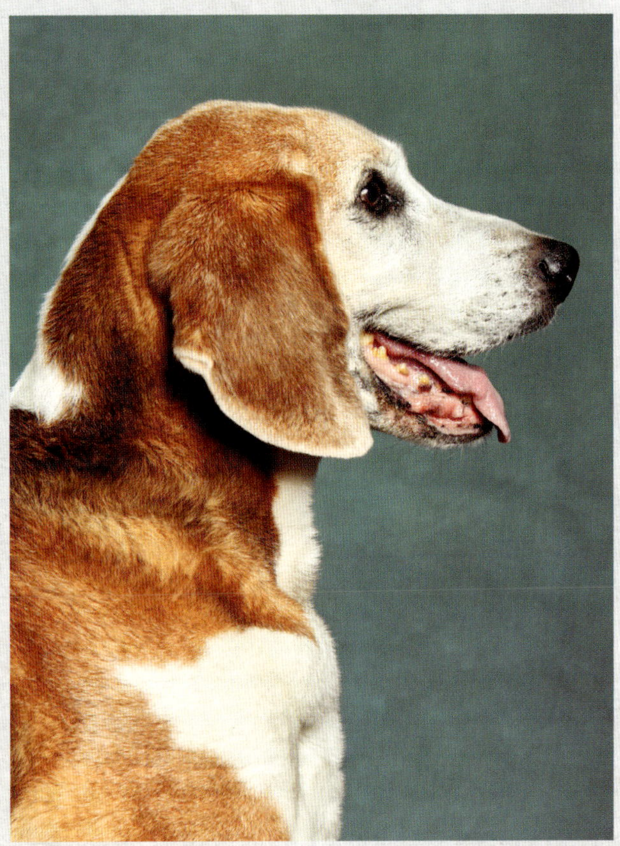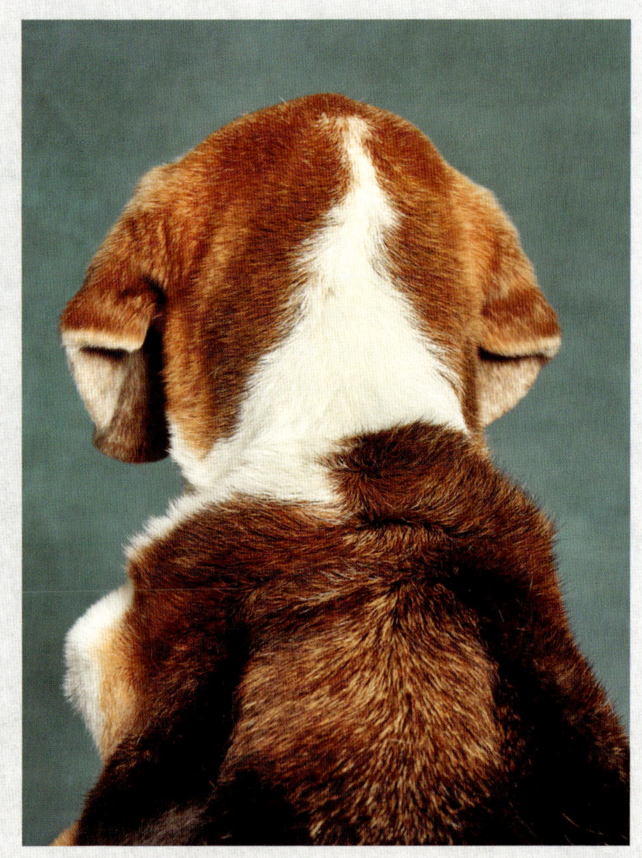

D, Harley

ALIASES: Harlequin / Old Man / Dog

BORN: 06/09/2000   TRADE: Food Connoisseur   BREED: Beagle

BUILD: Broad & Tall   EYES: Brown   HEIGHT: 75cm   HAIR: Tri Colour

MARKS: Has scar on front leg

PECULIARITIES: Is generally in a state of aloofness

M.O: ETC. Food Obsession, can sense when food is near and drools immediately upon detection.

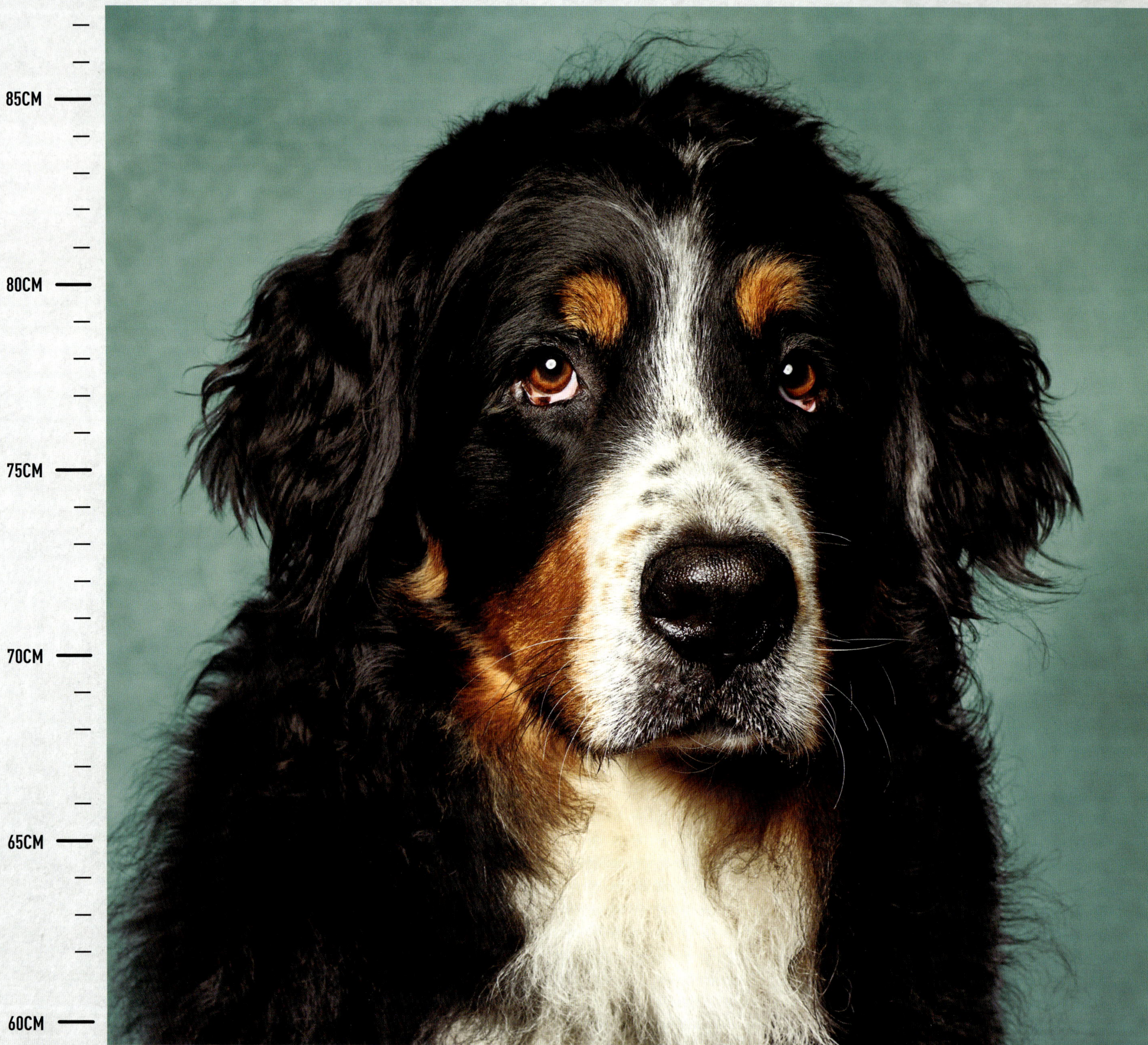

85CM
80CM
75CM
70CM
65CM
60CM

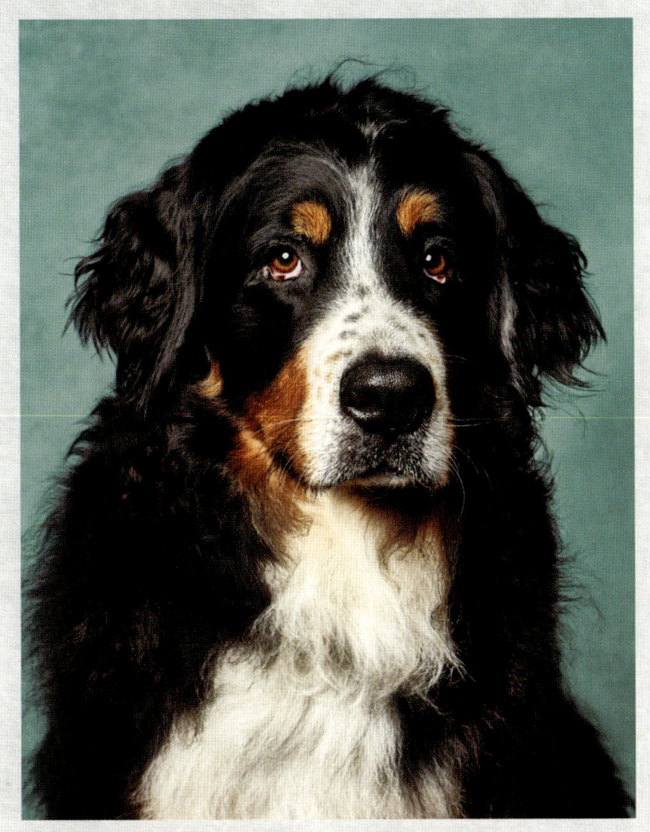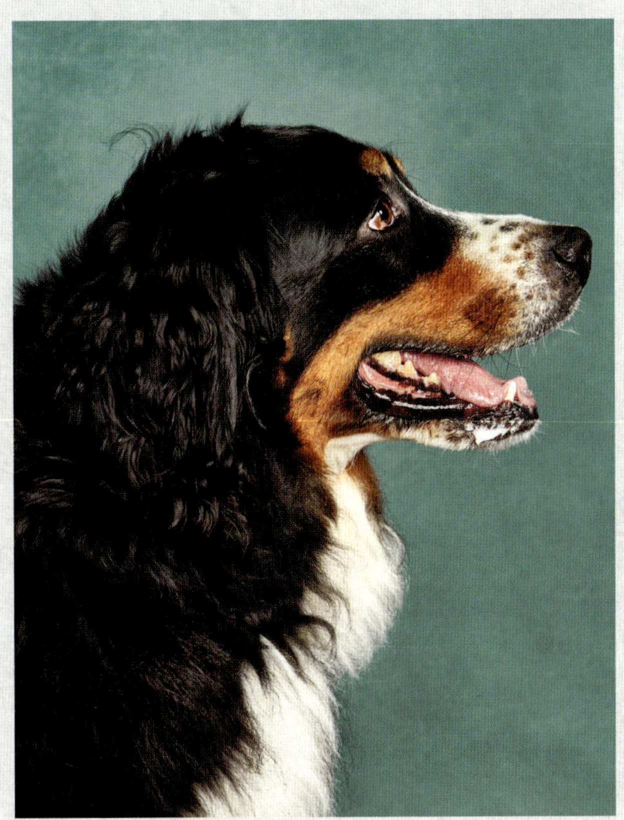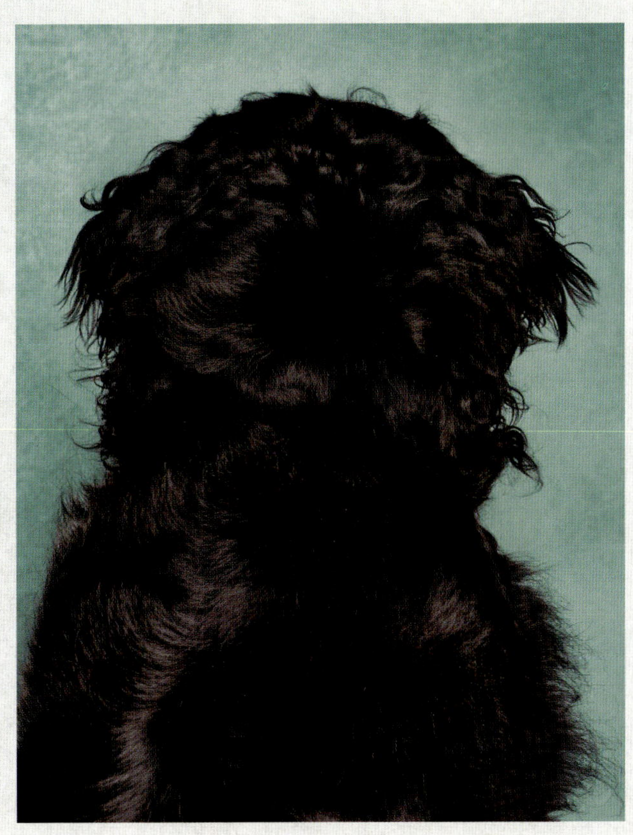

G, Dio

ALIASES:

BORN: 20/09/2010 TRADE: Sensitive Artful Dodger BREED: Bernese Mountain Dog

BUILD: Mountain Size EYES: Brown HEIGHT: 85cm HAIR: Black / Tan / White

MARKS: Freckles

PECULIARITIES: Has eyebrows that look like eyes when sleeping

M.O: ETC. Master of theft — has been able to stealthily steal, consume and return to innocent exterior before his victims realised their cake was missing.

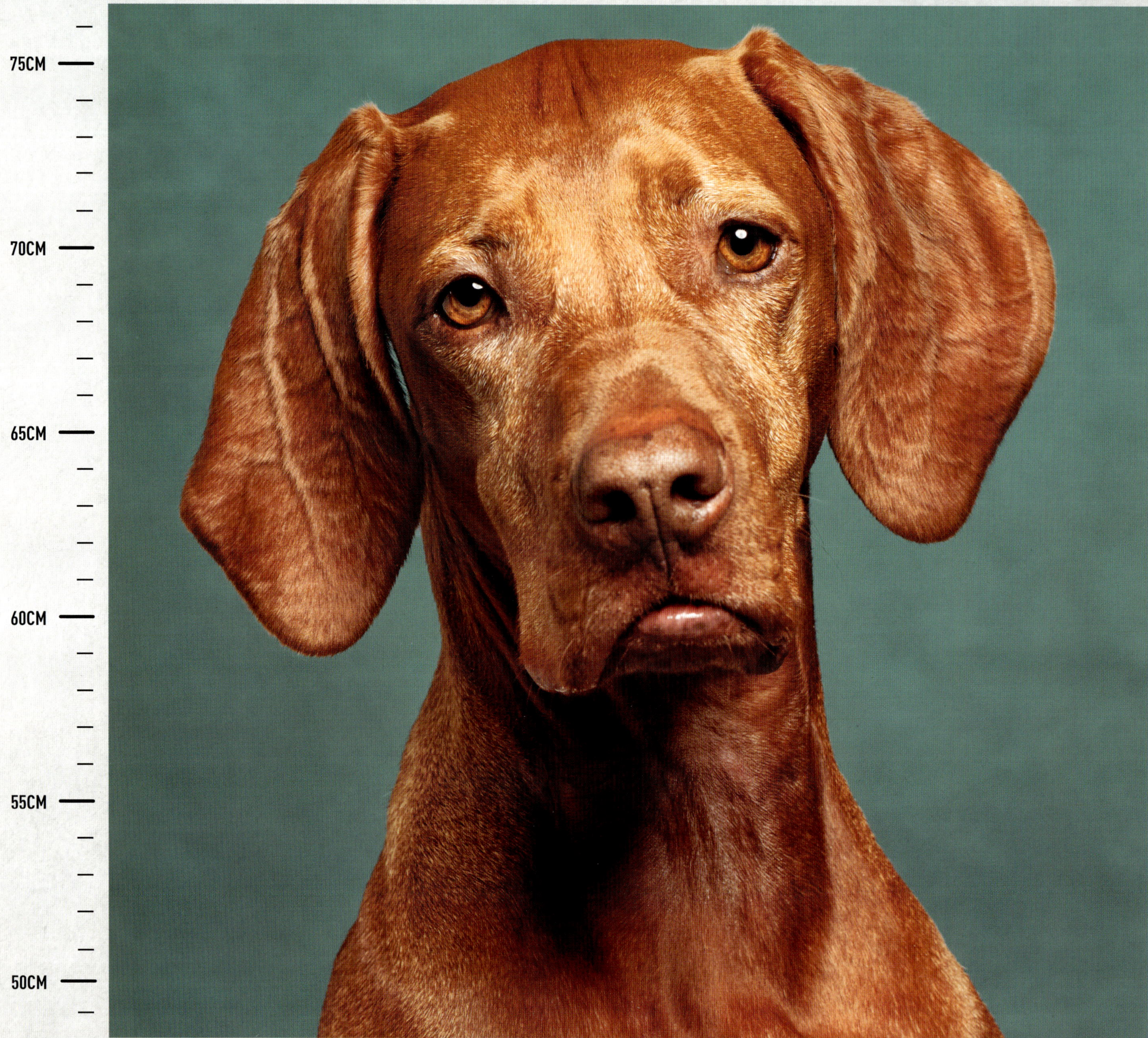

75CM
70CM
65CM
60CM
55CM
50CM

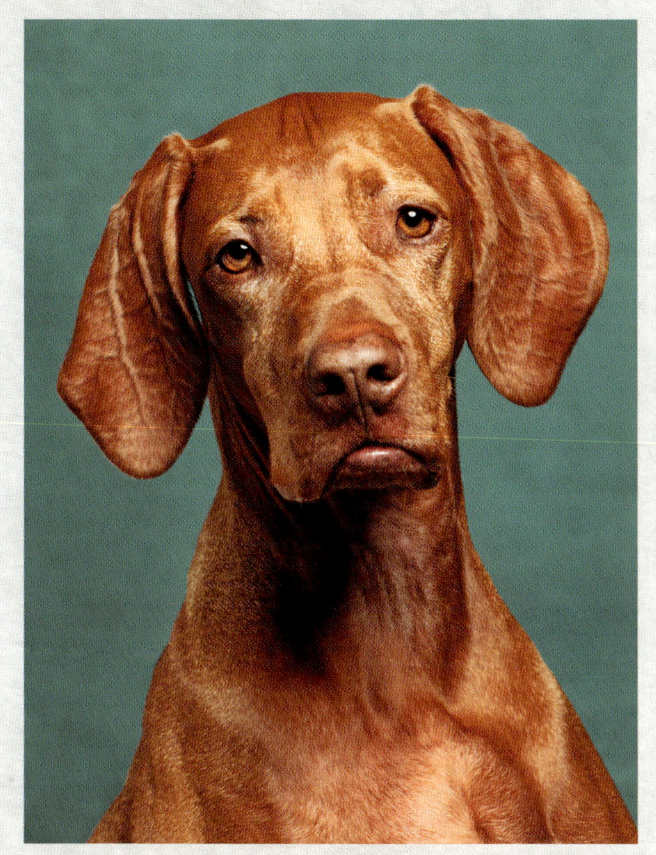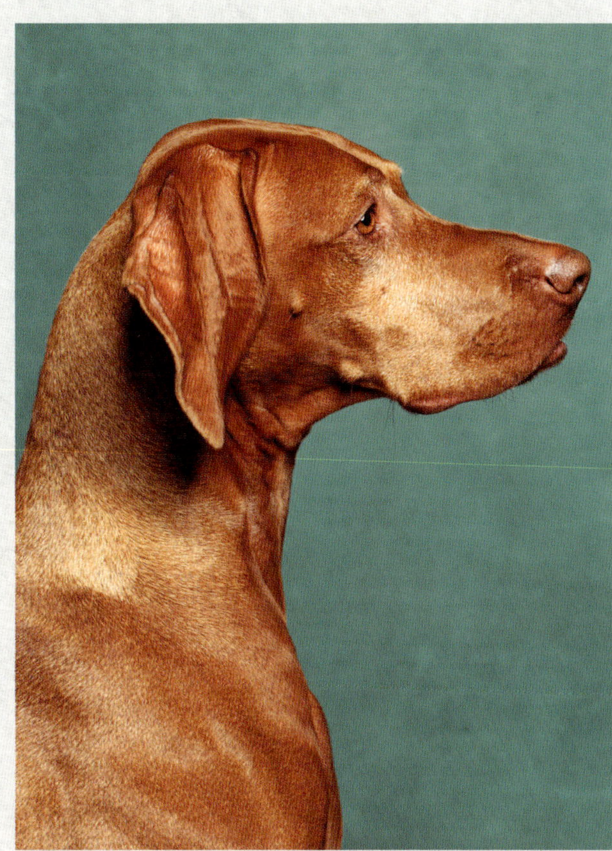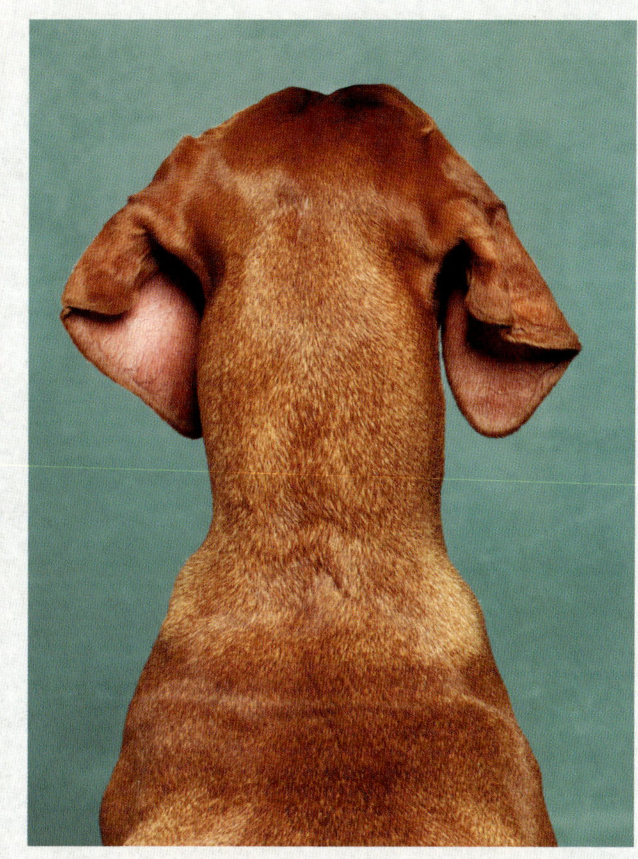

G, Lilly

ALIASES: Lillian (when in trouble)

BORN: September 2010 TRADE: Athlete BREED: Hungarian Vizsla

BUILD: Olympic Swimmer EYES: Brown HEIGHT: 76cm HAIR: Copper / Red

MARKS: Strong presence of veins in ears resembling autumn leaves

PECULIARITIES: Very smart and very clingy

M.O: ETC. Has a stash of stuffed teddies — large 'Elephant Ted' is her favourite.
Does not sit. For anyone.

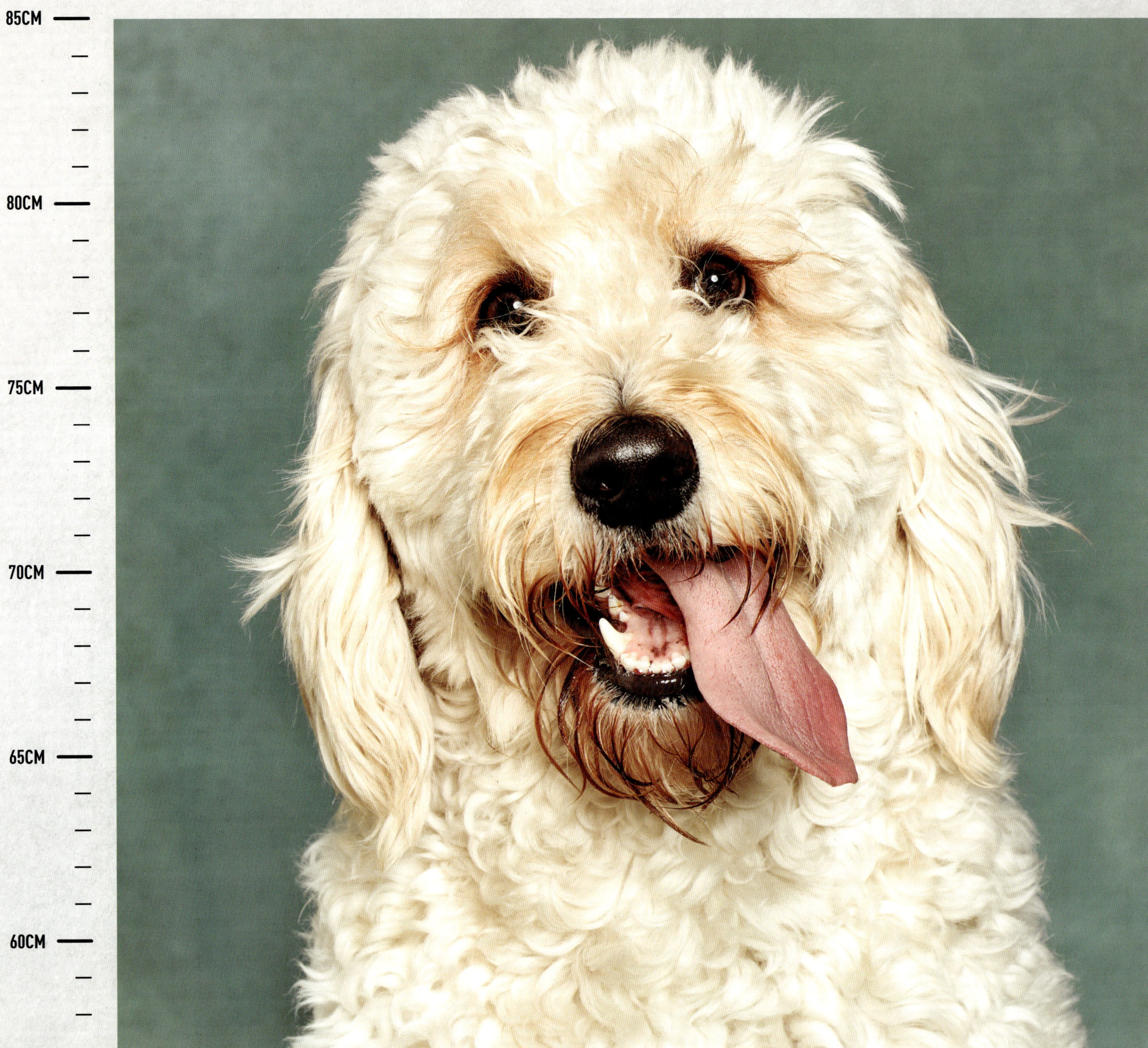
85CM
80CM
75CM
70CM
65CM
60CM

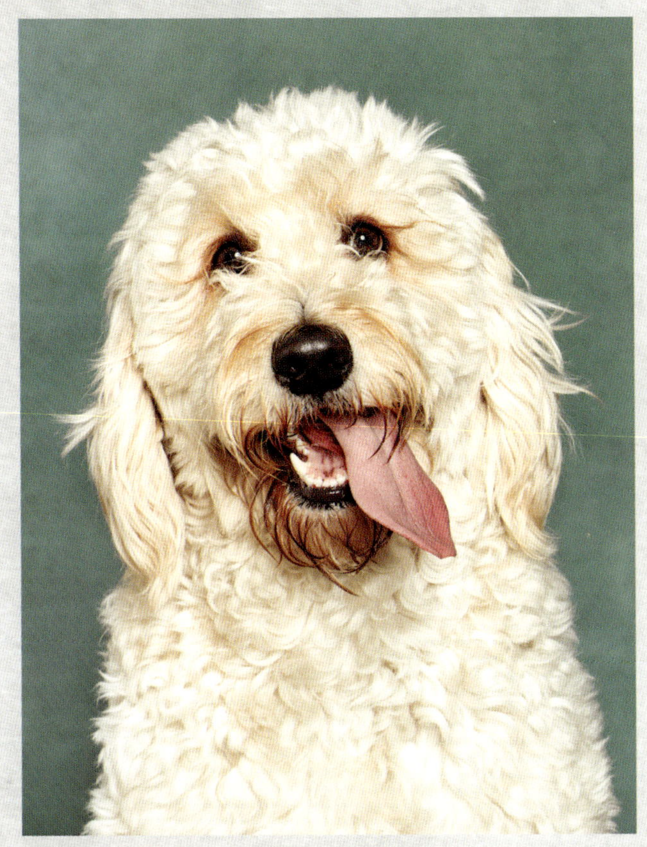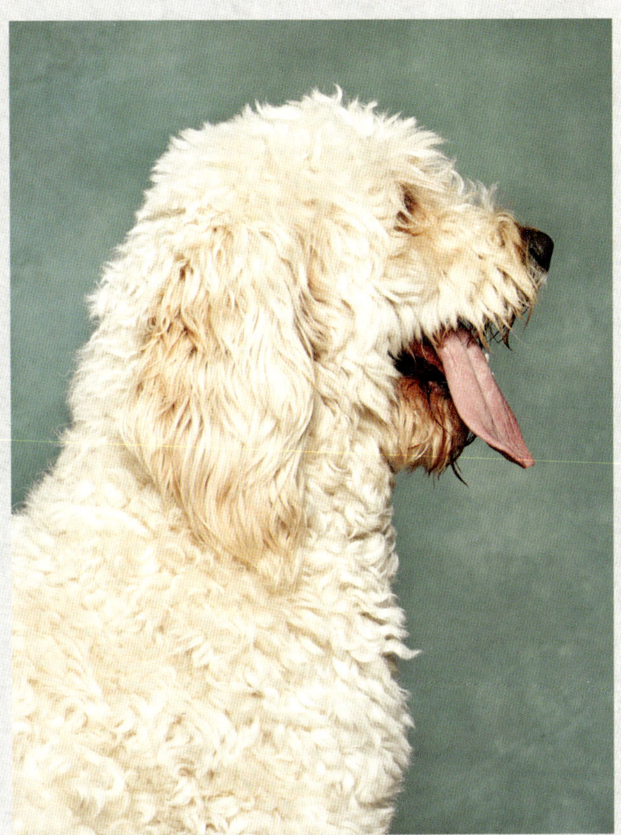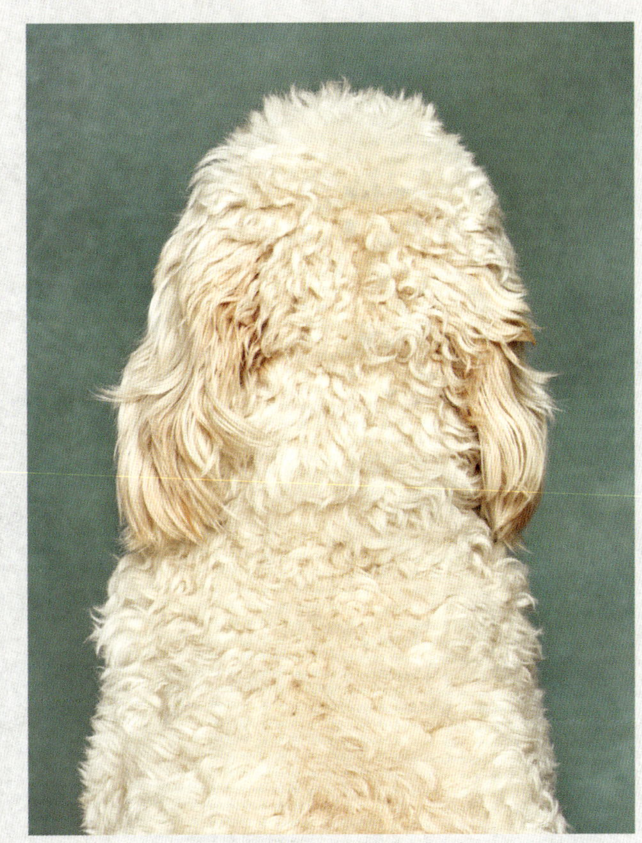

E, Benji

ALIASES:	Lazza / Little Guy

BORN: 01/09/2015	**TRADE:** Goof-ball	**BREED:** Groodle
BUILD: Tall & Floofy	**EYES:** Brown	**HEIGHT:** 85cm **HAIR:** Golden

MARKS:

PECULIARITIES: His Badonk — has a waggle when he walks

M.O: ETC. His smile has been known to have the opposite intention. It has been reported that a man ran the other way when his smile was deployed.

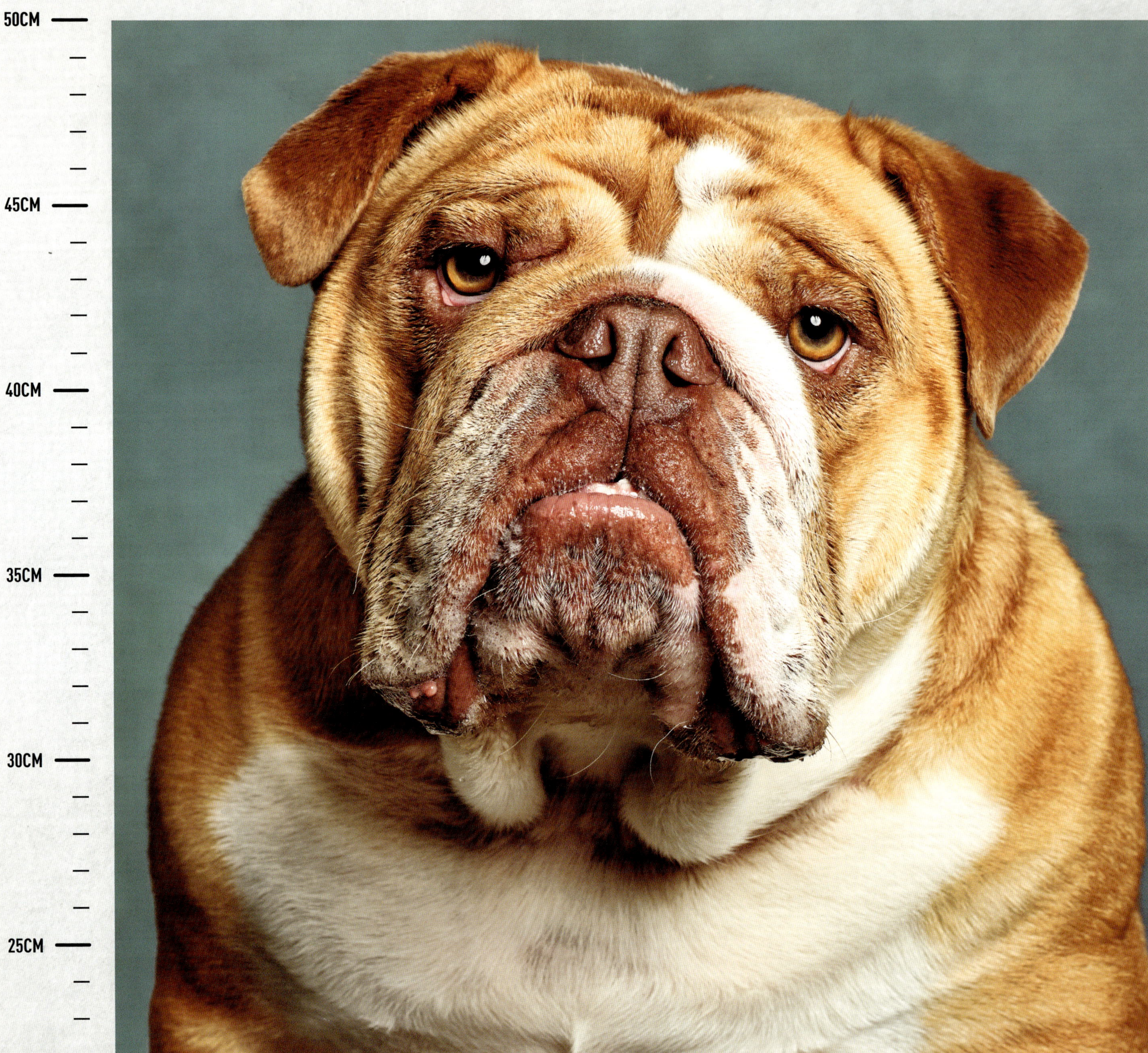
50CM
45CM
40CM
35CM
30CM
25CM

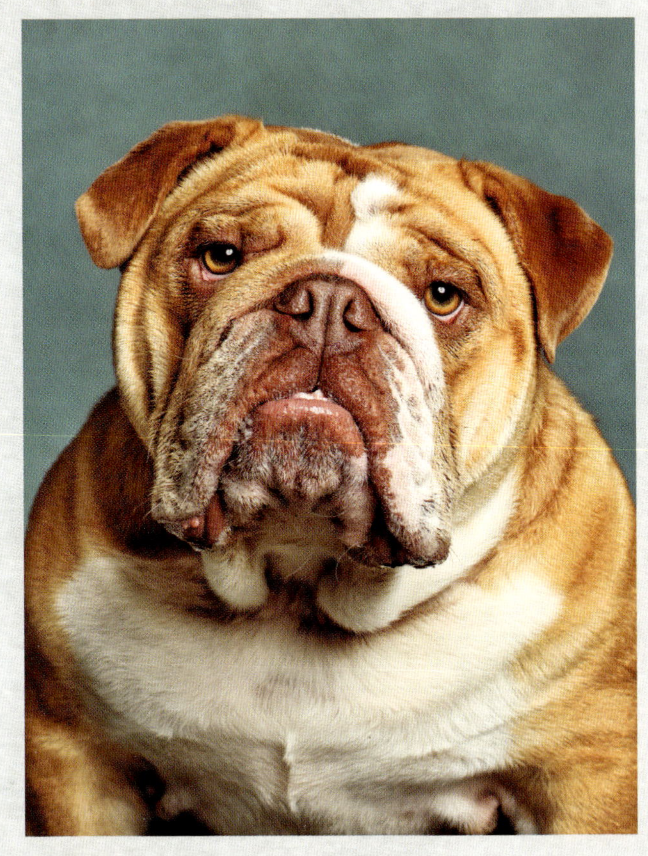 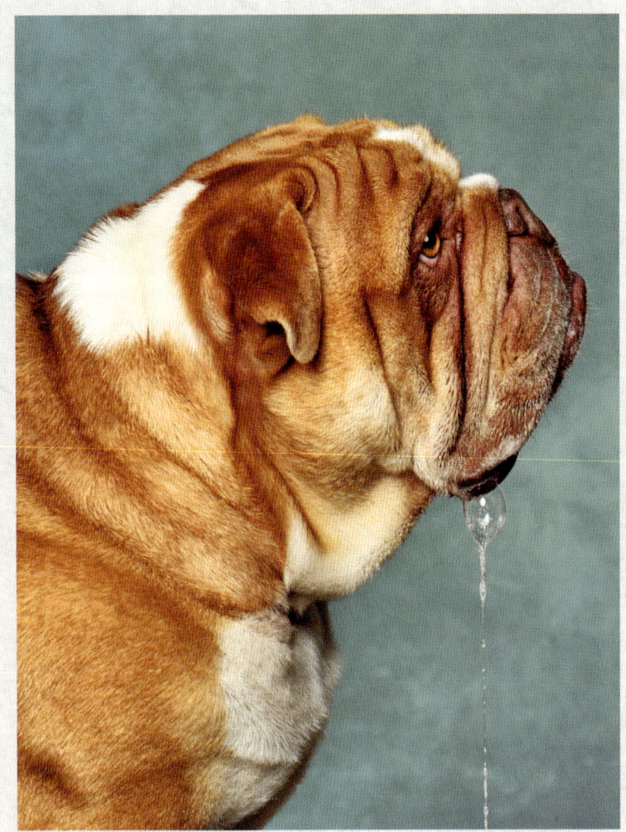 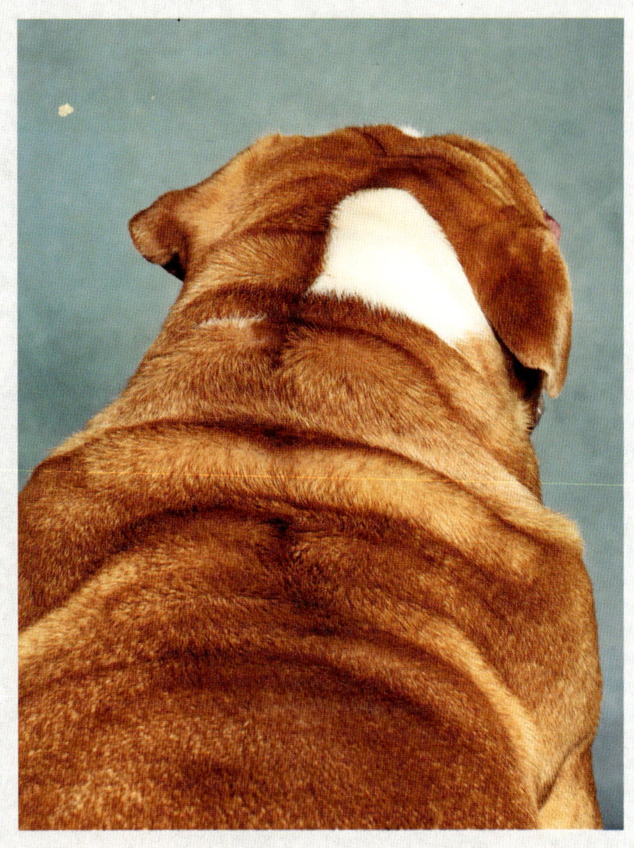

W, Benson

ALIASES: Bee Bee

BORN: 21/10/2015   TRADE: Lover not a Fighter   BREED: Australian x English Bulldog

BUILD: Rolly   EYES: Copper Brown   HEIGHT: 50cm   HAIR: White / Copper / Brown

MARKS: White patch on back of neck behind right ear

PECULIARITIES: Will eat terracotta pots to satisfy hunger when food is restricted

M.O: ETC. Seeks out neighbourhood cats, but when confronted has been known to squeal and flee.

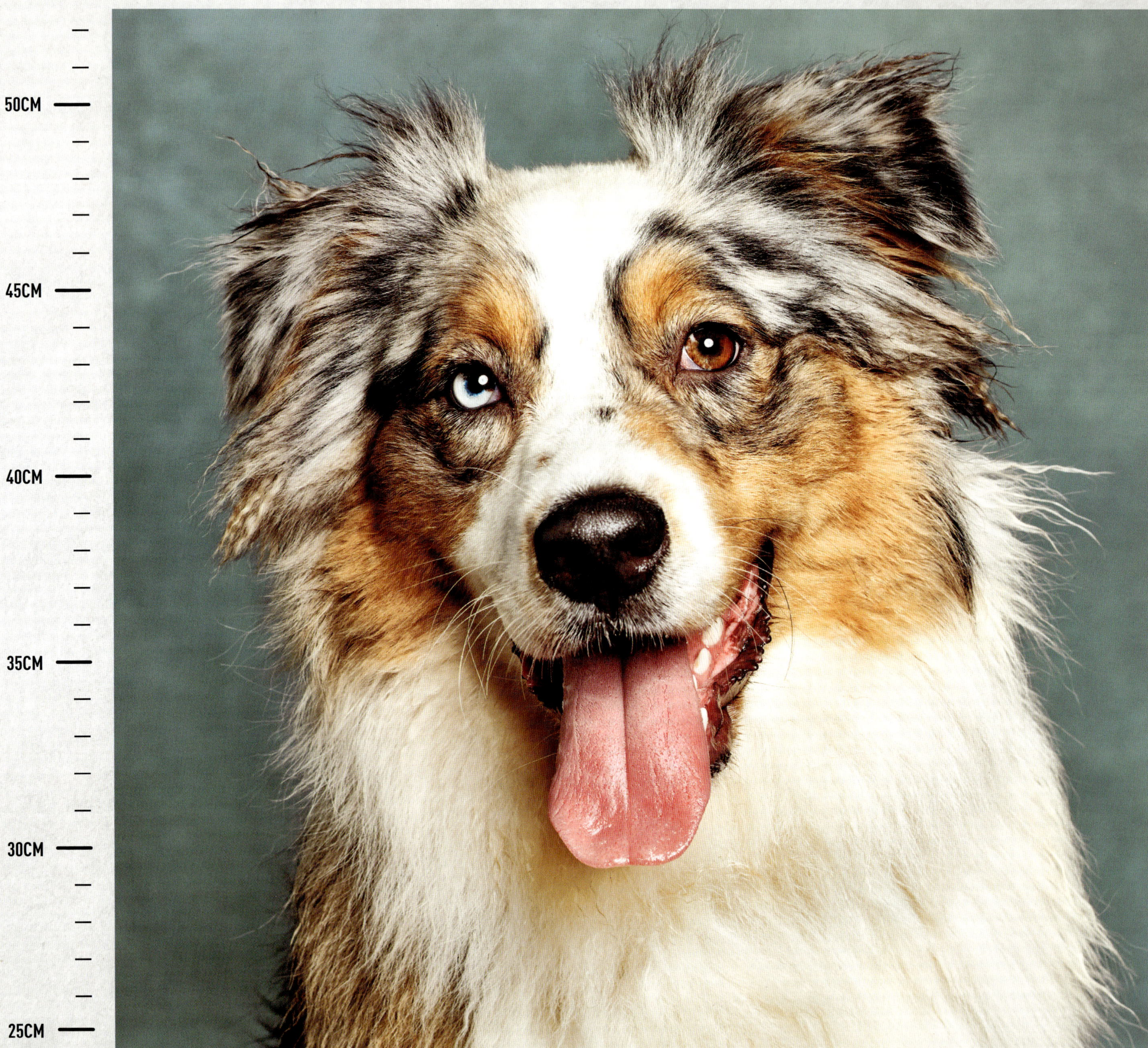

50CM
45CM
40CM
35CM
30CM
25CM

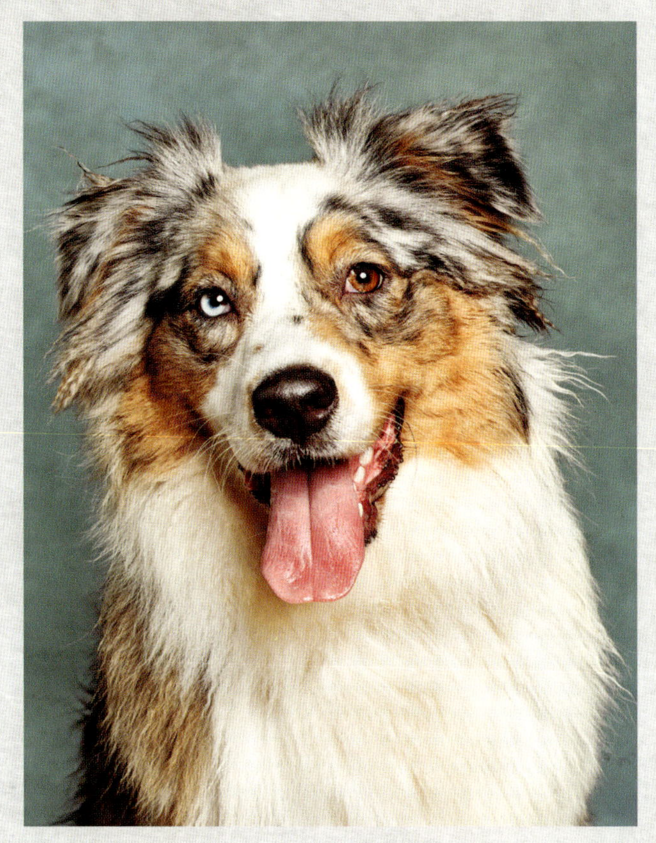 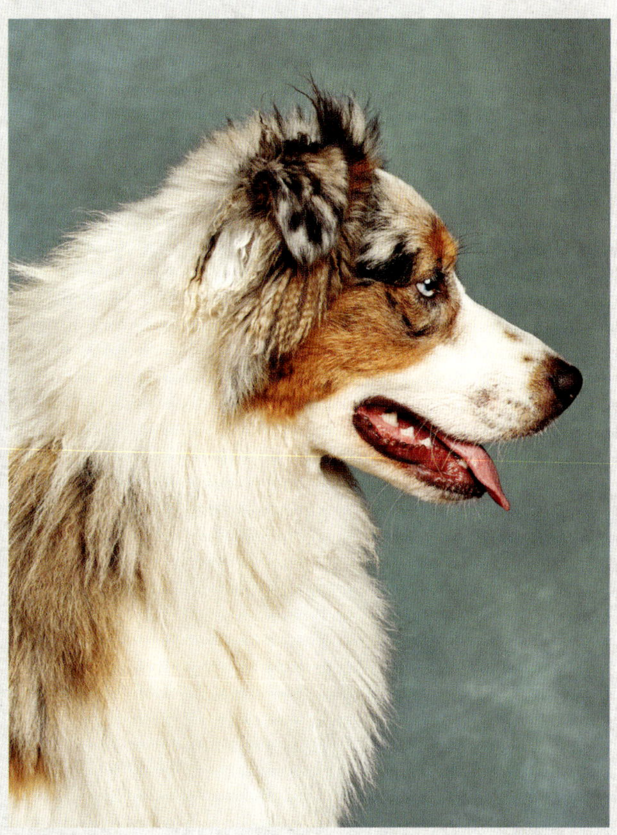 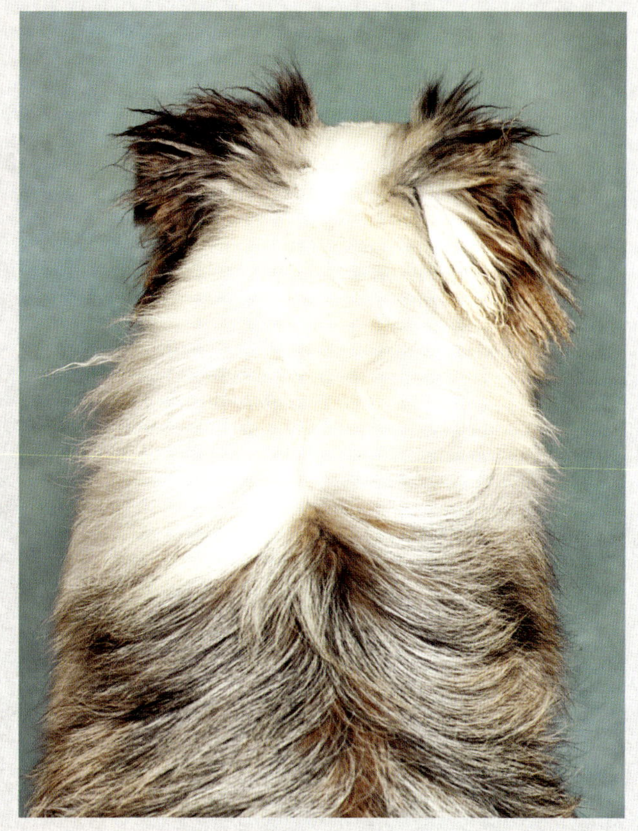

S, Pepper

ALIASES:	

BORN: 26/08/2016	**TRADE:** Explorer	**BREED:** Australian Shepherd

BUILD: Fluffy **EYES:** Blue & Brown **HEIGHT:** 57cm **HAIR:** White / Tan / Grey / Black

MARKS: Black 'pepper' like flecks around her face and ears

PECULIARITIES: Maintains strict eye contact with her humans at all times.

M.O: ETC. Has been known to stick her nose into everything — fridges, dishwasher and washing machine. Known to escape confinement in order to partake in a late night 'game' on a busy road with her counterpart, Benson.

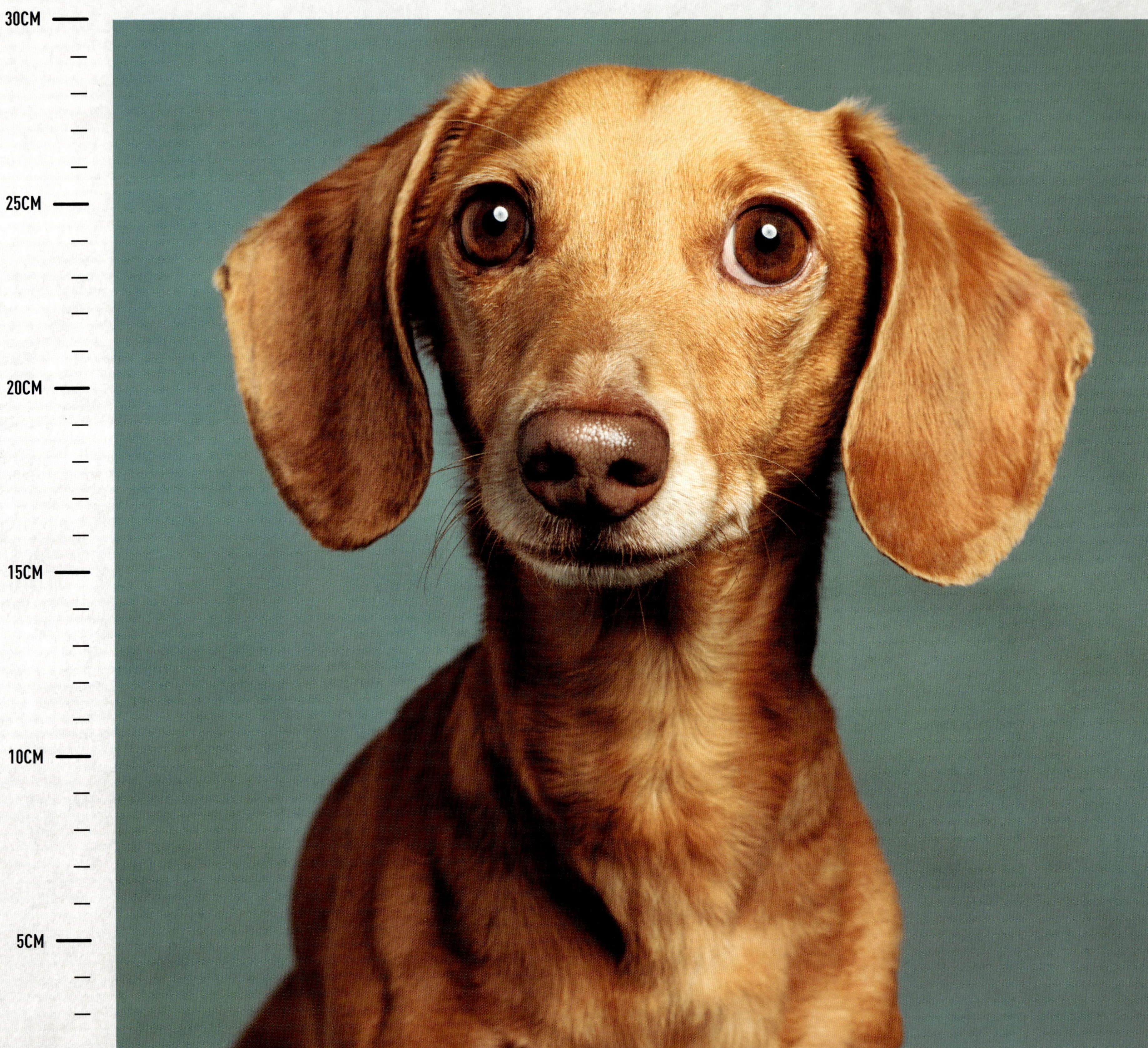
30CM
25CM
20CM
15CM
10CM
5CM

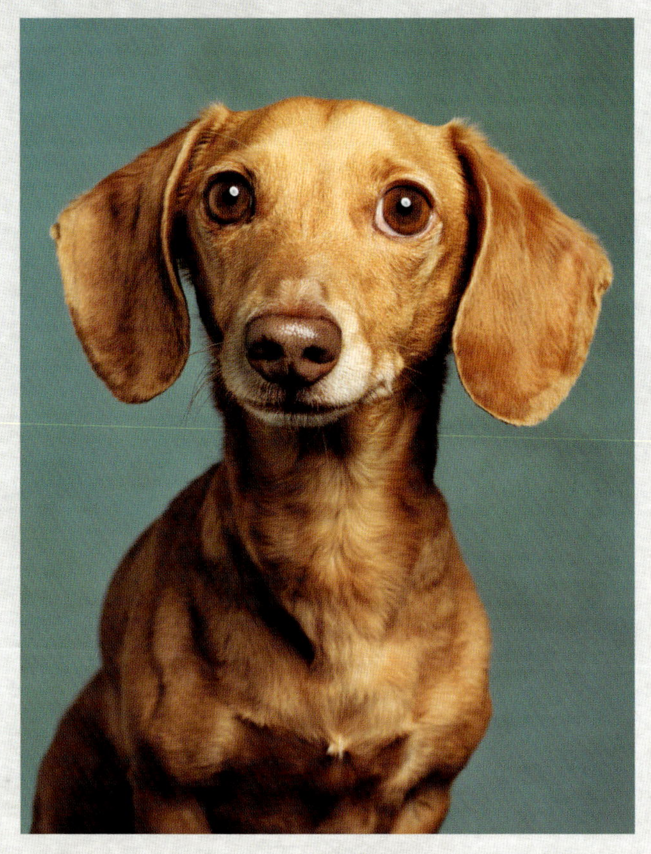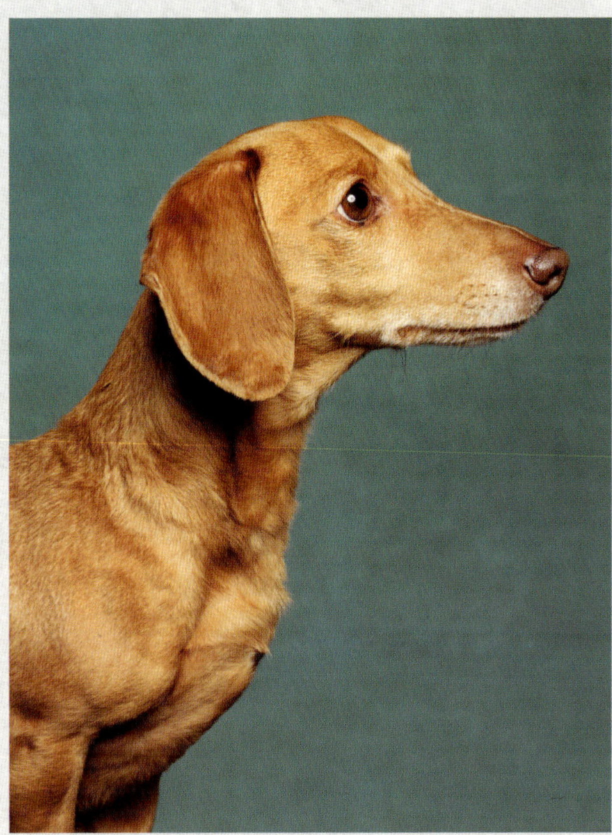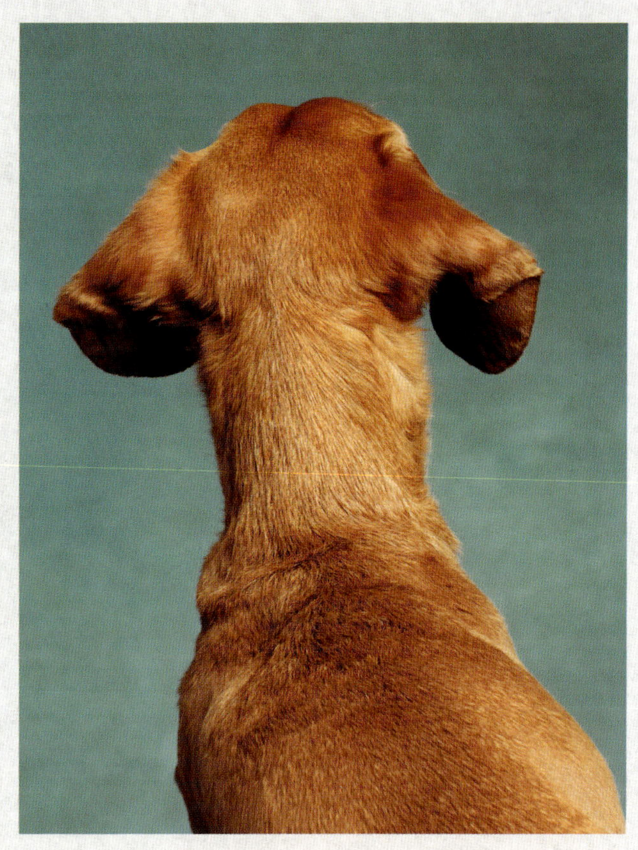

D, Brian

ALIASES: Mighty Mouse / Muppet / Mouse / B-Man

BORN: 26/12/2010   TRADE: Sentinel   BREED: Miniature Dachshund

BUILD: Teeny   EYES: Brown   HEIGHT: 27cm   HAIR: Tan

MARKS: Lightening of fur around muzzle area

PECULIARITIES: Has been known to army crawl around the house to express happiness.

M.O: ETC. Always alert and ready to vocalise the presence of other dogs. Understands human words and listens into phone calls — when the phrase 'I'll see you soon' is uttered, he will race to the door and sit waiting to leave.

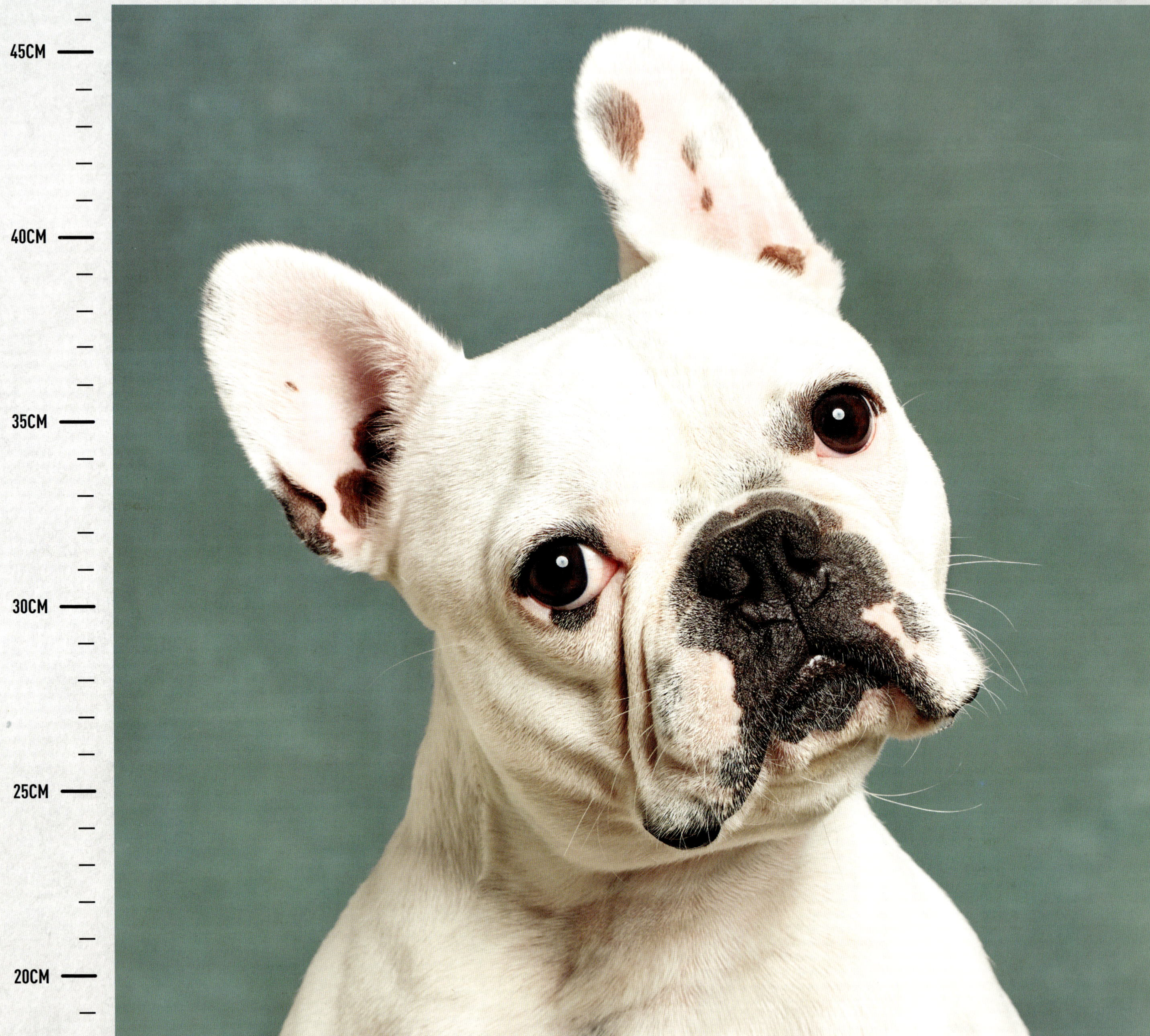
45CM
40CM
35CM
30CM
25CM
20CM

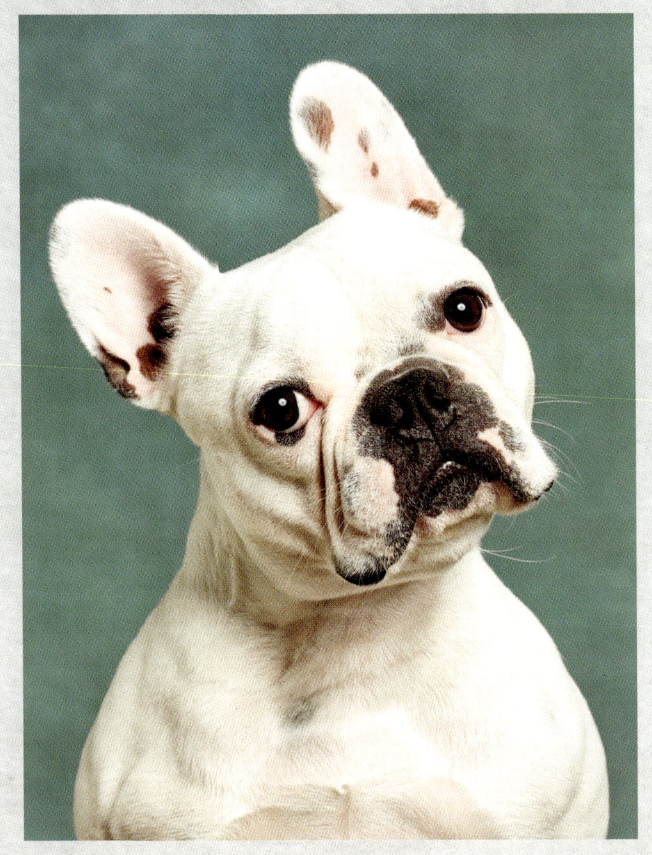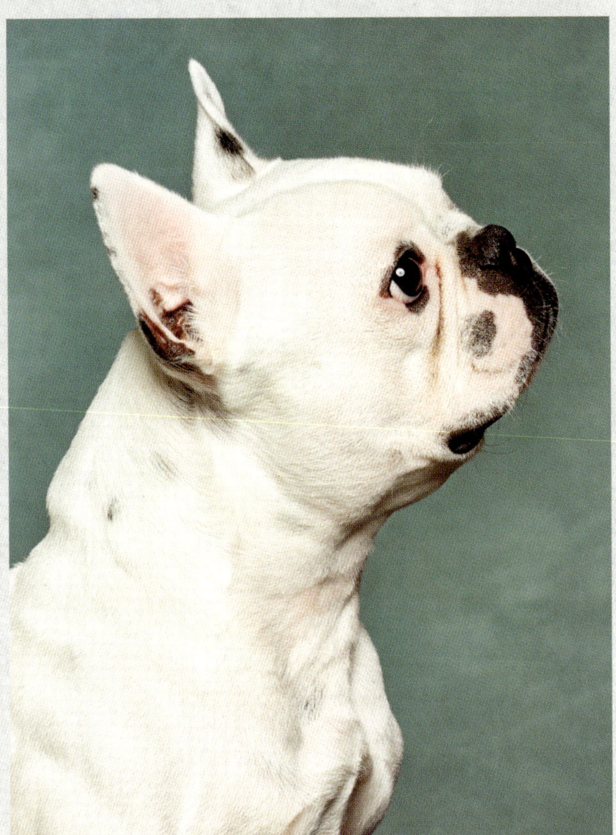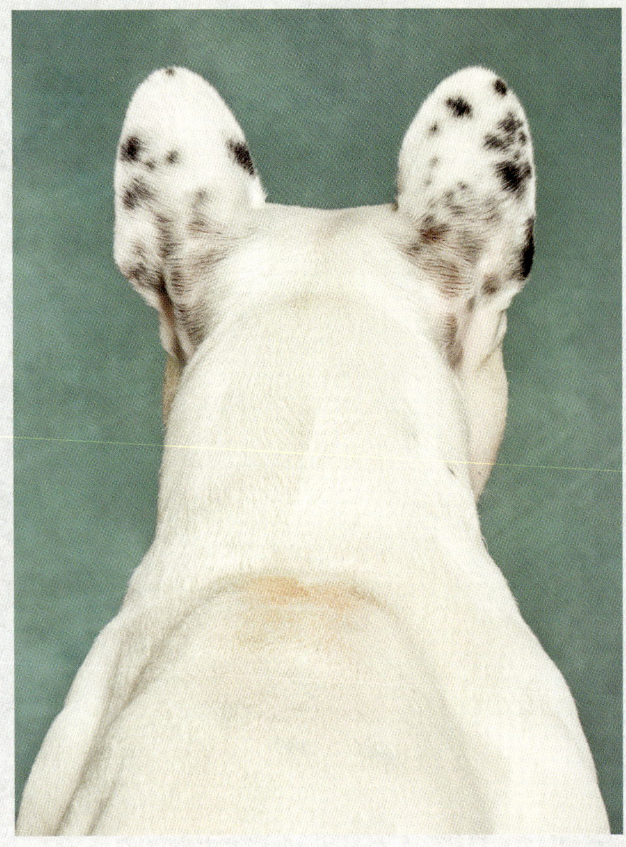

G, Duke

BORN: 22/05/2015	**TRADE:** Ball Chaser	**BREED:** French Bulldog
BUILD: Ripped	**EYES:** Brown	**HEIGHT:** 46cm **HAIR:** White / Black

MARKS: Black spots dotted around ears

PECULIARITIES: Has been known to do random army rolls around the floor

M.O: ETC. Will do anything to obtain his property. After a little jump test to size up a large jump to a mantle, witnesses report seeing him launch towards the prize only to see him miscalculate and face-plant into the fire grill — he was not harmed.

DUKE
THE BIG DOG IN A SMALL PACKAGE

Duke — though the smallest of his litter and resembling a little piglet when his humans adopted him, has the largest personality.

Ball obsessed, he loves playing with balls by himself and strategically *accidentally* rolling balls under tables he cannot fit underneath as a ploy to get humans to play with him.

THINGS DUKE LOVES:

- Stealing balls at the beach
- Doing random army rolls
- Snoozing
- Heat — sun baking, laying in front of the fire, on top of floor vents, being underneath duvets

THINGS DUKE HATES:

- Missing out on what the humans are doing
- Vegetables

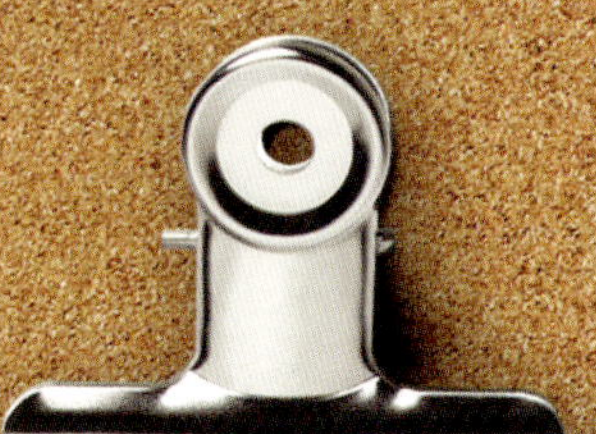

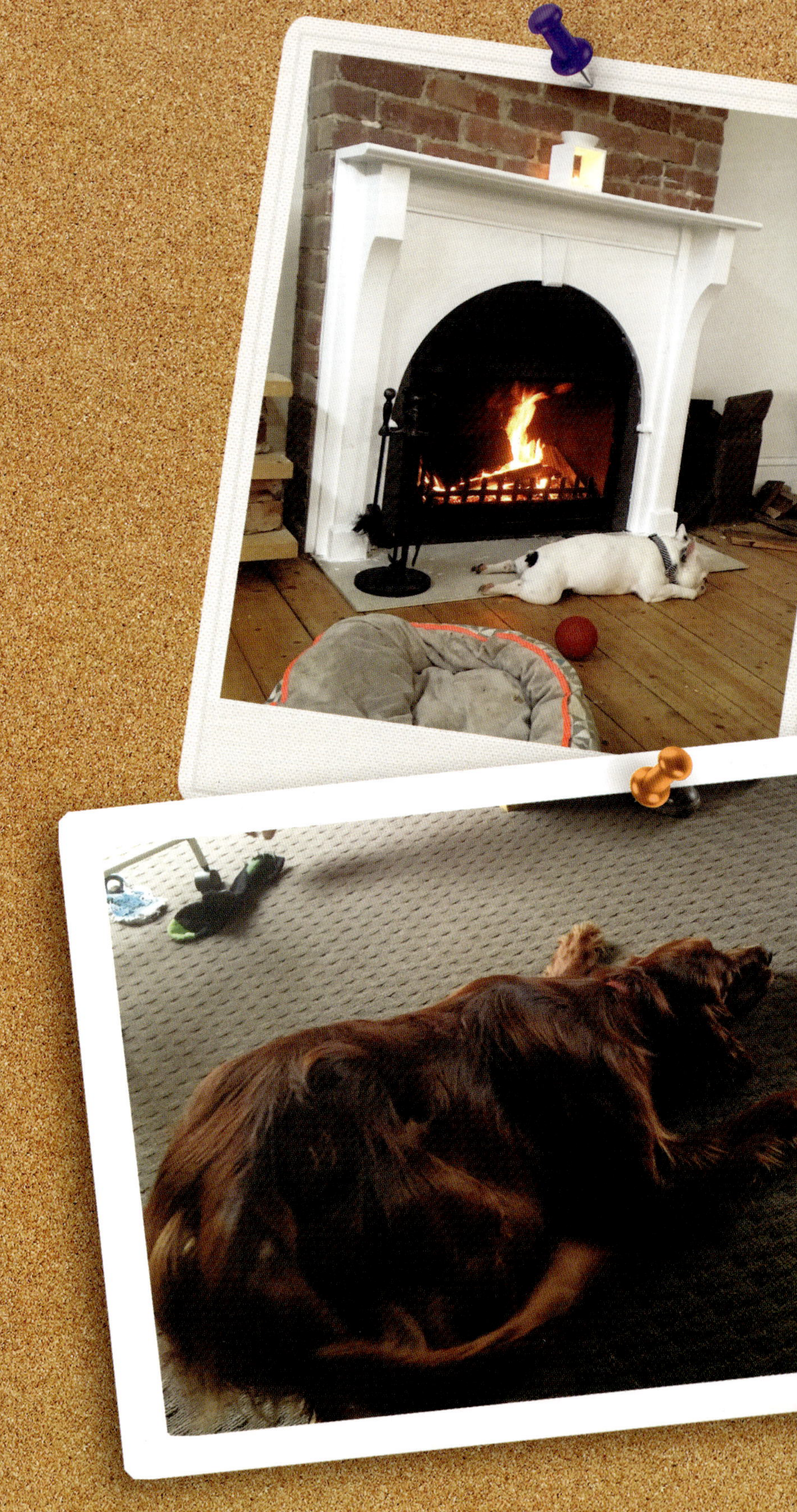

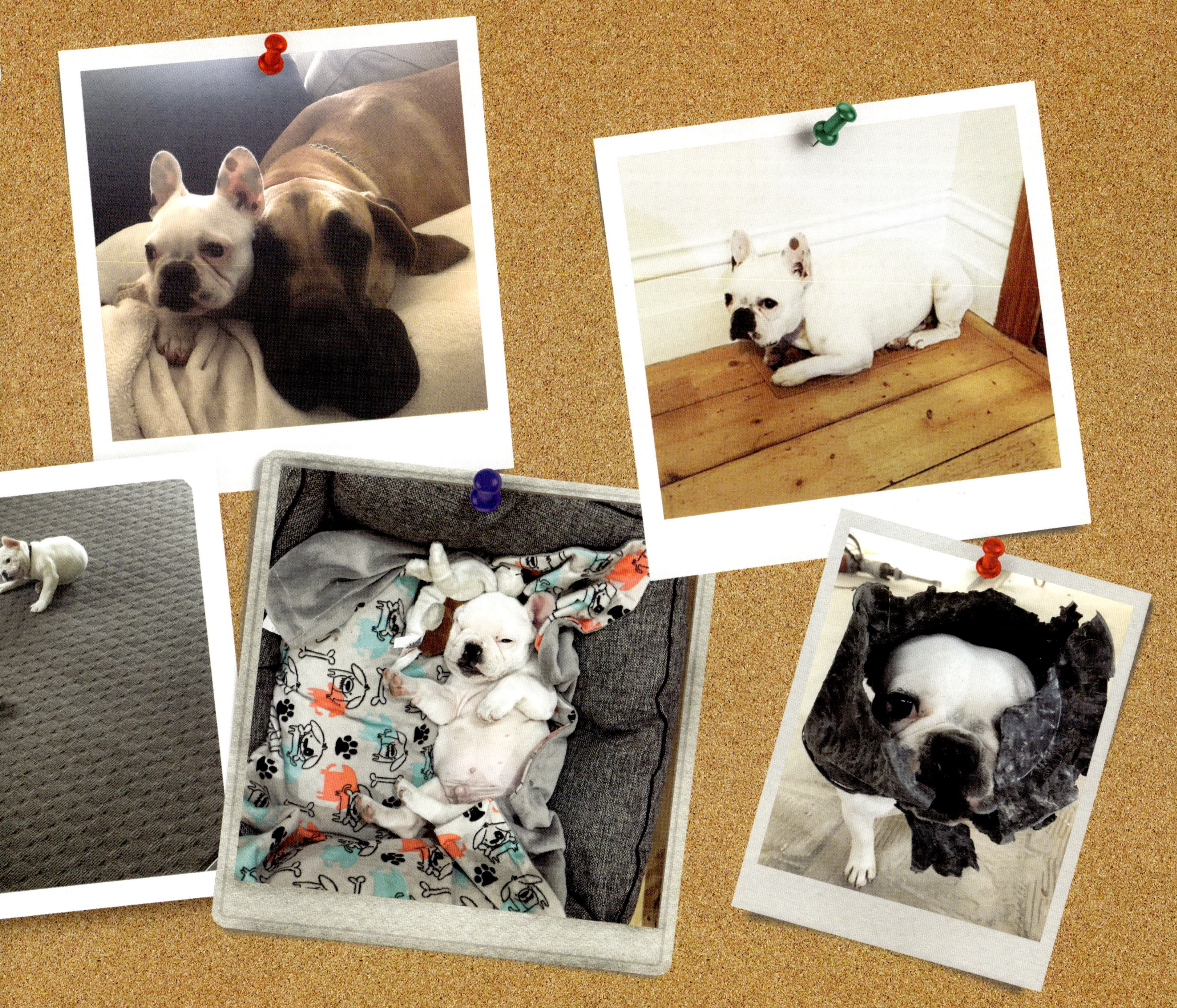

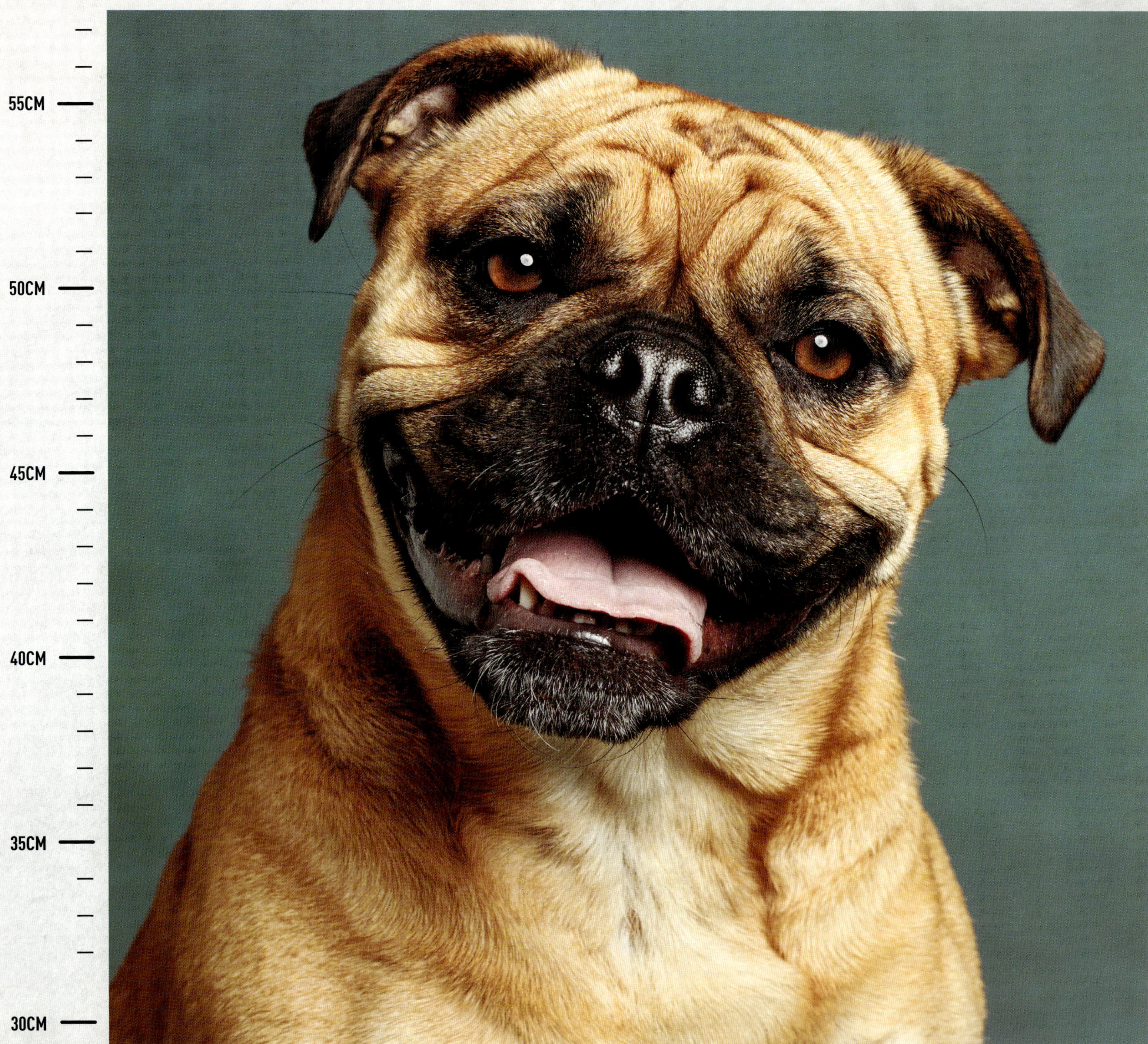

55CM
50CM
45CM
40CM
35CM
30CM

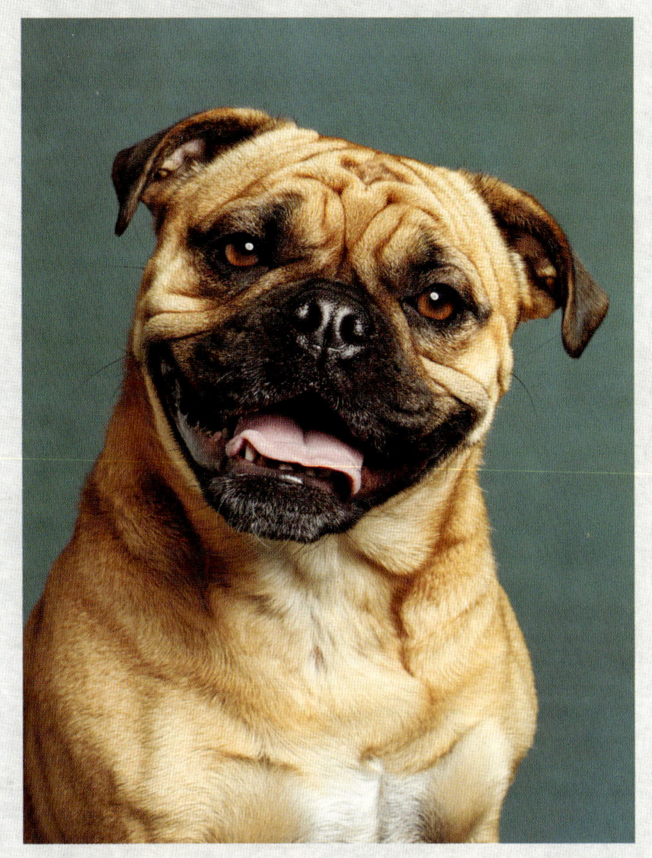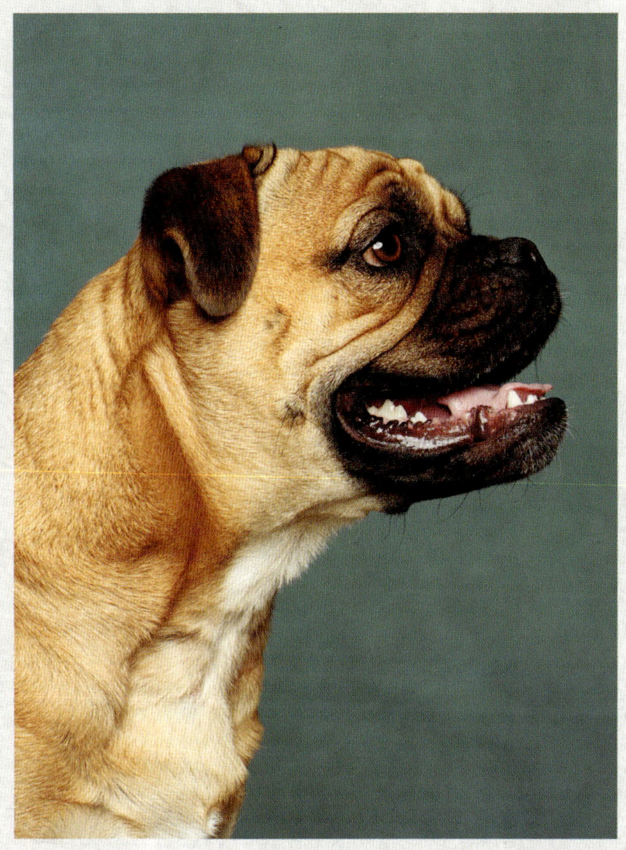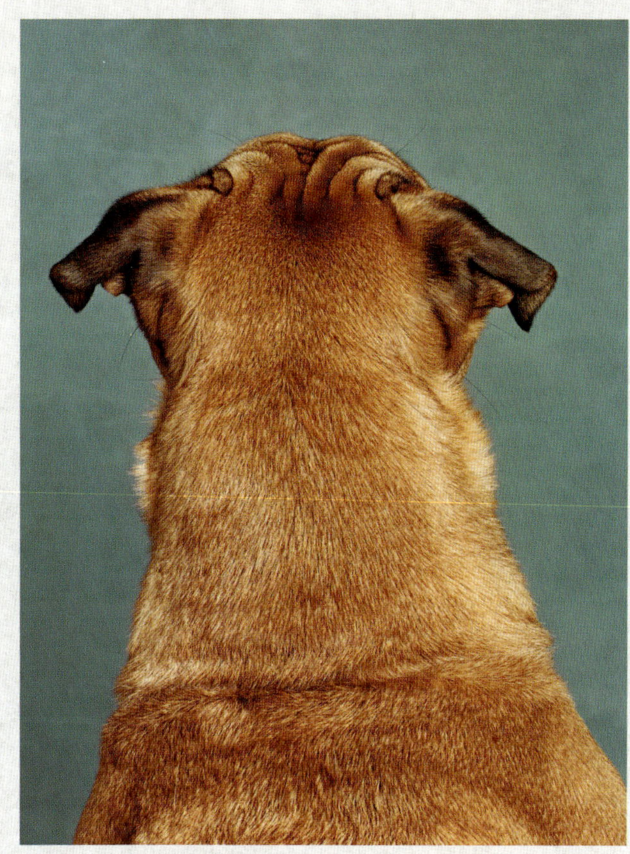

M, Bronte

ALIASES: Nugget

BORN: 11/01/2015   TRADE: Dummy Collector   BREED: British Bulldog x Pug

BUILD: Giant Pug   EYES: Brown   HEIGHT: 57cm   HAIR: Tan / Black / Brown

MARKS: Little patch of white on tummy

PECULIARITIES: Is a surprisingly excellent swimmer

M.O: ETC. Has a knack for finding baby dummies — then proceeds to suck them like a baby. When excited, has been observed shaking her coiled pug tailed posterior.

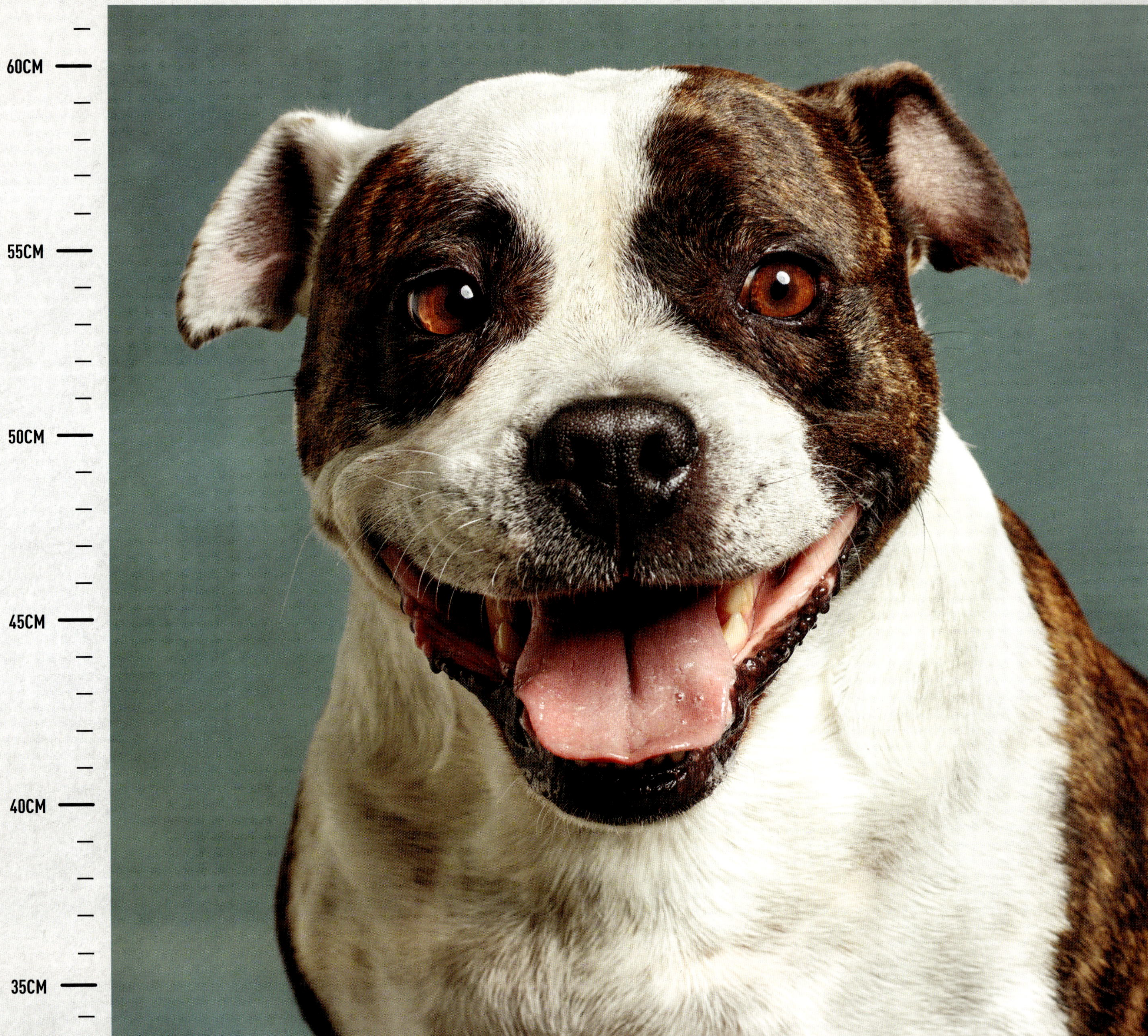

60CM
55CM
50CM
45CM
40CM
35CM

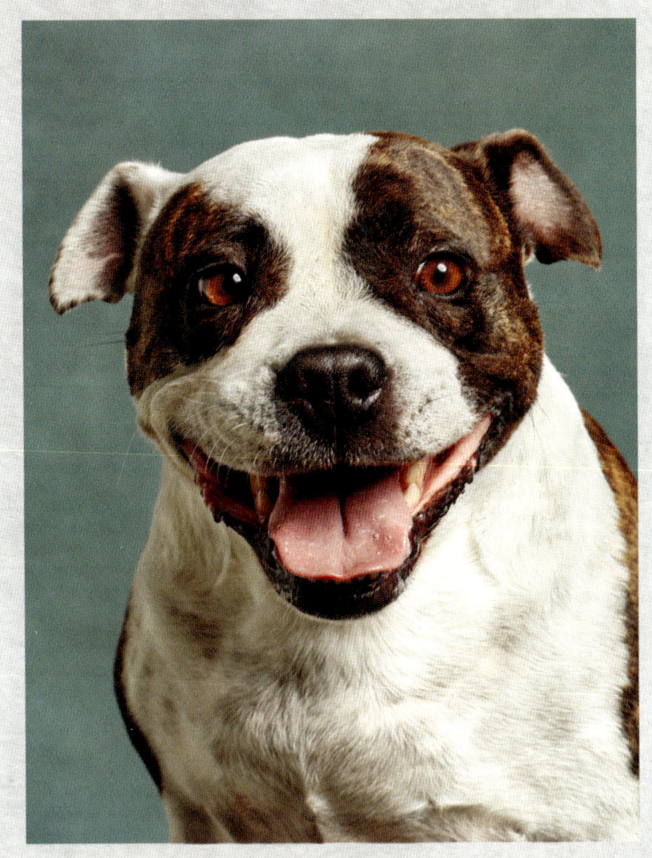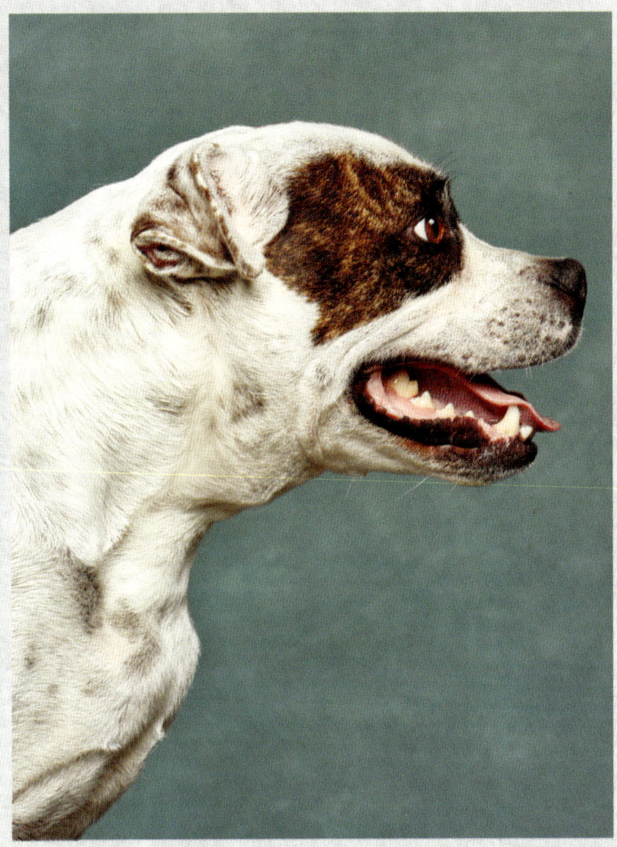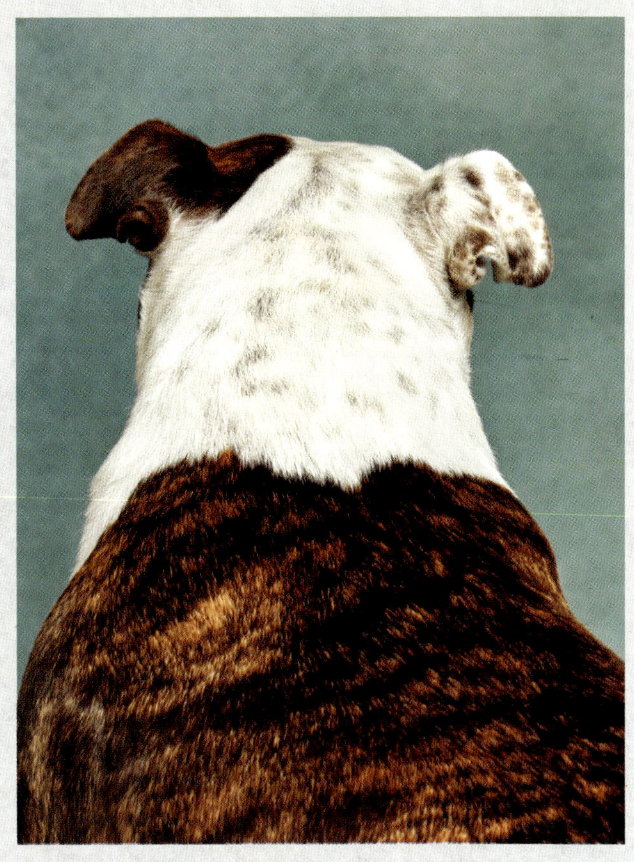

GG, Dracula

ALIASES: Drac / Wootsie / Wiggles

BORN: 11/11/2011 TRADE: Cat in a Dog's Body BREED: English Bulldog x Staffy

BUILD: Stocky EYES: Brown HEIGHT: 60cm HAIR: White / Brindle

MARKS: One brindle ear, one white ear

PECULIARITIES: Exhibits a 'wiggle bottom dance' when excited

M.O: ETC. Frequently attempts to enter a stealth mode — using this to sneak onto a couch one paw are at a time as if he were a 15kg ball of invisible.

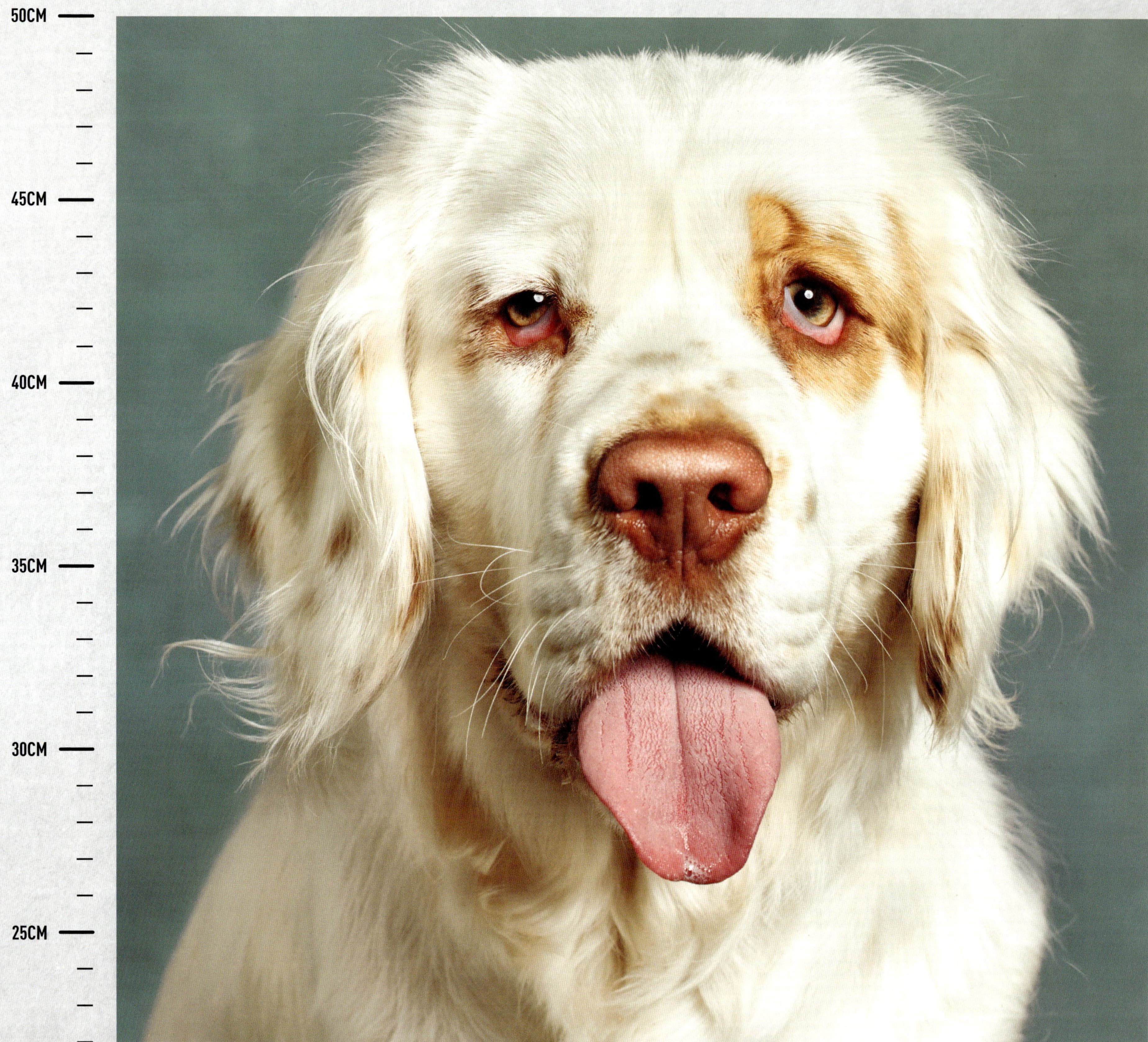

50CM
45CM
40CM
35CM
30CM
25CM

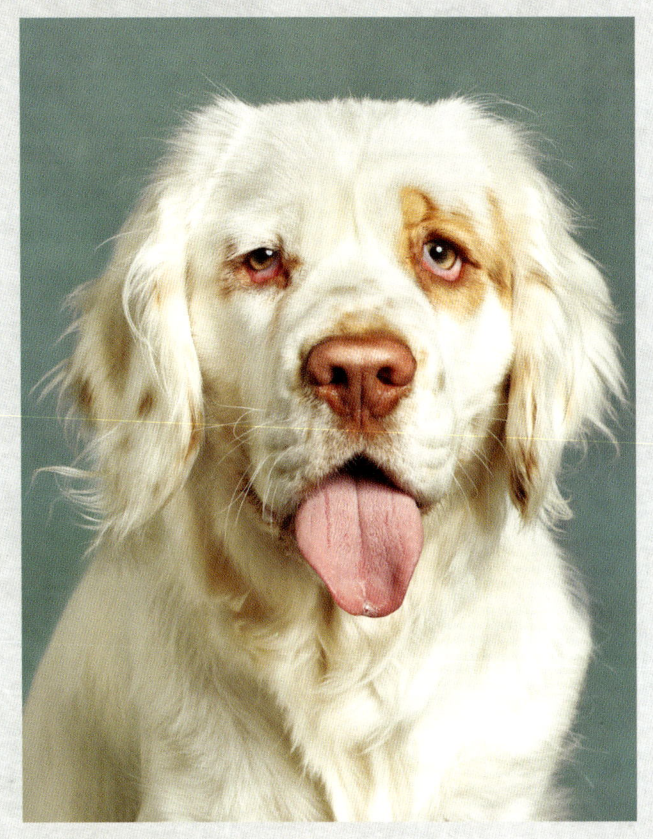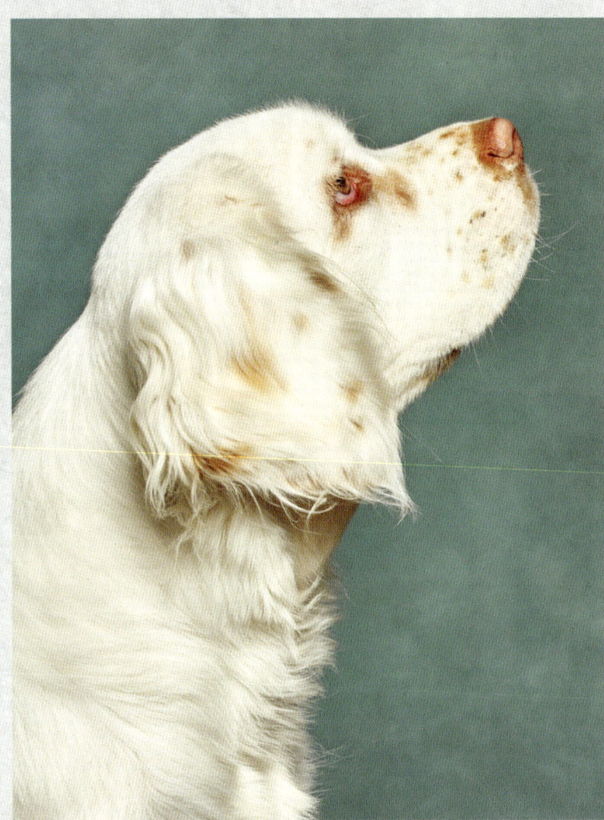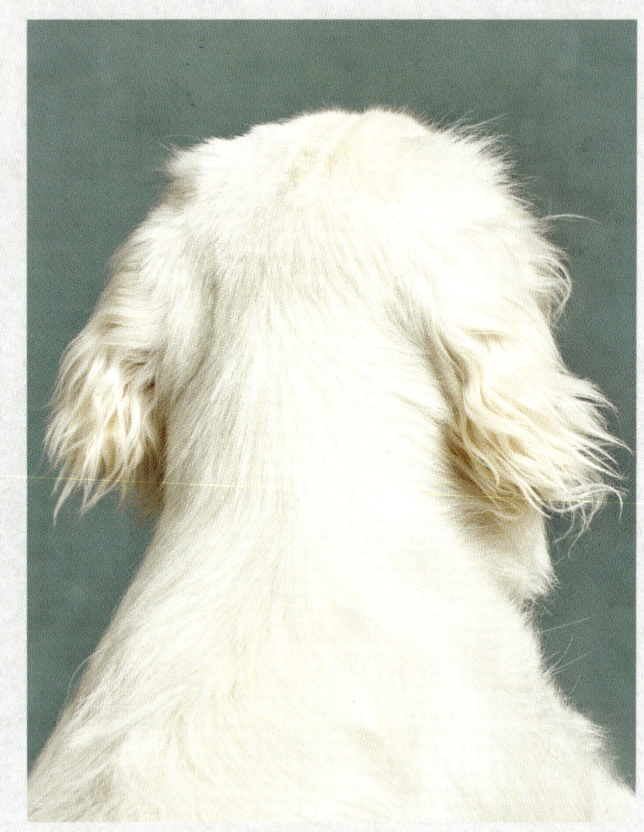

GG, Peach

BORN: 15/11/2016   **TRADE:** Sloth   **BREED:** Clumber Spaniel

BUILD: Stocky   **EYES:** Copper   **HEIGHT:** 50cm   **HAIR:** White / Light Brown

MARKS: Little brown patch on left eye

PECULIARITIES: If one wishes to see her eyes they must direct her gaze upwards

M.O: ETC. Stores bounty — toys, tiny human's toys, shoes and articles of clothing — within her bed.

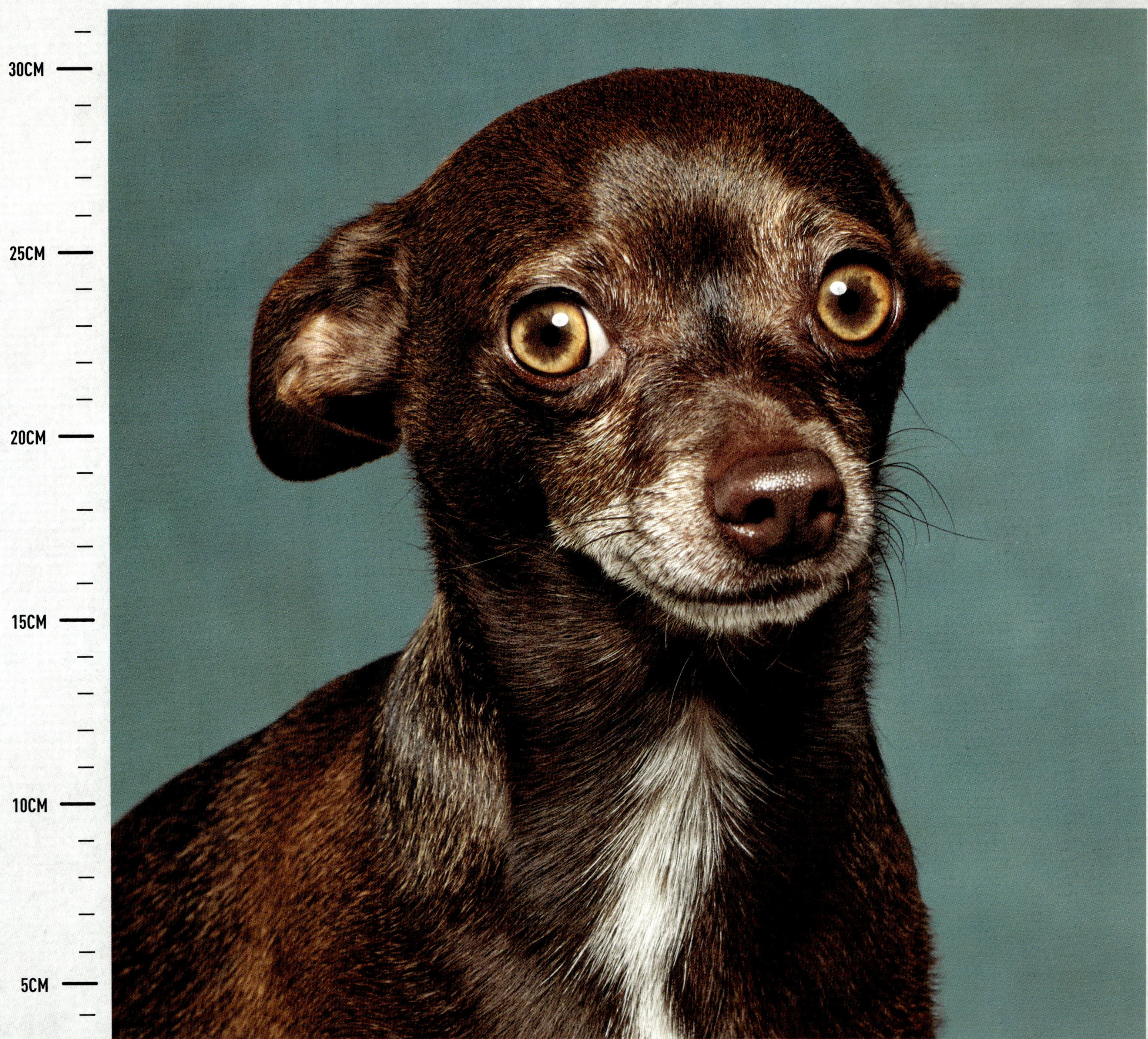

30CM
25CM
20CM
15CM
10CM
5CM

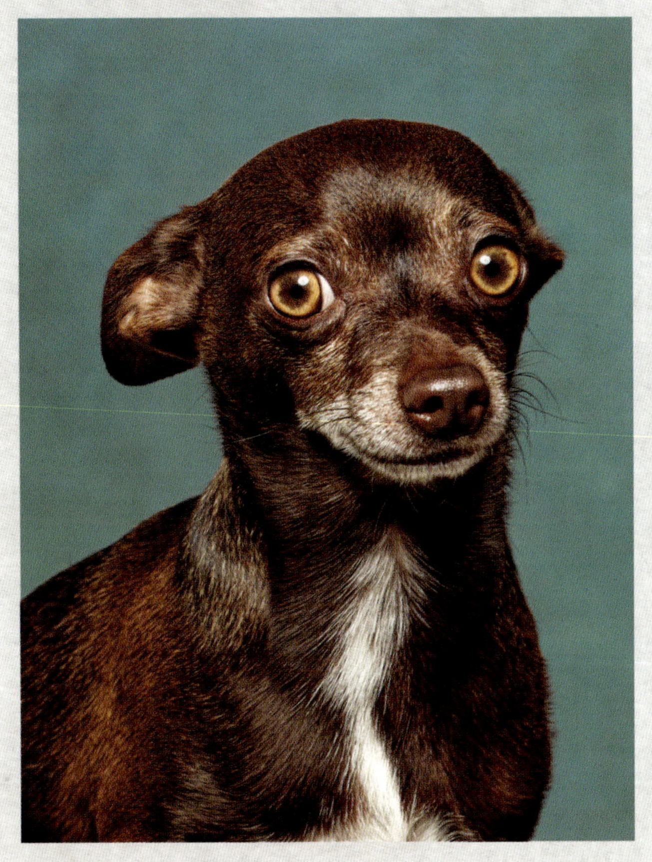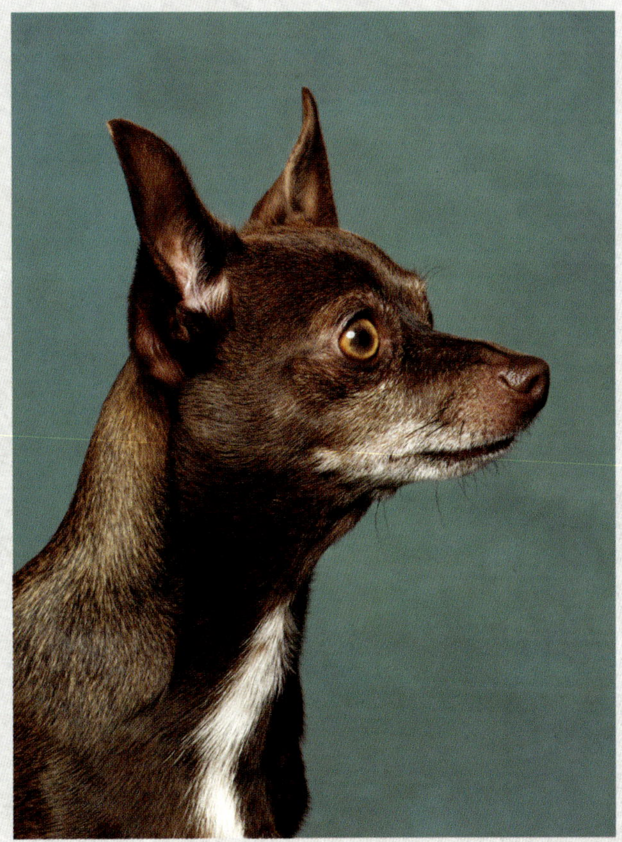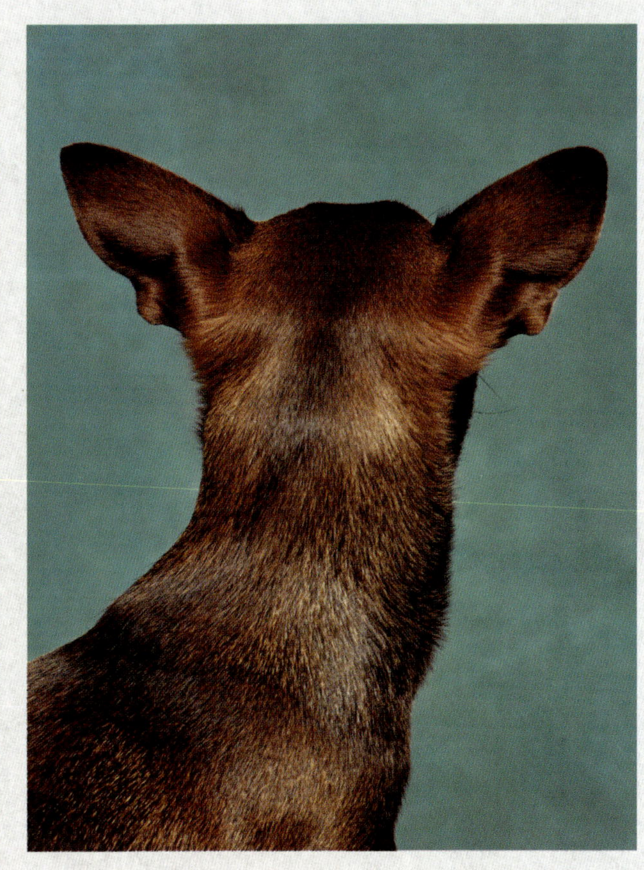

J, Eddie

ALIASES:

BORN: 27/03/2015   TRADE: Boss   BREED: Chihuahua

BUILD: Tiny Package   EYES: Copper Brown   HEIGHT: 30cm   HAIR: Brown / White

MARKS: Patches of white around mouth and down chest

PECULIARITIES: A small package but a big personality

M.O: ETC.   Has been frequently observed chewing on his feline companion's ears.

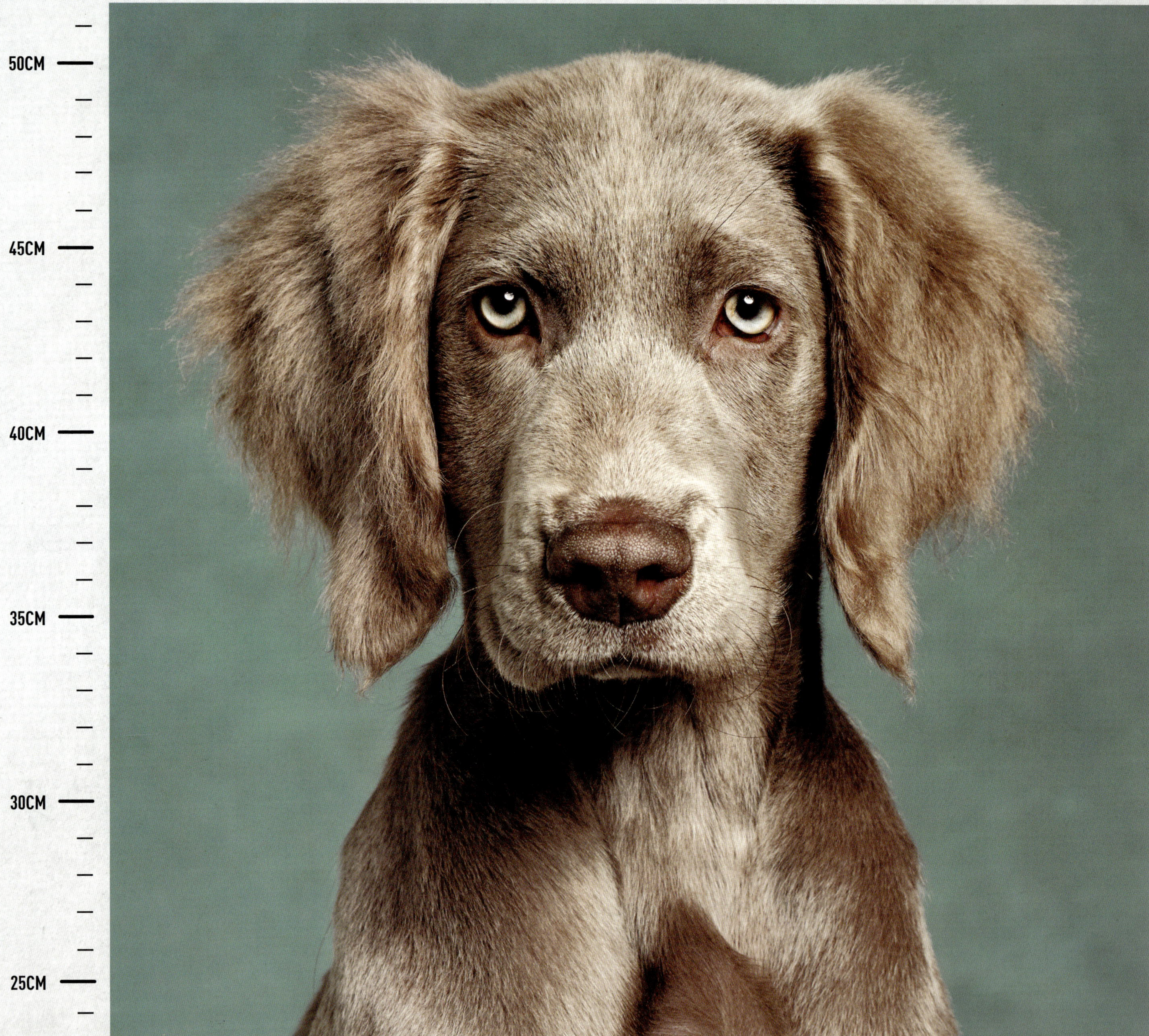

50CM
45CM
40CM
35CM
30CM
25CM

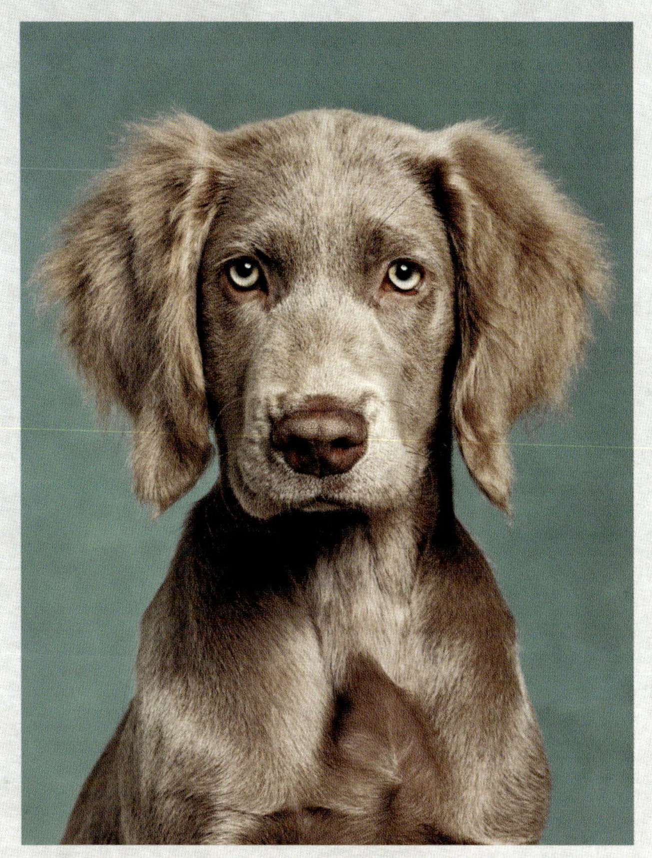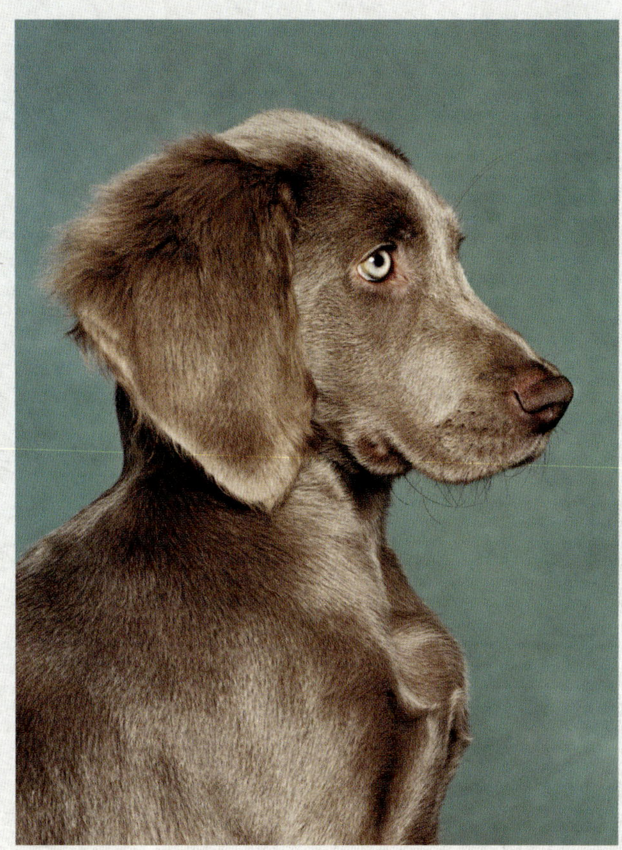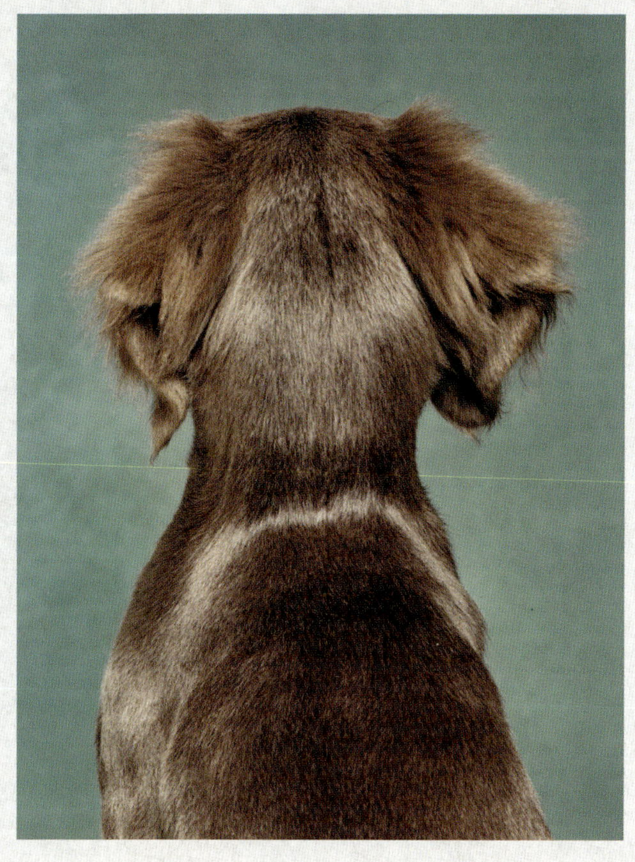

K, Elka

ALIASES: Pink Lemonade

BORN: 28/02/2017　　TRADE: Socialite　　BREED: Long Haired Weimaraner

BUILD: Sleek　　EYES: Ice Blue　　HEIGHT: 50cm　　HAIR: Mouse Grey

MARKS: Those ice blue eyes

PECULIARITIES: Has long hair

M.O: ETC. Has a fascination with slippers — especially those with human feet inside, has been seen launching herself at the slippers with lightning speed trying to eat them.

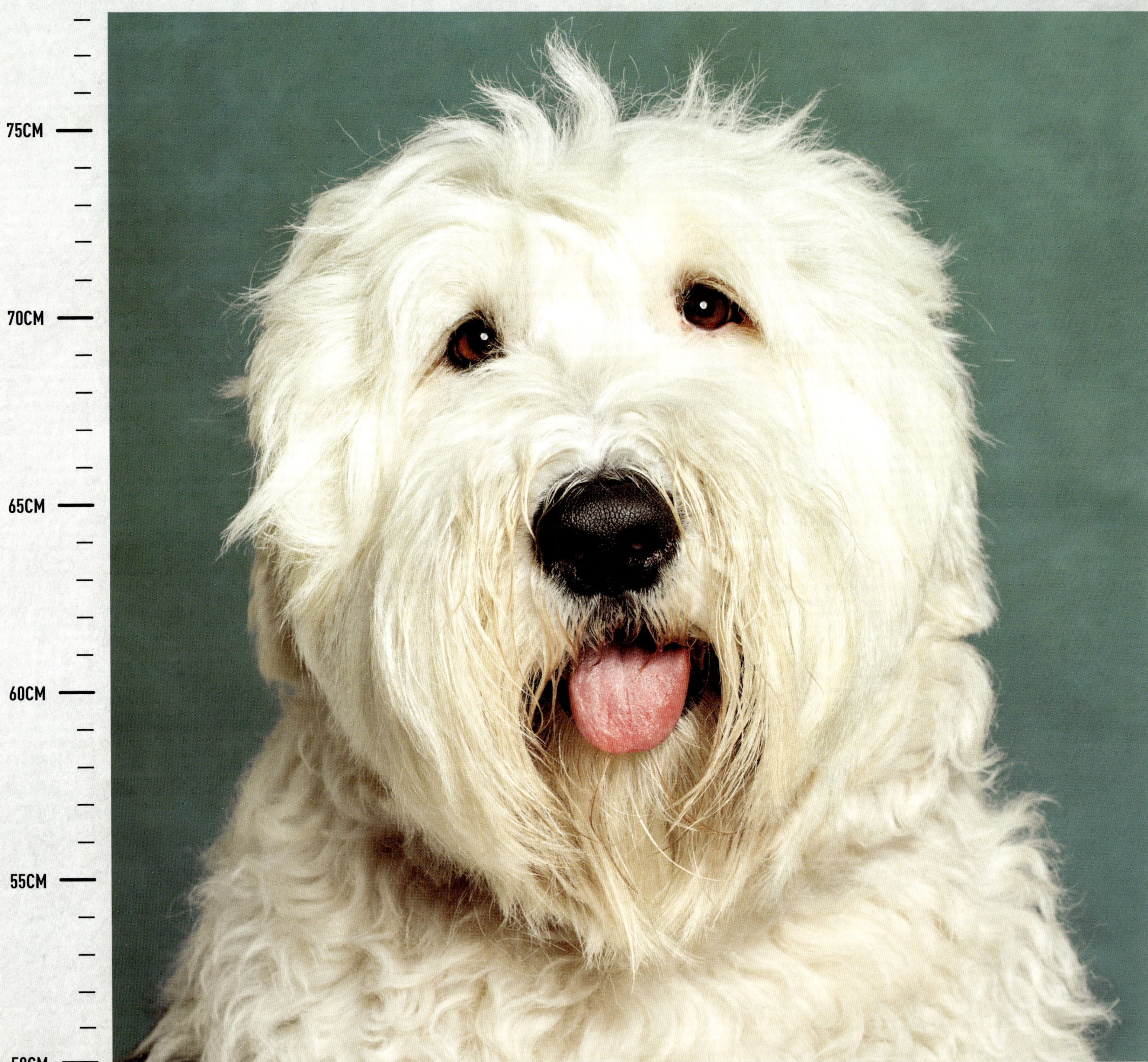
75CM
70CM
65CM
60CM
55CM
50CM

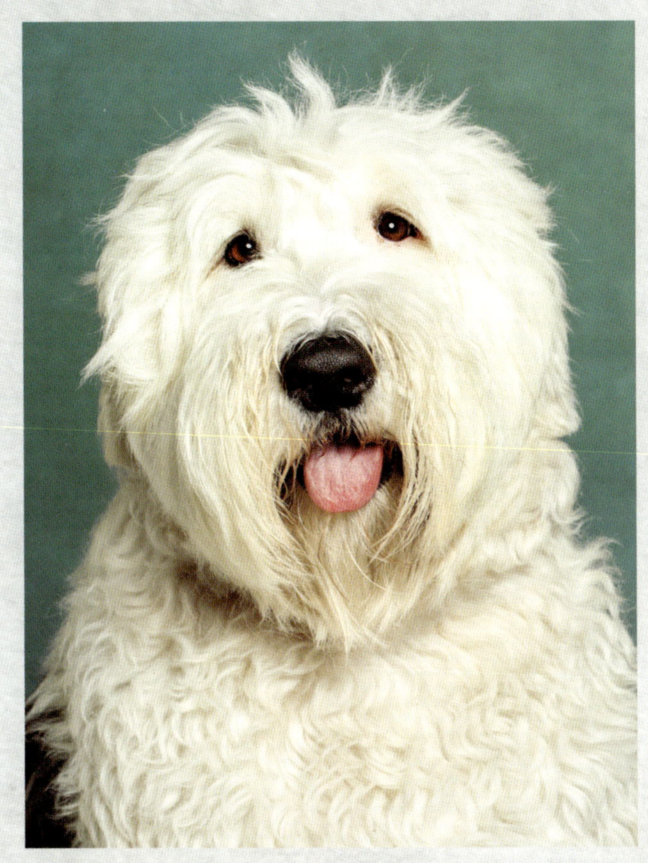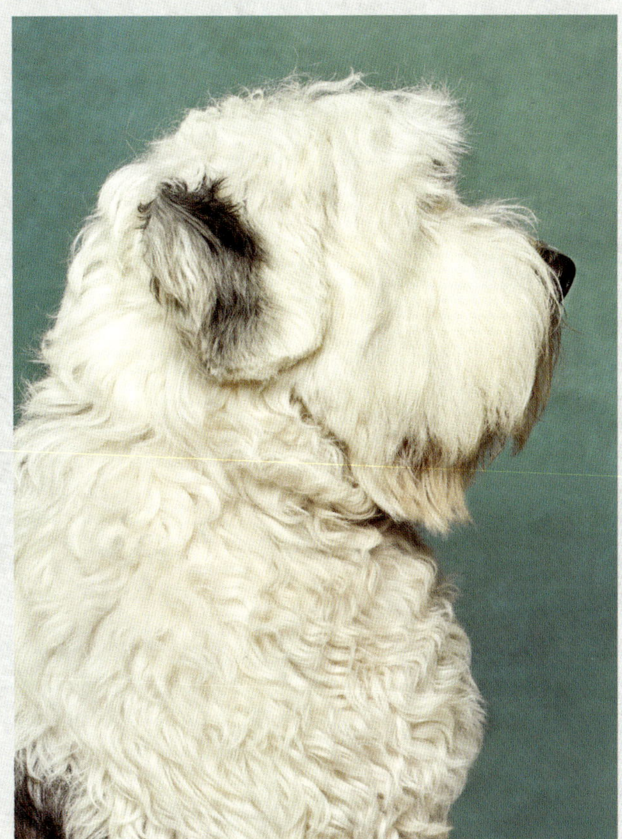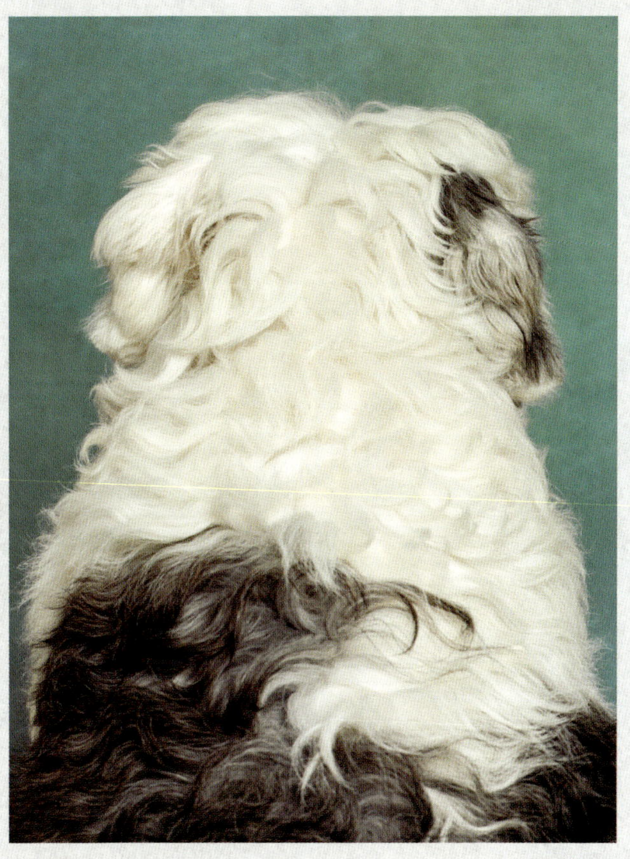

K, Holly

ALIASES:

BORN: 20/10/2014 **TRADE:** Local Celebrity **BREED:** Old English Sheepdog

BUILD: Tall & Floofy **EYES:** Brown **HEIGHT:** 78cm **HAIR:** White / Grey

MARKS: Little grey patch on right ear

PECULIARITIES: Resembles a giant teddy bear

M.O: ETC. Has been known to 'fight' on couches with feline best mate 'Kenny'. Has a frequent relationship with the local press — has been featured in newspapers and on the front of a bag of food.

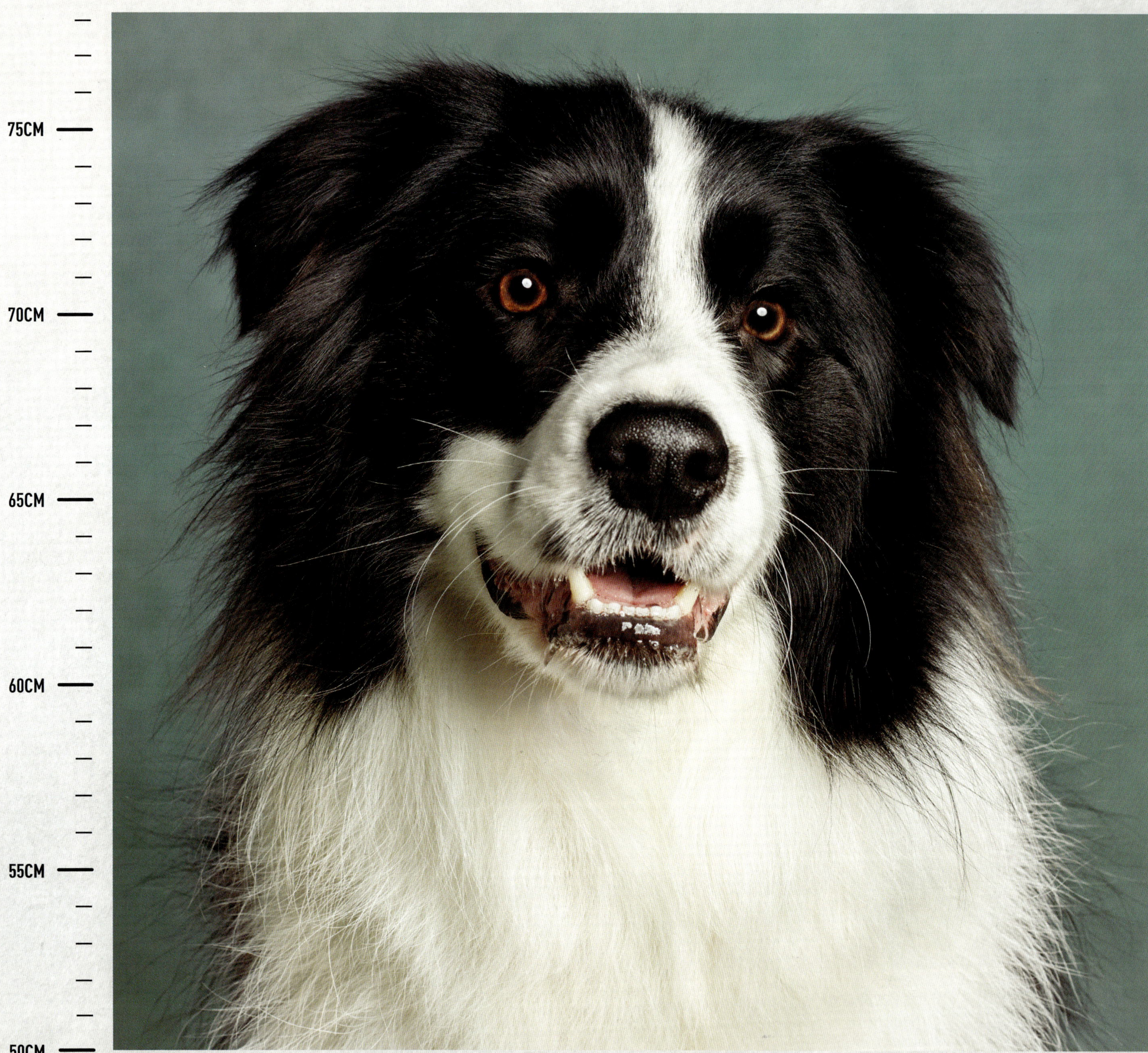75CM
70CM
65CM
60CM
55CM
50CM

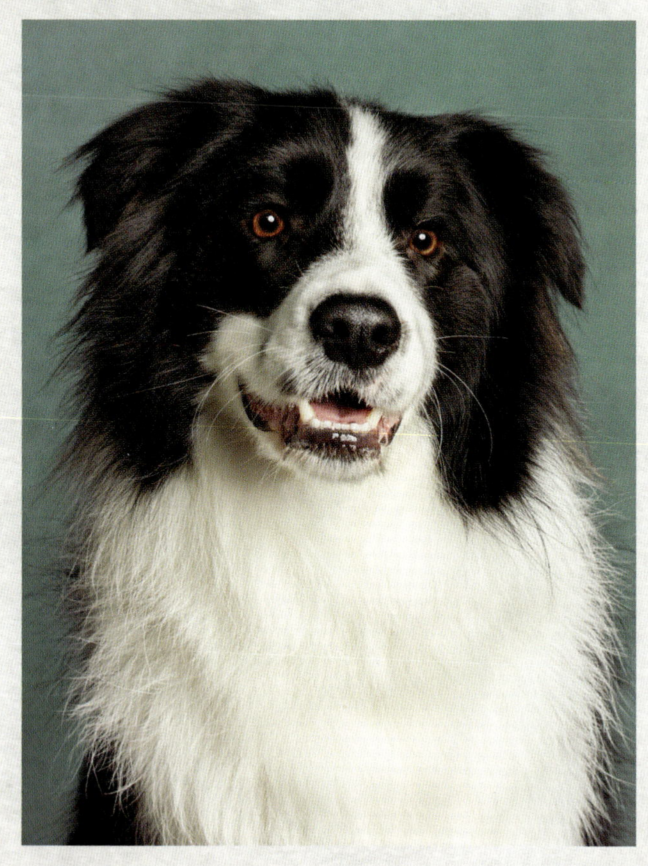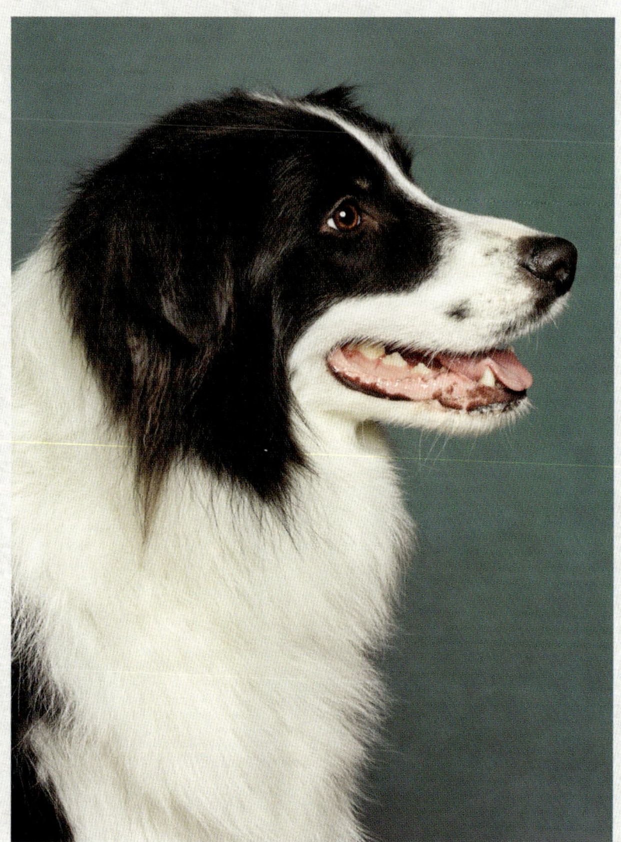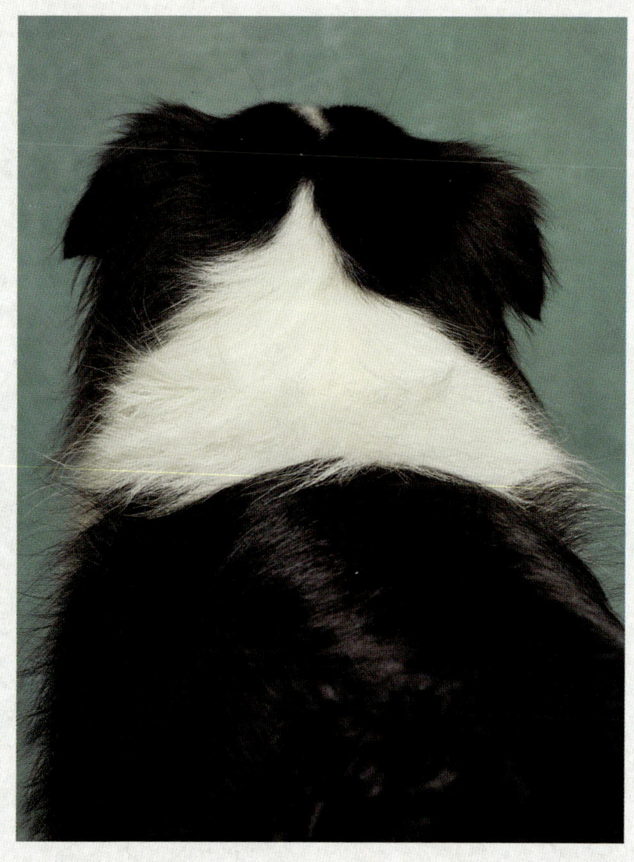

T, Horace

ALIASES: Horacito / Mr Dribbles

BORN: 11/11/2014   **TRADE:** Español Translator   **BREED:** Border Collie

BUILD: Sleek   **EYES:** Brown   **HEIGHT:** 77cm   **HAIR:** Black / White

MARKS: Such a smooth and shiny coat

PECULIARITIES: Enjoys having conversations with his female human in Español

M.O: ETC. Has a fussy palate. Passes on the beef flavoured treat (which may hold a tablet) in favour of the old half of a lemon left in the rubbish bin. Would be an excellent door greeter — always exhibiting overwhelming excitement when his humans come home.

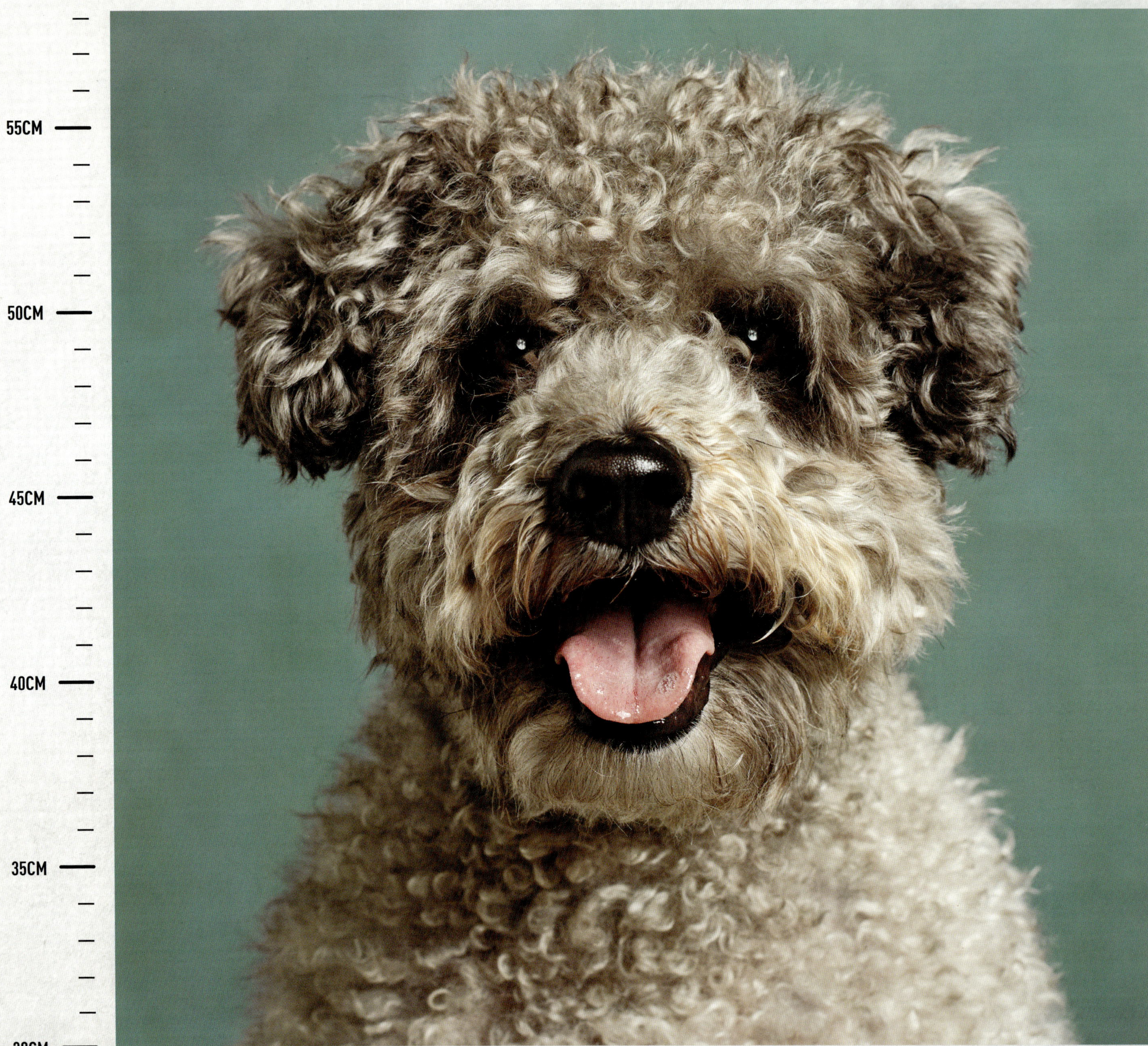

55CM
50CM
45CM
40CM
35CM
30CM

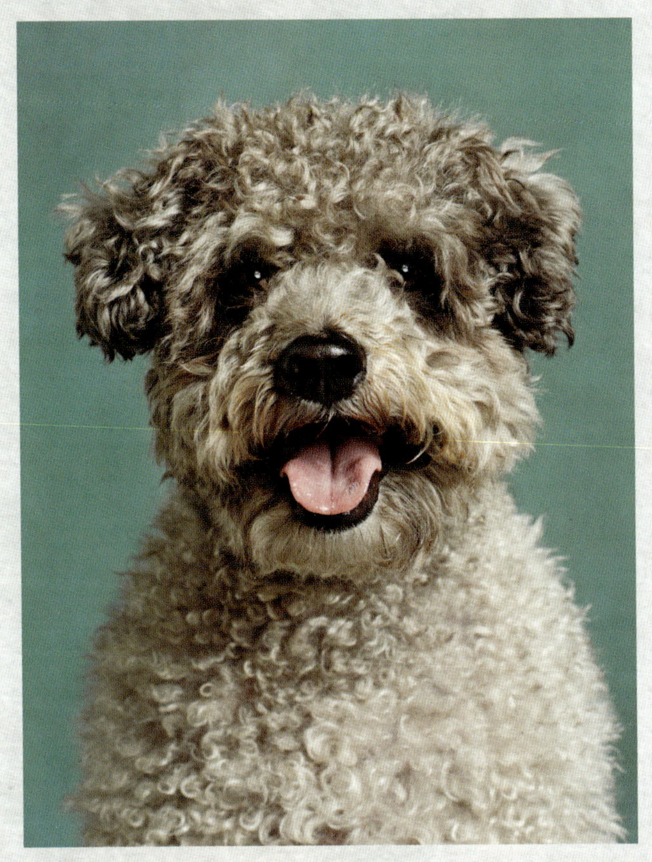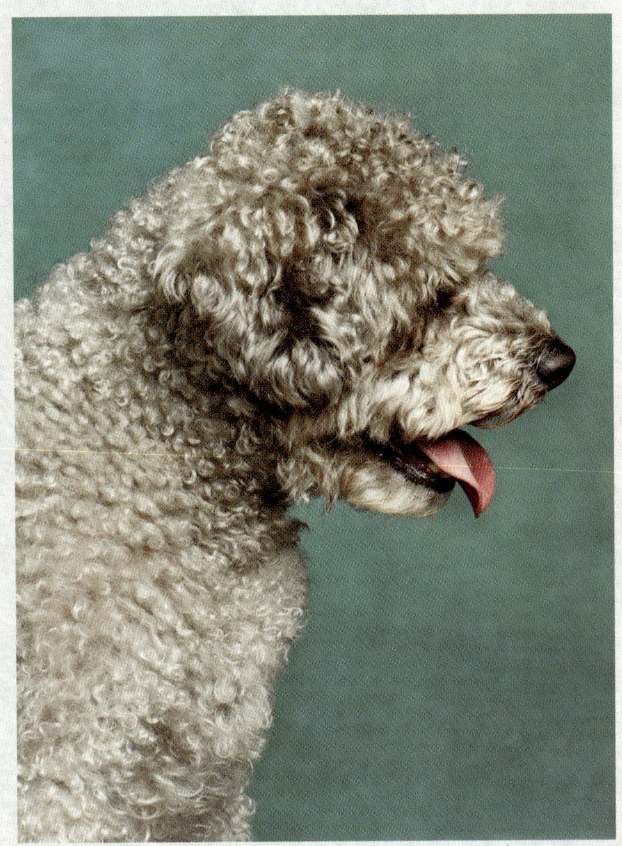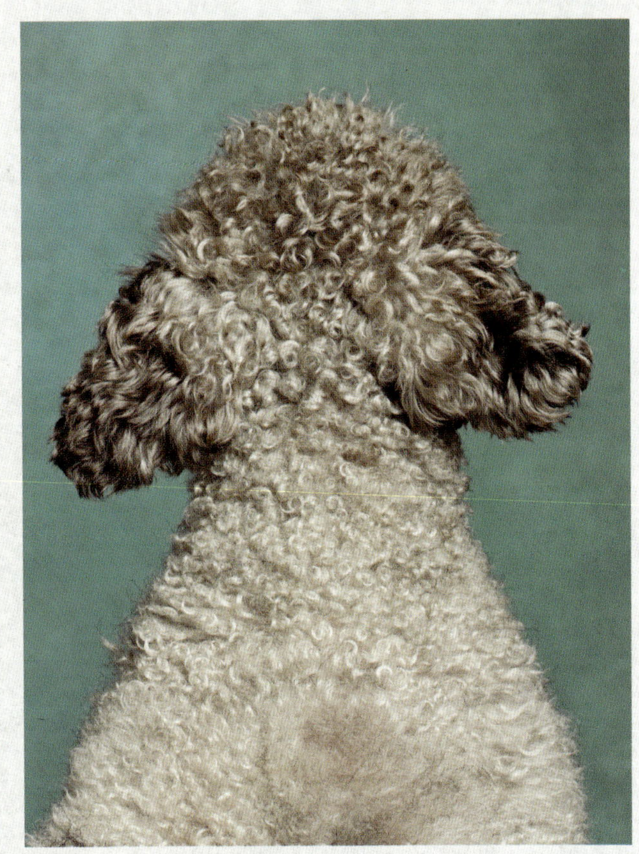

C, Iggy Pup

ALIASES: Iggy / Moose / Ignatius

BORN: 23/11/2013   TRADE: Sous-Chef / Food Taster   BREED: Miniature Schnoodle

BUILD: Like a Lamb   EYES: Brown   HEIGHT: 57cm   HAIR: Grey / Salt & Pepper

MARKS: Still has patches of puppy fur on back

PECULIARITIES: Resembles a Muppet — unconfirmed reports he is actually Sprocket from 'Fraggle Rock'

M.O: ETC.   Has been known to taunt humans with their own possessions if he is feeling neglected. Extremely apt at acquiring food from any source — out of human hands, steaks sitting on plates, an entire sponge cake.

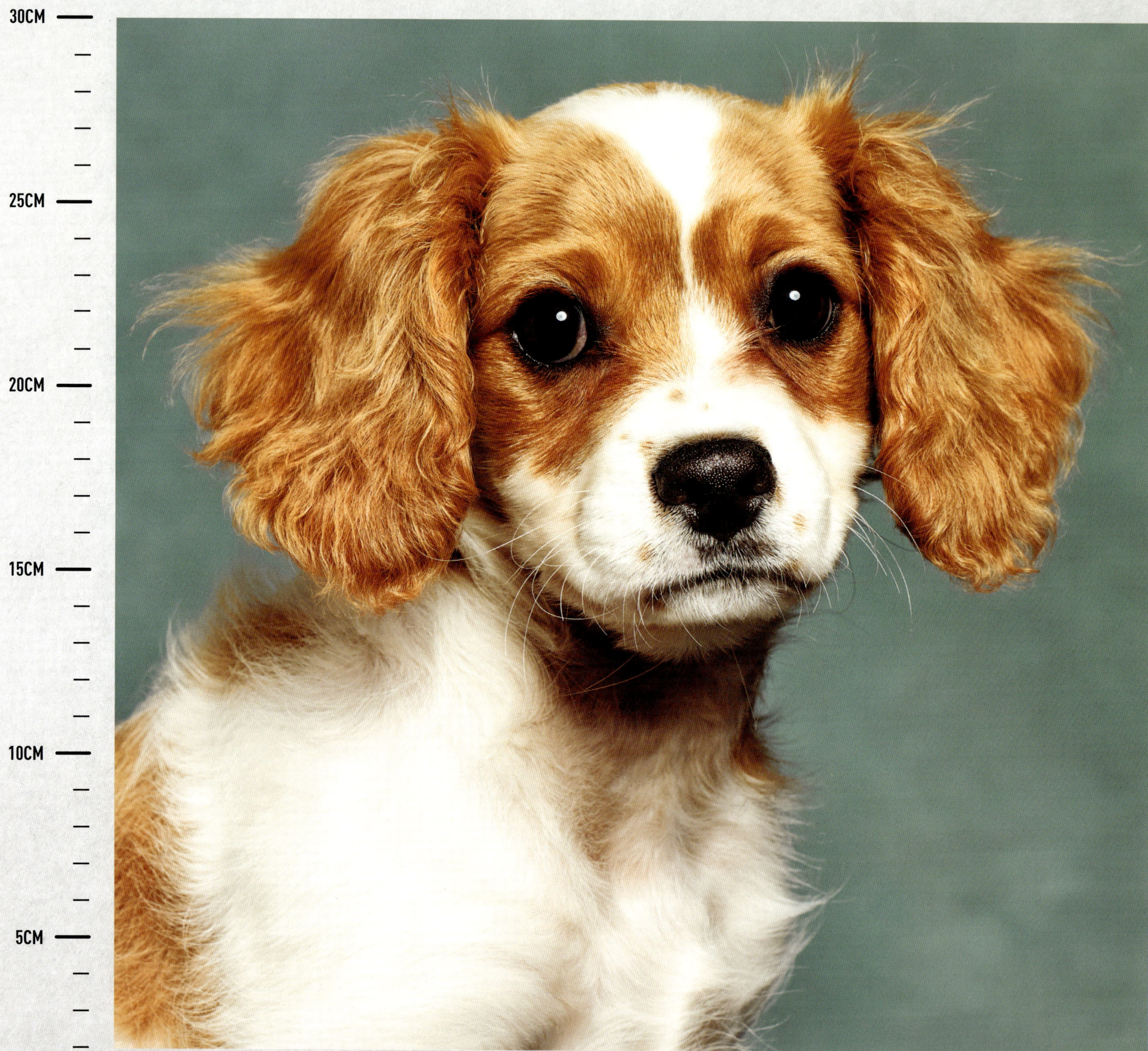

30CM
25CM
20CM
15CM
10CM
5CM

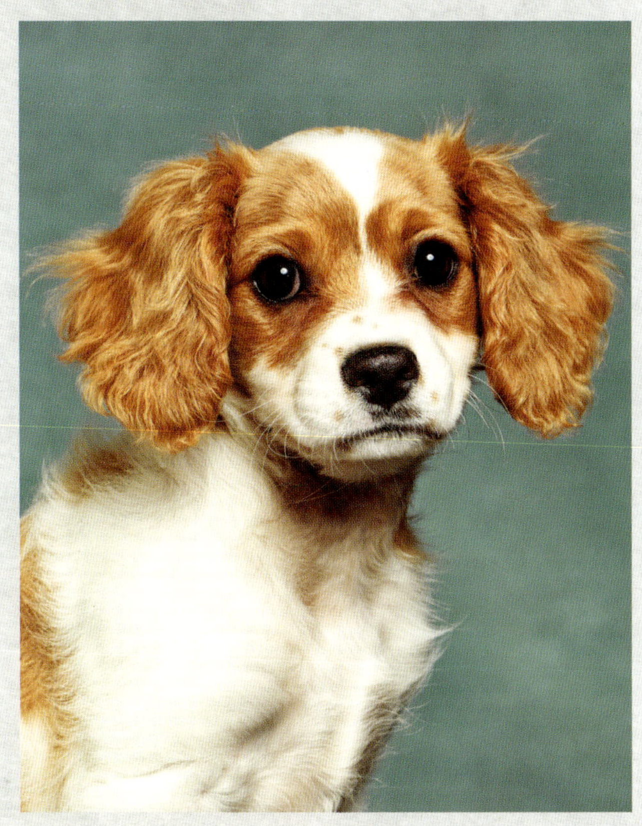 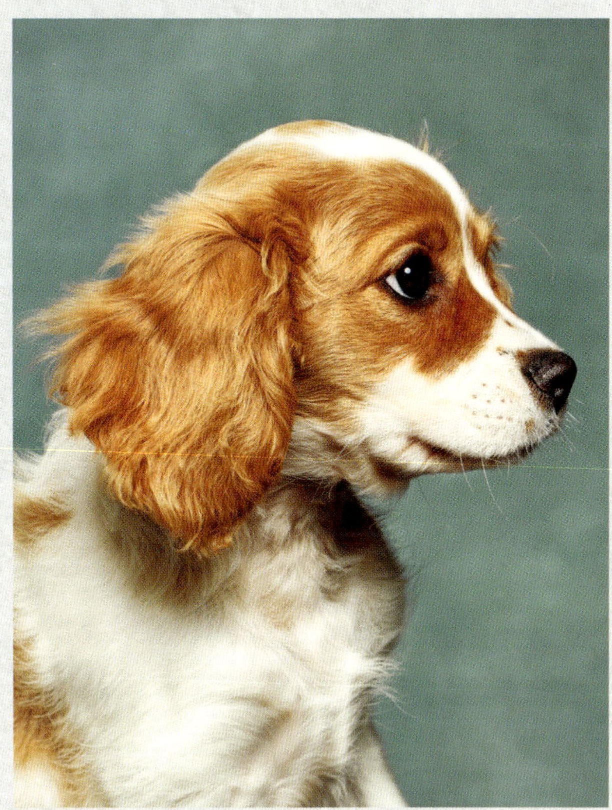 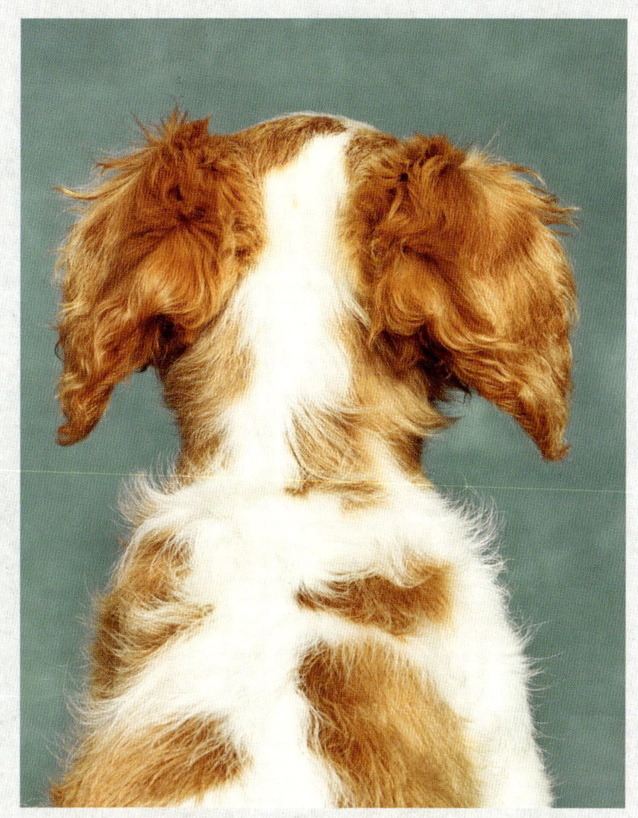

D, Koda

BORN: 02/07/2017   TRADE: Dogfather in Training   BREED: King Charles Cavalier

BUILD: Big Dog in Small Package   EYES: Brown   HEIGHT: 50cm   HAIR: White / Chestnut Brown

MARKS: Nose freckles and curly ears

PECULIARITIES: Fearless, despite his size

M.O: ETC.   Holds his own around four other big companions — he bites and steals toys and food to remind them who is boss.

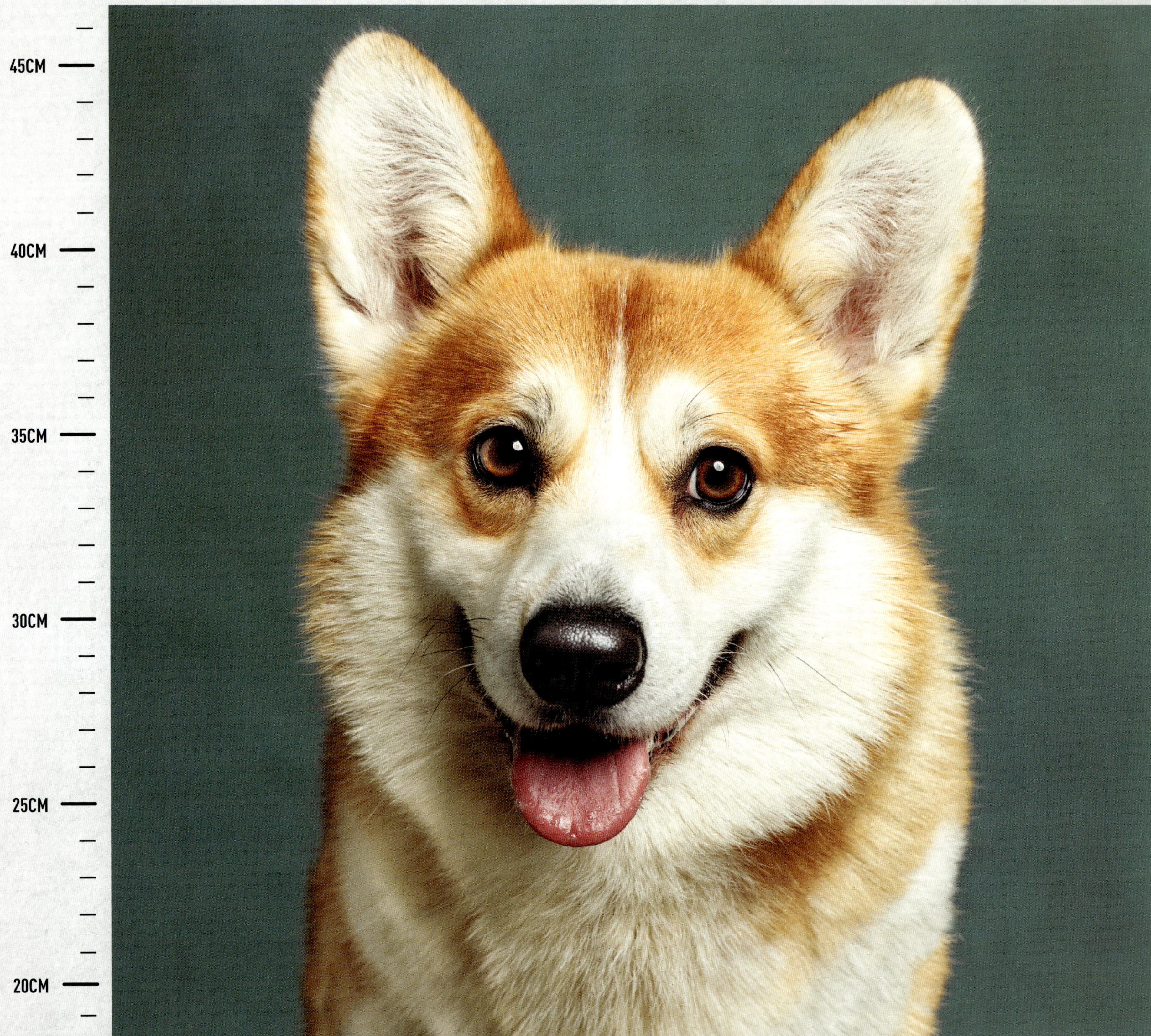

45CM
40CM
35CM
30CM
25CM
20CM

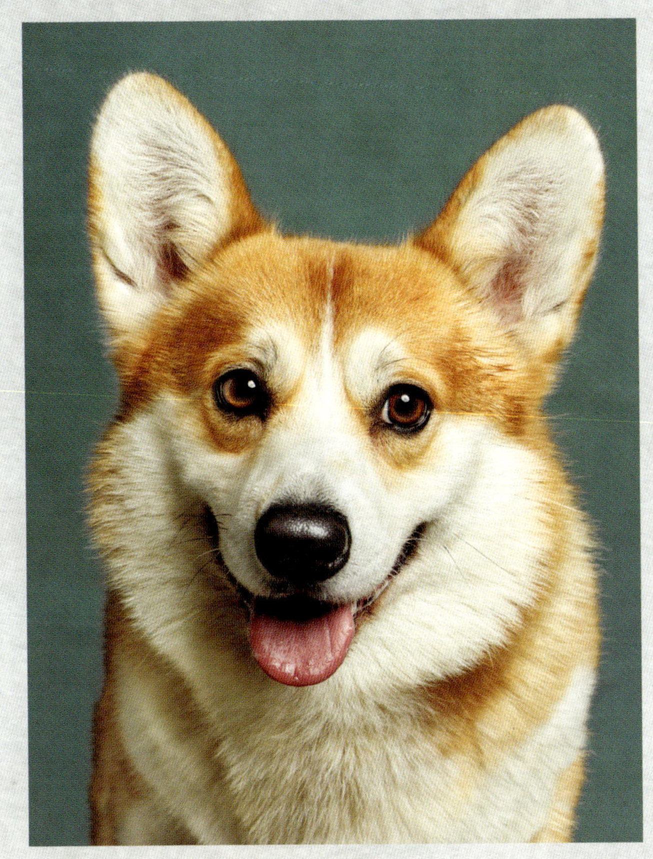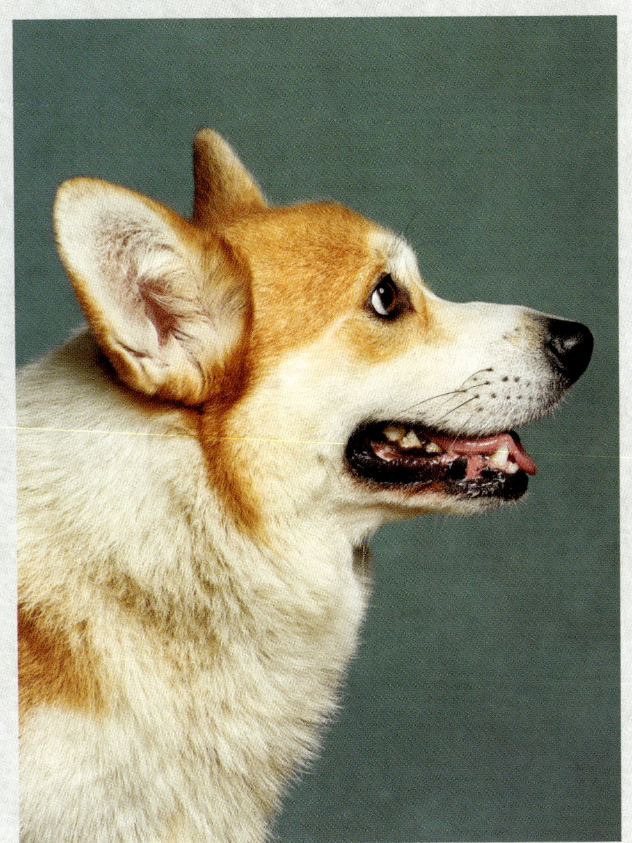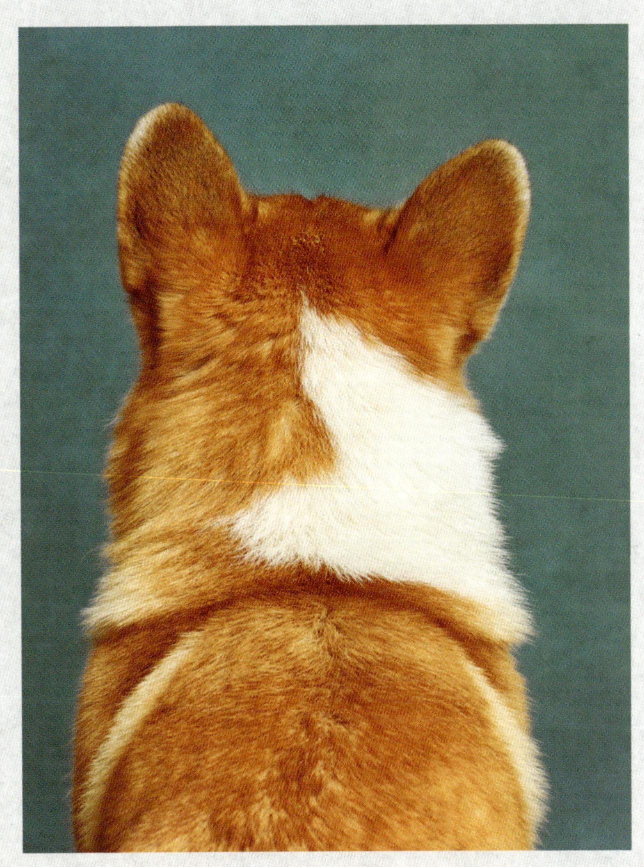

C, Kiwi

ALIASES:	
BORN: 28/02/2015	**TRADE:** Insta Model **BREED:** Pembroke Welsh Corgi
BUILD: Stocky	**EYES:** Brown **HEIGHT:** 46cm **HAIR:** Blonde / White
MARKS: Natural bobtail	

PECULIARITIES: Odd habit of sucking on soft toys — especially when they are bone-shaped

M.O: ETC. Has been observed digging and hiding toys out in the garden, but when told off has to improvise by hiding them under his bed in the house to 'dig' them up again.

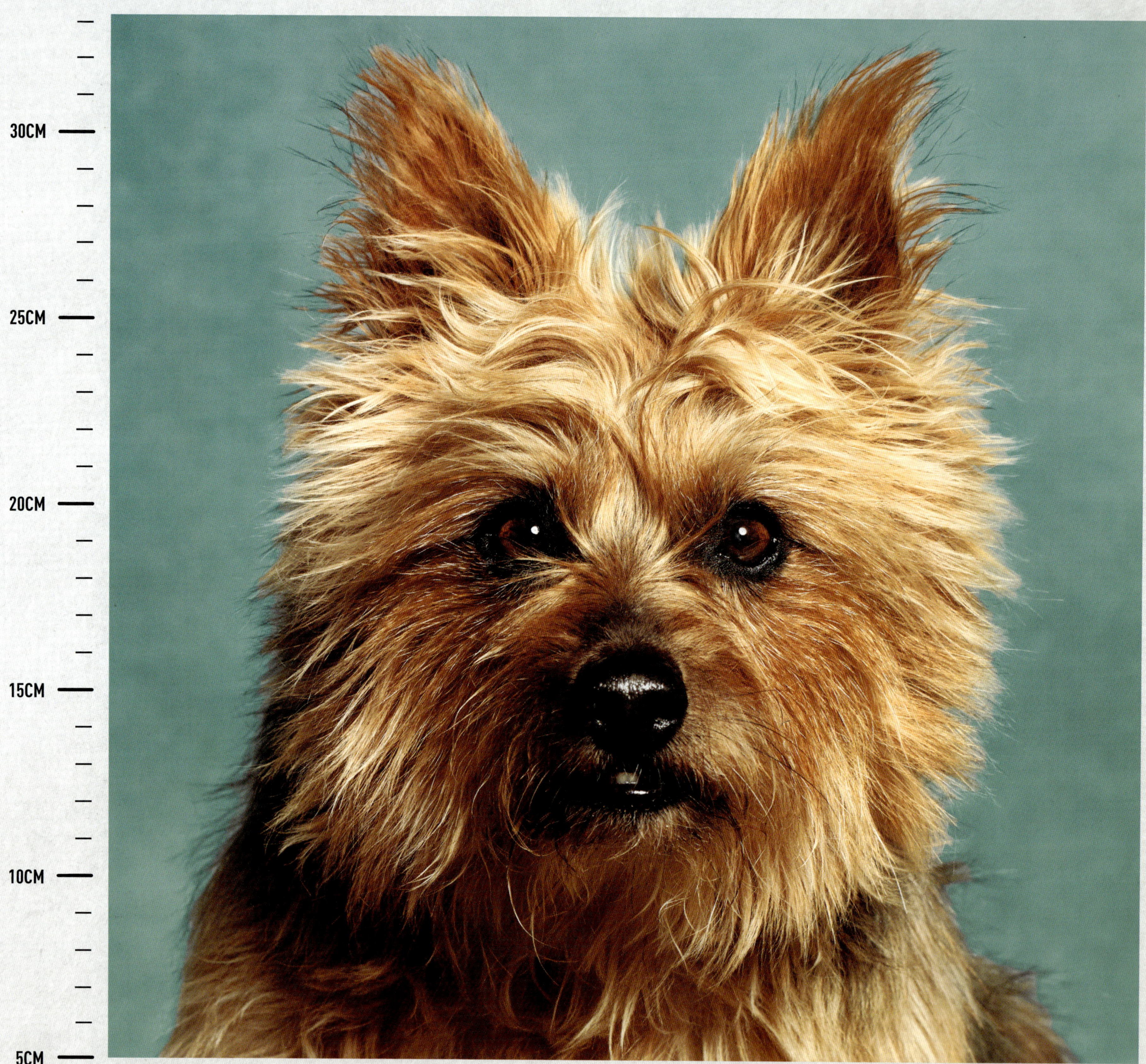

30CM
25CM
20CM
15CM
10CM
5CM

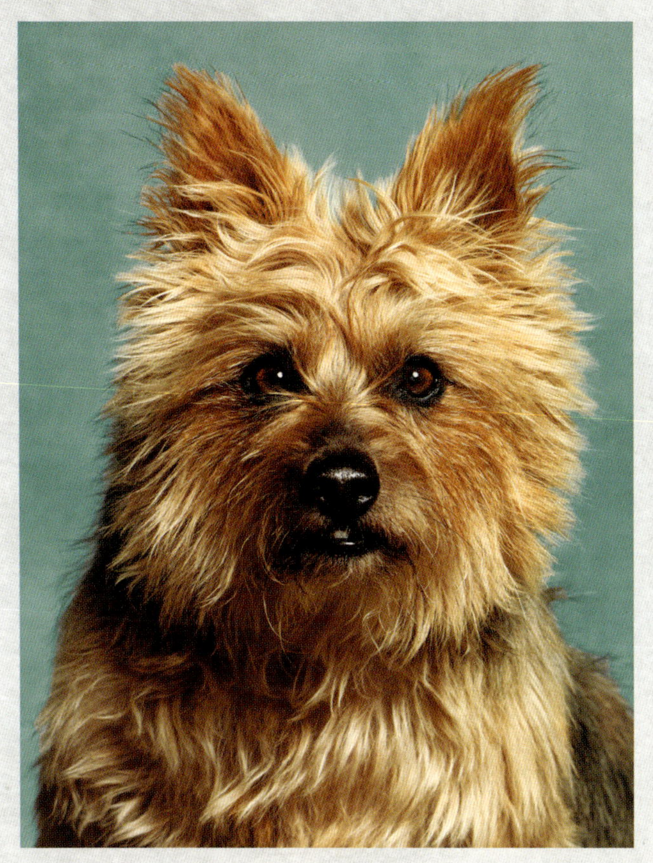
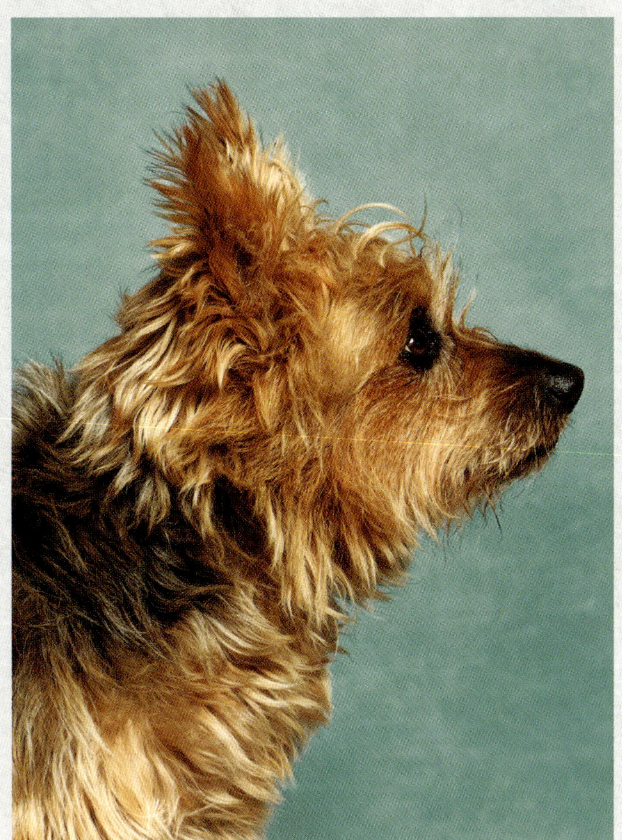
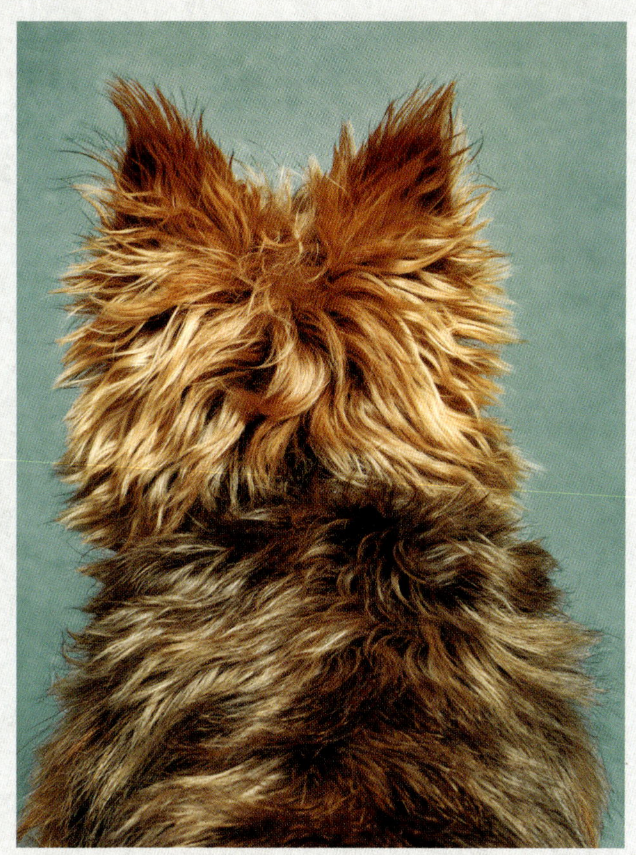

D, Piper

ALIASES: Pop / Popper / Poopy

BORN: 22/08/2006   TRADE: Cloud 9 Farm Vacuum   BREED: Australian Terrier

BUILD: Round   EYES: Brown   HEIGHT: 33cm   HAIR: Tan / Blonde / Grey

MARKS: Bottom teeth pop out a bit

PECULIARITIES: Enjoys midnight snacks — brings in outside carcasses/creatures to chomp on

M.O: ETC. Is quite the ambusher — often gets the upper hand on lead-restricted passers by. Has trained her brother to catch rabbits for her to eat.

75CM
70CM
65CM
60CM
55CM
50CM

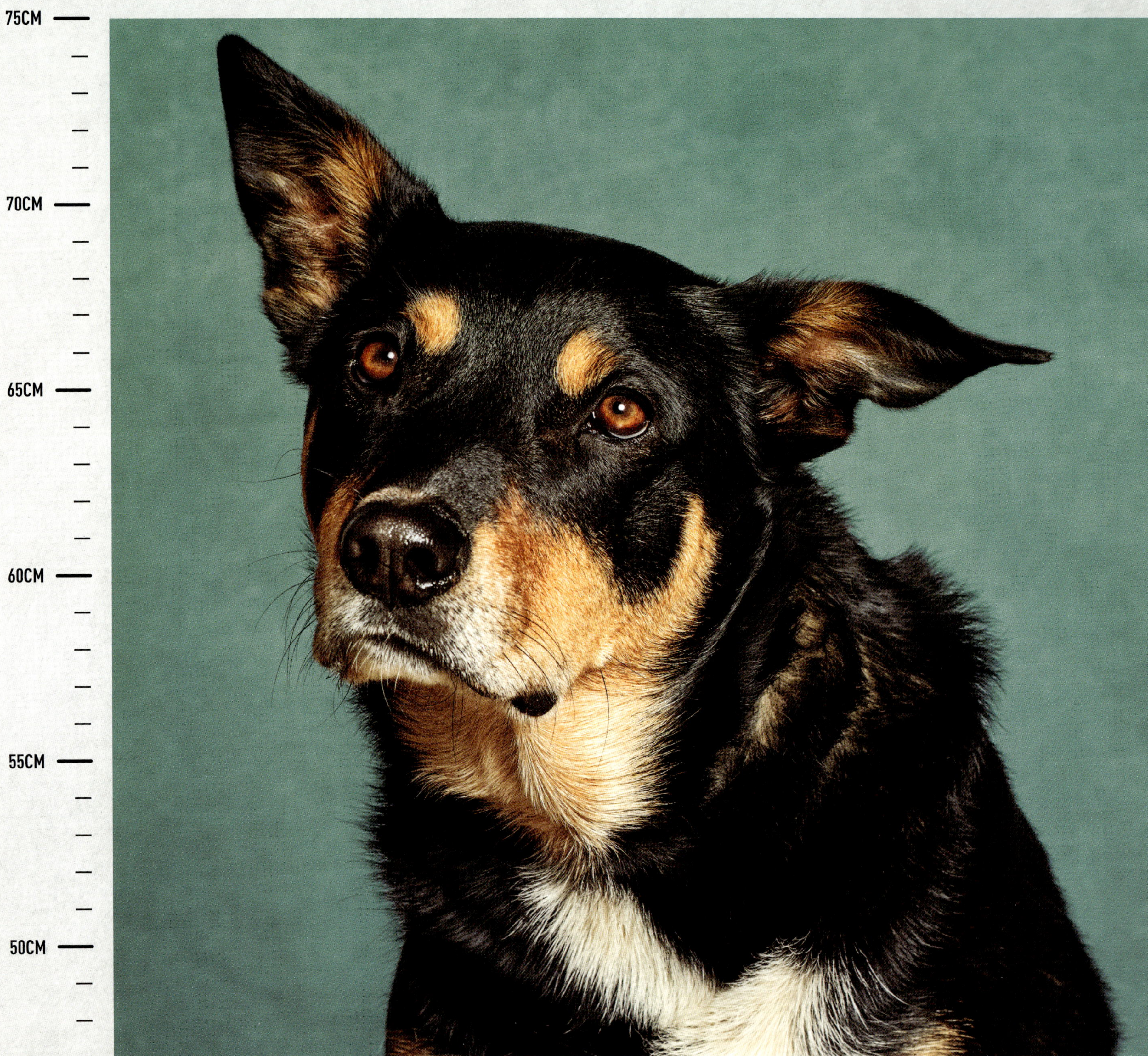

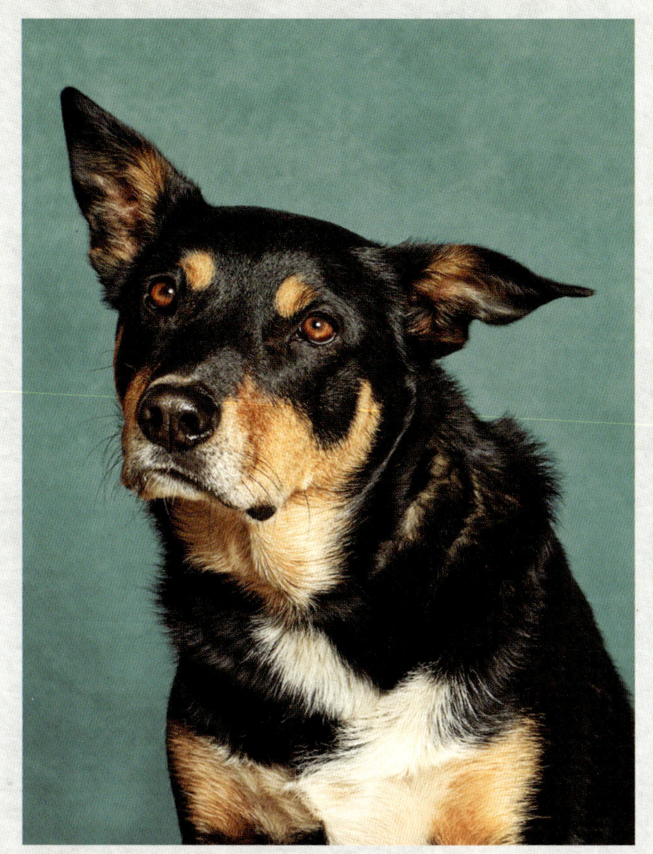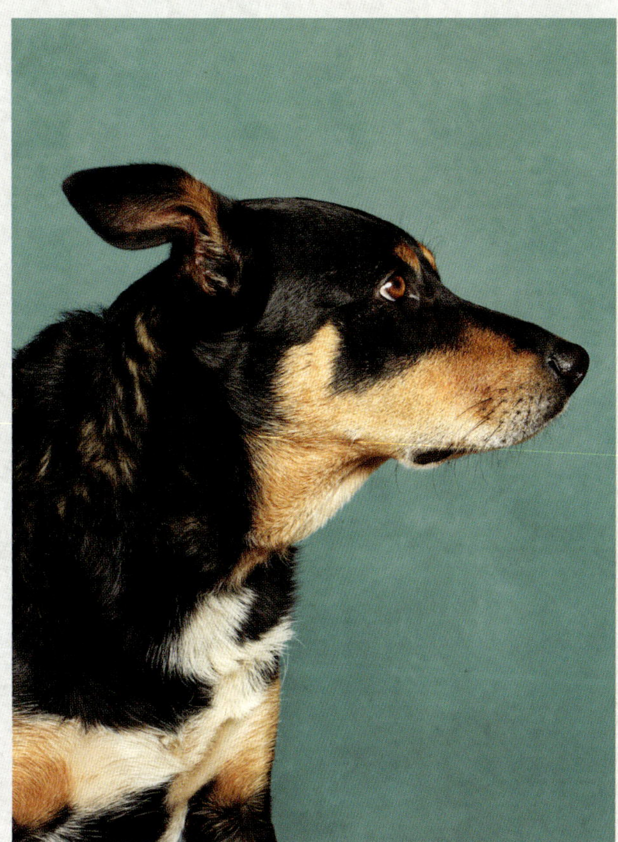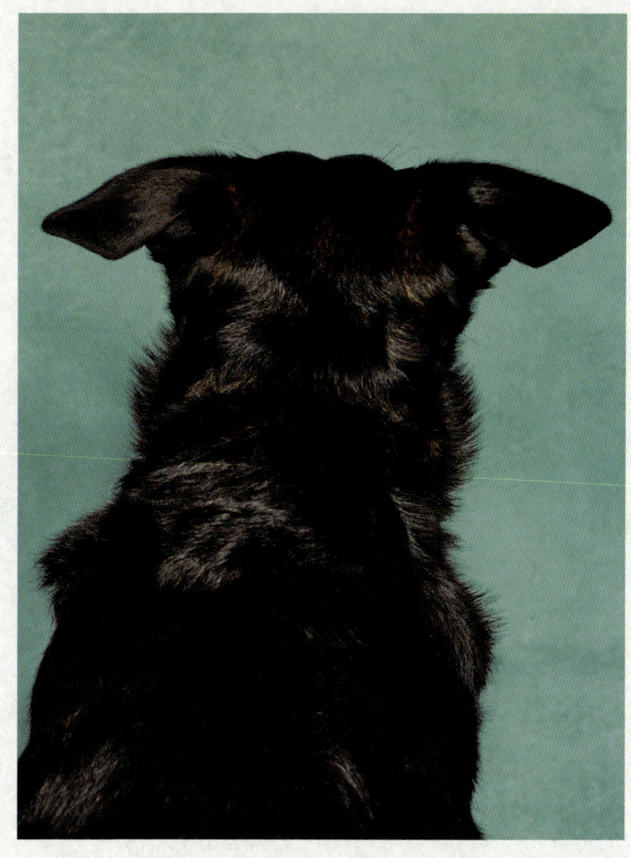

D, Roy

ALIASES: Roddy / Royd / Roy Boy

BORN: 09/12/2012   TRADE: Cloud 9 Farm Dog   BREED: Australian Kelpie

BUILD: Stockman   EYES: Copper Brown   HEIGHT: 75cm   HAIR: Black / Tan / White

MARKS: Tan eyebrows

PECULIARITIES: Enjoys sleeping with a blanket

M.O: ETC. Is a hard worker but beware — when left alone no soft furnishing is safe, not even his prized bed.

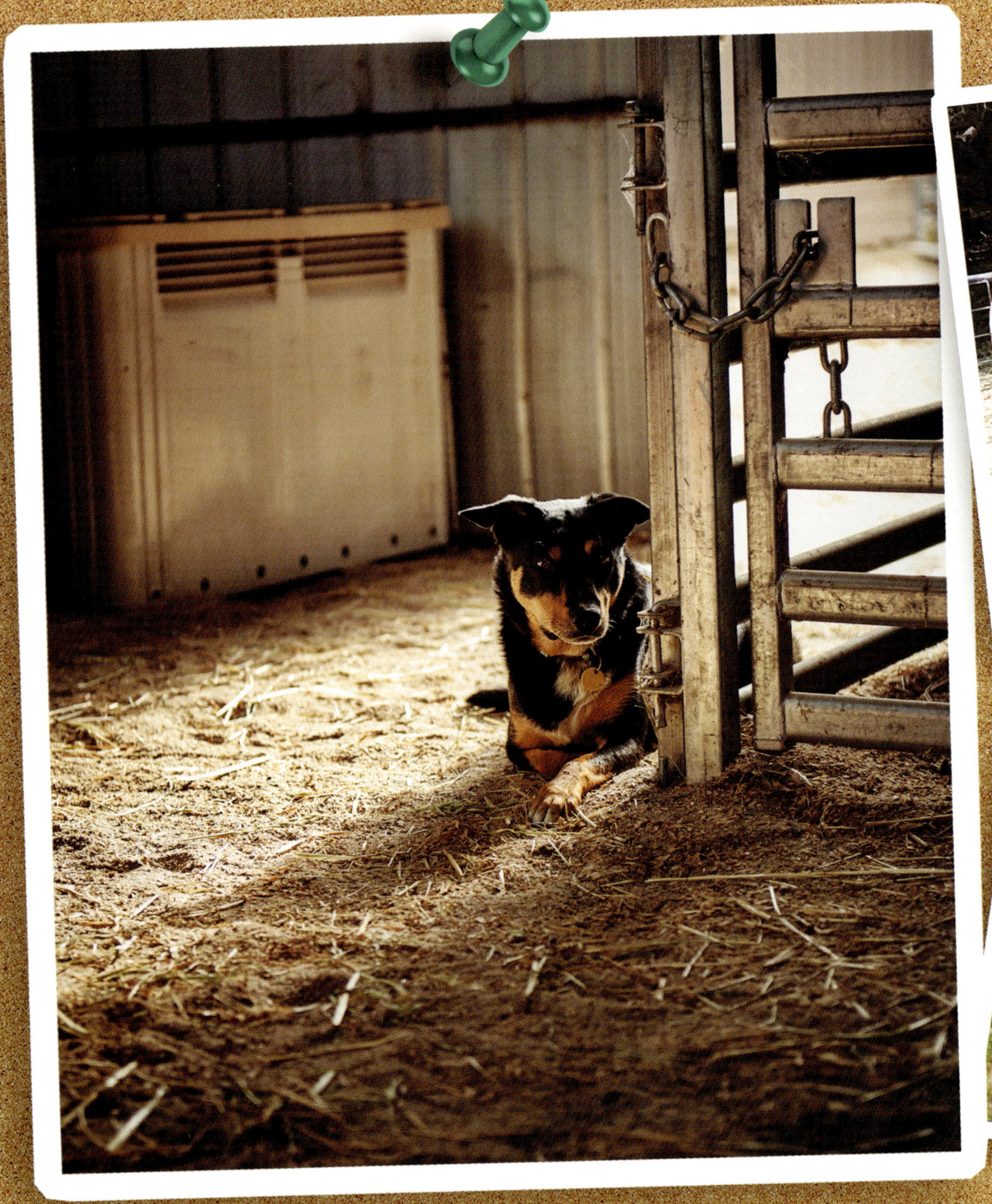

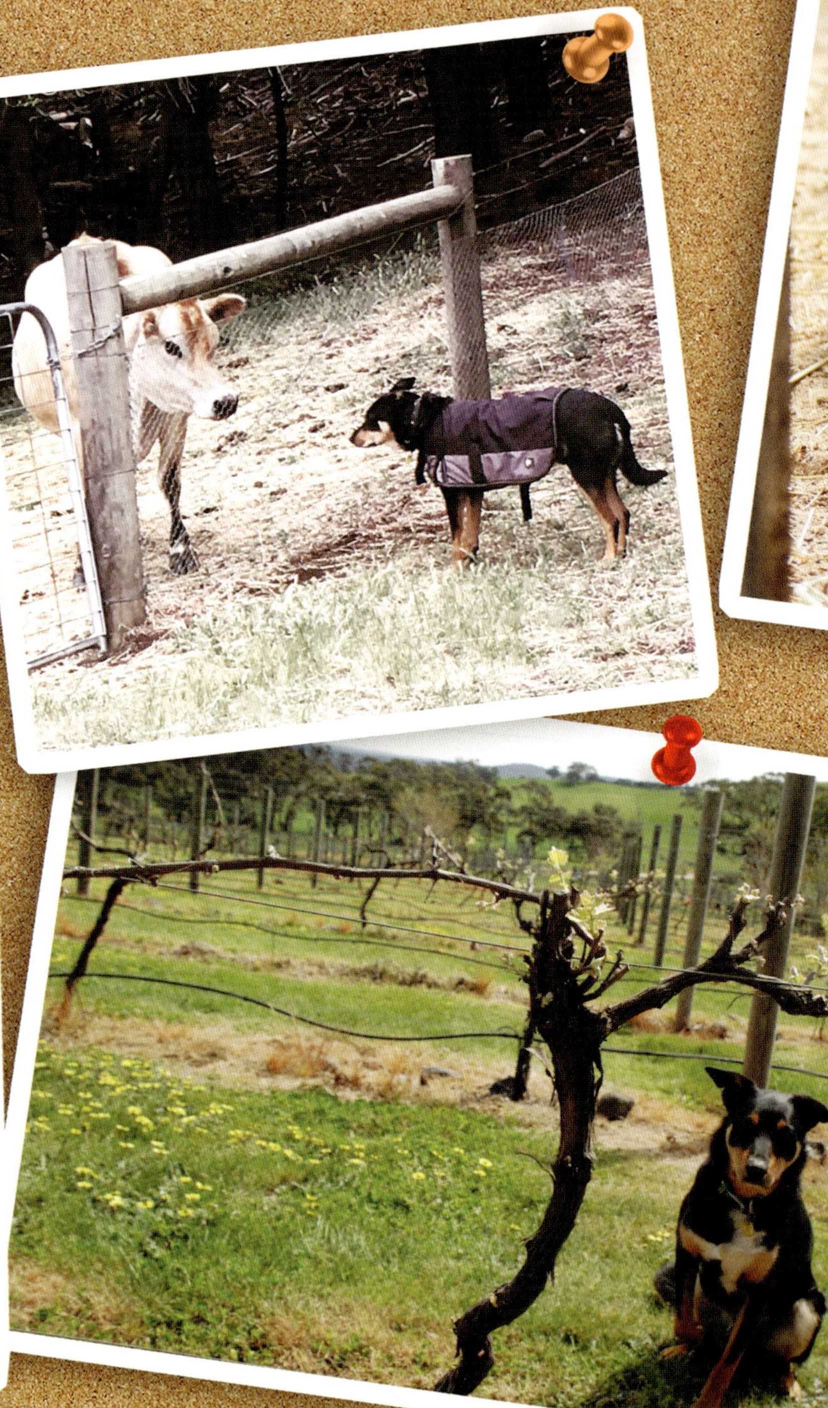

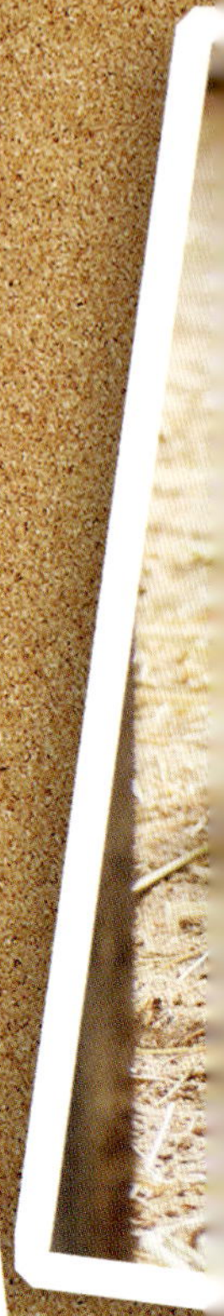

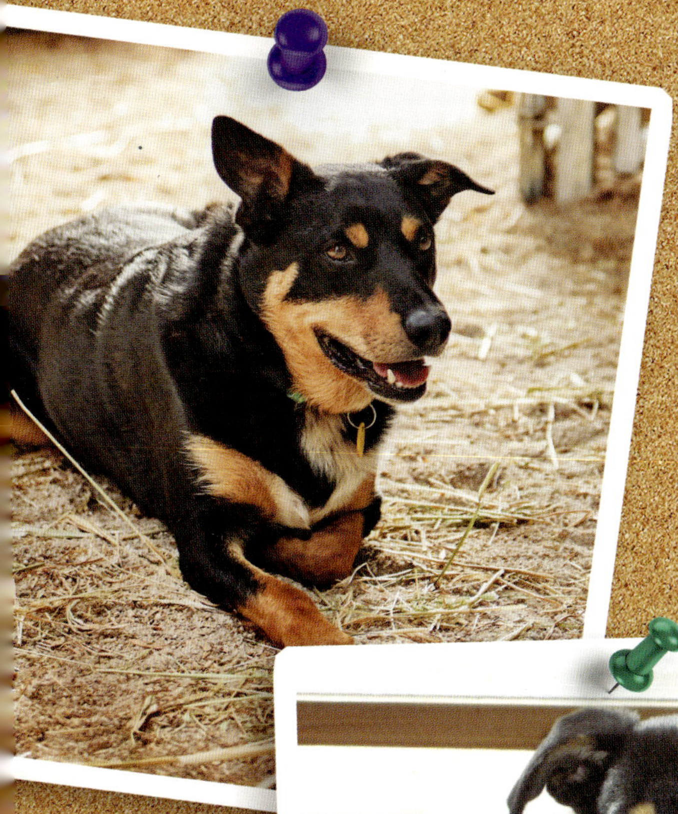

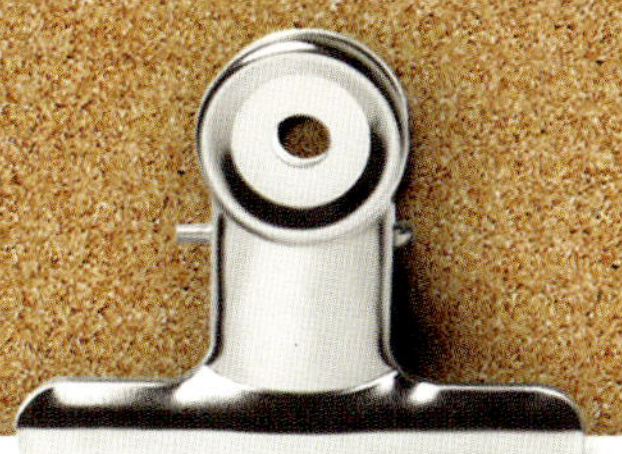

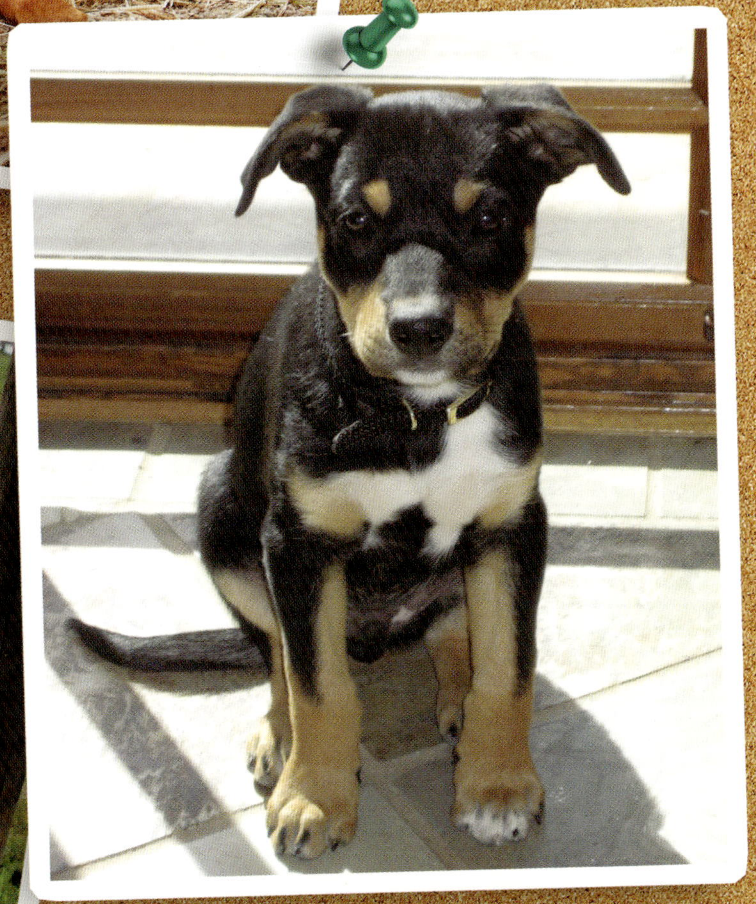

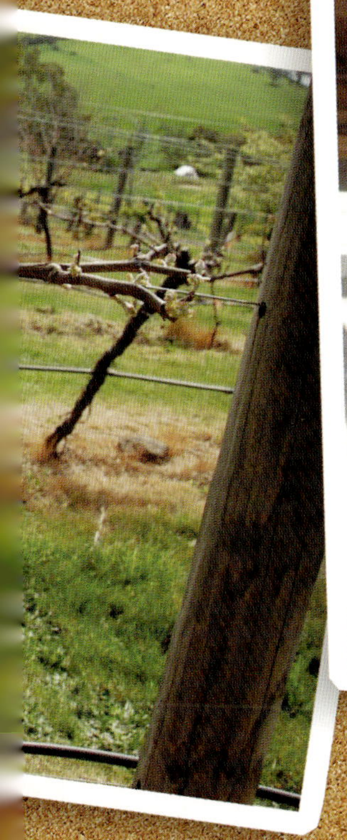

ROY
THE FARM DOG

Roy is the farm dog at Cloud 9 Farm, located just outside Kyneton in Victoria's countryside.

Along with his farm duties he is a champion cattle and sheep dog.

He has won employee of the year for the last two years, and keeps Winemaker Alan in line.

He is very vocal every morning and makes sure he talks to everyone in the house, getting them ready for the day ahead.

In Roy's spare time, he enjoys eating the Persian rug and ripping apart any manchester in sight — including couch cushions and his bed.

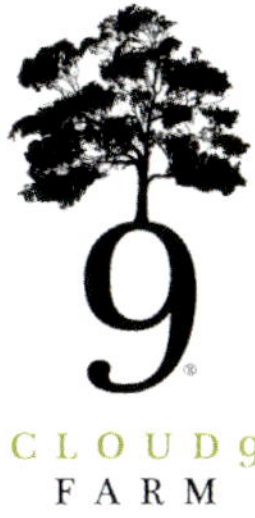

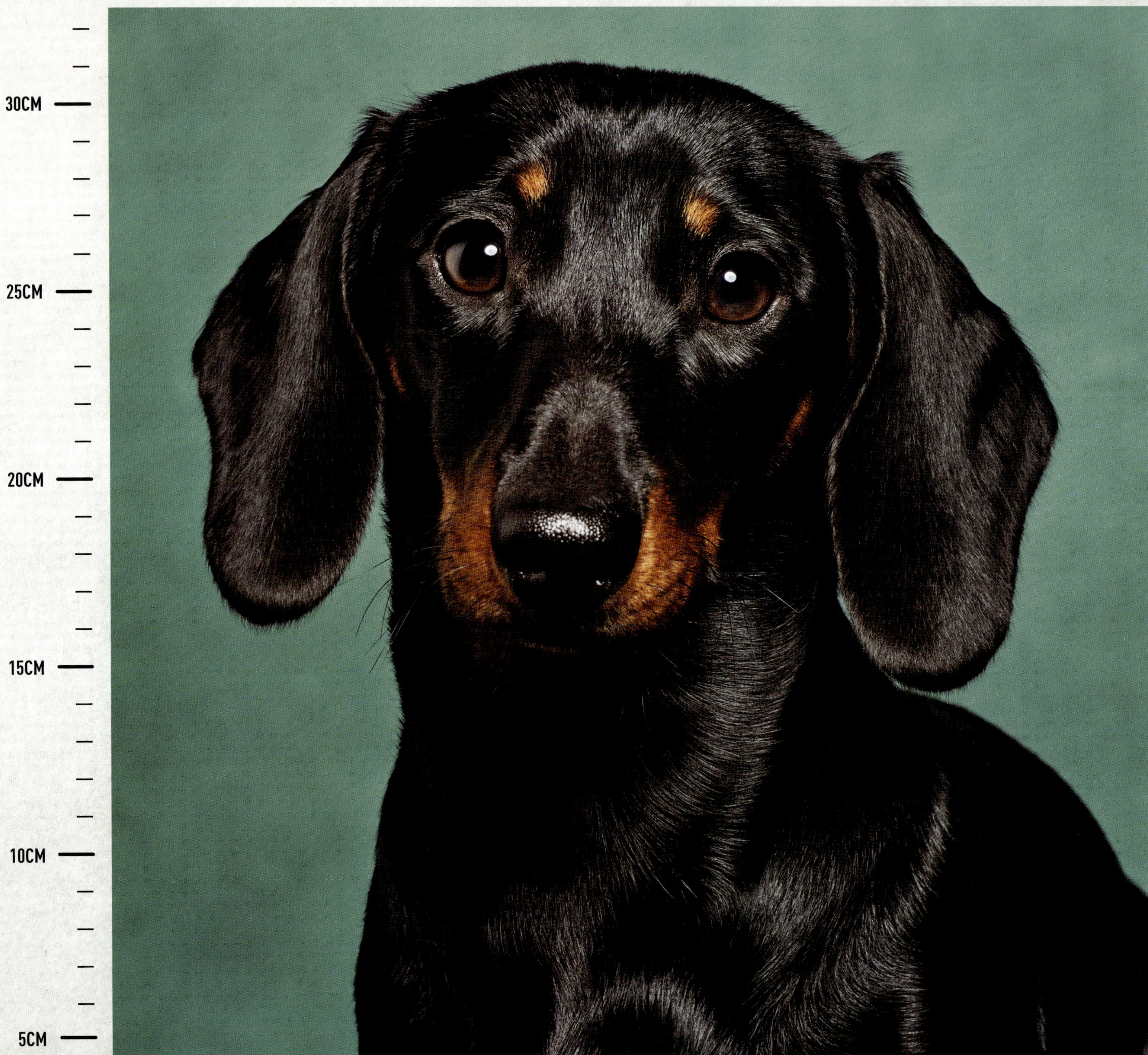

30CM
25CM
20CM
15CM
10CM
5CM

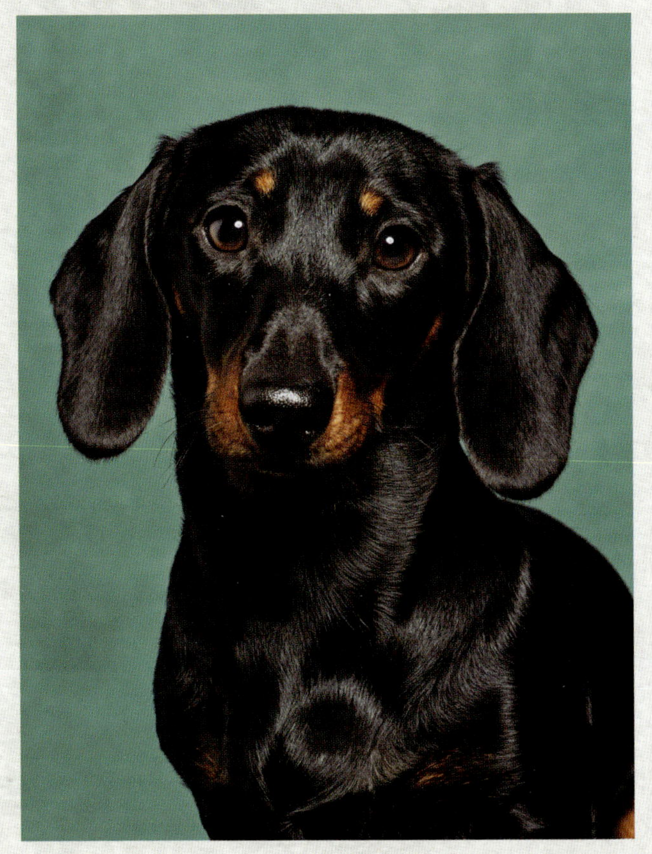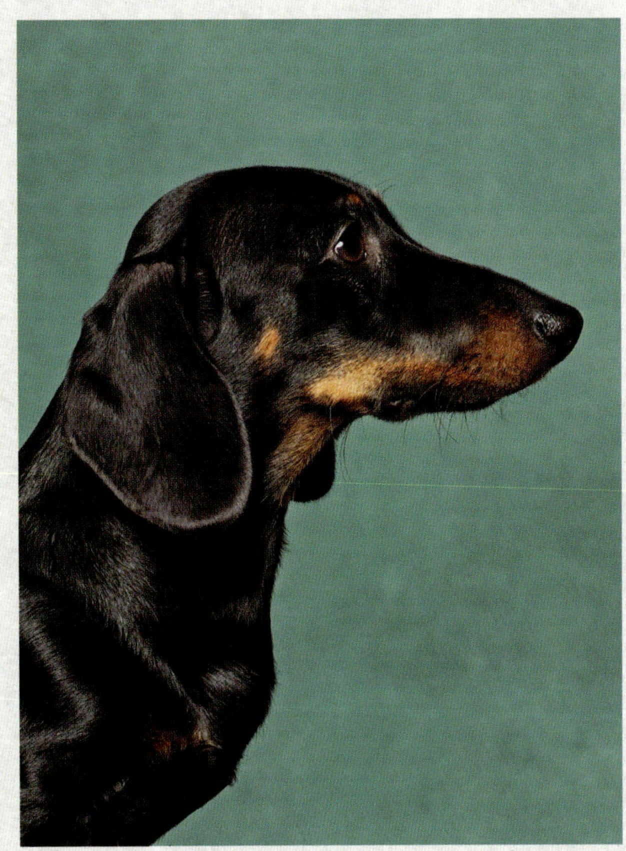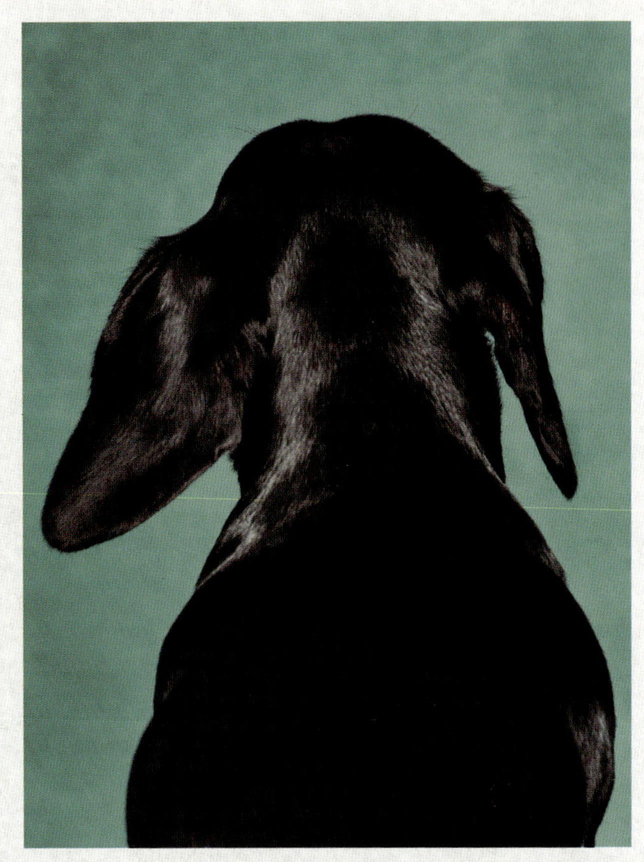

Dr. Derek

BORN: 24/09/2016   **TRADE:** Mini Torpedo   **BREED:** Dachshund

BUILD: Long   **EYES:** Brown   **HEIGHT:** 31cm   **HAIR:** Black / Tan

MARKS: Super sleek coat

PECULIARITIES: Is not in fact a registered doctor

M.O: ETC. Has a laser beam snout attack causing destruction in his tiny wake — often in the pursuit of chicken.

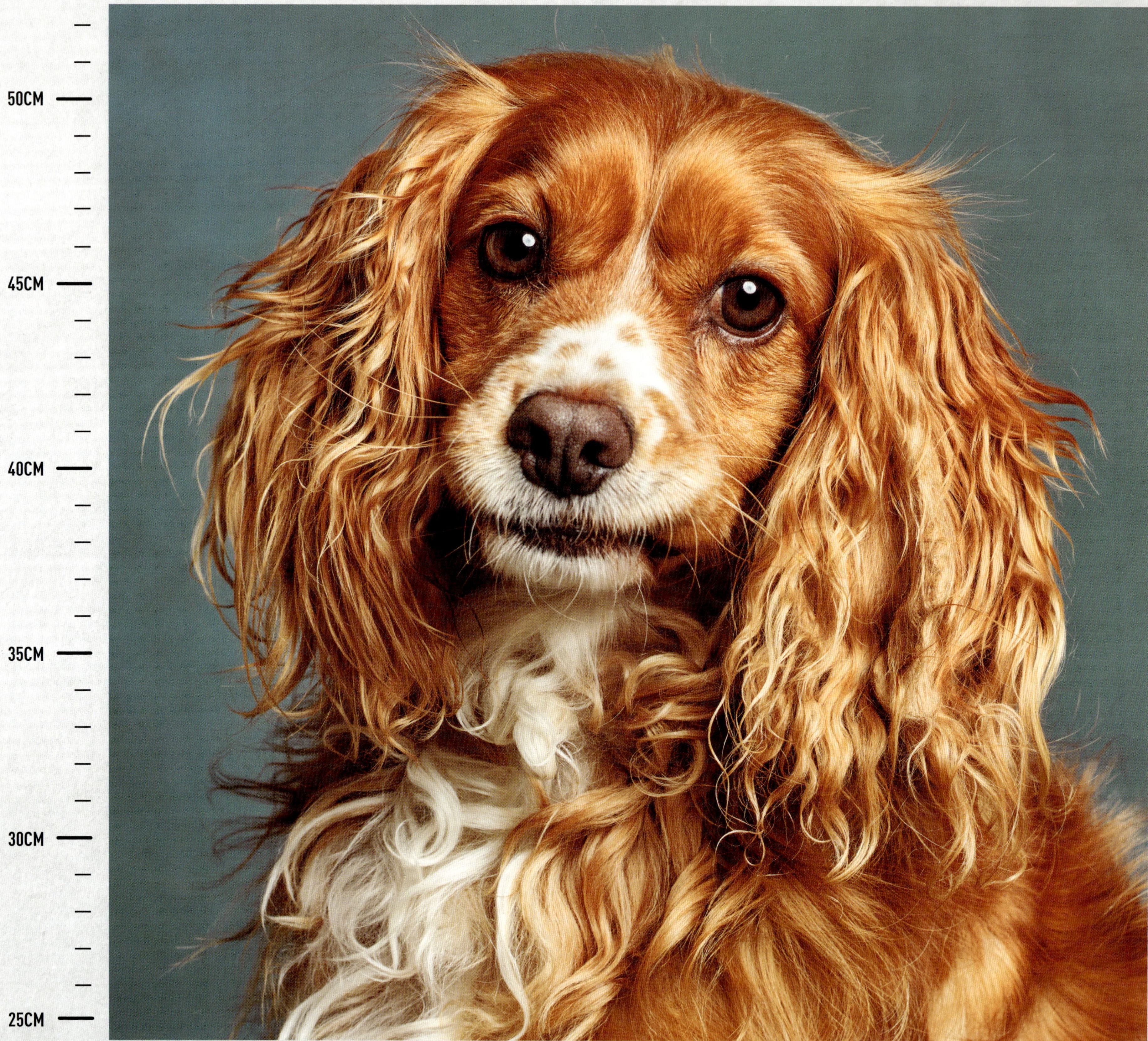

50CM
45CM
40CM
35CM
30CM
25CM

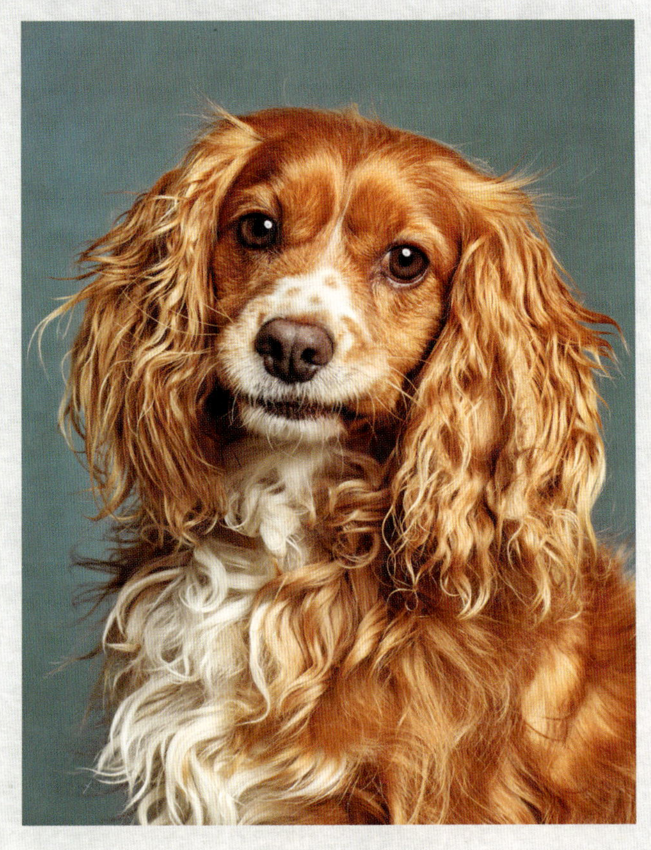 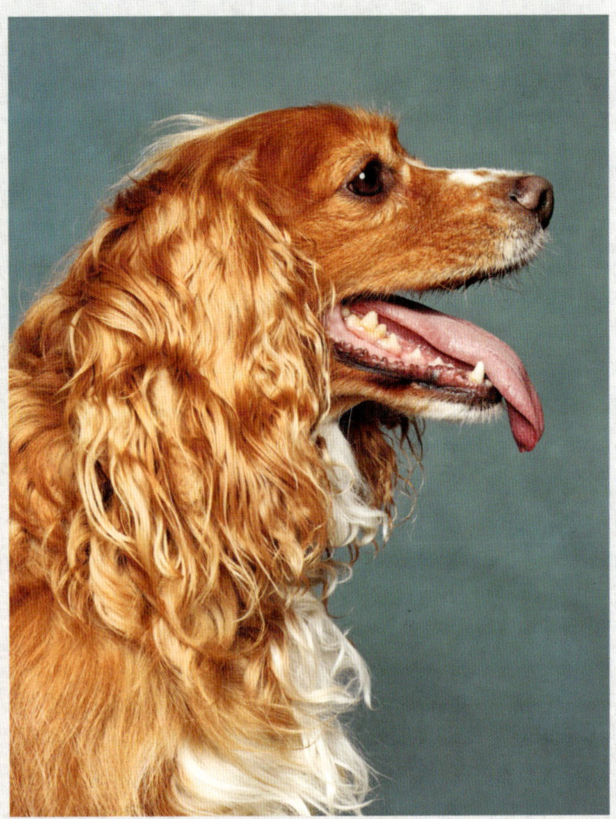 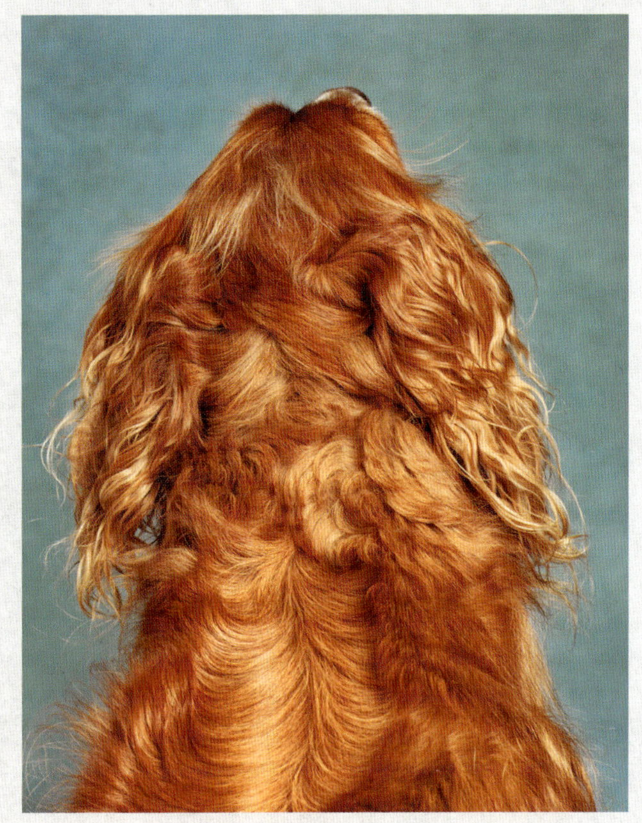

S, Pepe

ALIASES:

BORN: December 2010   TRADE: Positivity Motivator   BREED: Cavoodle x Spoodle

BUILD: Wavy   EYES: Brown   HEIGHT: 52cm   HAIR: Copper / White

MARKS: Freckles

PECULIARITIES: Tail seemingly never stops wagging

M.O: ETC. Has been known to 'catch' bubbles. Has an affinity for his soft toys, especially if they are not his.

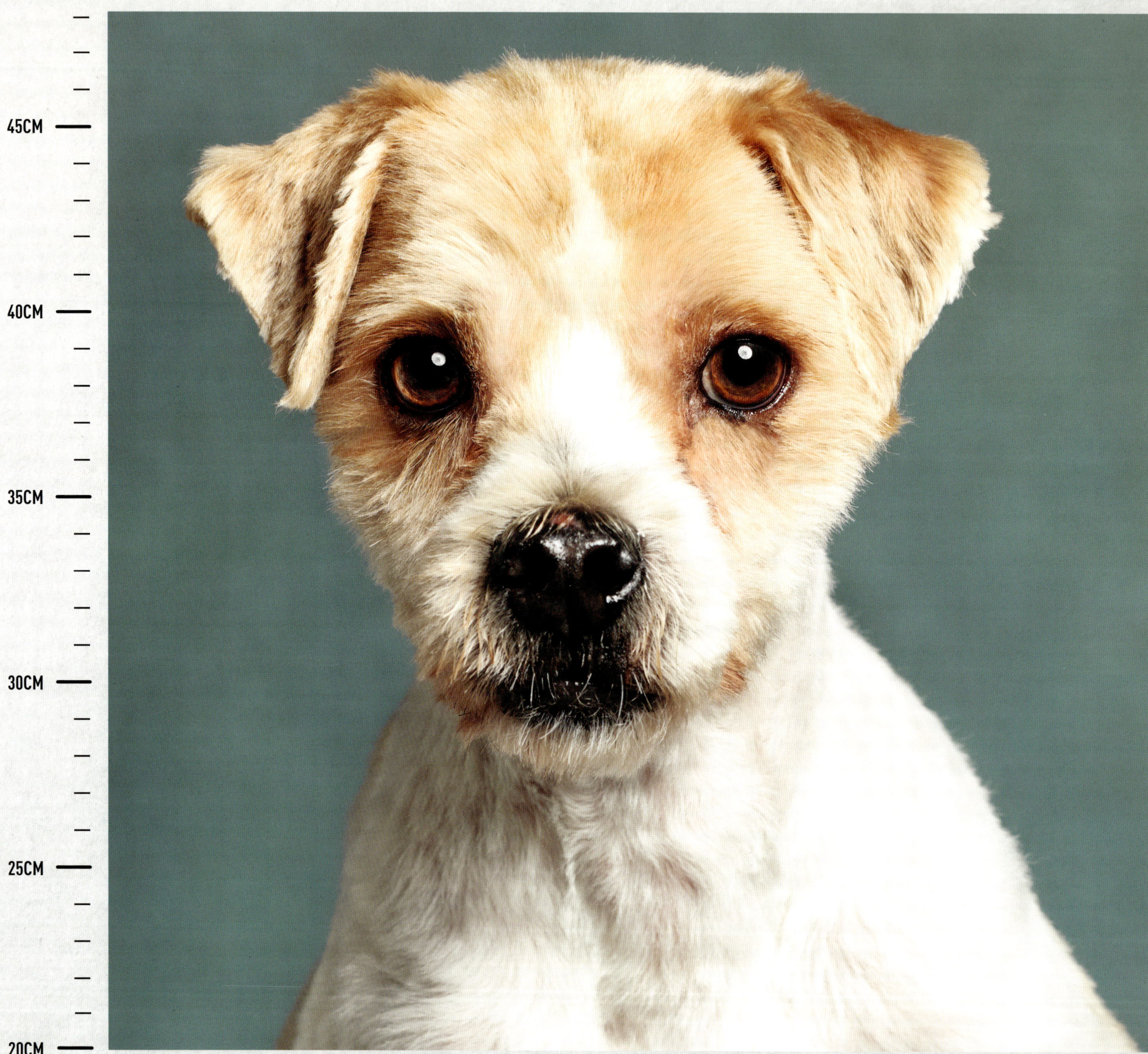

45CM
40CM
35CM
30CM
25CM
20CM

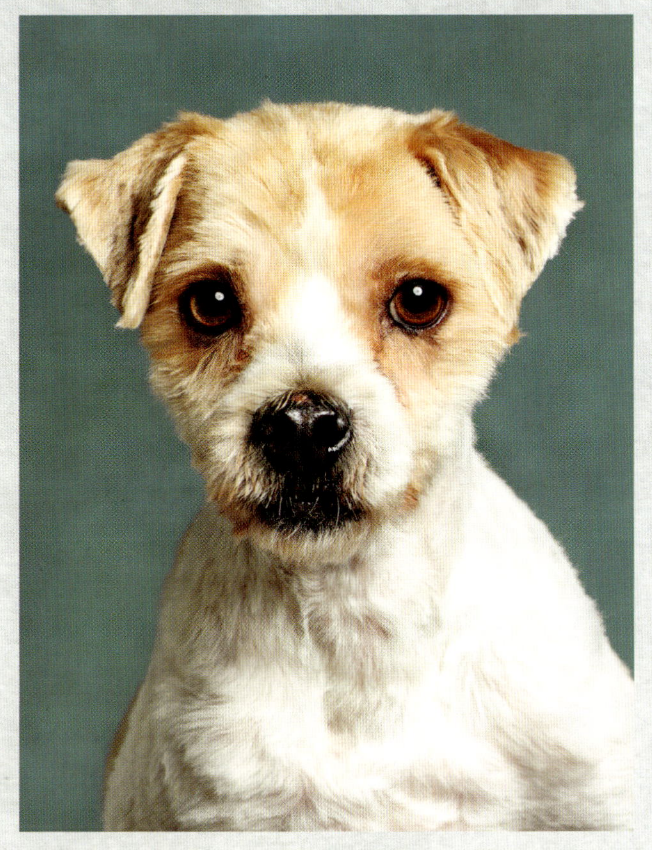 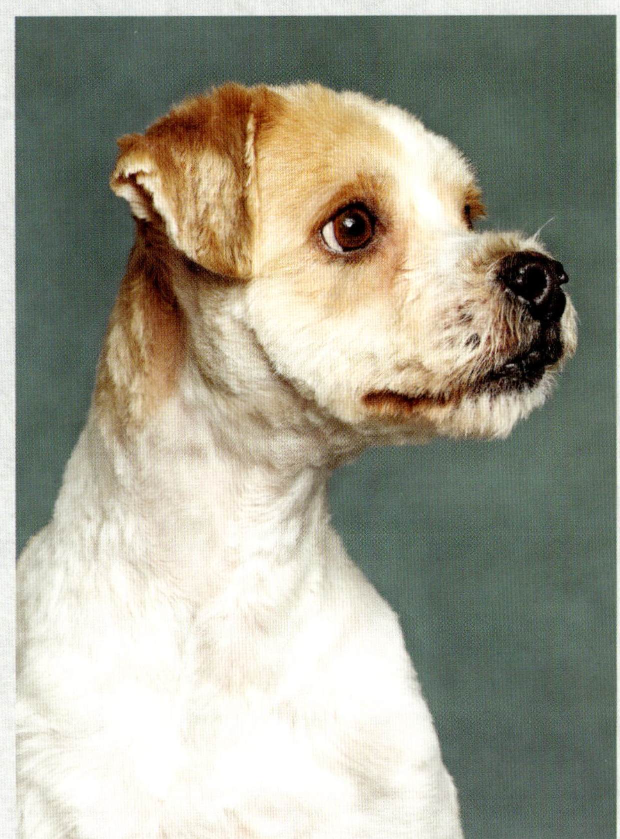 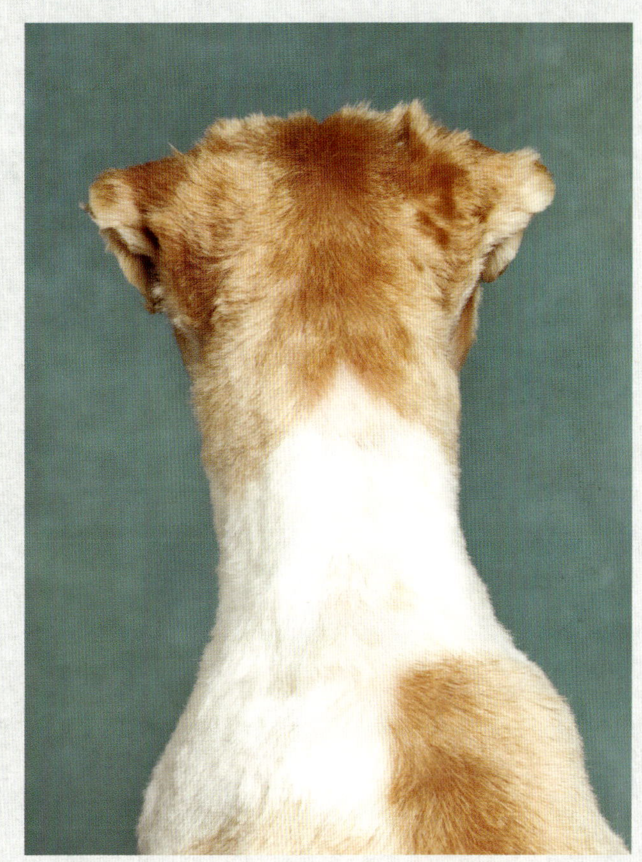

S, Lapooh

BORN: November 2009 **TRADE:** Risk Assessor **BREED:** Mystery Mutt

BUILD: Petite **EYES:** Brown **HEIGHT:** 47cm **HAIR:** White / Light Brown

MARKS: Pink spot on top of nose

PECULIARITIES: Has quite a small face — which is more evident post haircut

M.O: ETC. Originally scared of walking up stairs — has been known to climb half way, pause and call for assistance to be carried the rest of the way.

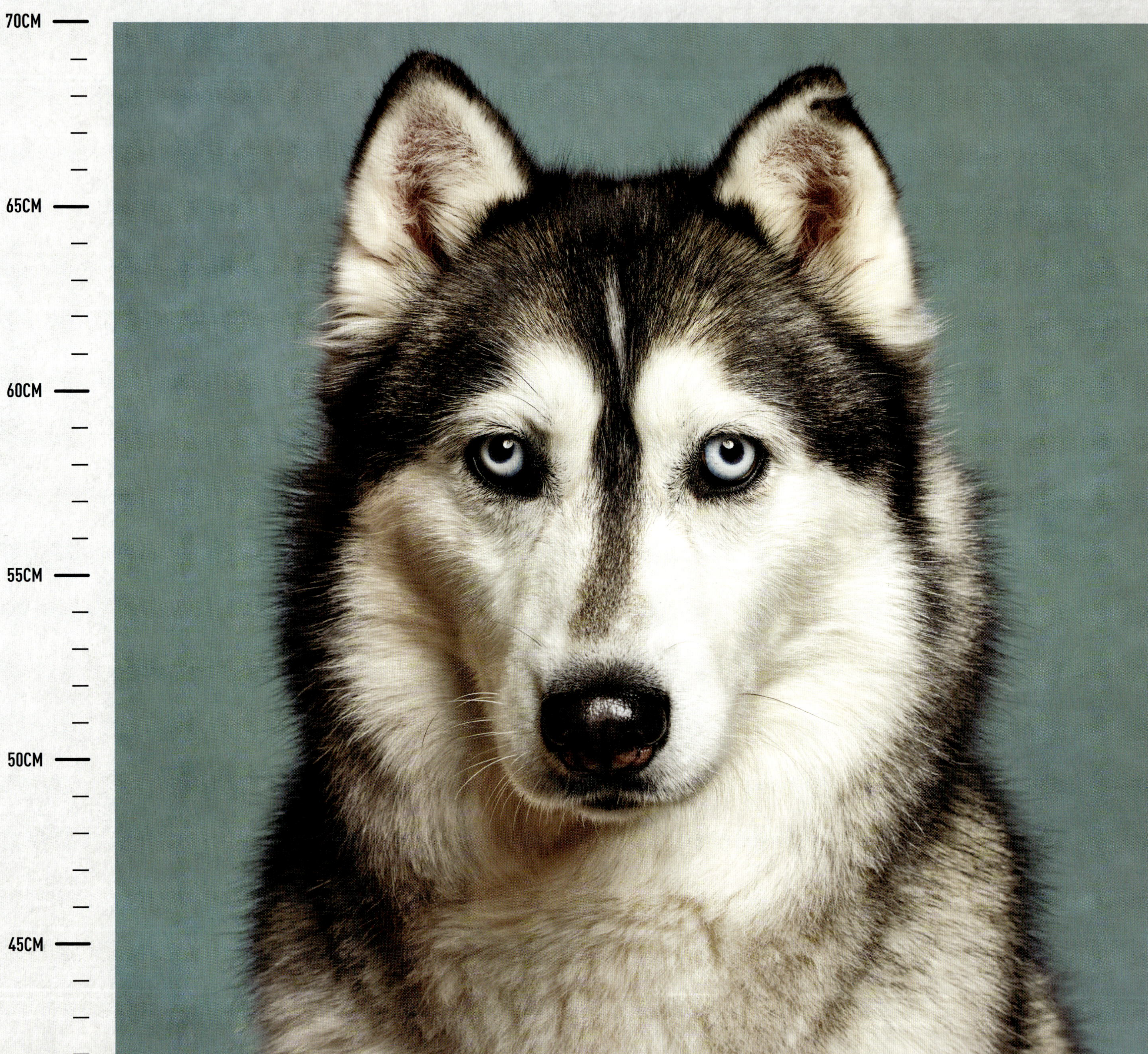

70CM
65CM
60CM
55CM
50CM
45CM

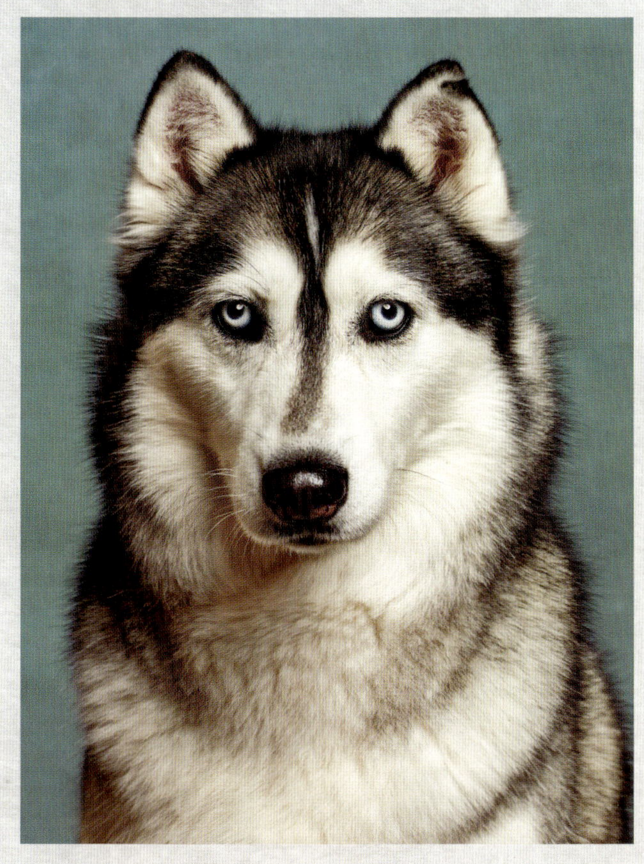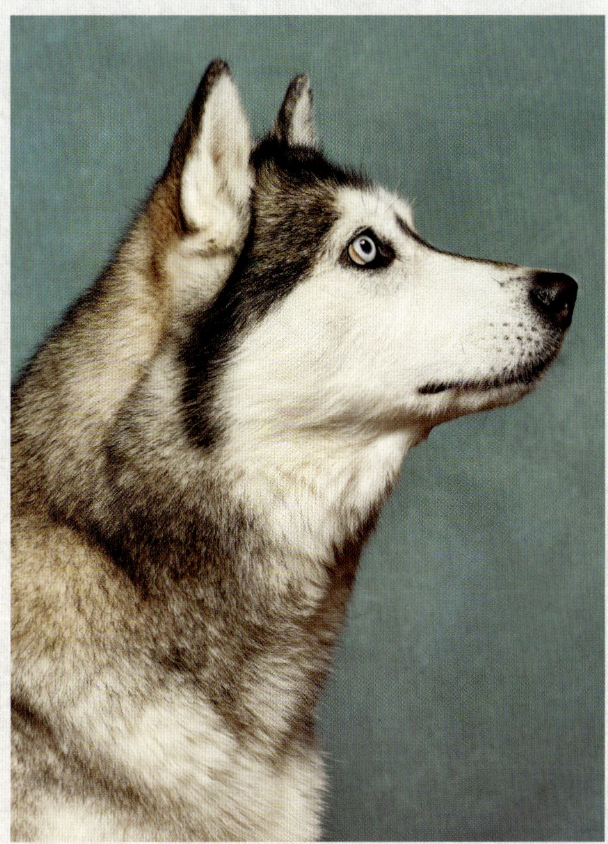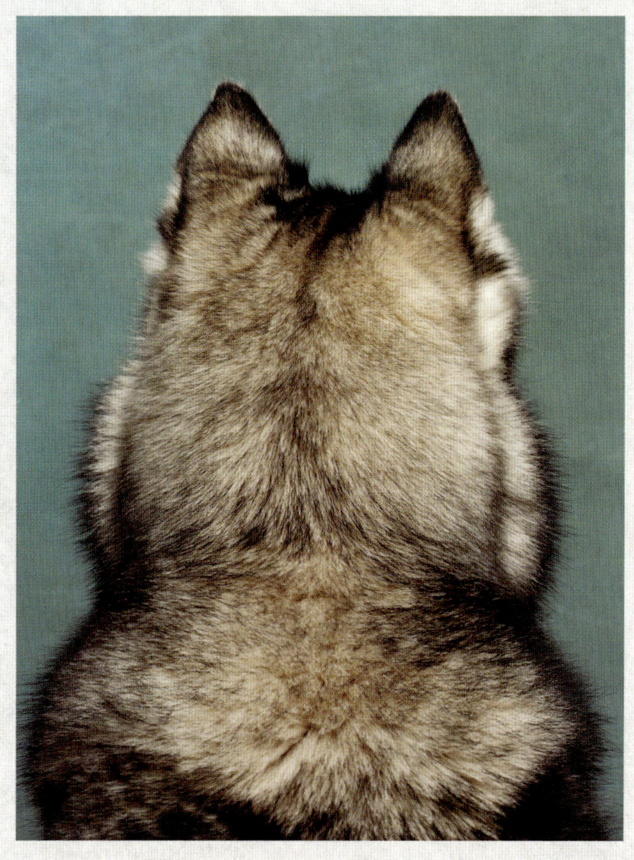

T, Mishka

BORN: November 2010   **TRADE:** Queen   **BREED:** Siberian Husky

BUILD: Floofy   **EYES:** Ice Blue   **HEIGHT:** 70cm   **HAIR:** Grey / White

MARKS: Slit in left ear — battle scar from her sister's puppy teeth

PECULIARITIES: Ate rat bait... Twice

M.O: ETC. Is particularly sassy — has mastered the look of judgement. Will do what her humans ask of her... if she feels like it.

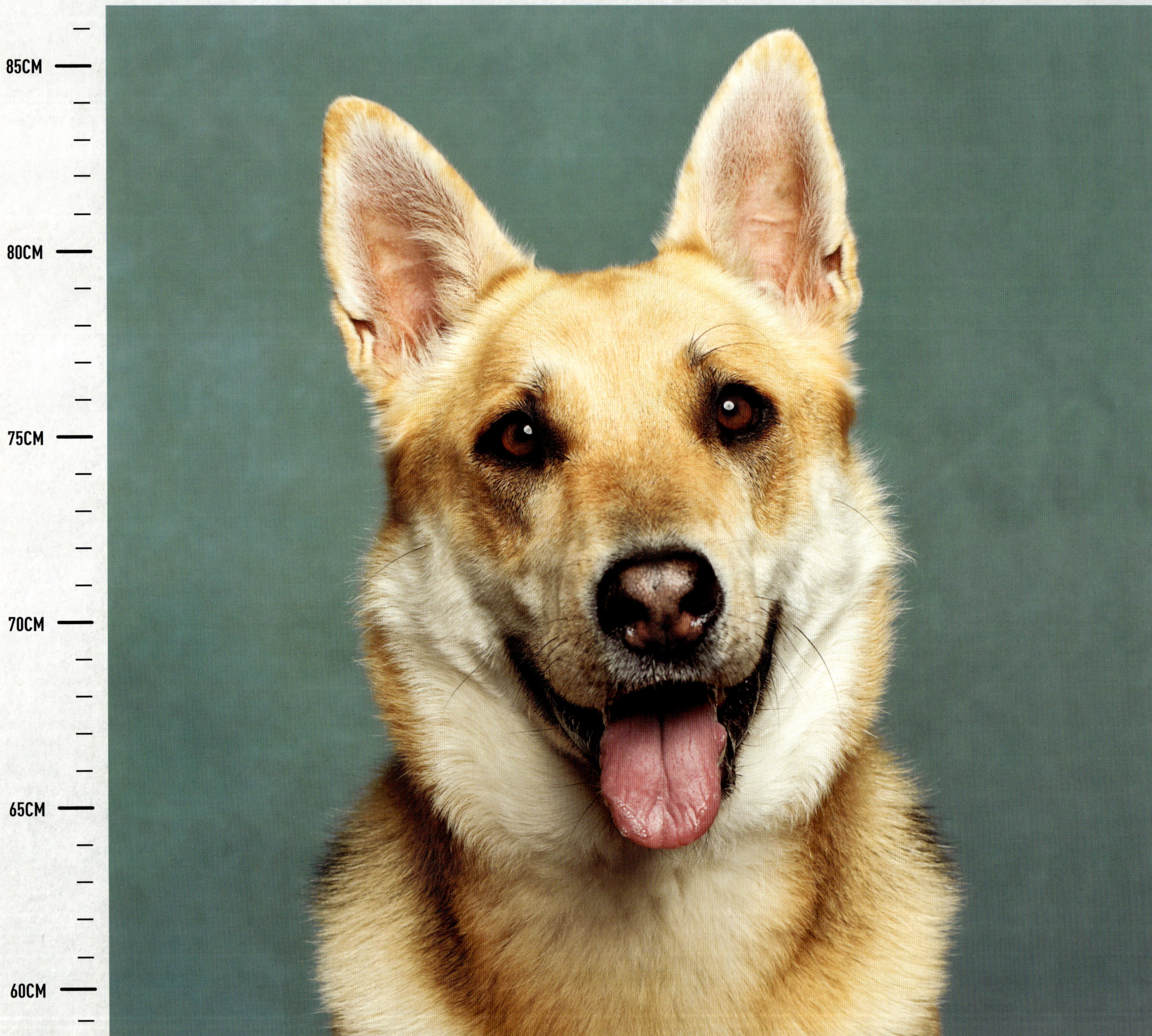
85CM
80CM
75CM
70CM
65CM
60CM

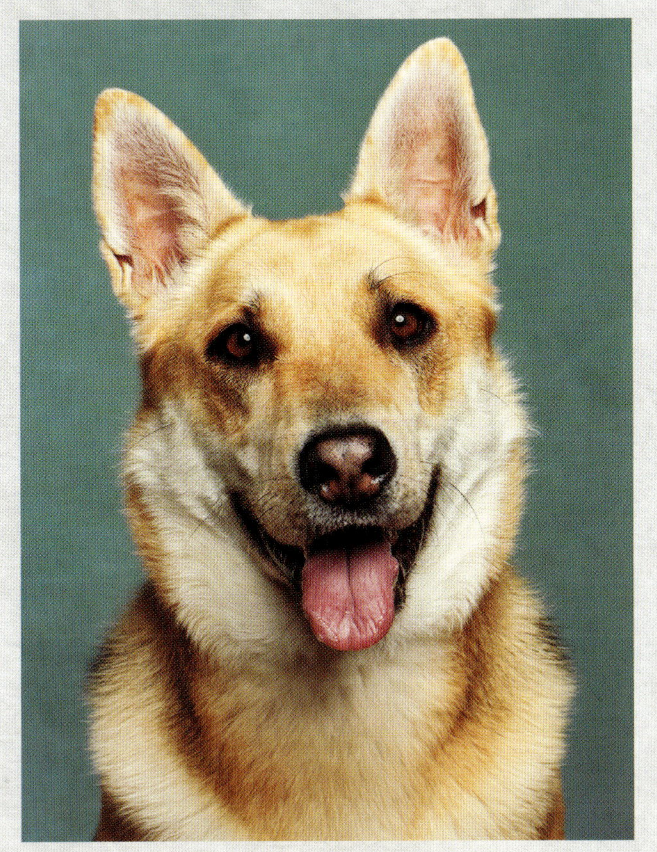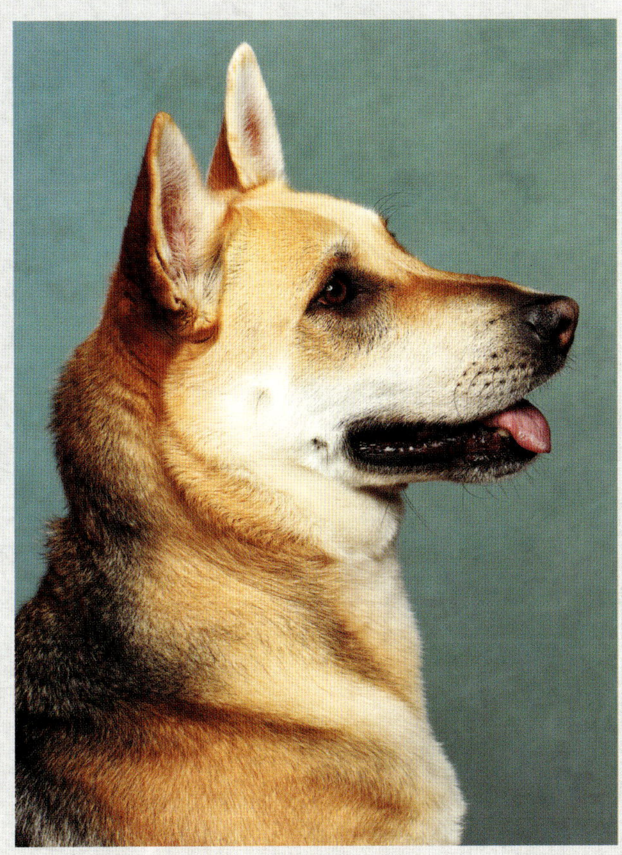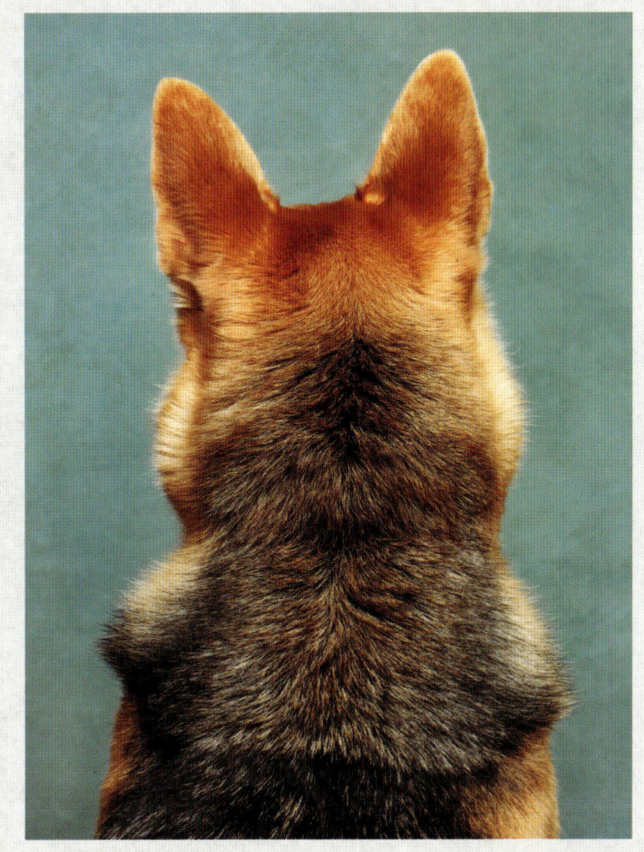

T, Aspen

ALIASES: Aspy / Aspo / Dogzilla / Destructor

BORN: March 2013   TRADE: Fetch Master   BREED: German Shepherd Cross

BUILD: Bootylicous   EYES: Brown   HEIGHT: 86cm   HAIR: Blonde / White / Black

MARKS: Pink tipped nose

PECULIARITIES: Exhibits a low long groan of happiness when sleeping comfortably

M.O: ETC. Saying she is fetch obsessed is an understatement. Has spilt blood for fetch and will no doubt do again in pursuit of the fetch object.

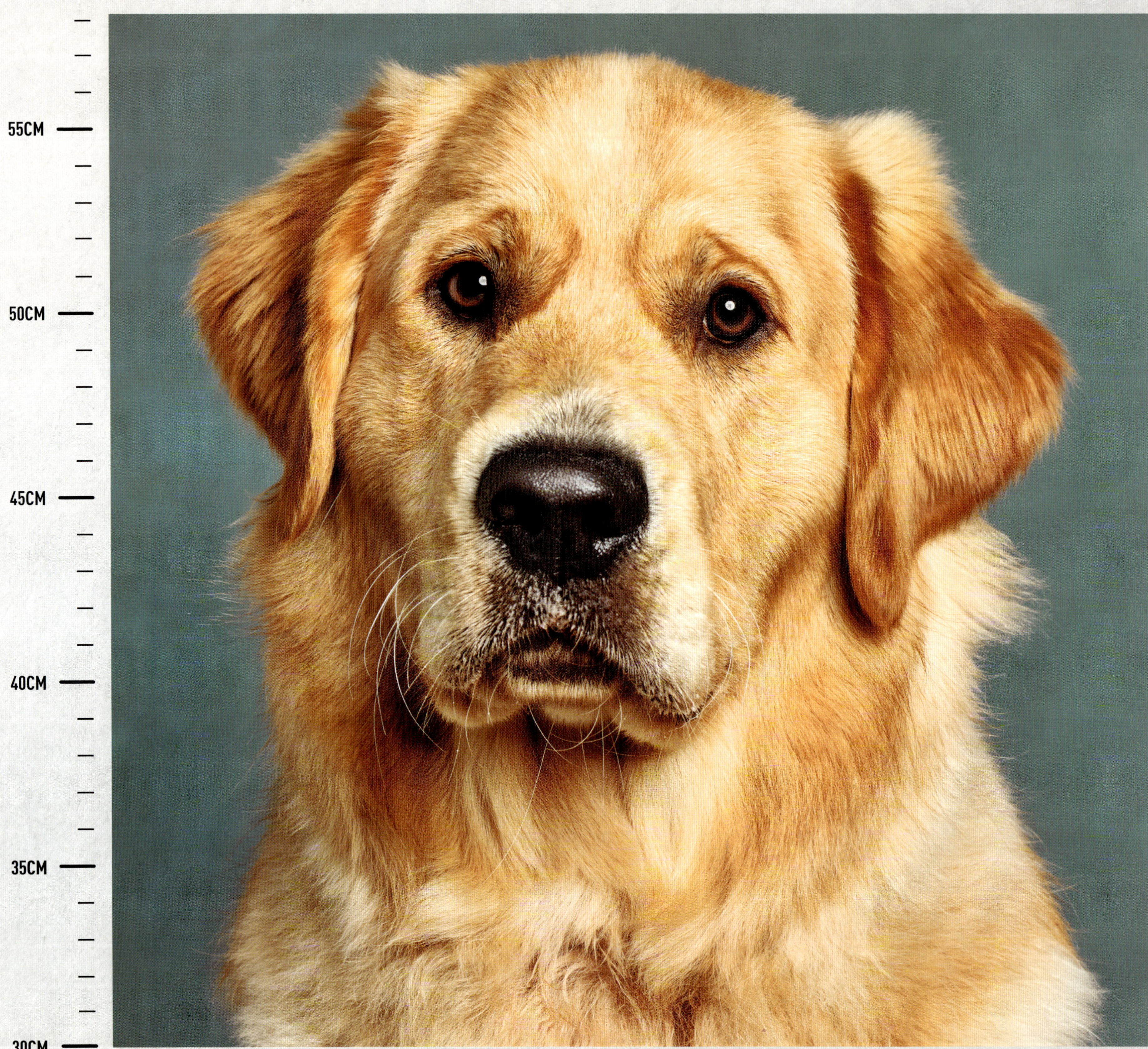

55CM
50CM
45CM
40CM
35CM
30CM

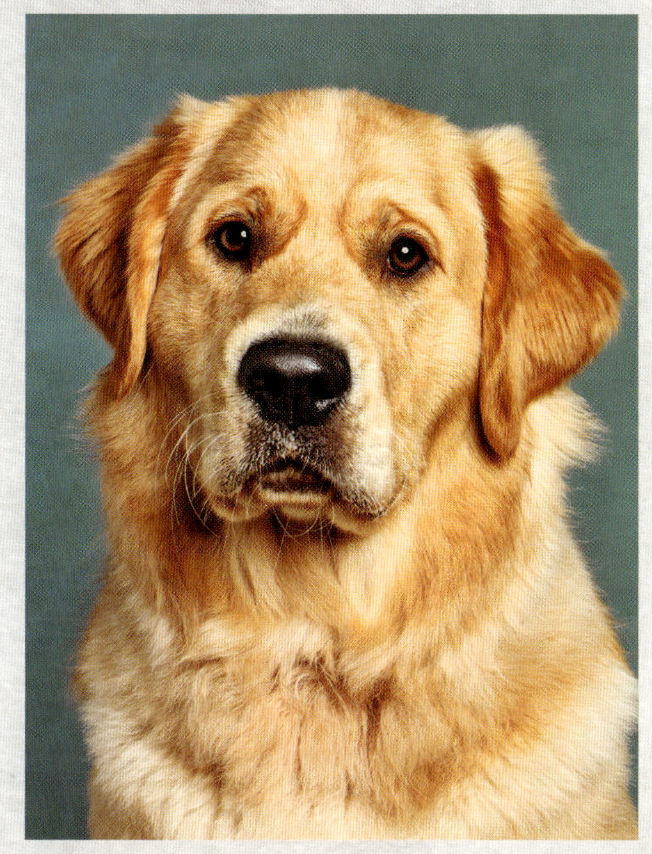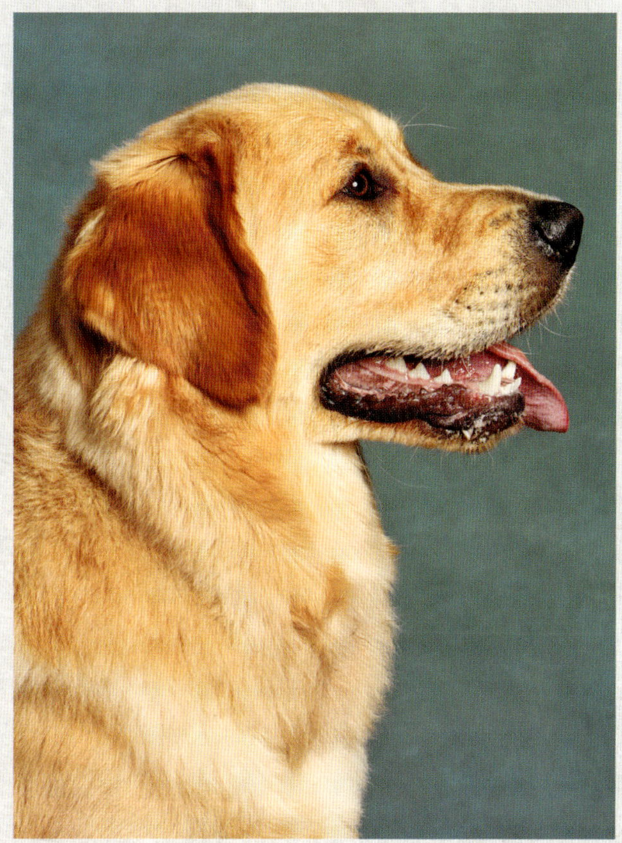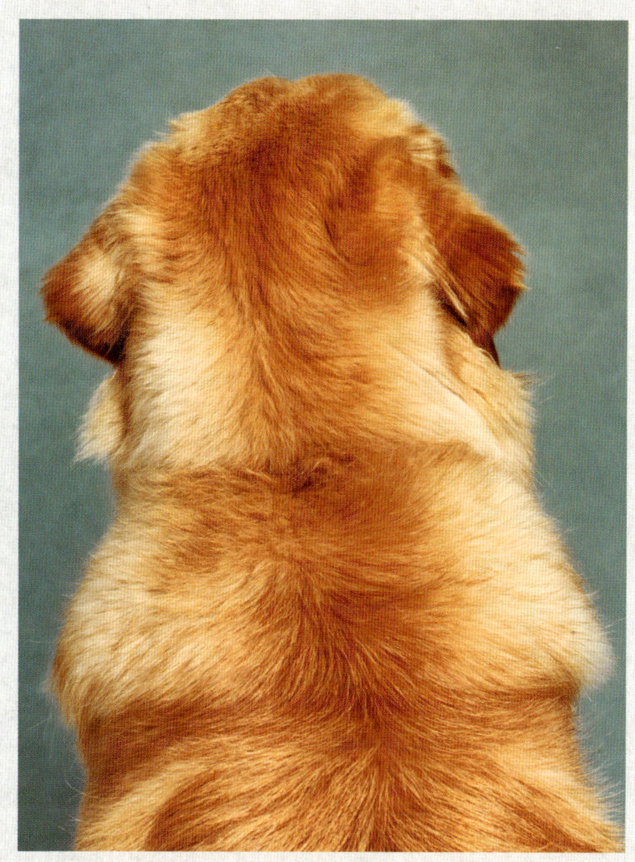

M, Ned

ALIASES: Nedmond / Nedster / Neddie

BORN: 16/08/2016   TRADE: Beach Comber / Land Seal   BREED: Golden Retriever

BUILD: Solid   EYES: Brown   HEIGHT: 57cm   HAIR: Golden

MARKS: Crimped ears

PECULIARITIES: Behind the adorable face lies a stubborn streak

M.O: ETC. May actually be a land seal — so drawn to the beach is he, that if he is being walked past the beach, not destined to go there, he will stop, lay down and refuse to move.

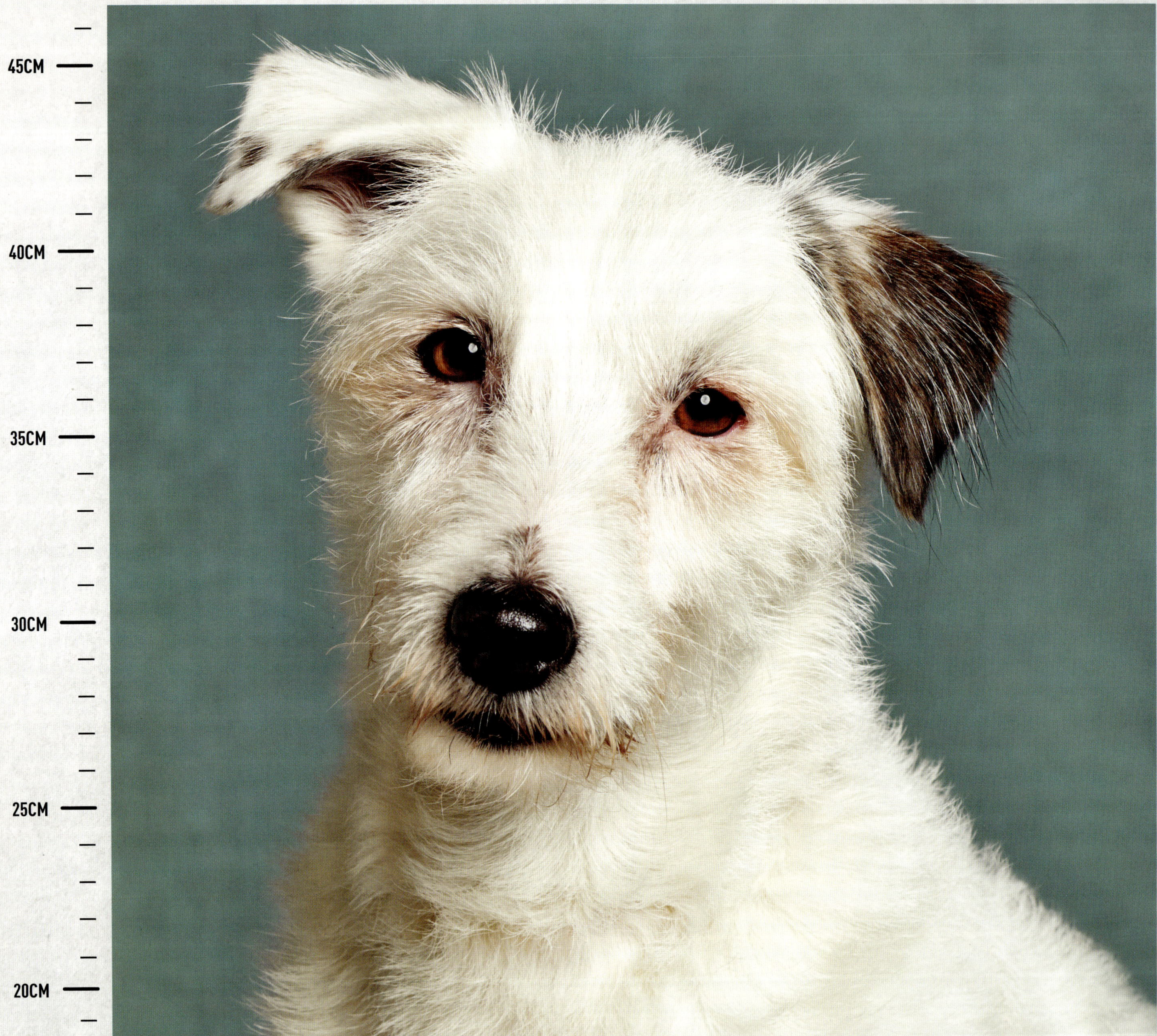
45CM
40CM
35CM
30CM
25CM
20CM

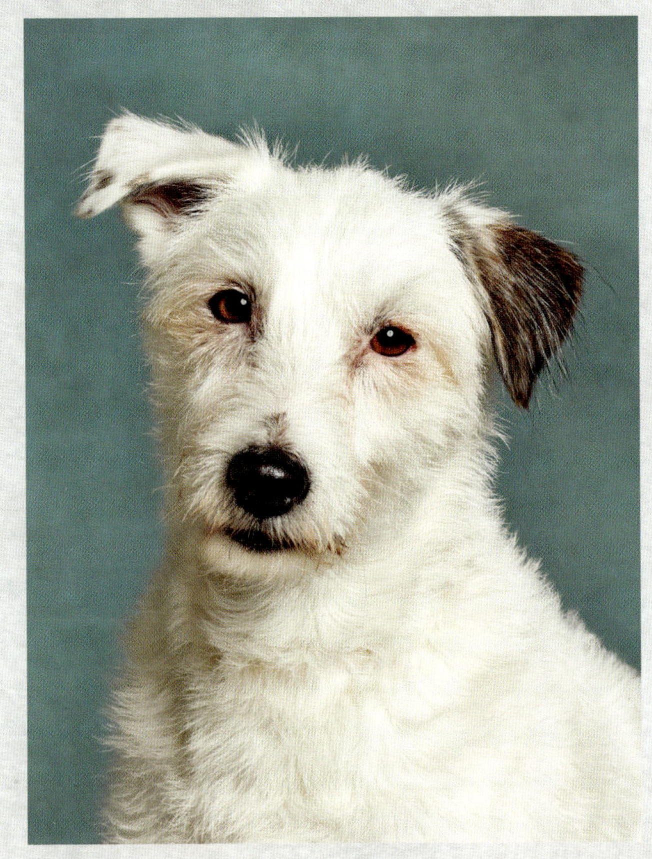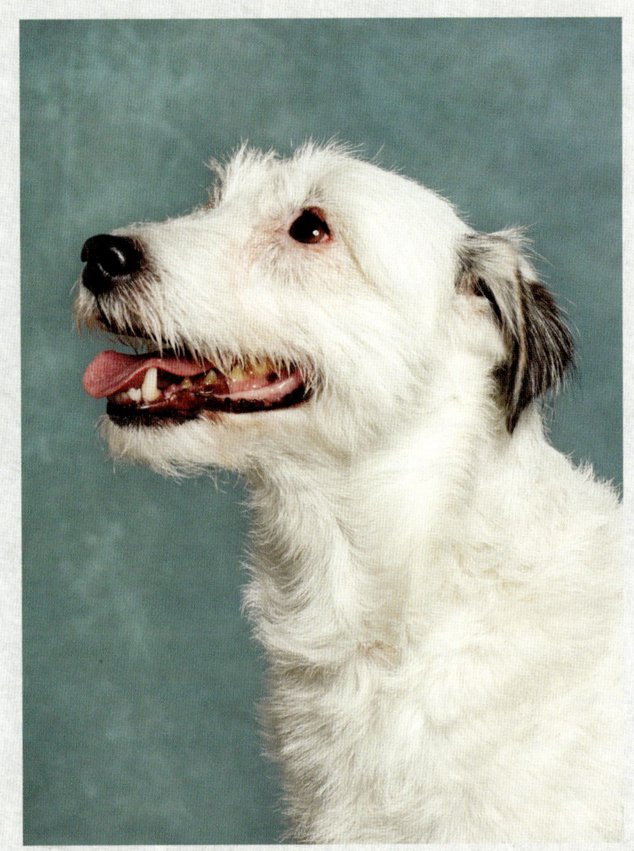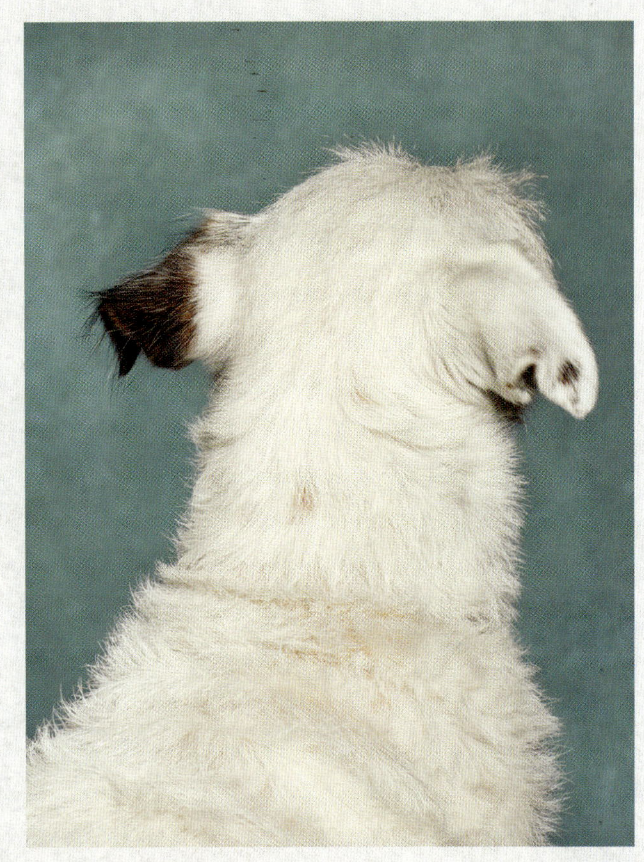

B, Matilda

ALIASES: Tilly / Till

BORN: 15/09/2004   TRADE: Treat Treasure Hunter   BREED: Rough Jack Russell Terrier

BUILD: Compact   EYES: Brown   HEIGHT: 45cm   HAIR: White / Brown

MARKS: One brown tipped ear

PECULIARITIES: Pursues possums

M.O: ETC. Has the ability to sniff out bounty from a mile away, including inside jacket pockets or in pants buried deep in laundry baskets.

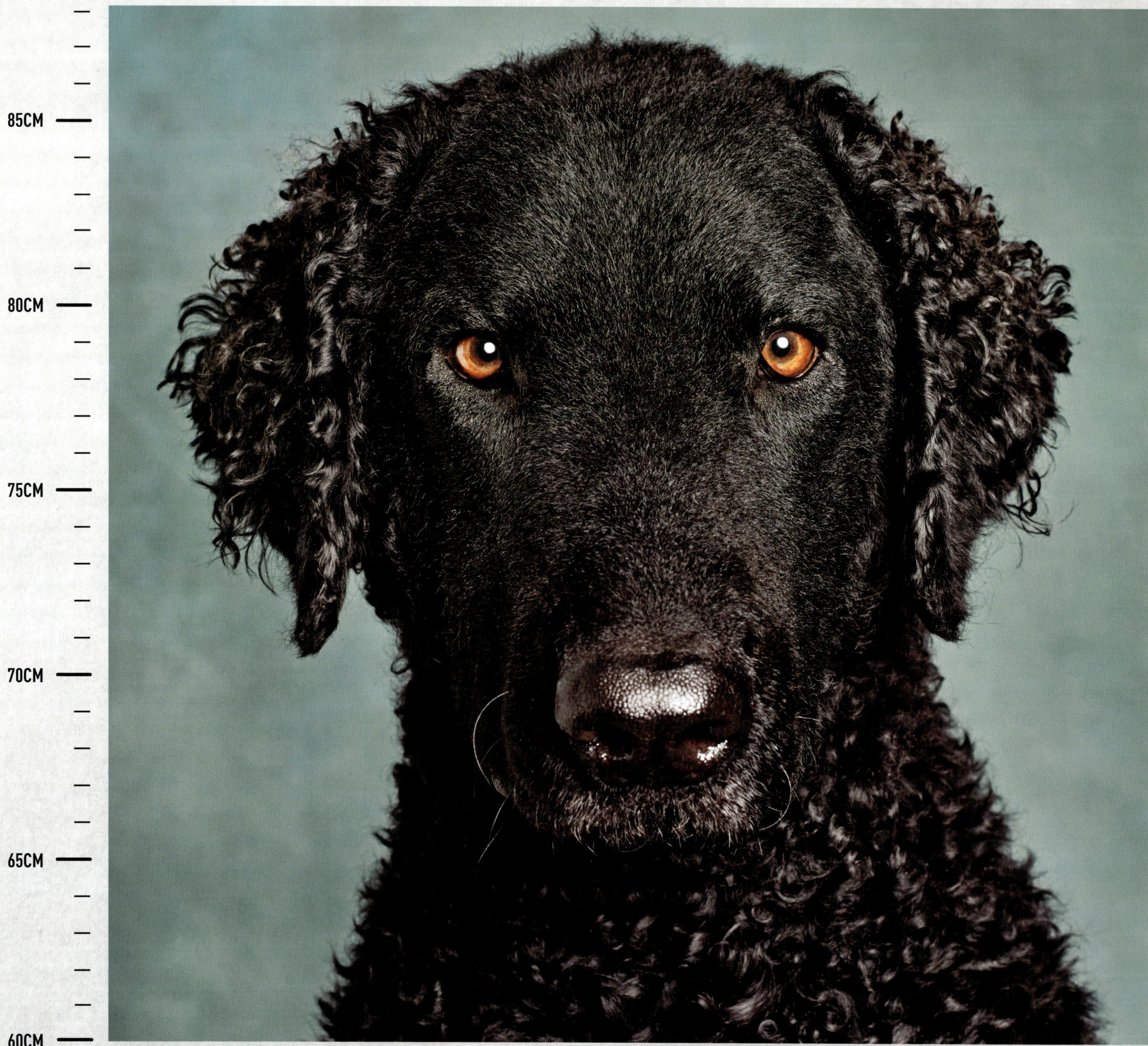
85CM
80CM
75CM
70CM
65CM
60CM

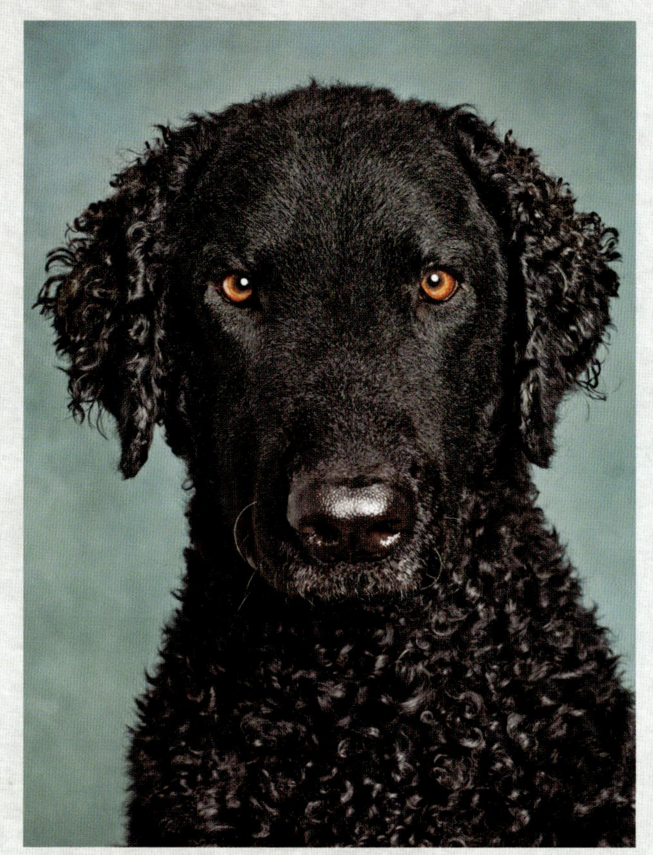 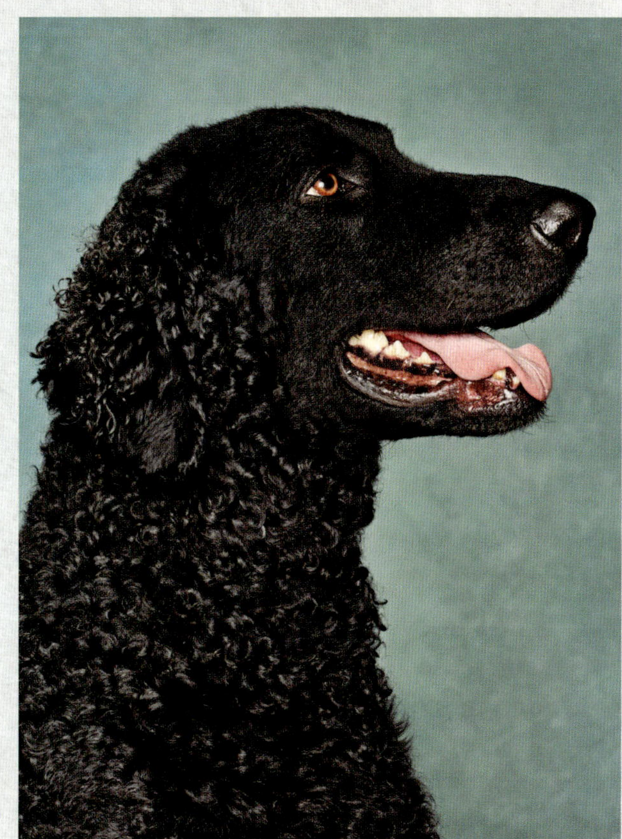 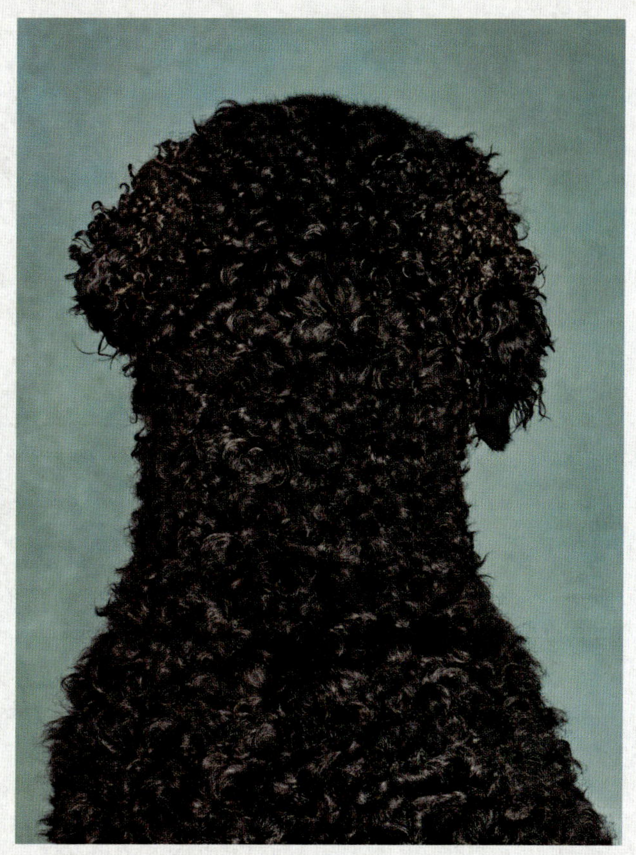

B, Java

ALIASES:

BORN: 02/12/2012   TRADE: Ambassador for Curls   BREED: Curly-Coated Retriever

BUILD: Curly   EYES: Brown   HEIGHT: 88cm   HAIR: Black

MARKS: Fur is naturally short and straight around her face area

PECULIARITIES: Intense eyes that can see into your soul

M.O: ETC. Has seemingly extendible front legs/arms that are frequently flung
at her human companions.

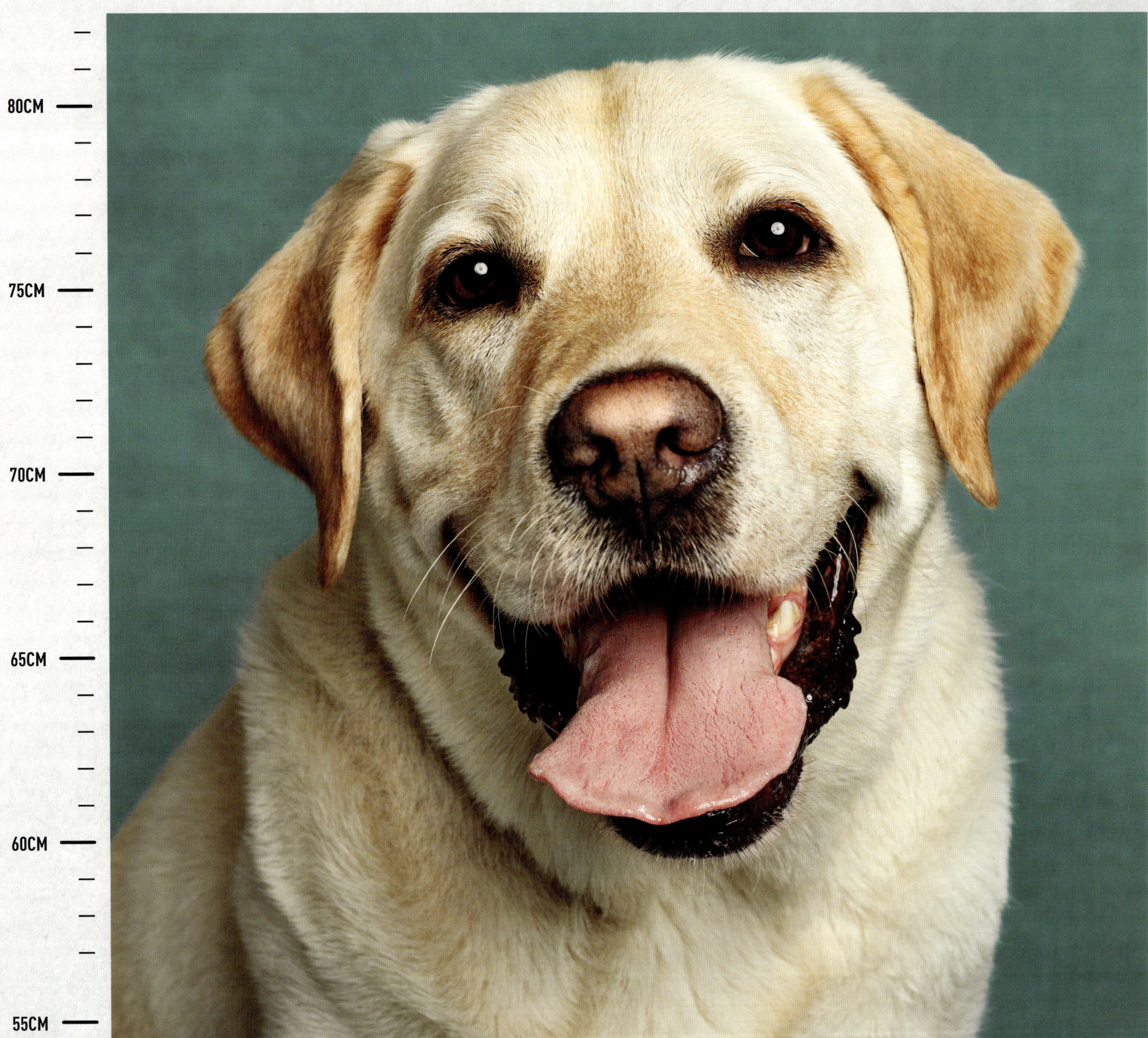

80CM
75CM
70CM
65CM
60CM
55CM

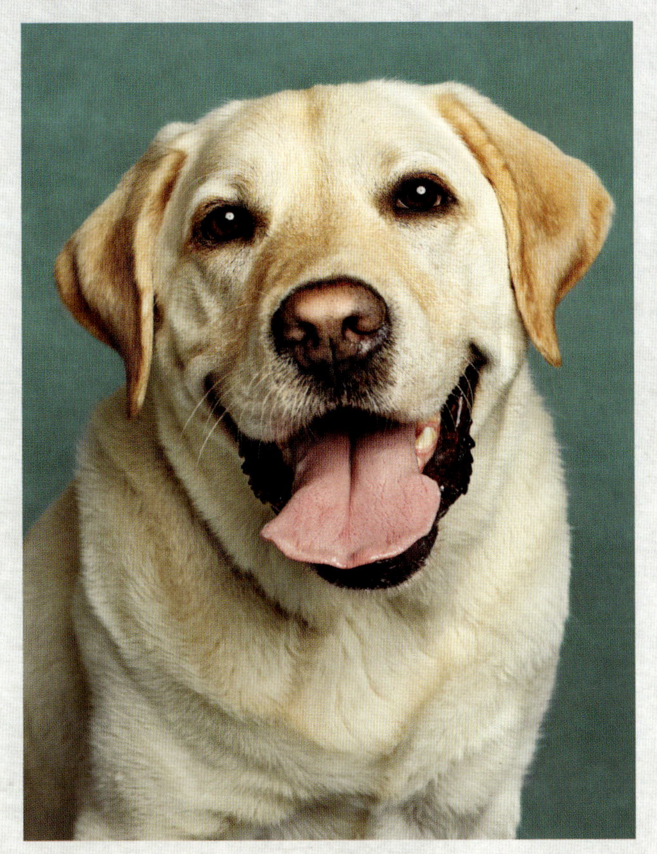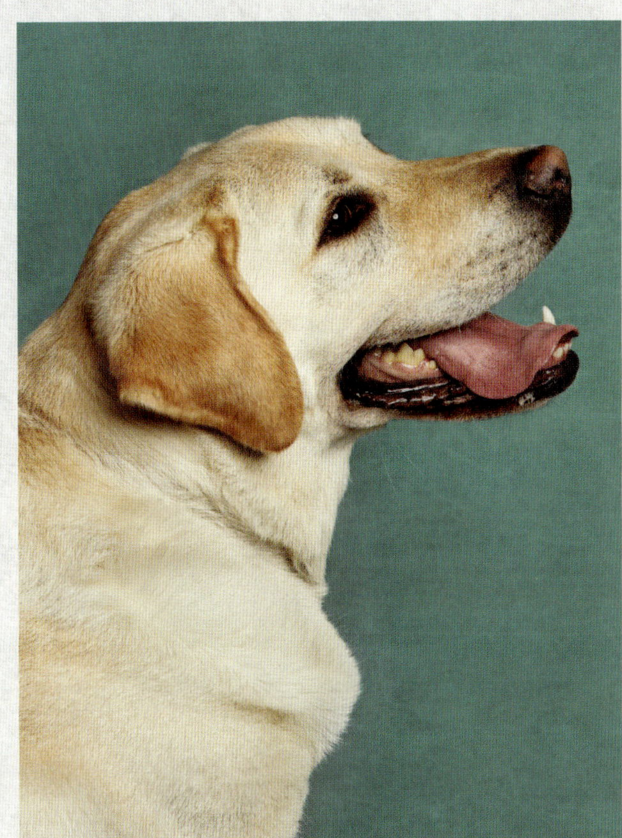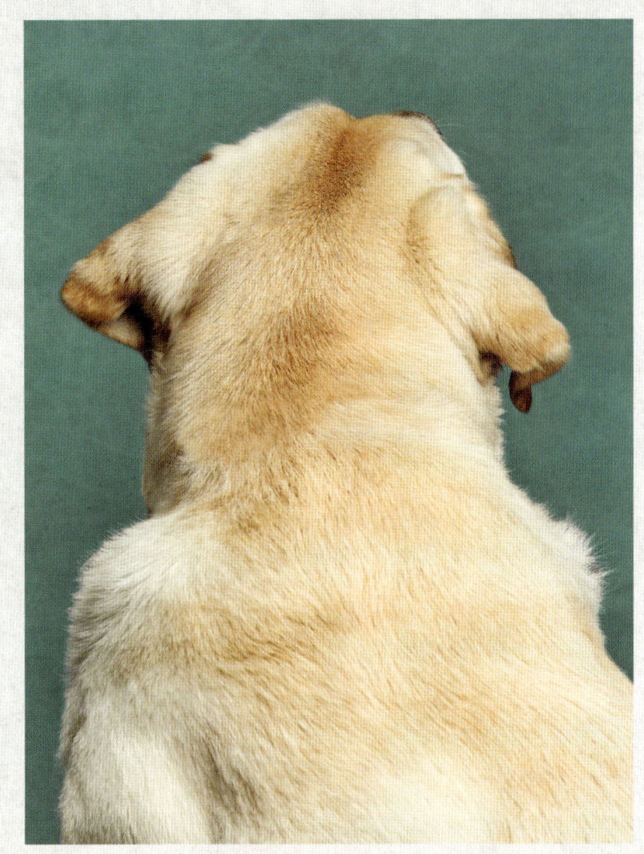

Murray

ALIASES: Muzz / Lance Bombardier Murray

BORN: 12/09/2012 TRADE: Army Dog BREED: Labrador Retriever

BUILD: Square EYES: Brown HEIGHT: 82cm HAIR: Golden

MARKS: Pink tipped nose

PECULIARITIES: He will trust, follow, bond and most importantly play with anyone

M.O: ETC. Described as the most obedient, relaxed and calm natured dog, all this changes if he sees birds. Known to chase birds for hours, then once tired, will stop right there to nap, knowing someone will eventually find and carry home his 40kgs+ body.

MURRAY
LANCE BOMBARDIER (16th ALR)

Murray the Labrador enlisted into the
Australian Army in 2014 as the unit mascot
of the 16th Air Land Regiment (16th ALR)
at Woodside. Murray was promoted to
Lance Bombardier in 2016.

Murray is a certified Operation K9 Dog — his
role is to support the mental health and
well-being of service personnel. Like all
Operation K9 dogs, Murray is trained to be
able to recognise and respond to heightened
anxiety, depression and night tremors
in his human colleagues.

He is partial to chicken nuggets and is
bird obsessed — often chasing them
around the base for hours.

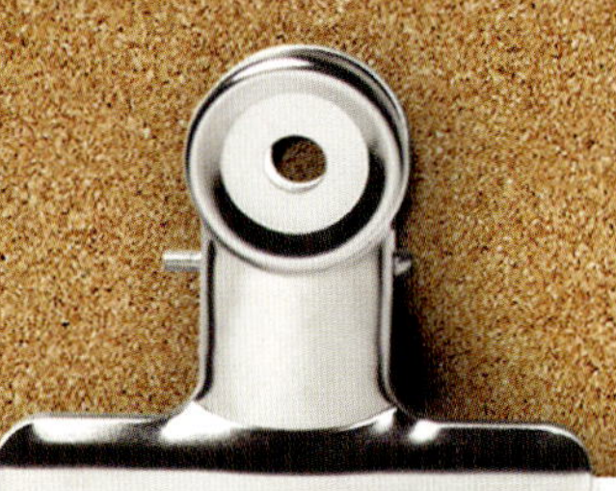

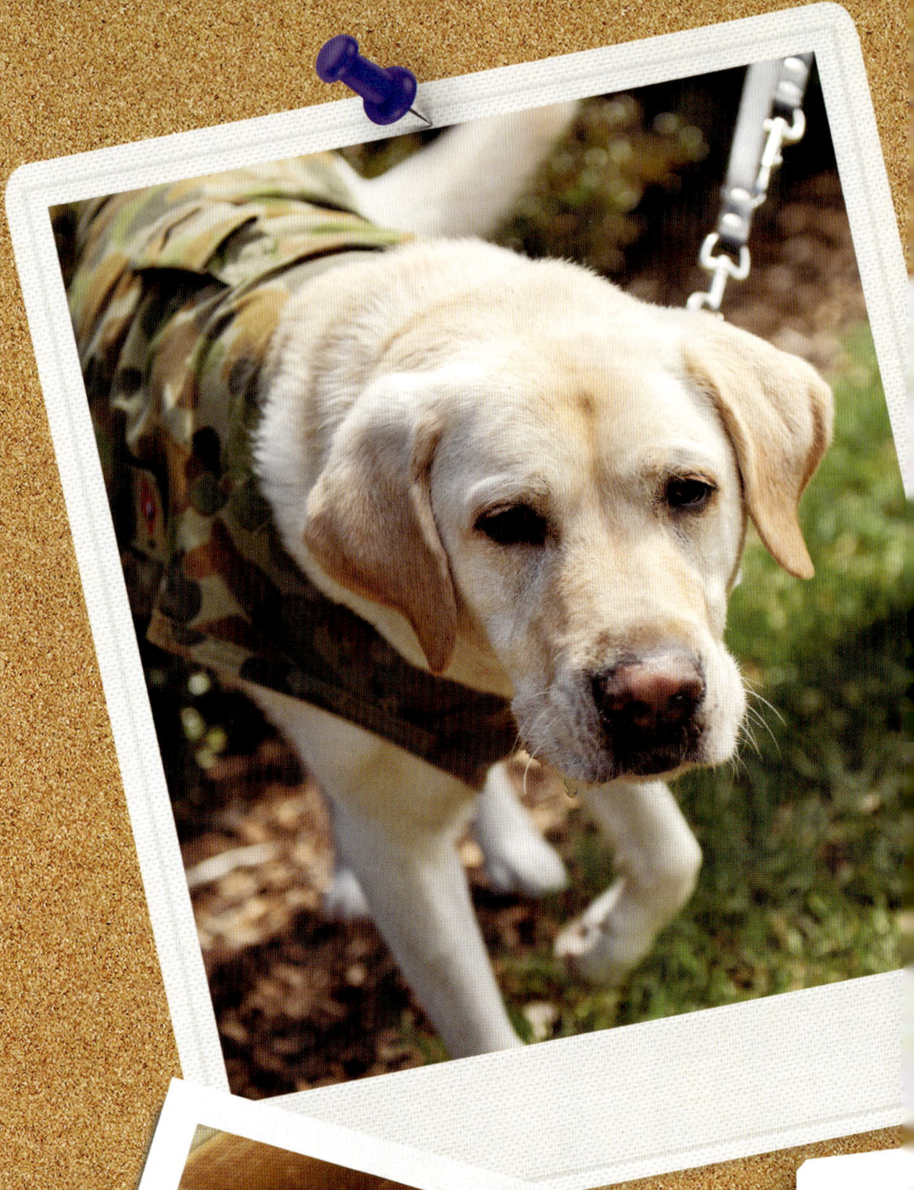

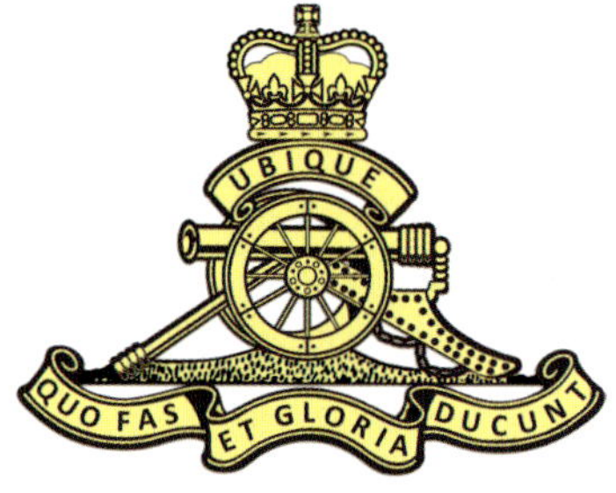

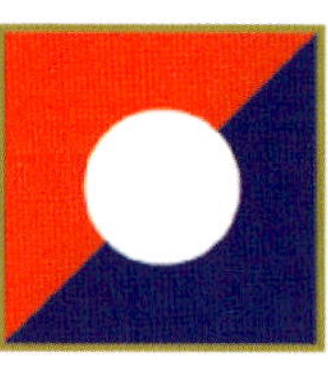

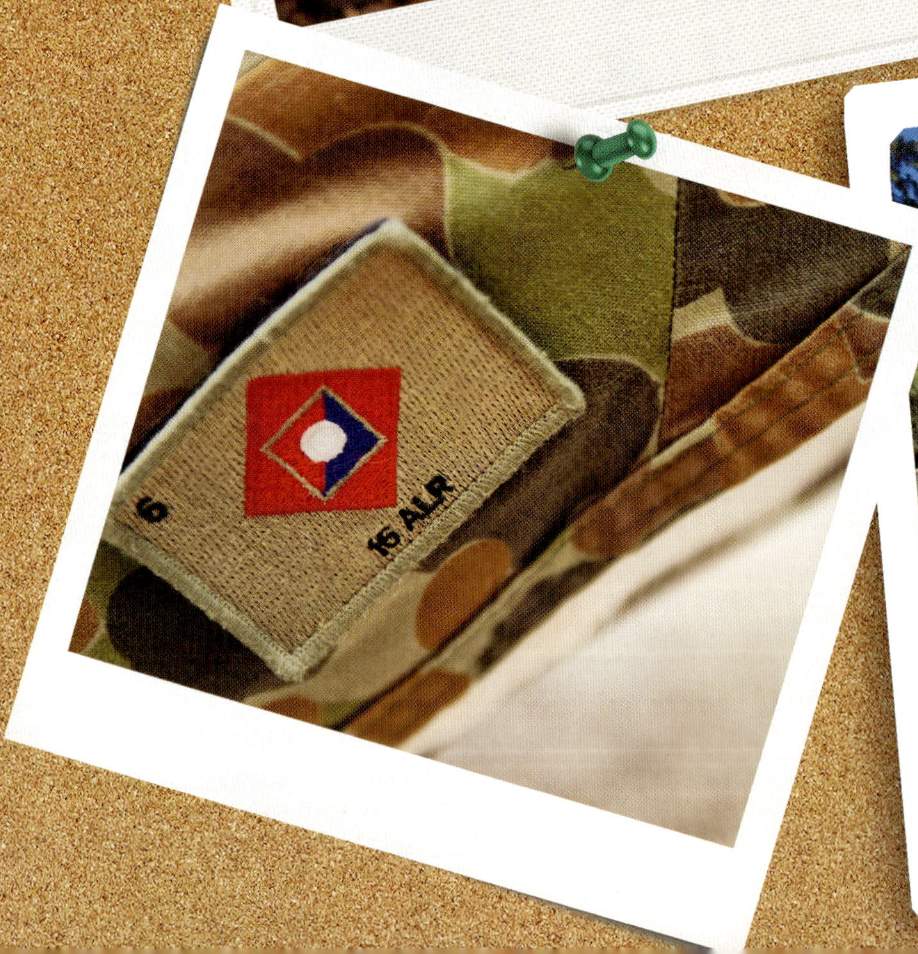

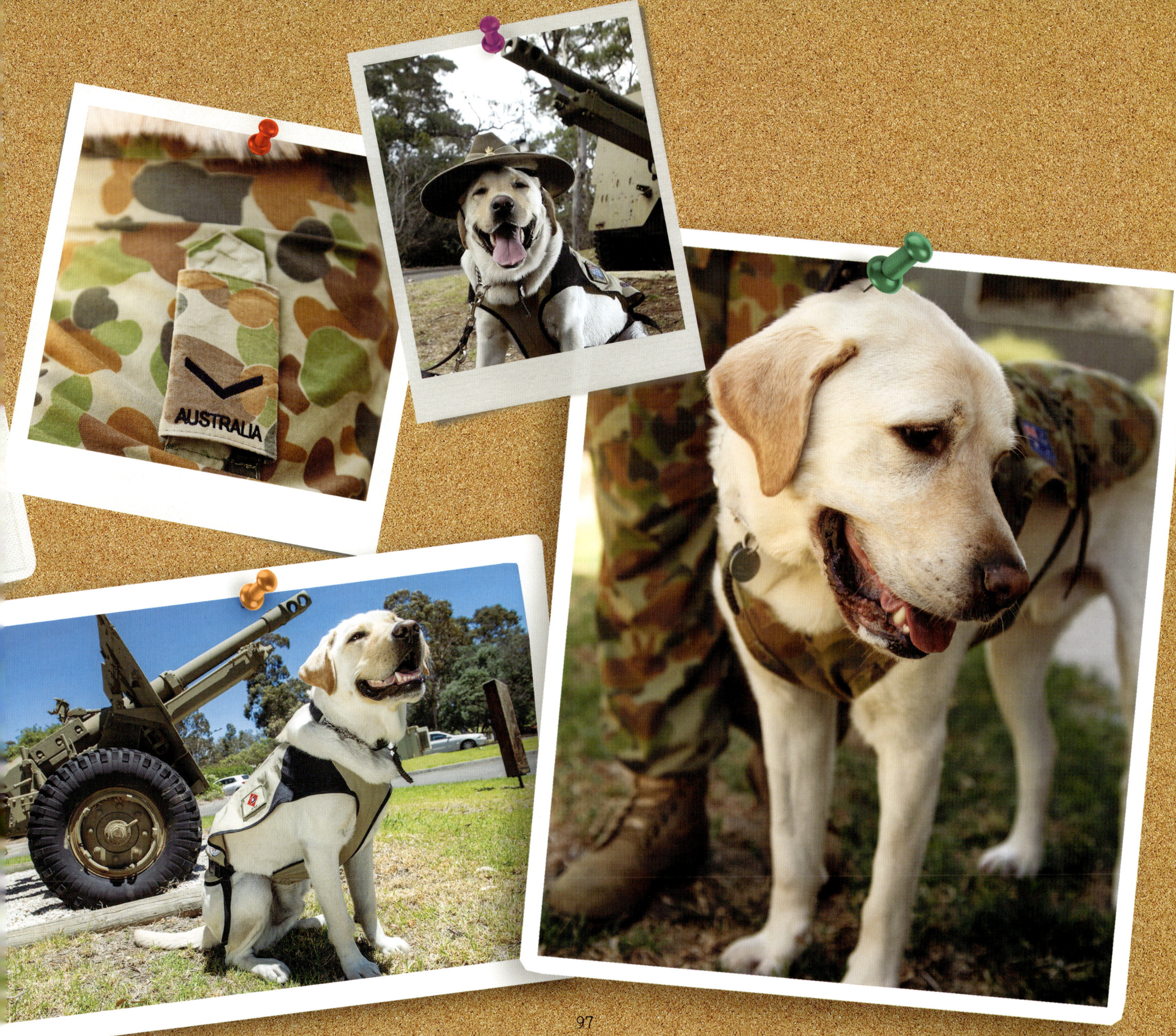

AUSTRALIA

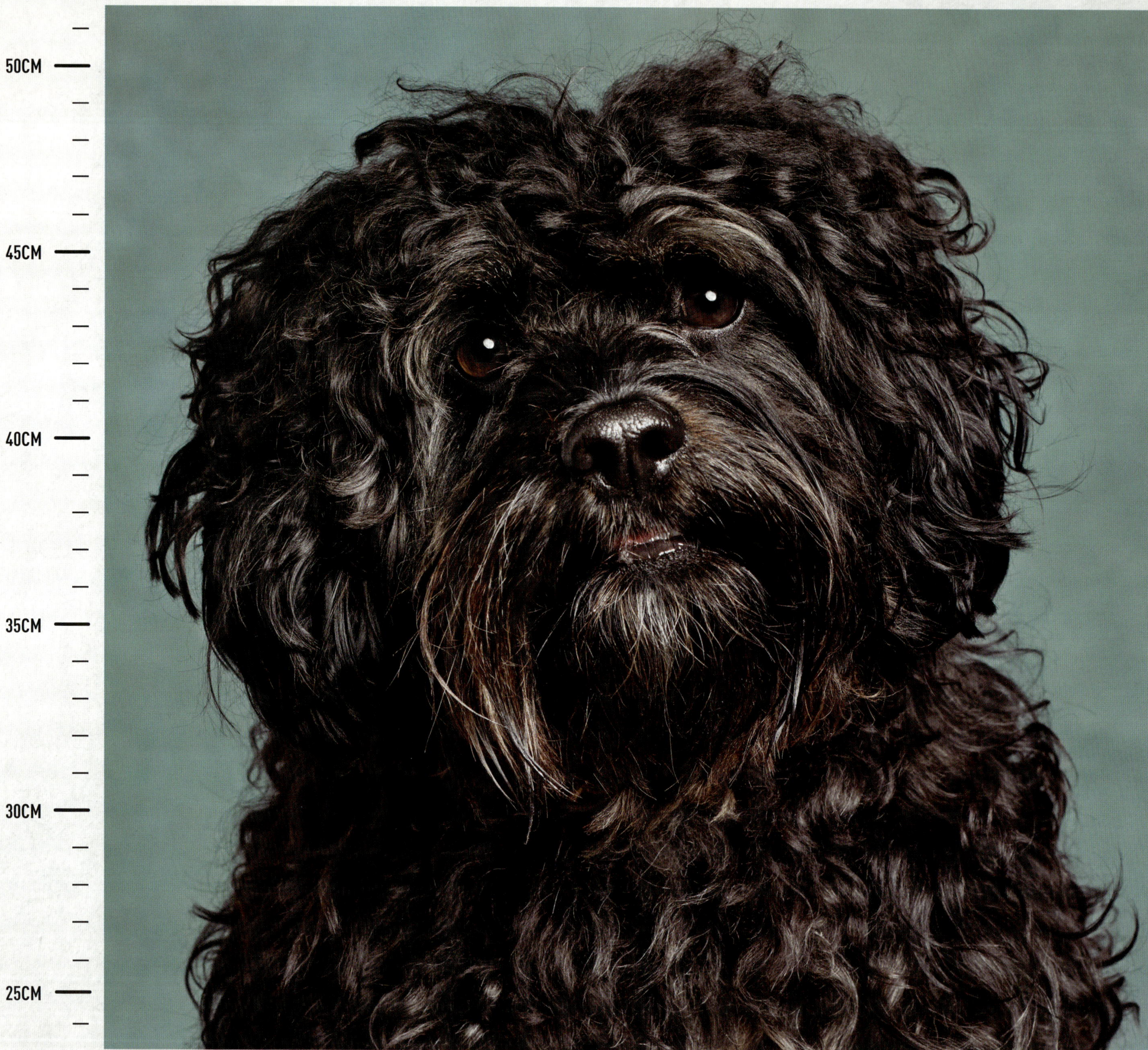
50CM
45CM
40CM
35CM
30CM
25CM

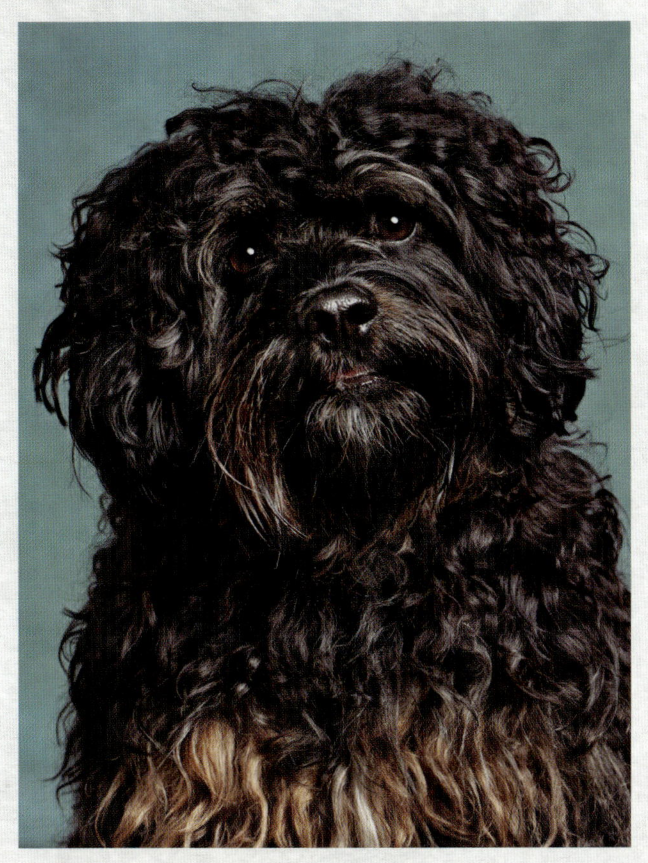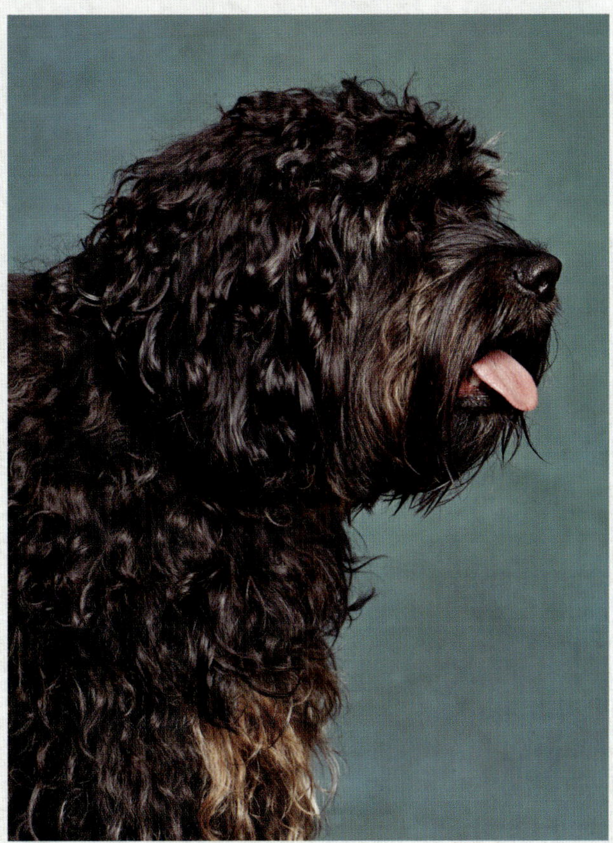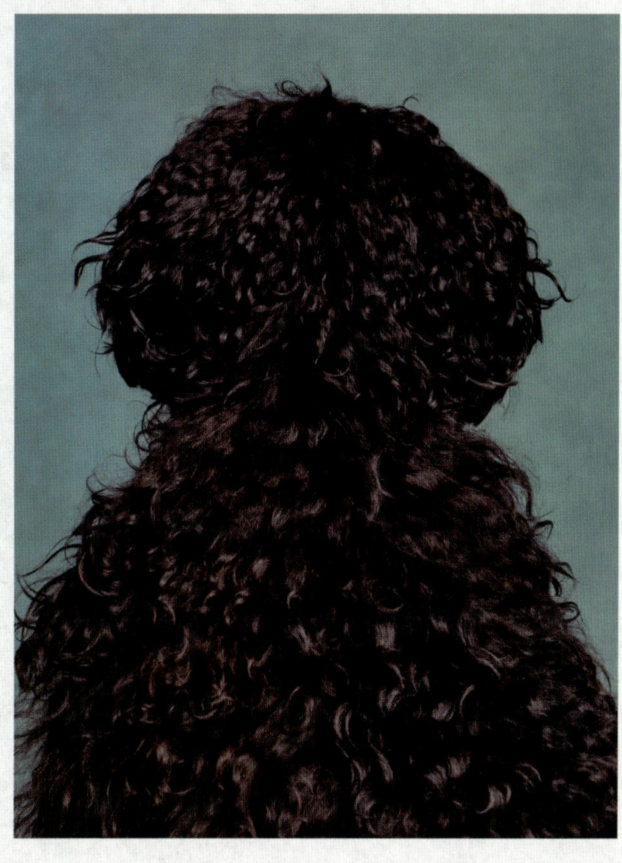

S, Miro

ALIASES: Moopy / Crumb / Sesame Puppet / Mooseppi

BORN: 27/04/2015   TRADE: Part Time Traceuse   BREED: Cavoodle

BUILD: Floofball   EYES: Brown   HEIGHT: 51cm   HAIR: Black / Brown

MARKS: Colourings resemble the current trend of Ombré hair

PECULIARITIES: Squeals loudly when the cross-walk sounds to walk — announcing to all it's time to go

M.O: ETC. Has an alter ego named 'Crumb' who sporadically appears. 'Crumb' runs laps of the room at high speed whilst doing parkour on the furniture. A major contrast to her usual sloth like personality.

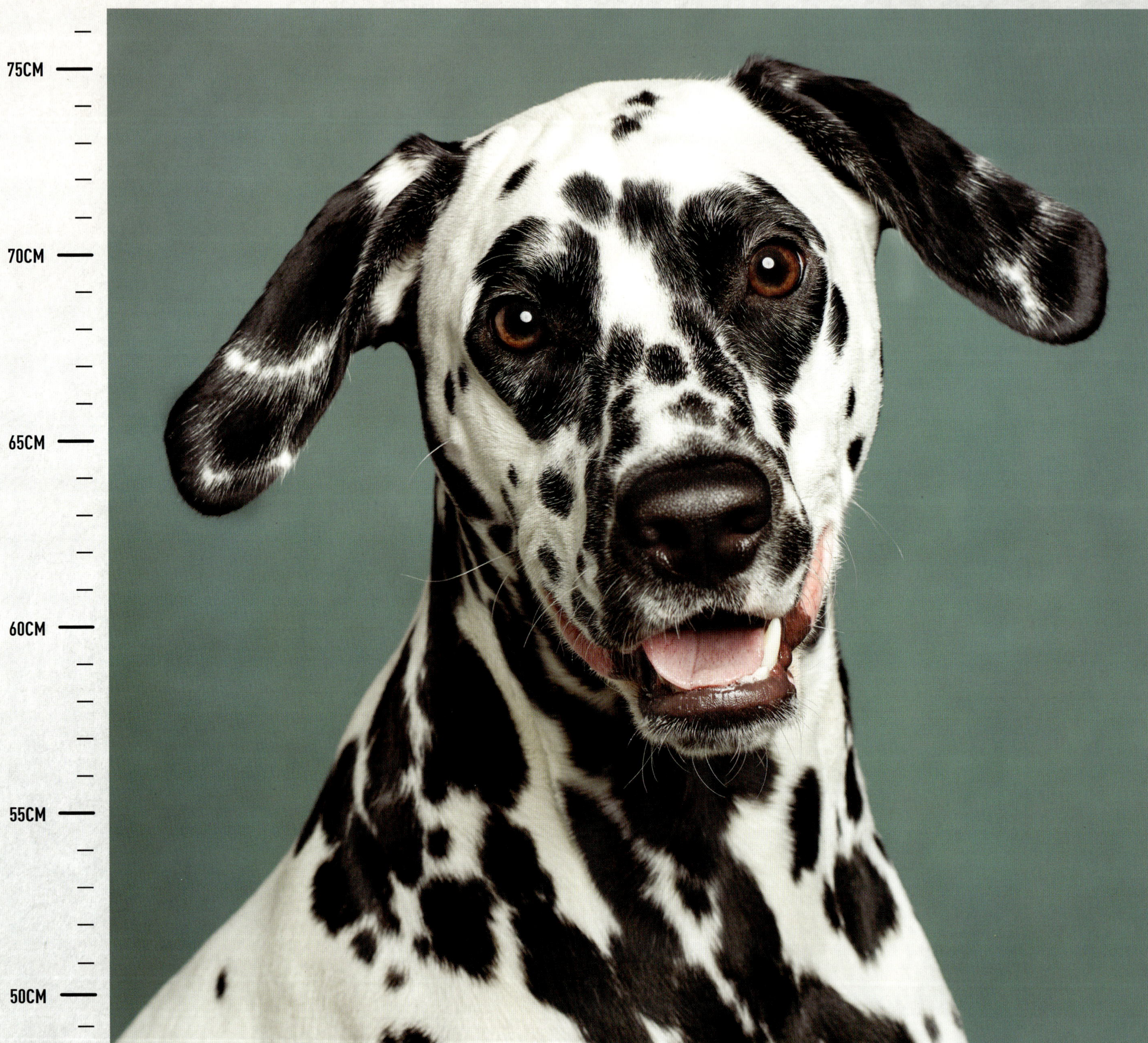

75CM
70CM
65CM
60CM
55CM
50CM

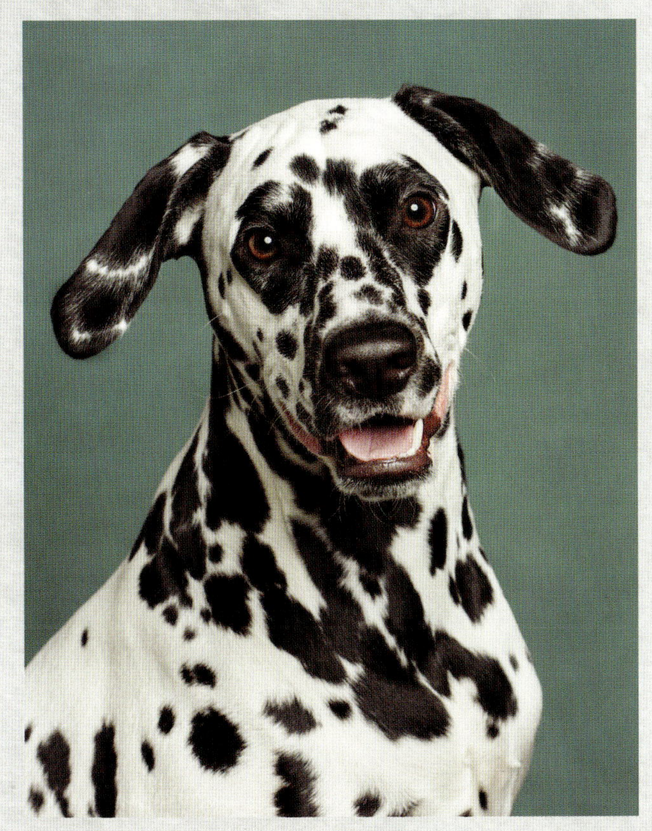 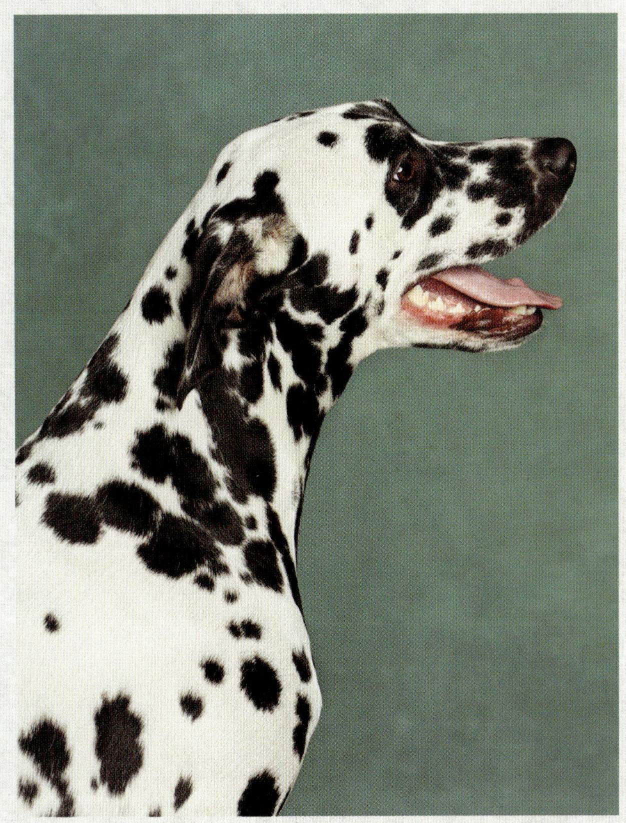 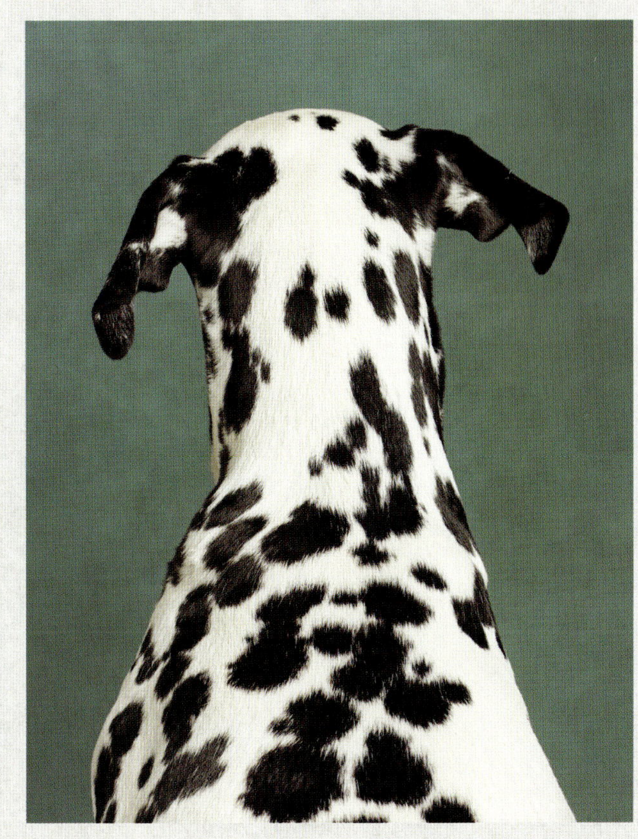

M, Lottie

ALIASES:

BORN: 05/03/2016   TRADE: Old Soul   BREED: Dalmatian

BUILD: Sleek   EYES: Brown   HEIGHT: 75cm   HAIR: Black / White

MARKS: Spots — a lot of them

PECULIARITIES: Has a particularly soft coat

M.O: ETC. Is not known to be particularly vocal, however has been observed frequently sighing and grumbling under her breath if she is displeased.

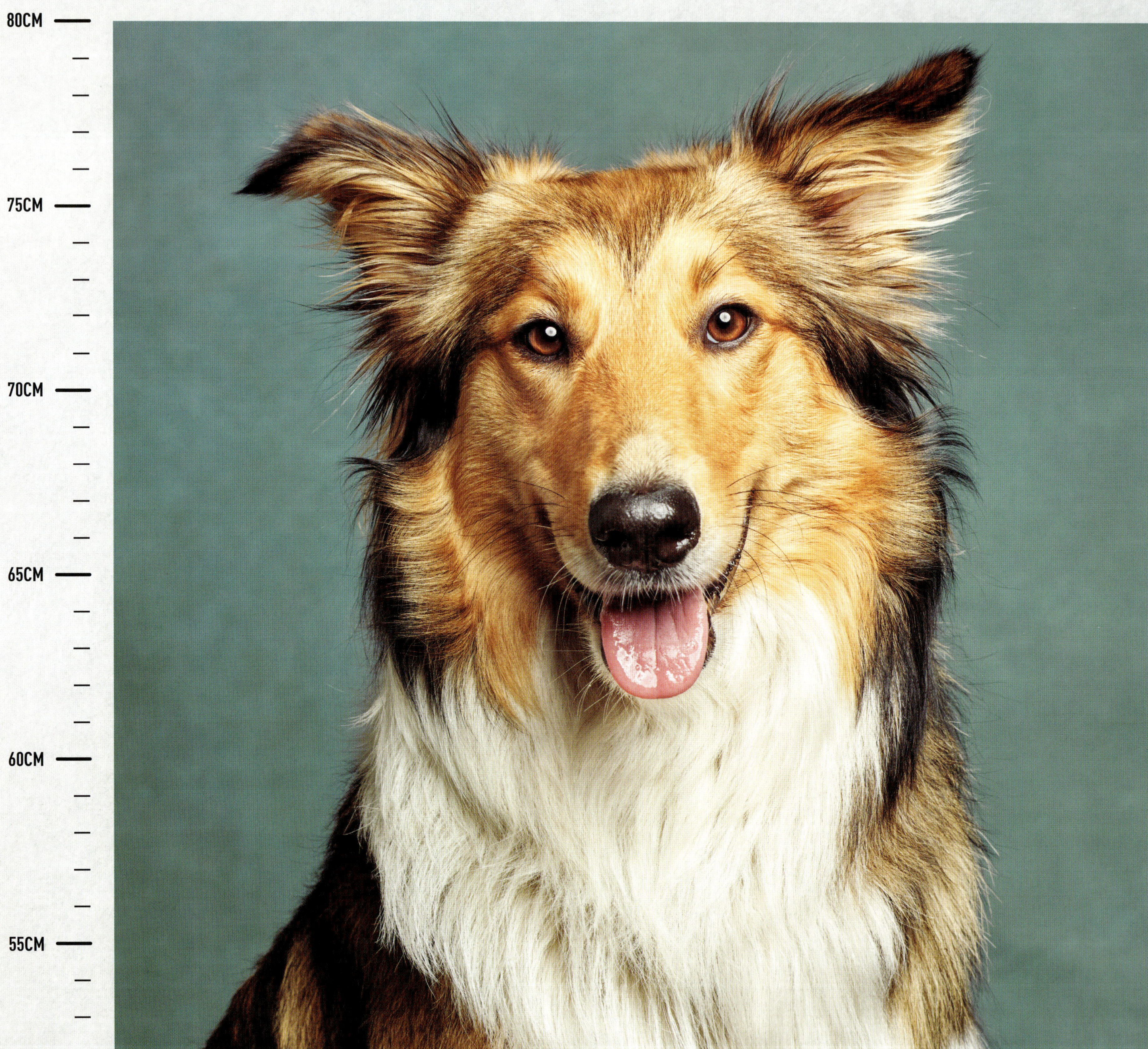

80CM
75CM
70CM
65CM
60CM
55CM

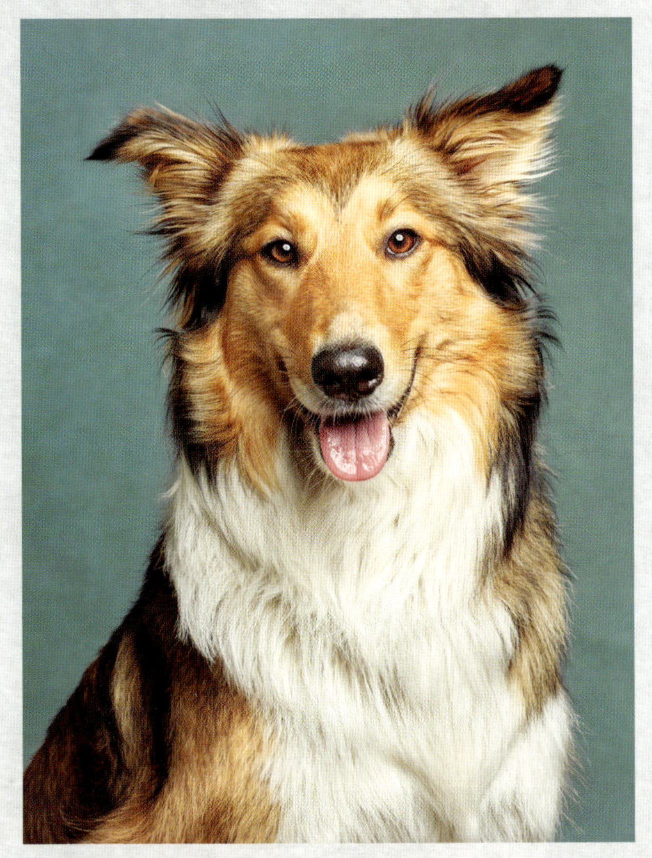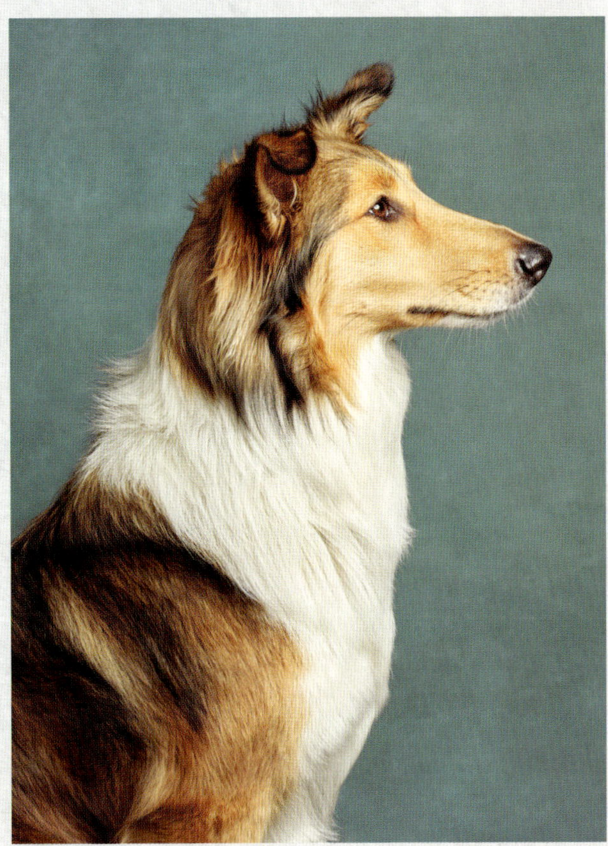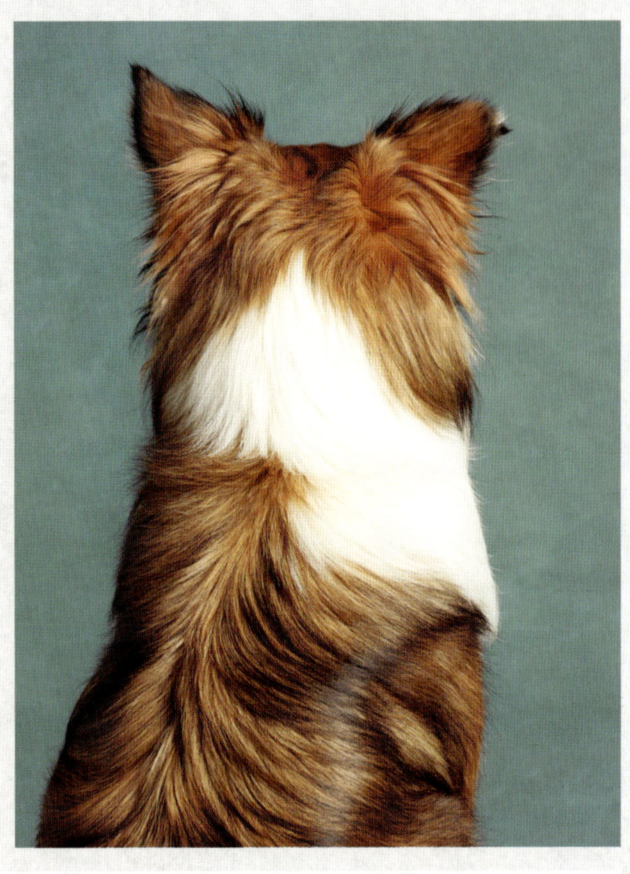

P, Olive

ALIASES:

BORN: 16/10/2015

TRADE: Model / Stunt Dog

BREED: Collie

BUILD: Slender & Sleek

EYES: Brown

HEIGHT: 80cm

HAIR: Tan / White / Black

MARKS: Dark tipped ends on coat

PECULIARITIES: Is extremely partial to sausage

M.O: ETC. Has mastered flashing a charming smile. Loves frisbees and has been known to jump into pools/bodies of water from a decent height.

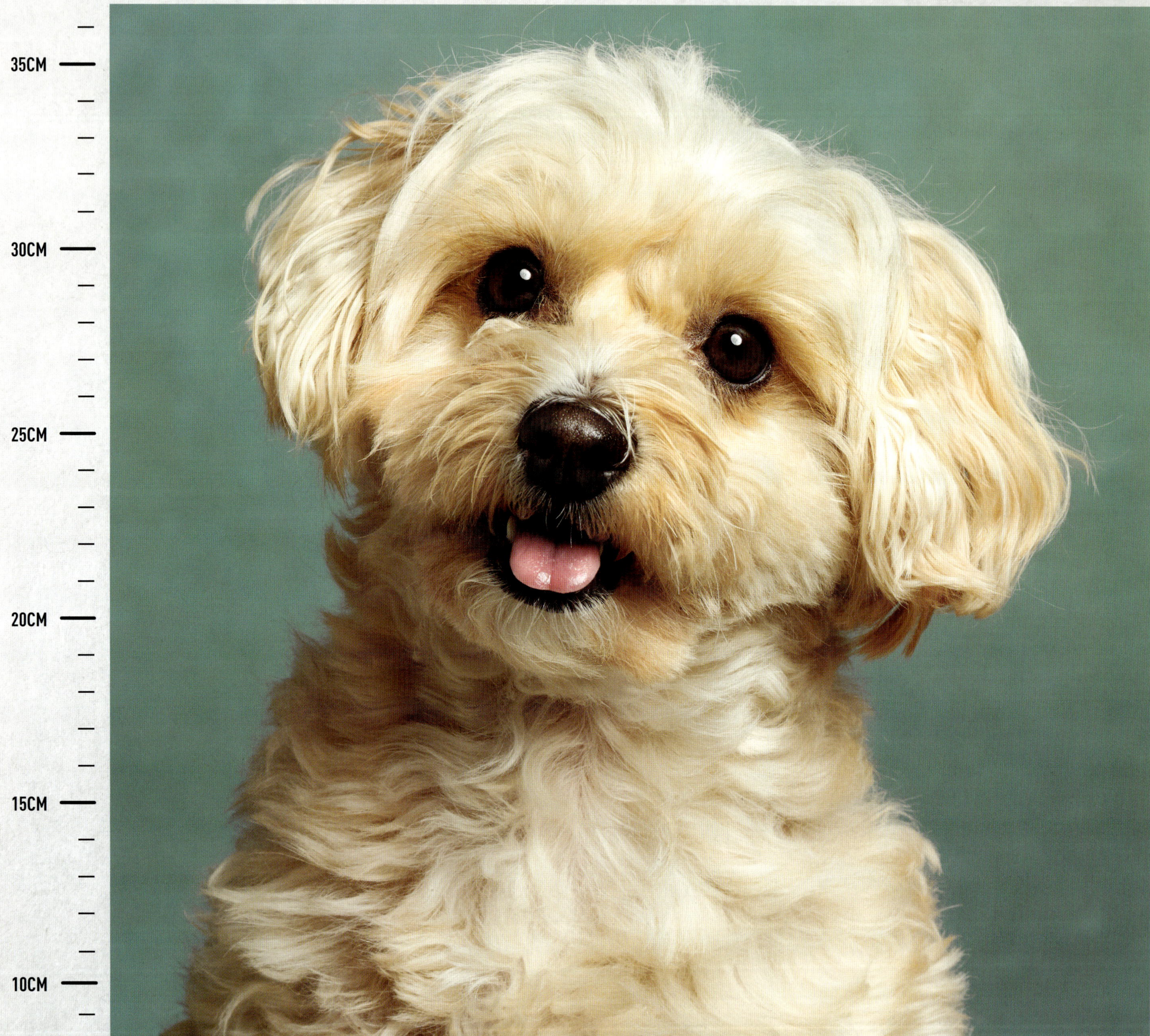

35CM
30CM
25CM
20CM
15CM
10CM

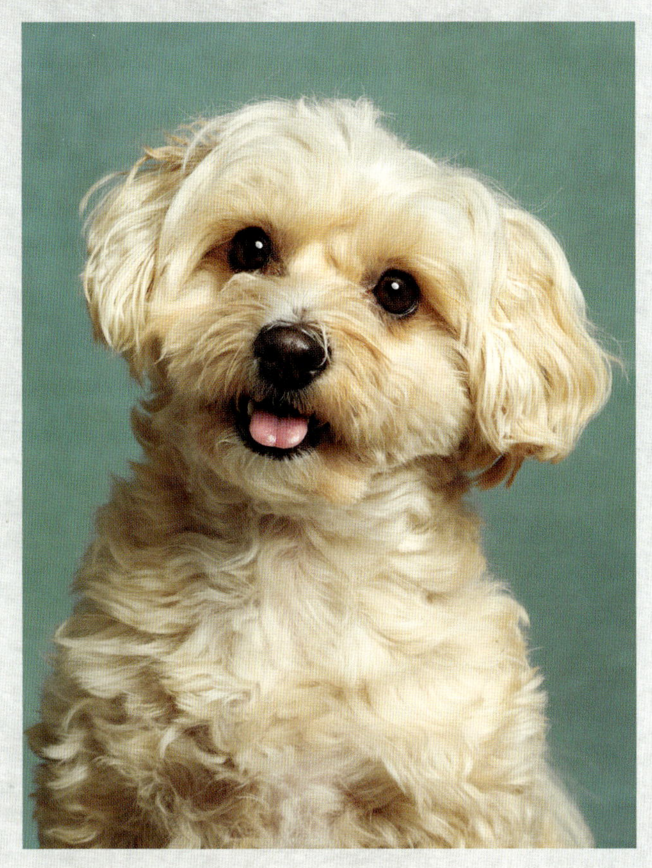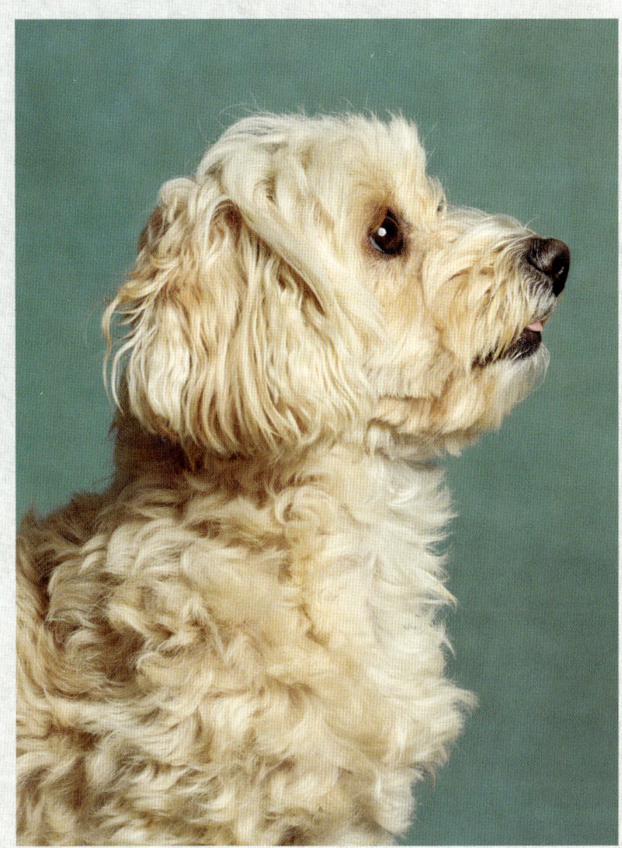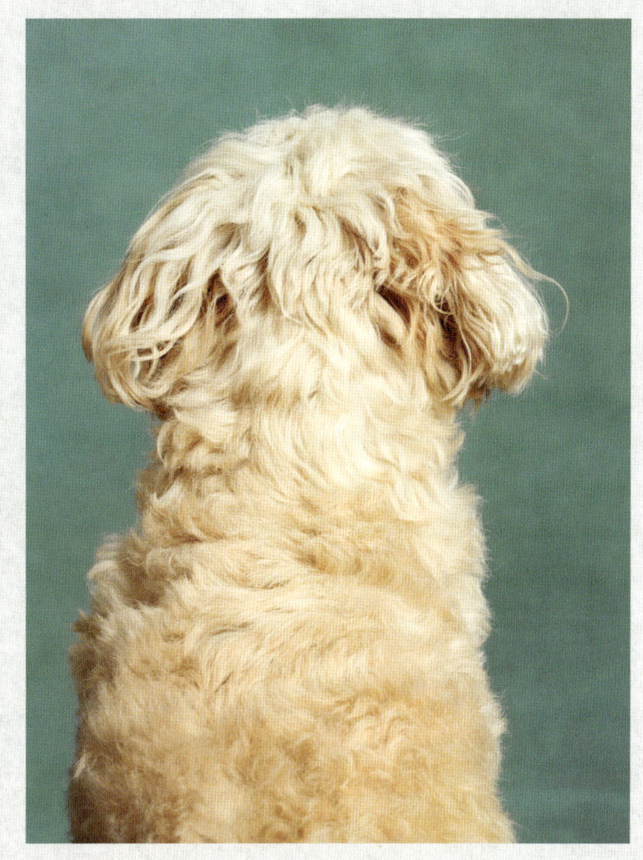

H, Nala

ALIASES: Nalski / Nals

BORN: 17/03/2015   TRADE: Love Guru   BREED: Moodle (Maltese / Poodle)

BUILD: Floofy   EYES: Brown   HEIGHT: 36cm   HAIR: Cream

MARKS: Little light tips throughout coat

PECULIARITIES: Is partial to a piece of salami or bacon

M.O: ETC. Has been known to run up to couples on the beach to interrupt their romantic encounters.

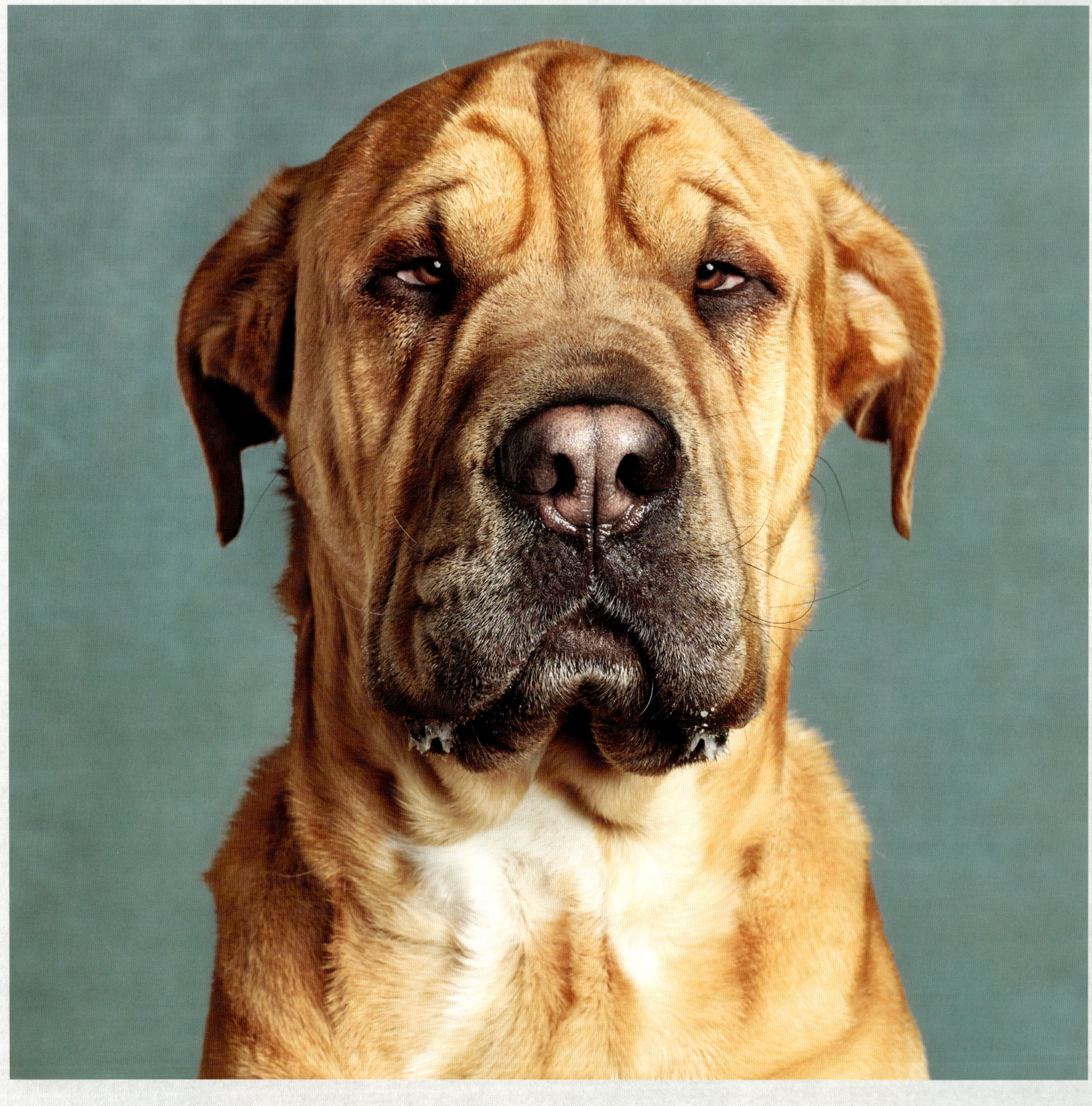
85CM
80CM
75CM
70CM
65CM
60CM

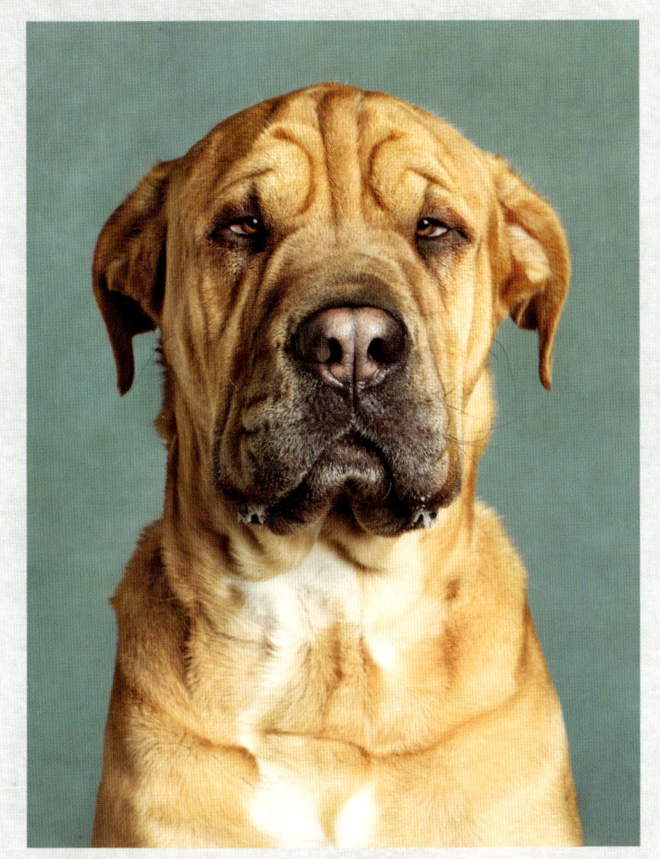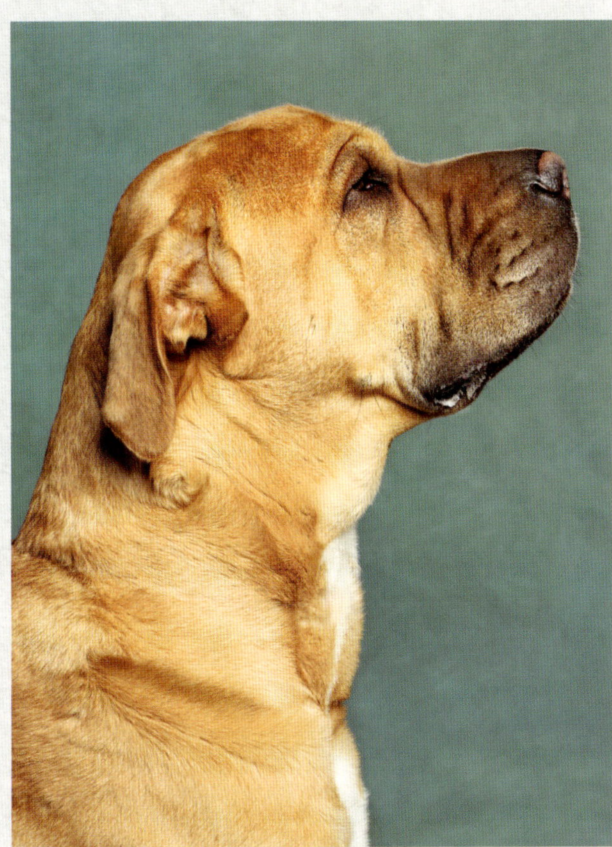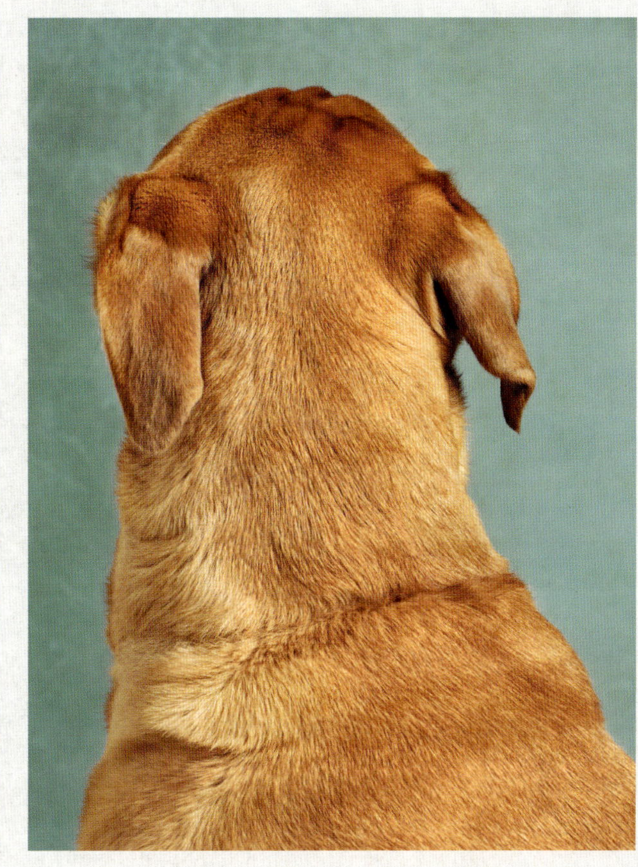

Z, Odin

ALIASES: Bubba Bear / Odie / Mr Handsome

BORN: 24/04/2015   **TRADE:** Mr Smooshy Face   **BREED:** Bull Mastiff x Shar Pei

BUILD: Wrinkly   **EYES:** Brown   **HEIGHT:** 88cm   **HAIR:** Brown / White / Black

MARKS: Nose has pinkish centre

PECULIARITIES: Had a rough start to life — a poisoning incident left him cross eyed

M.O: ETC. Loves water — will splash in it, go swimming in a pool, accompany humans in their showers — but will scream as if he is dying if taken to get washed. Has been known to intimidate his twin sister Bella into giving up her food by staring her down.

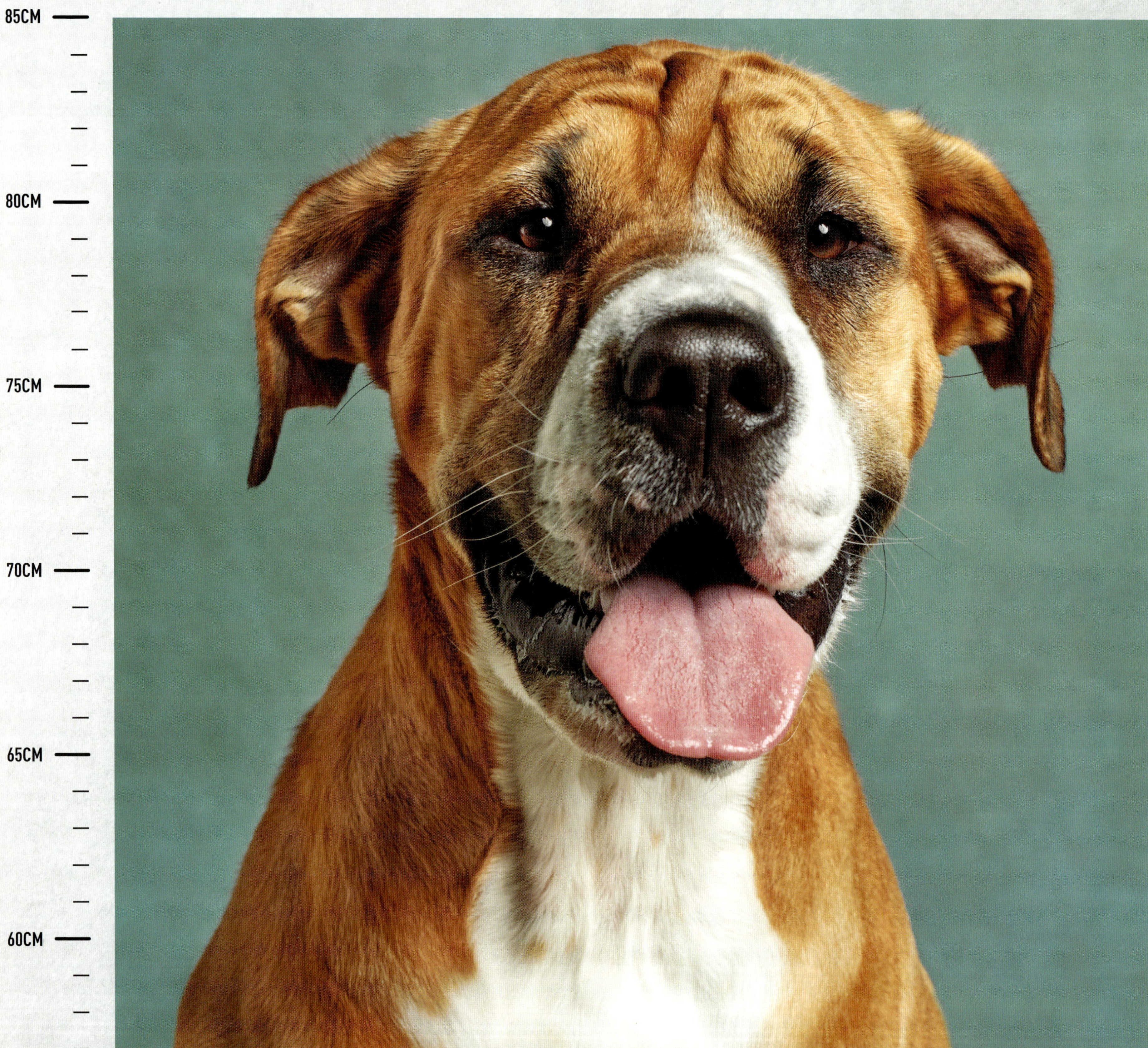

85CM
80CM
75CM
70CM
65CM
60CM

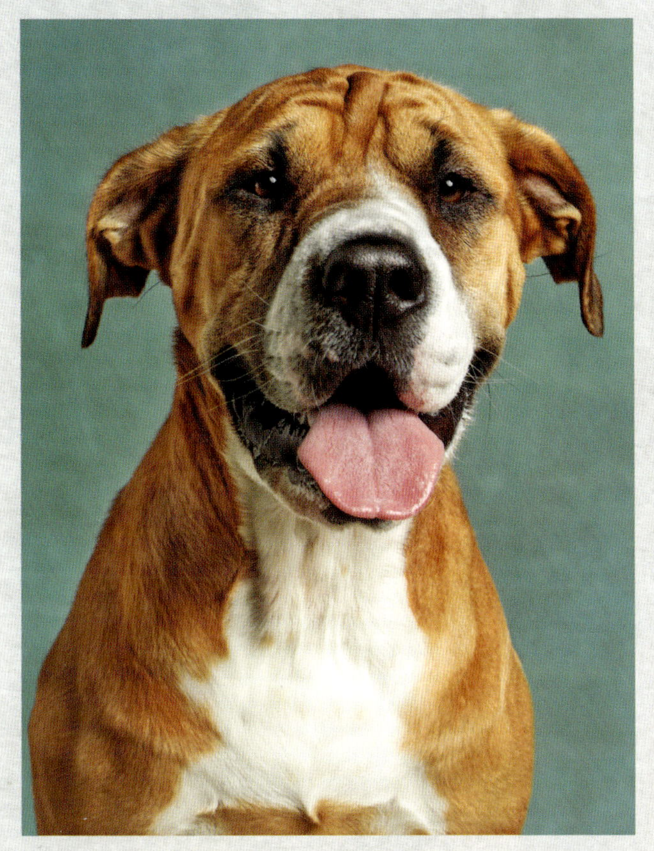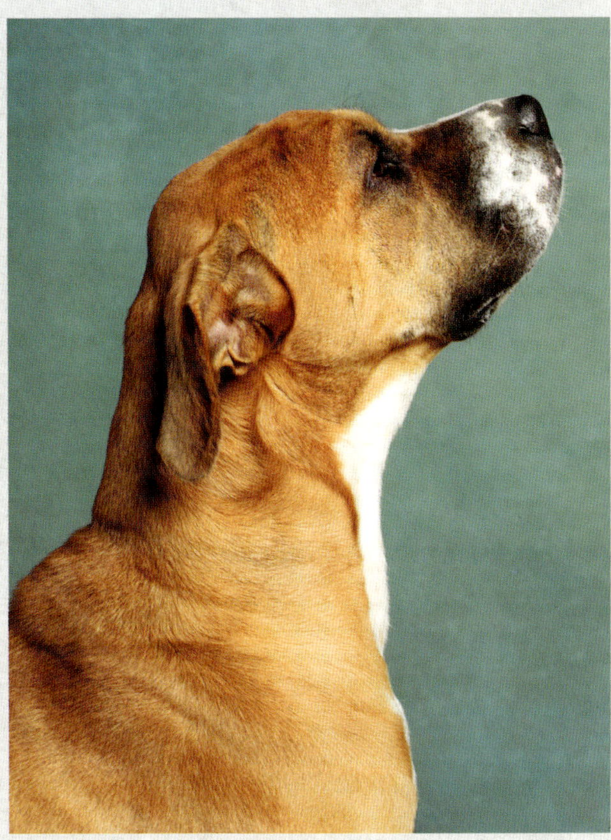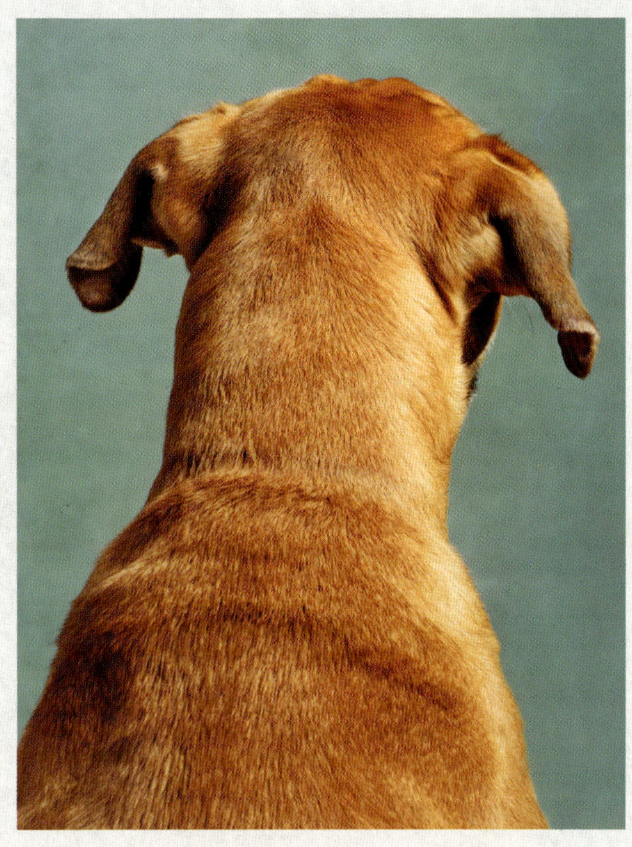

Z, Bella Bear

ALIASES: Belly / Monkey / Bear Bear

BORN: 24/04/2015   **TRADE:** Cuddle Monster   **BREED:** Bull Mastiff x Shar Pei

BUILD: Wrinkly   **EYES:** Brown   **HEIGHT:** 85cm   **HAIR:** Brown / White / Black

MARKS: Clown-like markings on face

PECULIARITIES: When human Grandma leaves she will wait at the front door all day — in case she comes back

M.O: ETC. Has been known to wait by the window for the curtain to be opened so she can sun bake. If there is no sun that day, she has been known to quietly cry to herself.

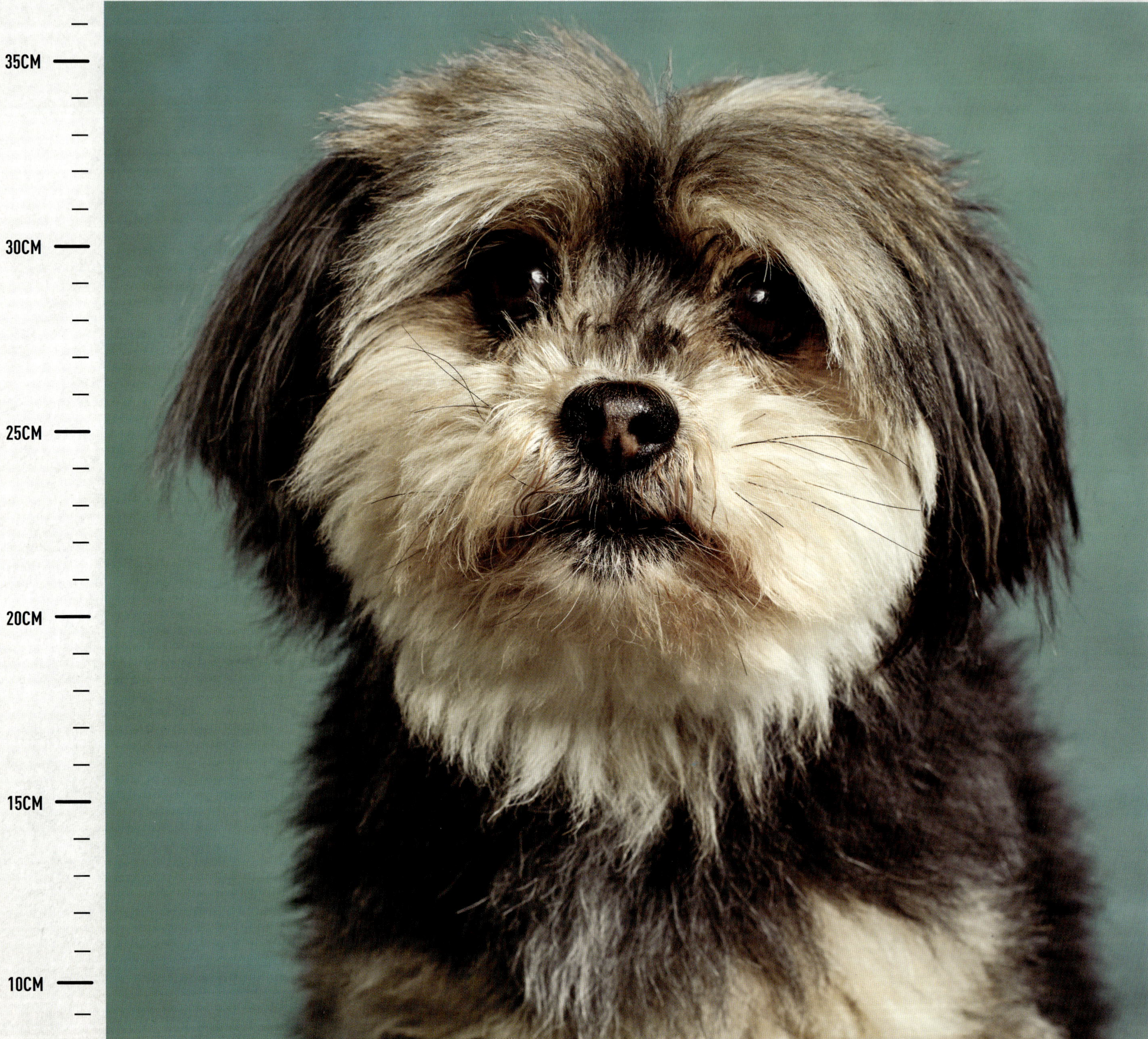

35CM
30CM
25CM
20CM
15CM
10CM

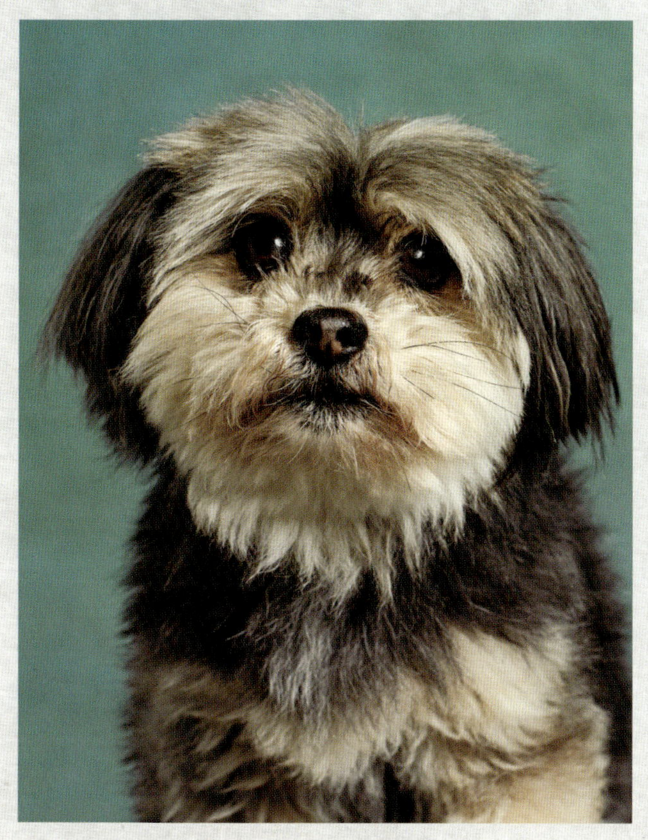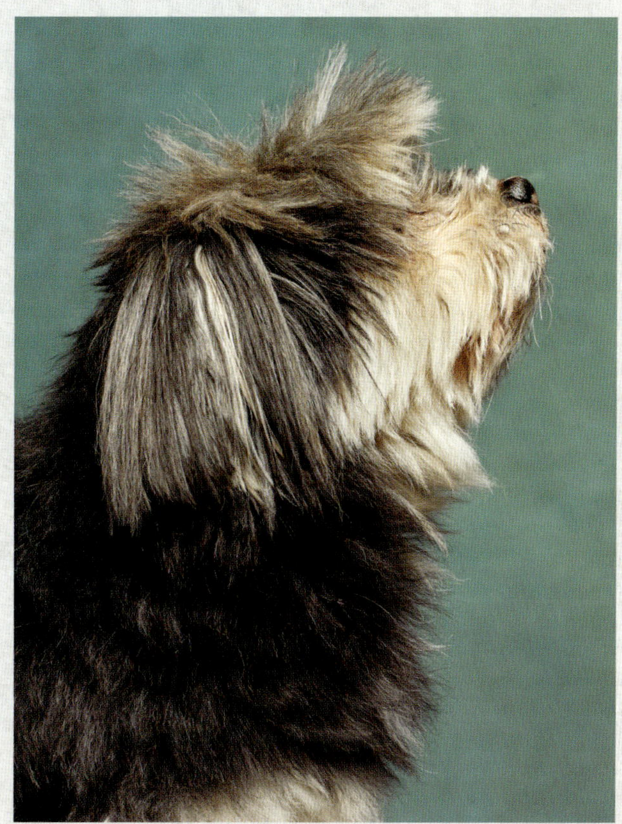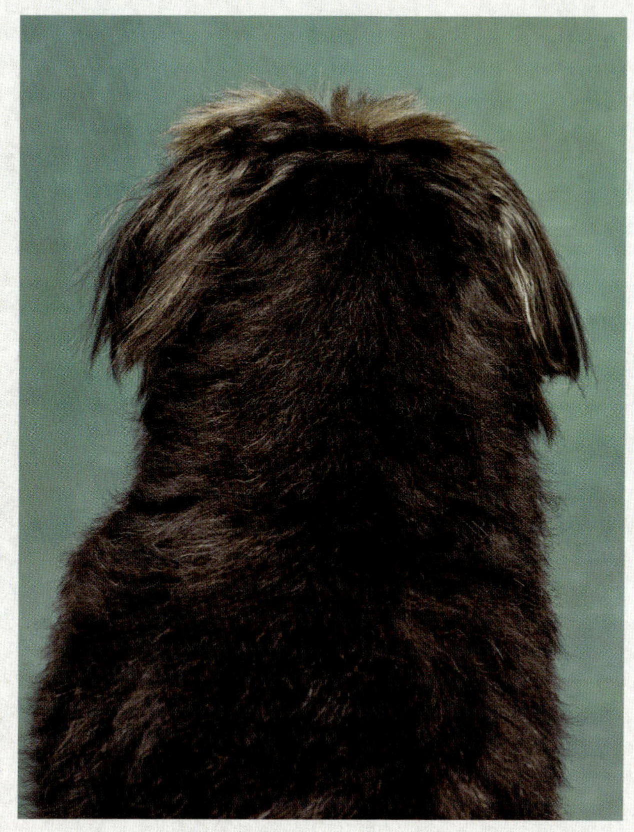

H, Ruby

ALIASES: Woob / Tuesday

BORN: 05/11/2003   TRADE: Matriarch   BREED: Maltese x Pomeranian

BUILD: Mini but Mighty   EYES: Brown   HEIGHT: 36cm   HAIR: Grey / Sand

MARKS: Little brown/pink spot on nose

PECULIARITIES: Hasn't always got the freshest of breath

M.O. ETC. Knows all the key canine players in the neighbourhood and barks in their direction when out on patrols, yet is confronted when faced with a paper bag blowing erratically down the street.

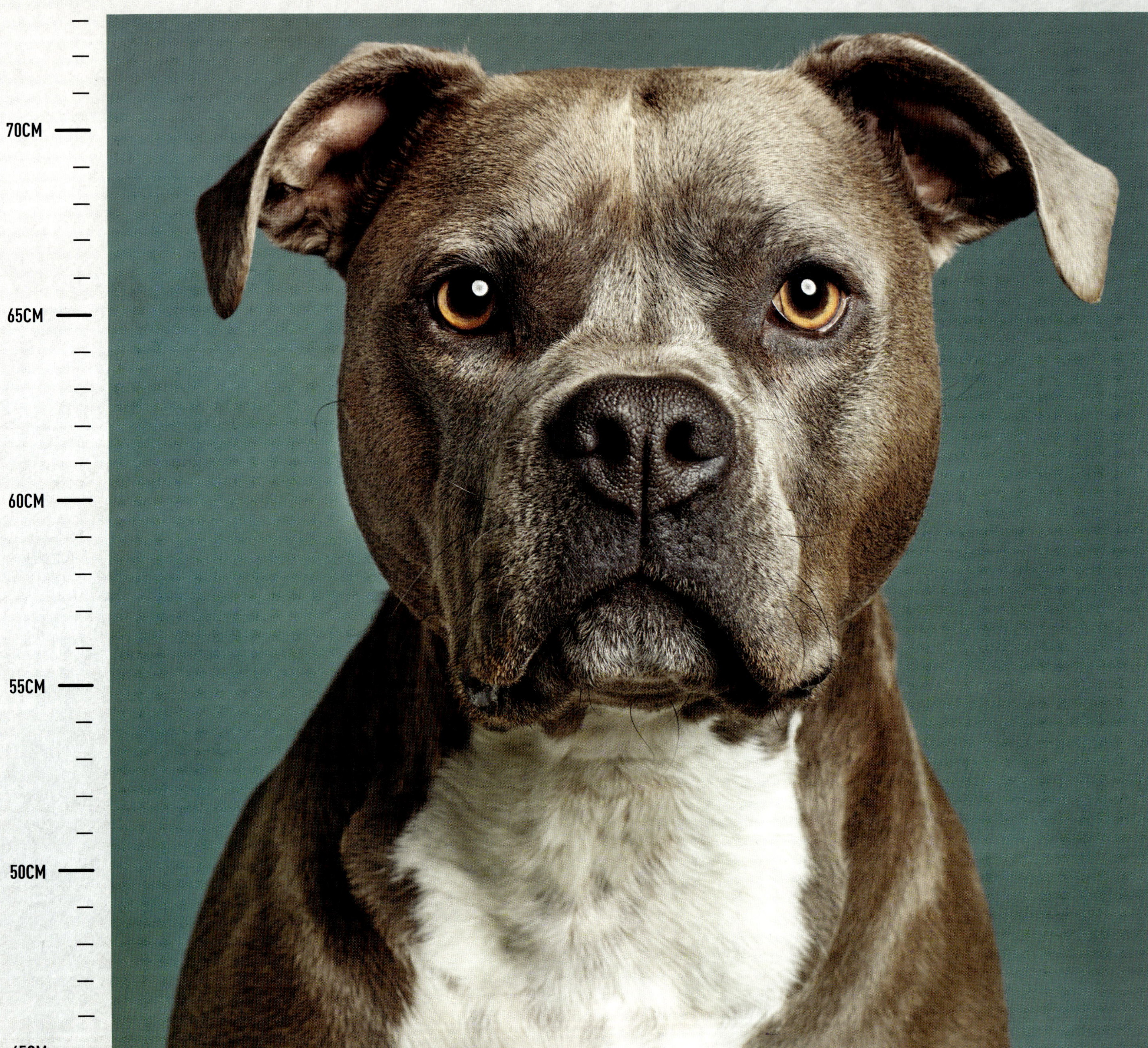

70CM
65CM
60CM
55CM
50CM
45CM

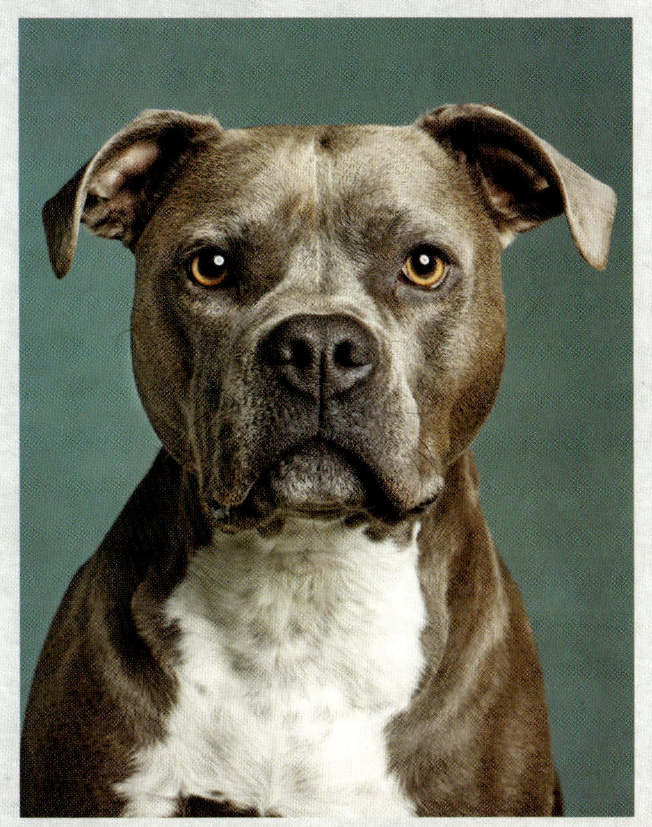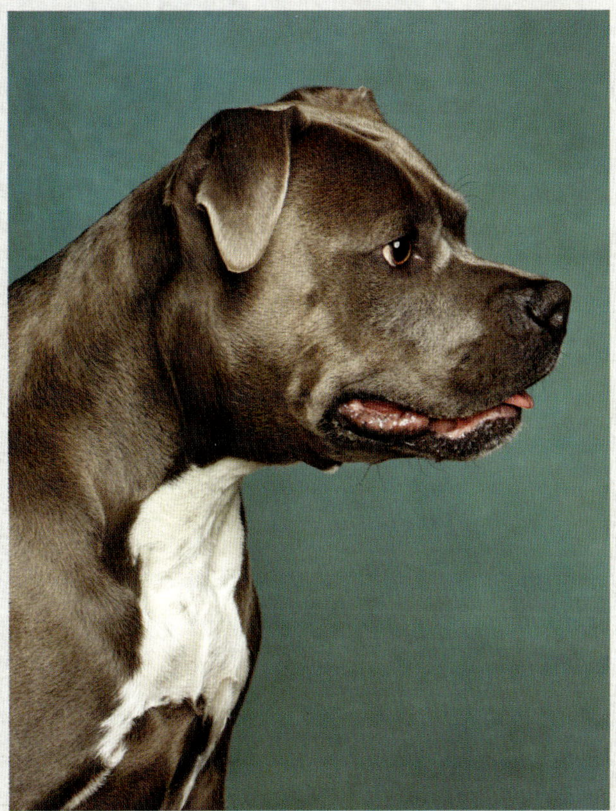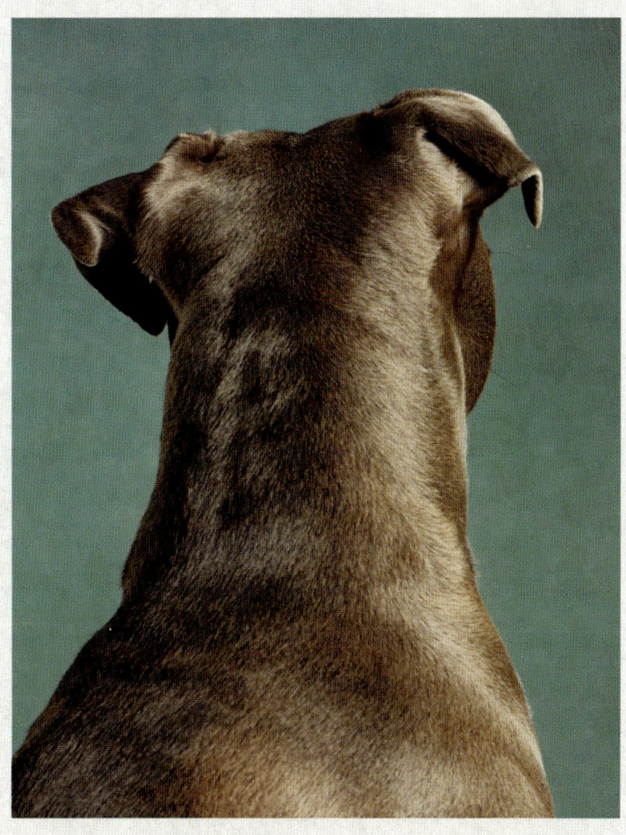

S, Jinx

ALIASES:

BORN: 25/09/2015   **TRADE:** Café Queen   **BREED:** American Staffordshire Terrier

BUILD: Solid yet Sleek   **EYES:** Copper Brown   **HEIGHT:** 73cm   **HAIR:** Grey / White

MARKS: Has a super shiny coat

PECULIARITIES: Underneath her serious exterior lies a gentle, affectionate soul

M.O: ETC. Has a regularly scheduled date every Sunday with her human, Brad, at her local cafe. She is on a first name basis with all the staff who promptly serve her favourite breakfast — a side of bacon. She has even featured on their Facebook page.

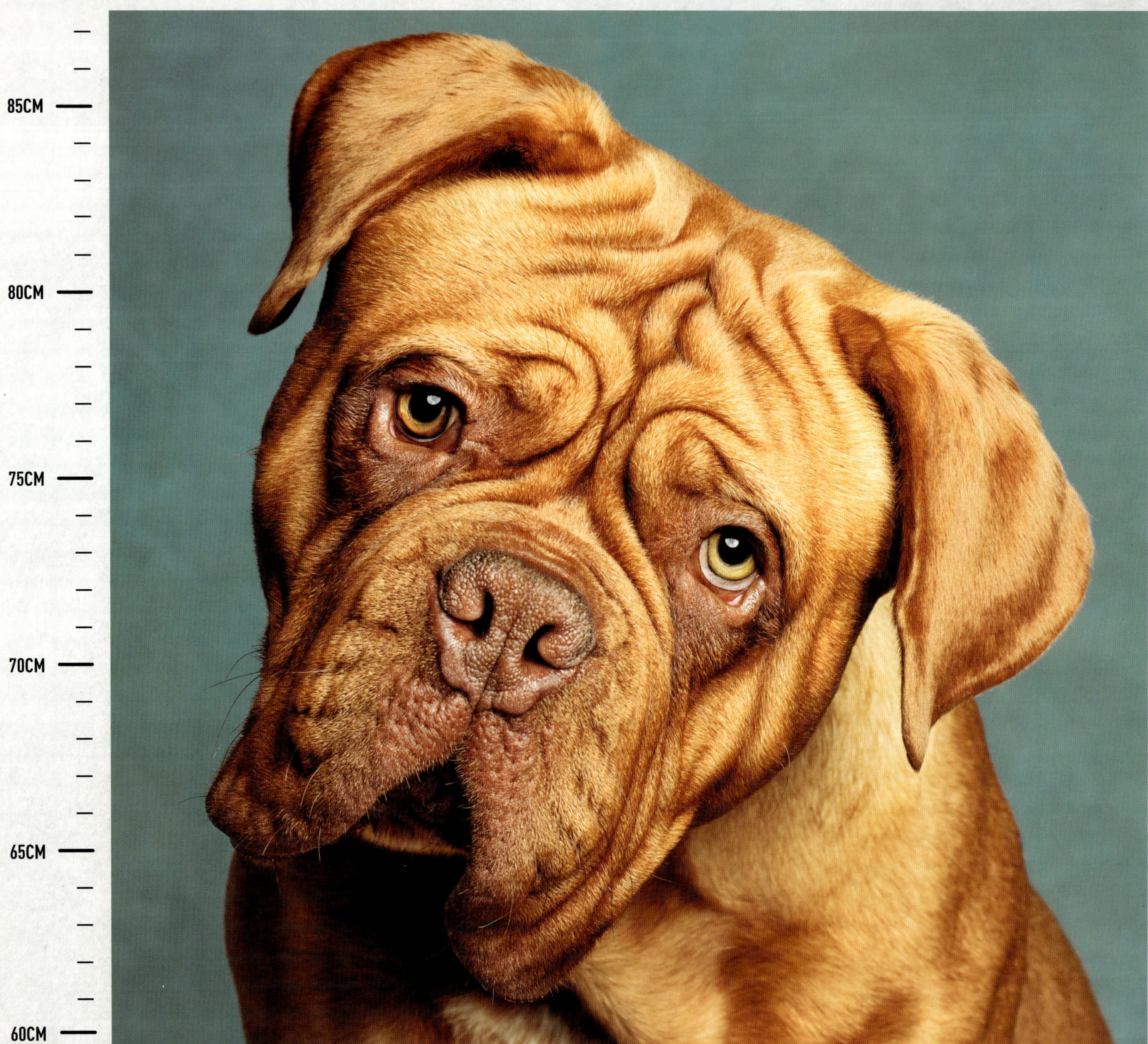

85CM
80CM
75CM
70CM
65CM
60CM

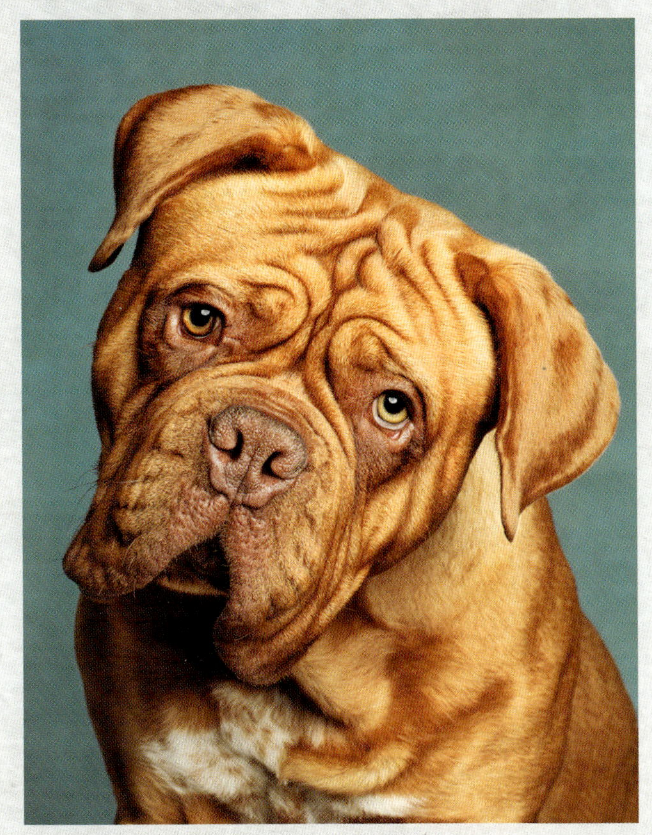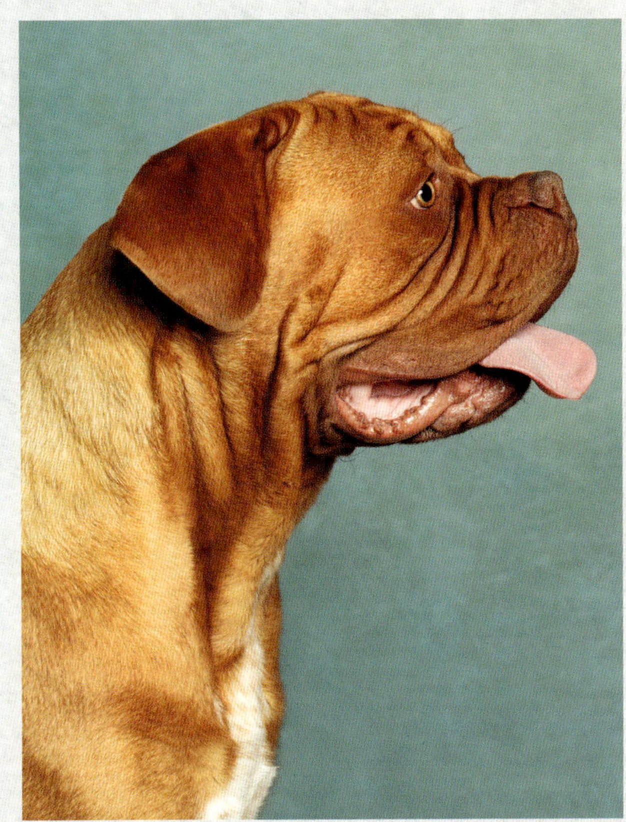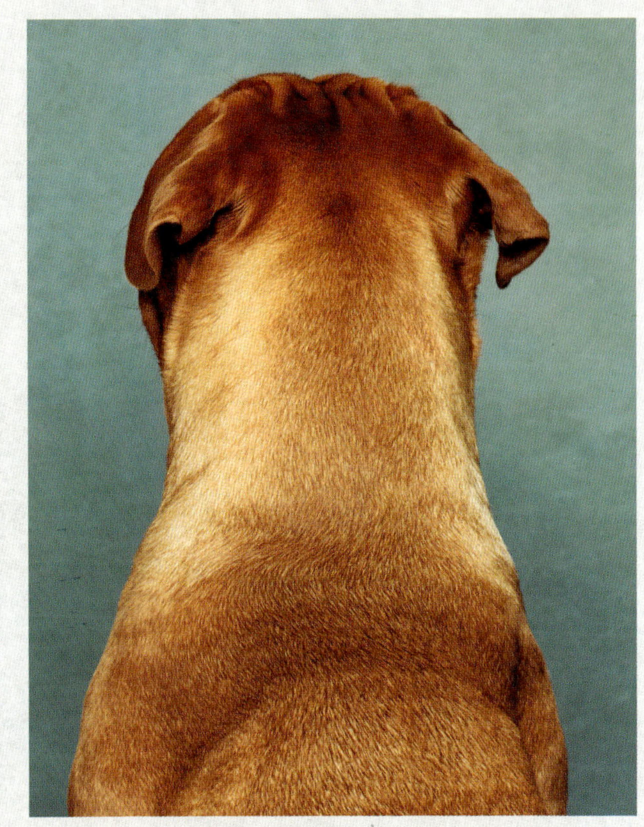

P, Pablo

ALIASES:

BORN: 05/11/2016   **TRADE:** Food Taster   **BREED:** Douge de Bordeaux

BUILD: Like a Tank   **EYES:** Brown & Green   **HEIGHT:** 87cm   **HAIR:** Copper / White

MARKS: One green eye, one brown eye

PECULIARITIES: Does not realise his size, beware — will sit on humans at any opportunity

M.O: ETC. Is known to be a speed eater — a plate left on the table was consumed in 30 seconds, post-theft he hid under the bed for about half an hour.

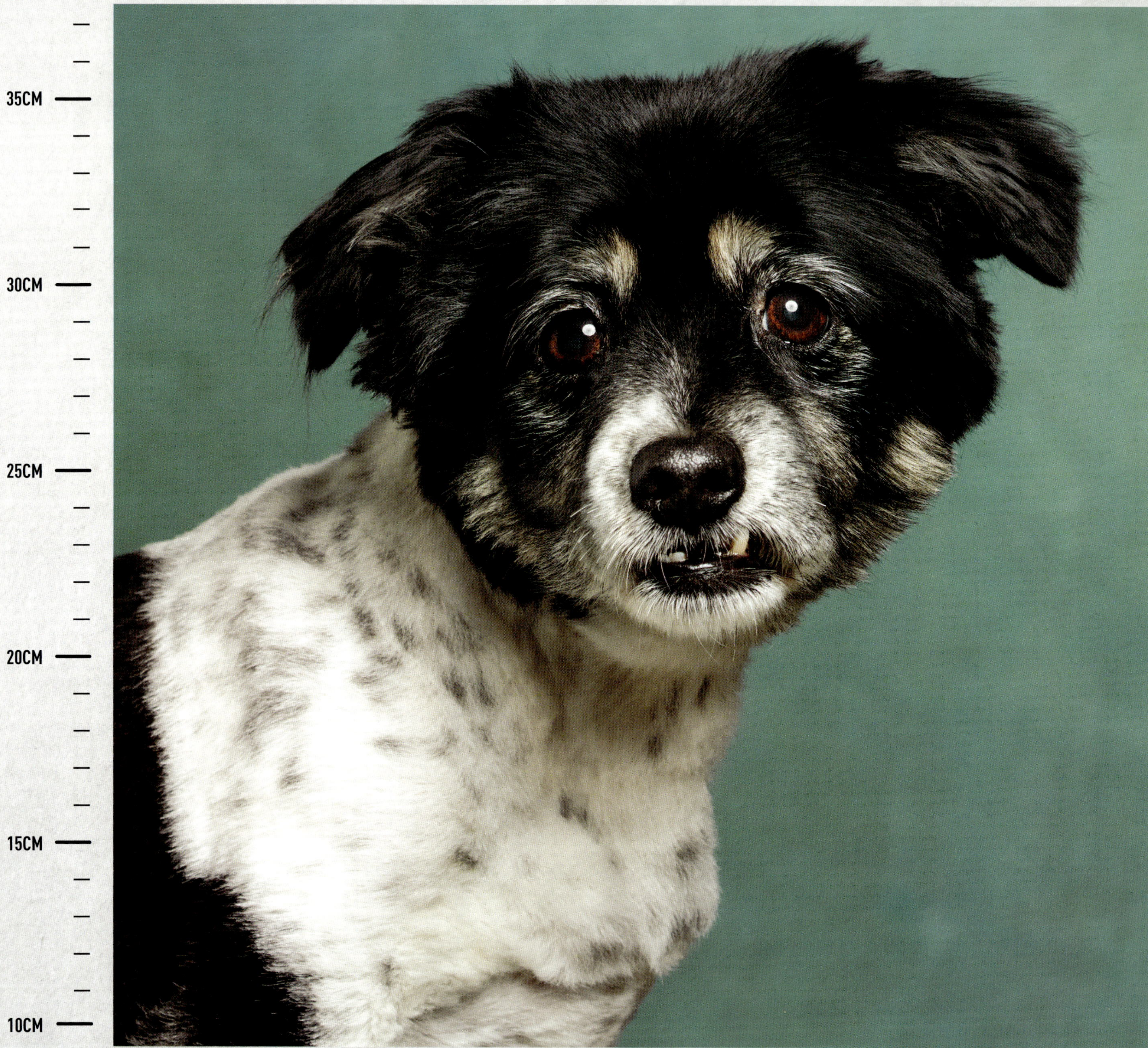

35CM
30CM
25CM
20CM
15CM
10CM

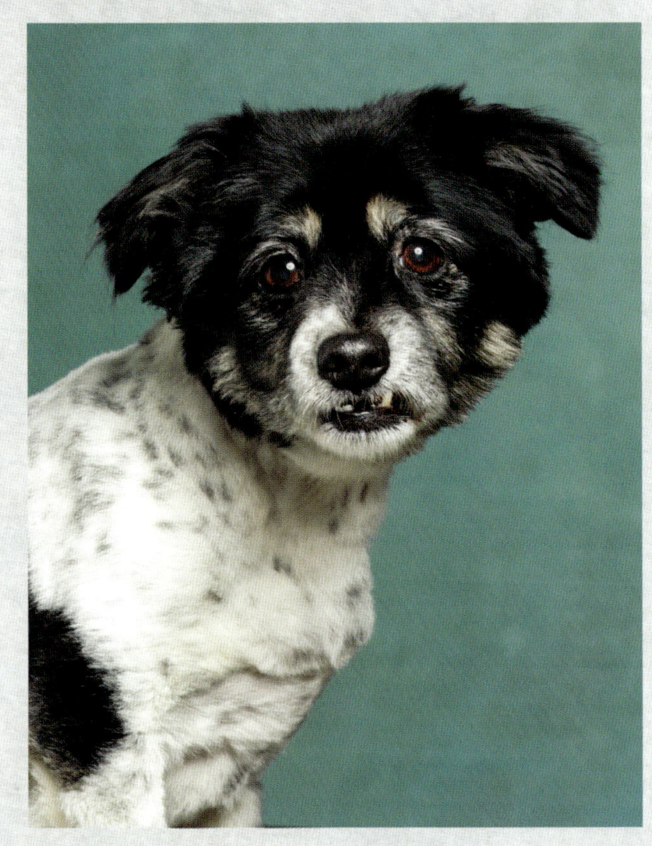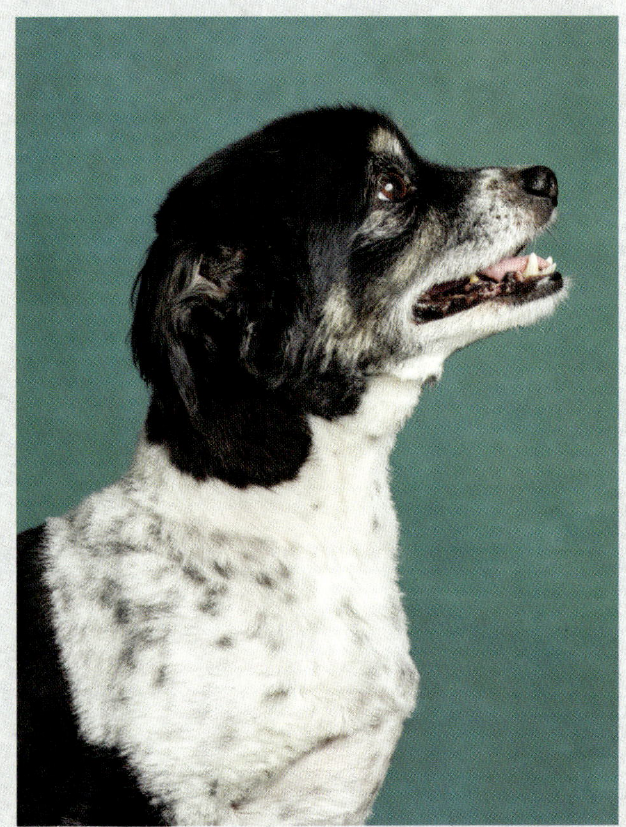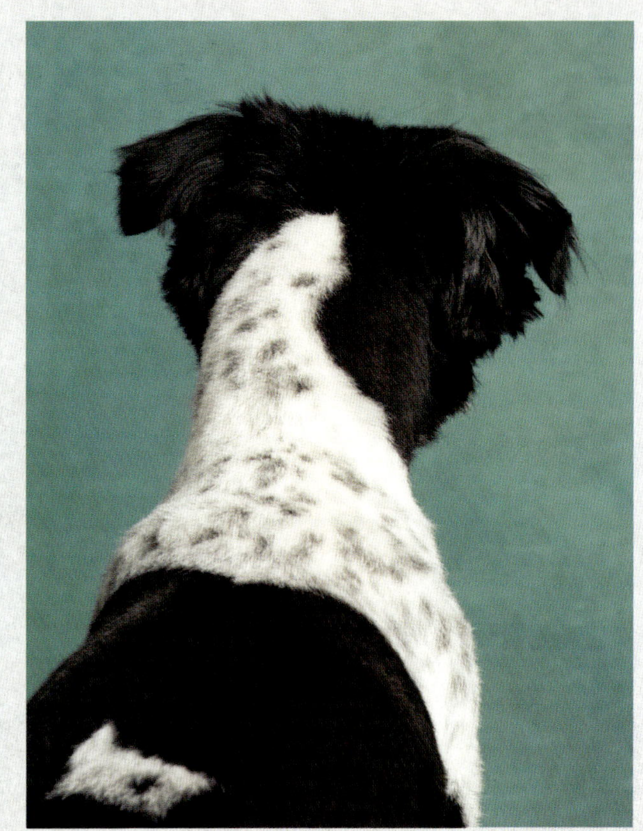

C, Ralph

ALIASES: Ralphy

BORN: Unknown, 14yrs **TRADE:** Retired **BREED:** Mystery Mutt

BUILD: Lightweight **EYES:** Brown **HEIGHT:** 37cm **HAIR:** Black / White / Blonde

MARKS: Cappuccino eyebrows

PECULIARITIES: Has a little snaggle tooth

M.O: ETC. Known to exhibit cat-like tendencies — has been seen sitting on top of couches.

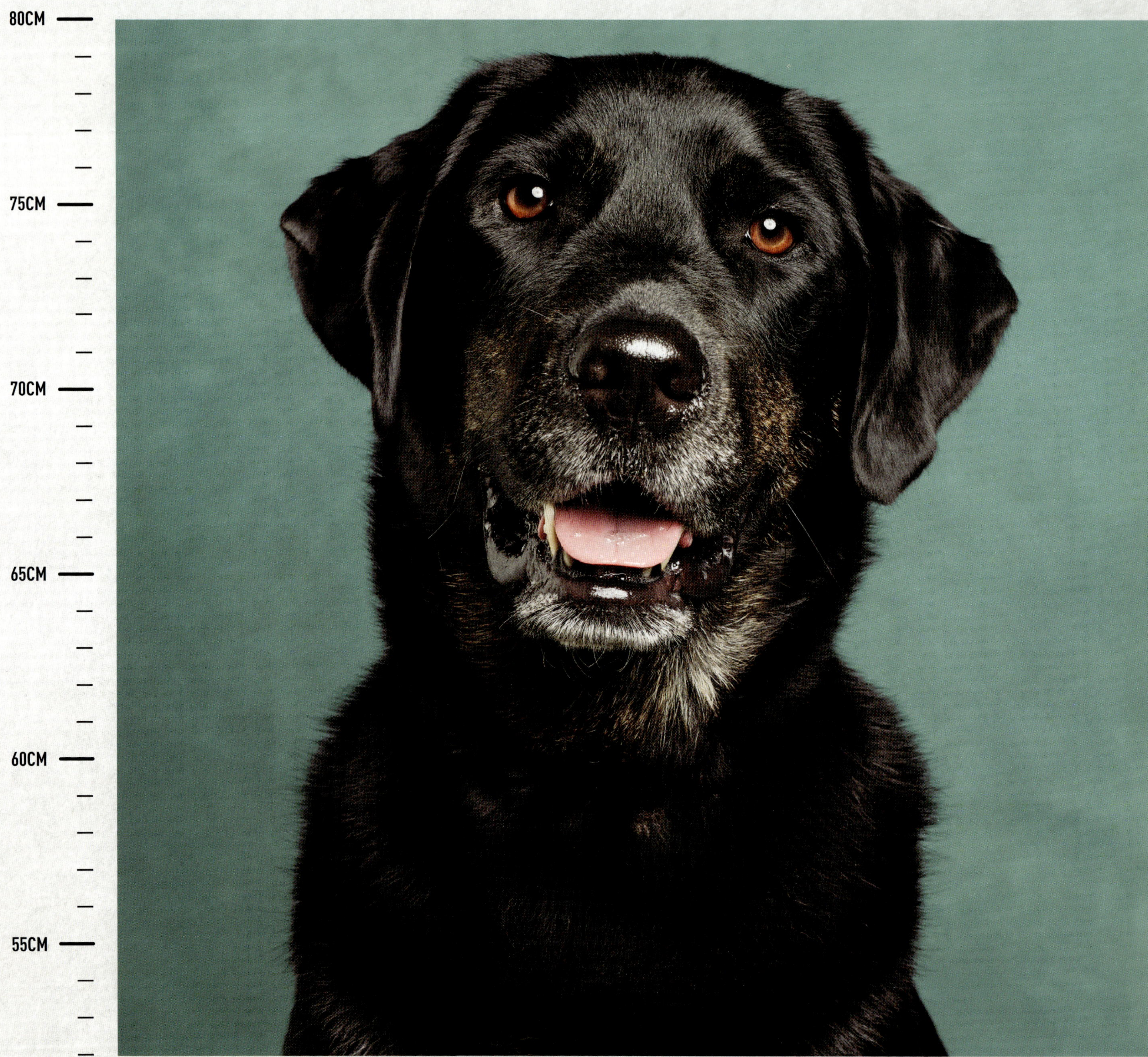

80CM
75CM
70CM
65CM
60CM
55CM

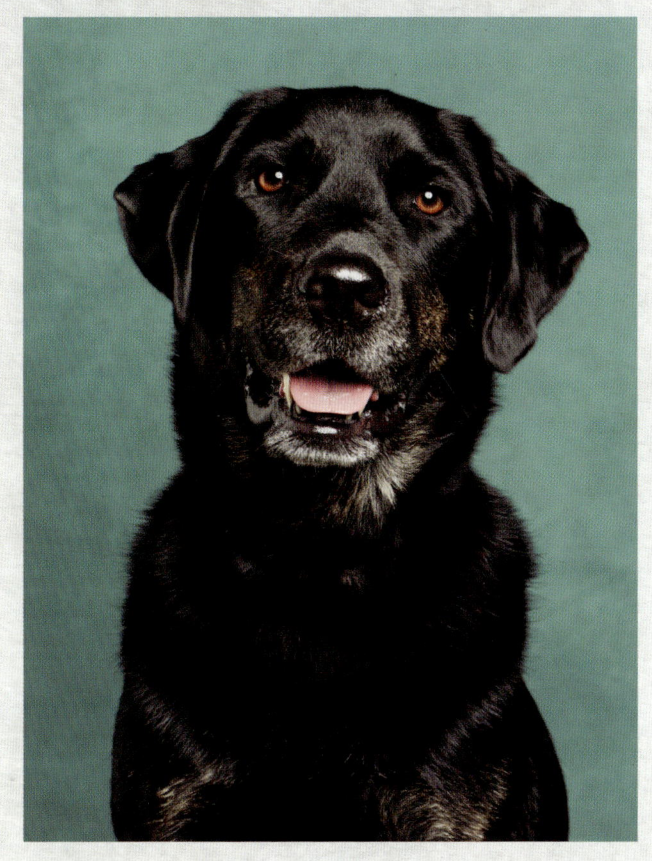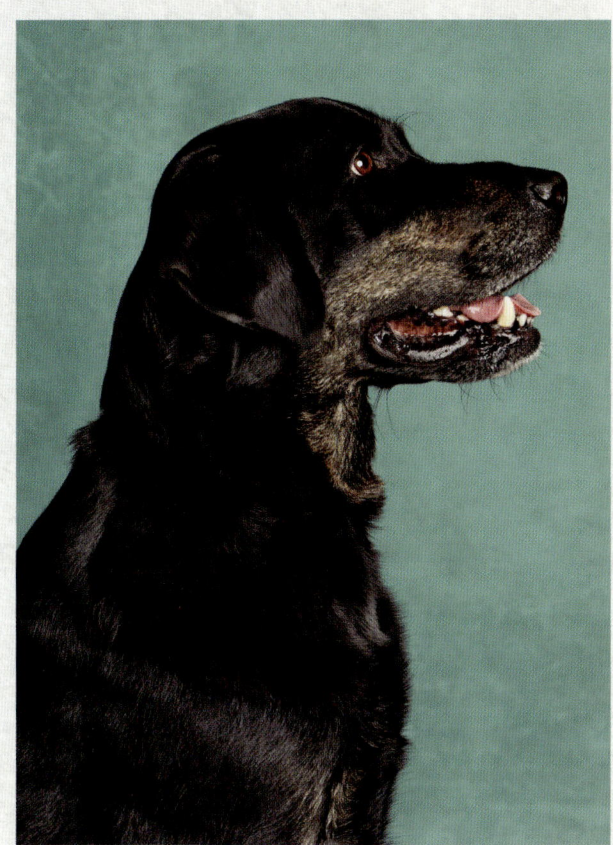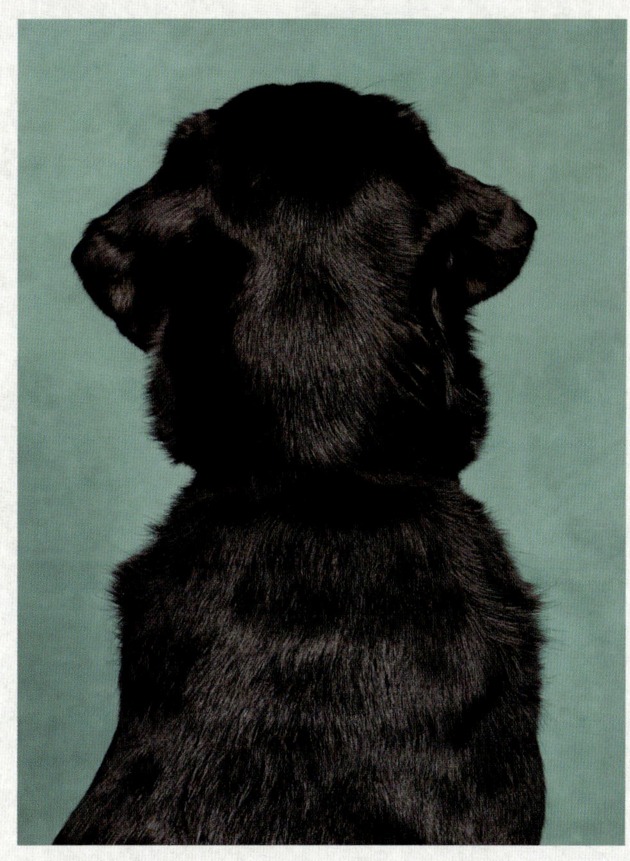

W, Elliott

ALIASES: El / Ellio / Smelliott / Joe

BORN: 21/02/2013   TRADE: Trainer   BREED: Labrador Retriever

BUILD: Reliable   EYES: Brown   HEIGHT: 80cm   HAIR: Black / Brindle

MARKS: Patches of Brindle

PECULIARITIES: The brindle present in his coat is rare — only occurring in 2% of Labradors

M.O: ETC. Is partial to a few hot chips at The Great Northern Hotel. Was cast in a movie which required he lick 33 litres of ice cream off an actress.

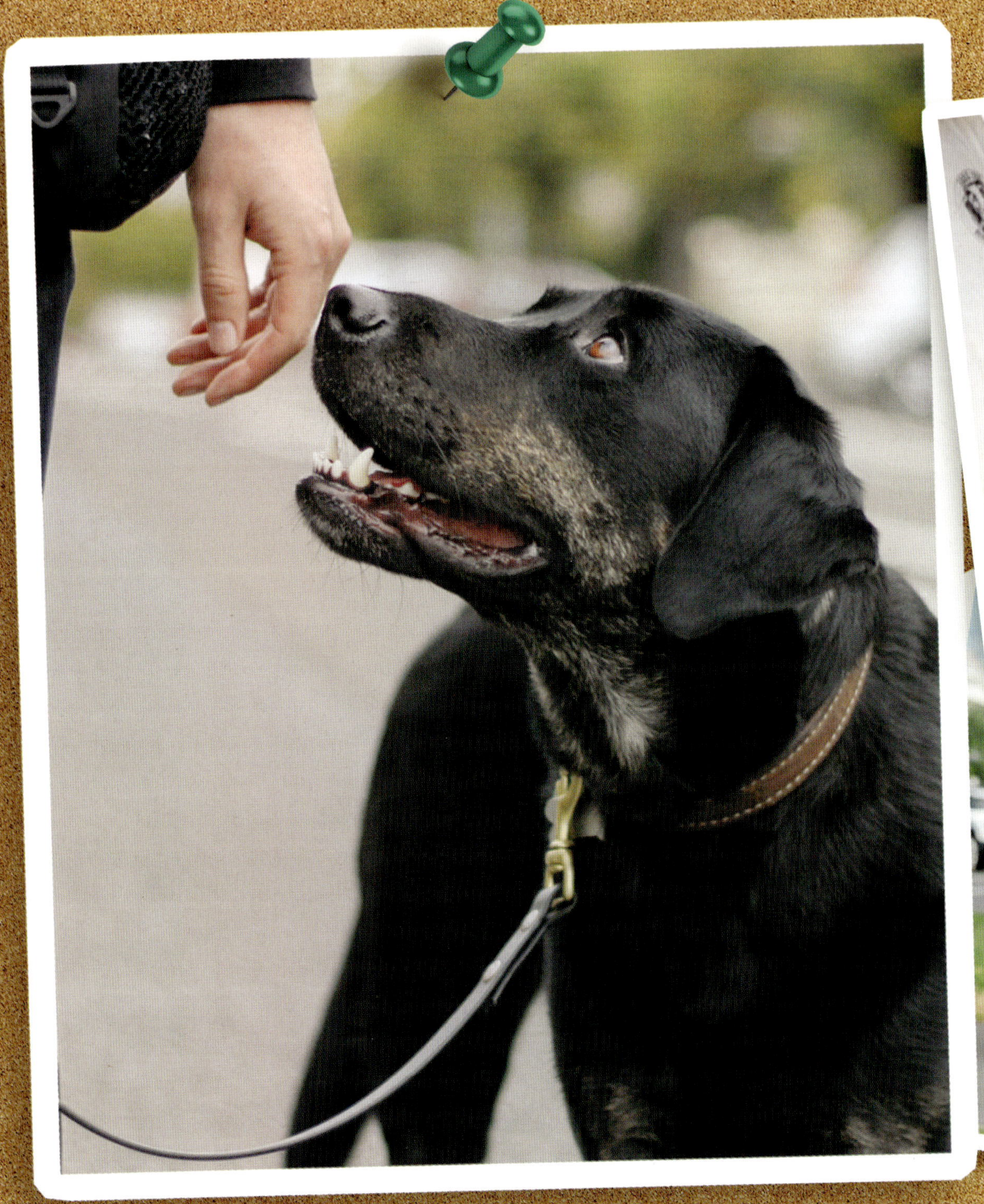

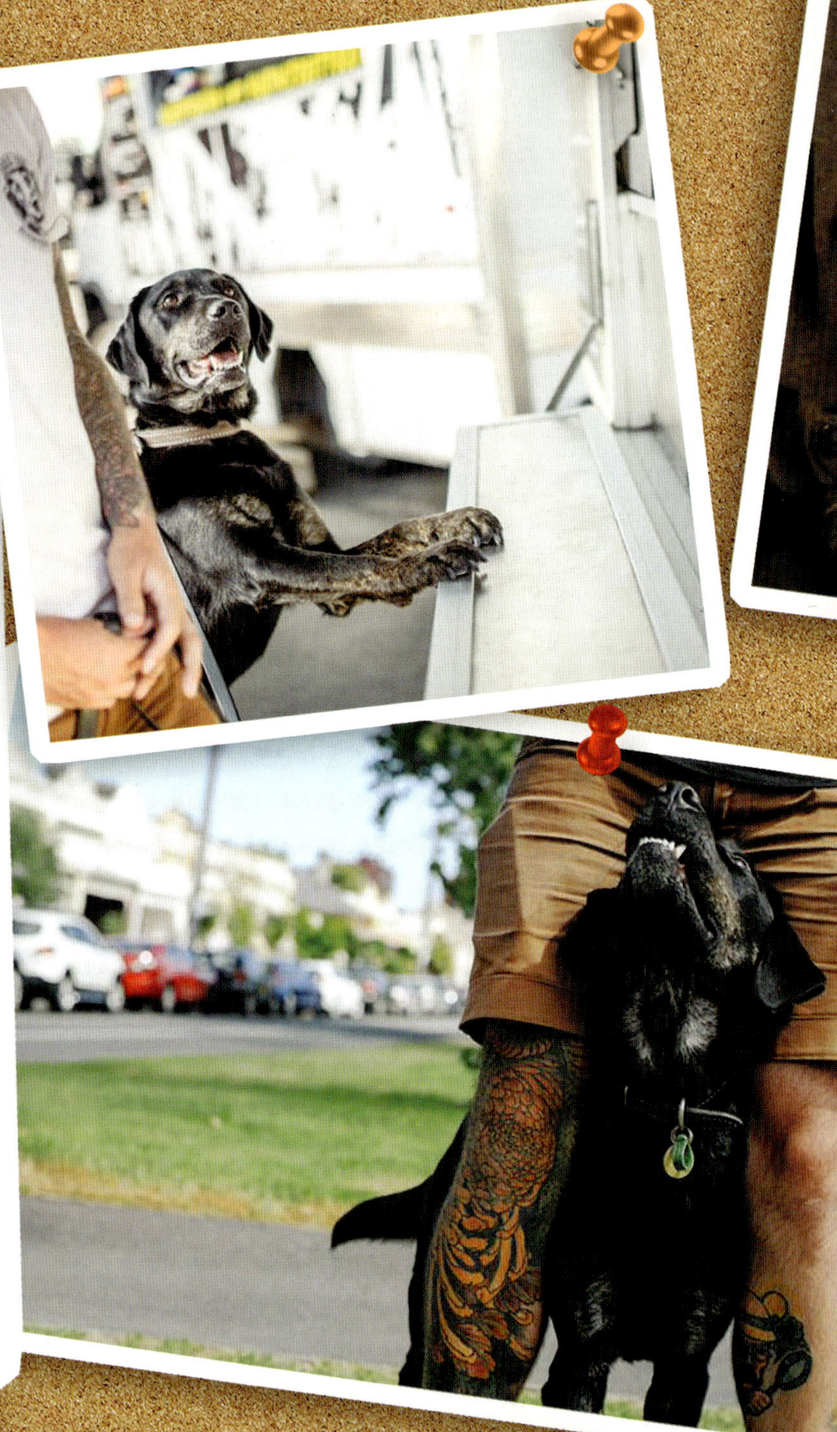

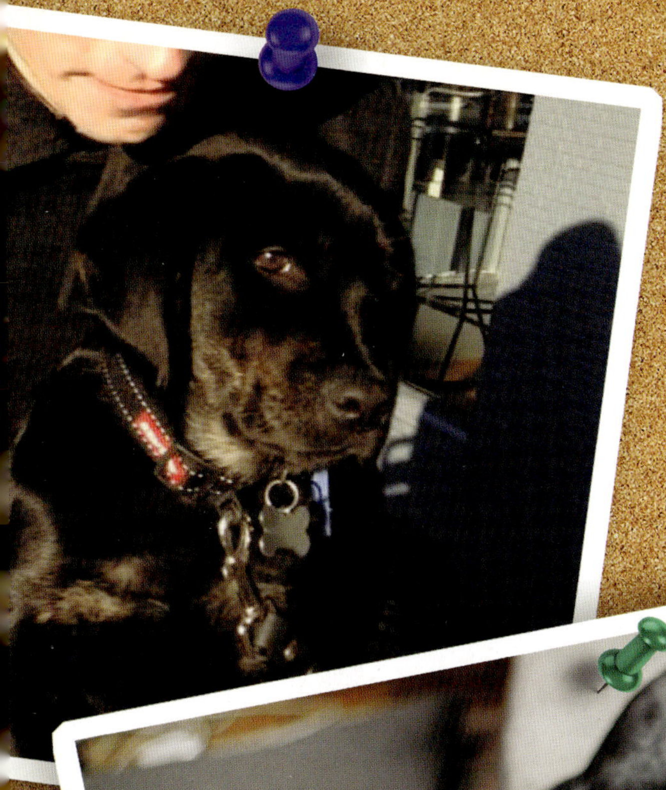

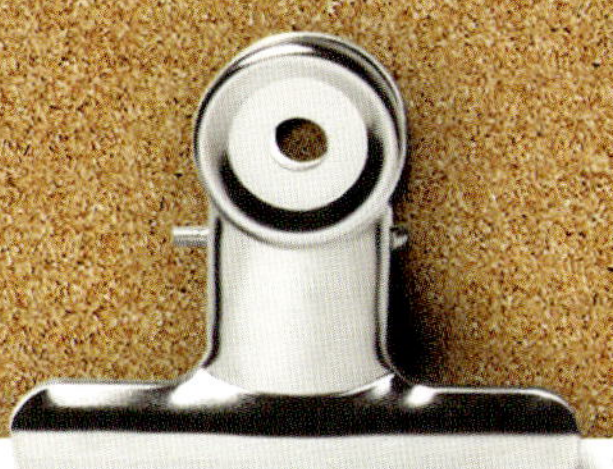

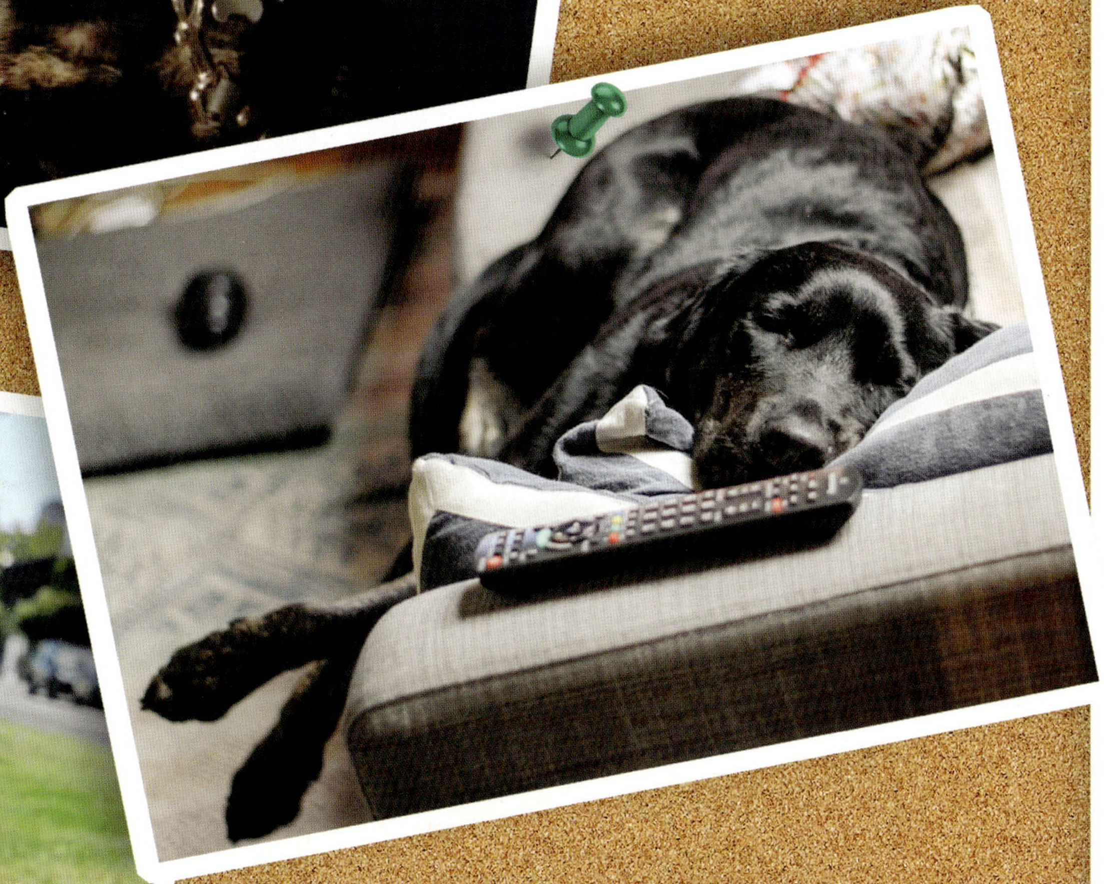

Elliott
THE TRAINER

Elliott was born on 21 February 2013 in
Pearcedale, Victoria. He is the Co-owner of
Good Dog, and often assists with the training
and rehabilitation of reactive, shy
and fearful dogs.

He is always lending trainer Tim a helpful paw
in connecting dogs and their owners, ensuring a
happy, healthy lifestyle for all.

In his downtime, you'll find Elliott curled up
on the couch, learning new tricks or trying
to hustle a hot chip from the bar staff at
The Great Northern Hotel.

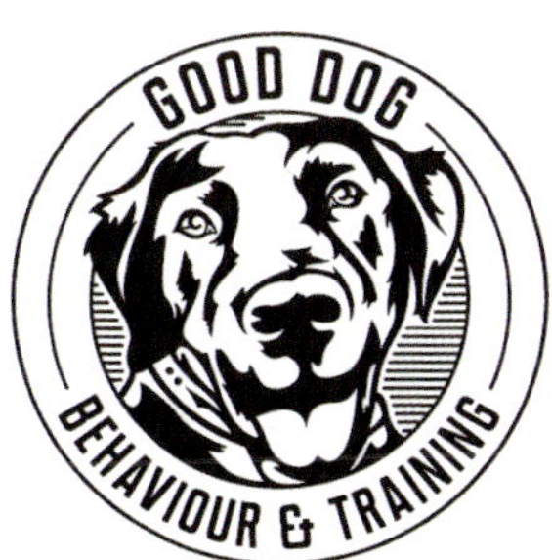

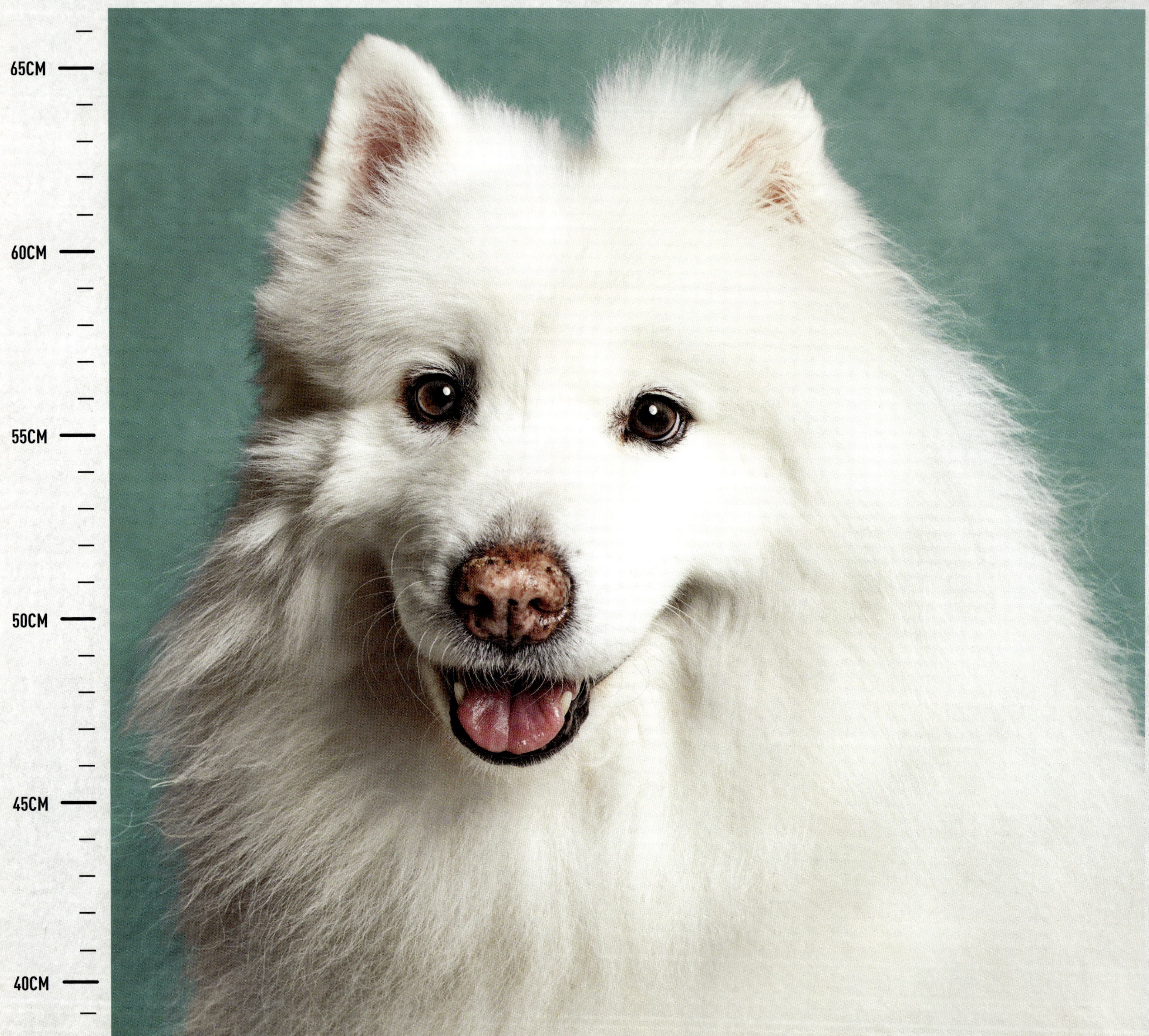

65CM
60CM
55CM
50CM
45CM
40CM

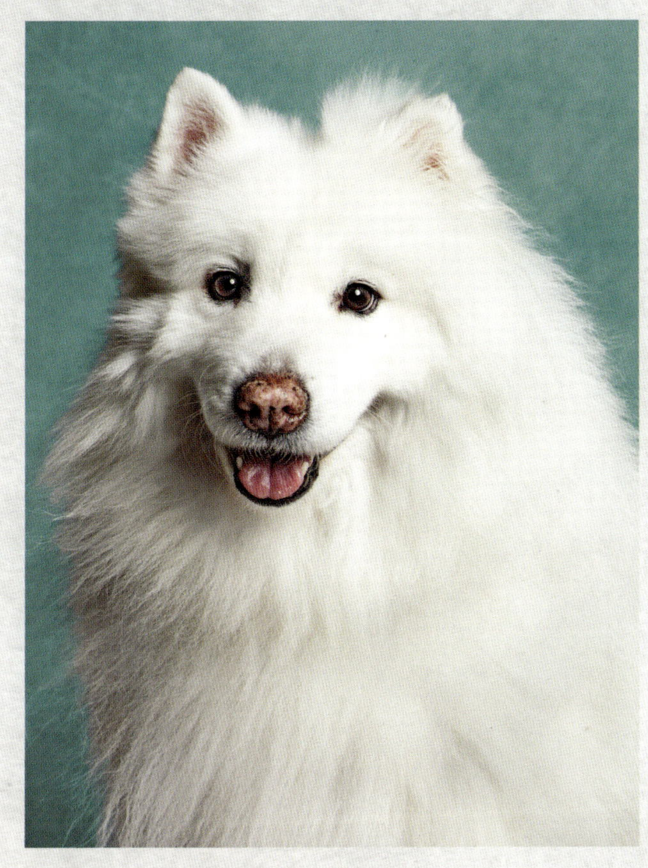 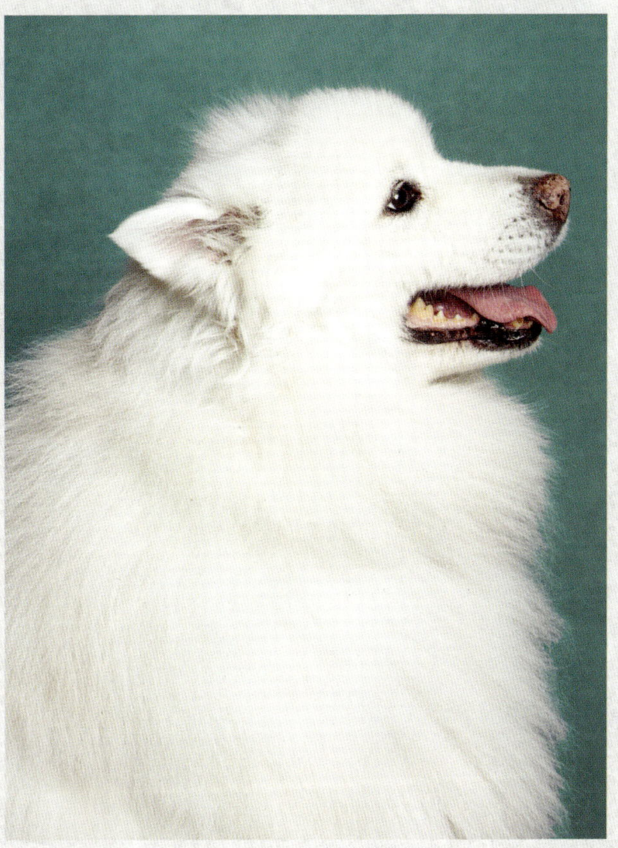 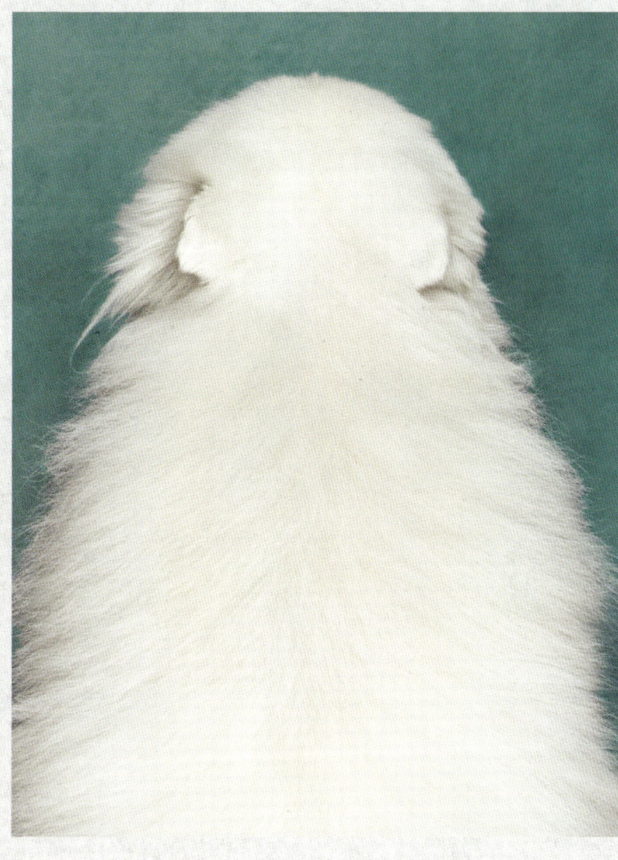

S, Mojo

ALIASES: Momo / Jo / Big Boy / Fluffy

BORN: Unknown, 15yrs   TRADE: Houdini Socialite   BREED: Samoyed

BUILD: Super Floofy   EYES: Brown   HEIGHT: 66cm   HAIR: White

MARKS: White eyelashes

PECULIARITIES: Although a senior at 15 years old, has the essence of a puppy.

M.O: ETC. Has a tendency to wander and not return in a rush — choosing instead to visit the local dogs, spending the day playing in their backyards and running around with their toys, much to the dismay of his smaller toy owners.

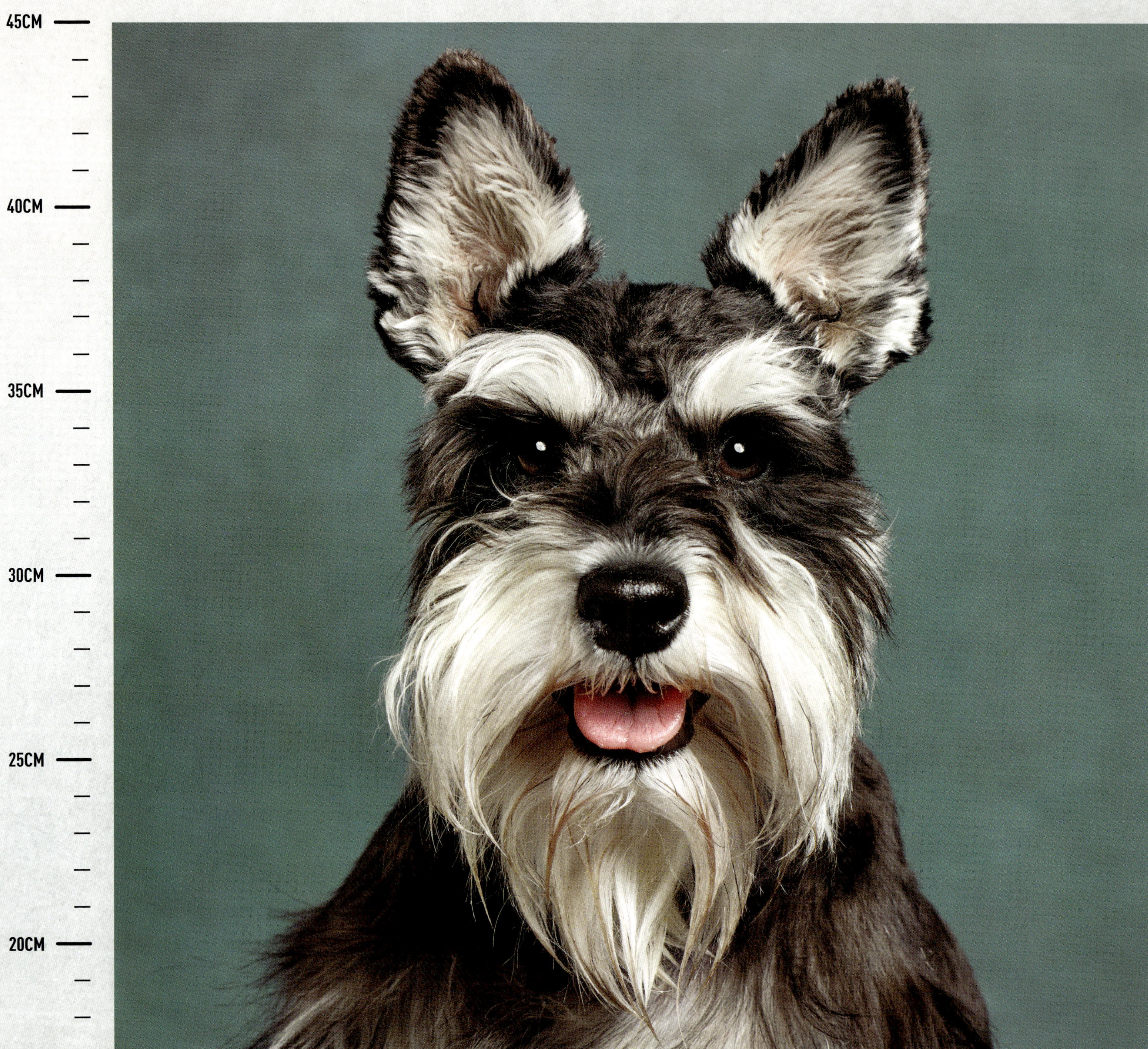

45CM
40CM
35CM
30CM
25CM
20CM

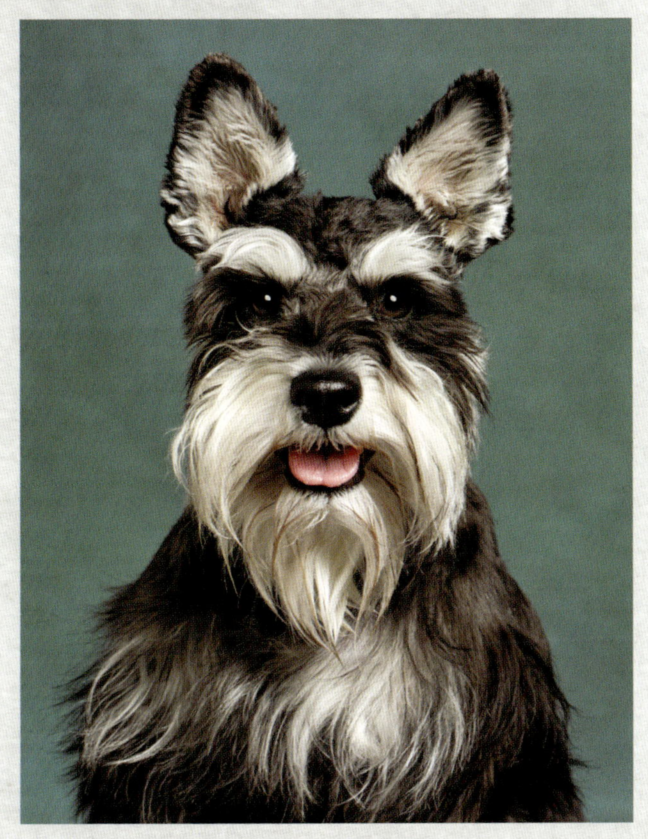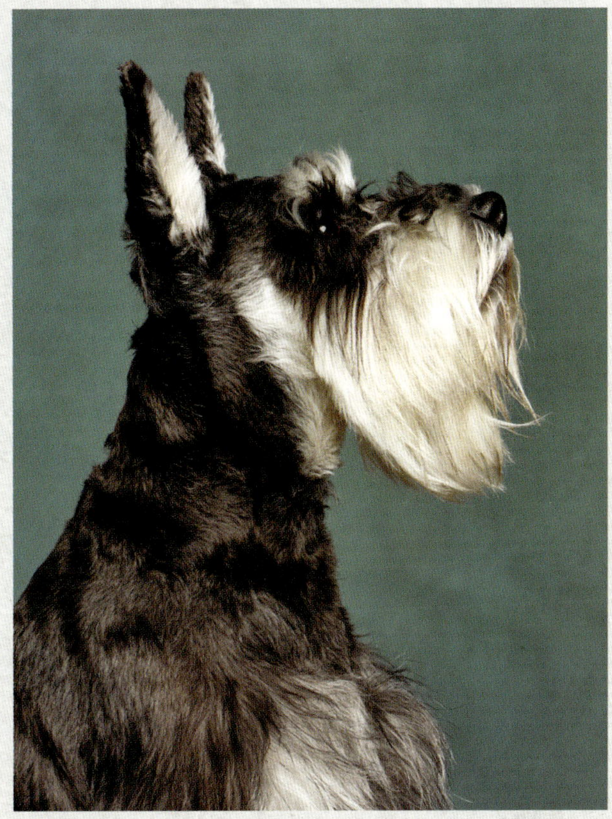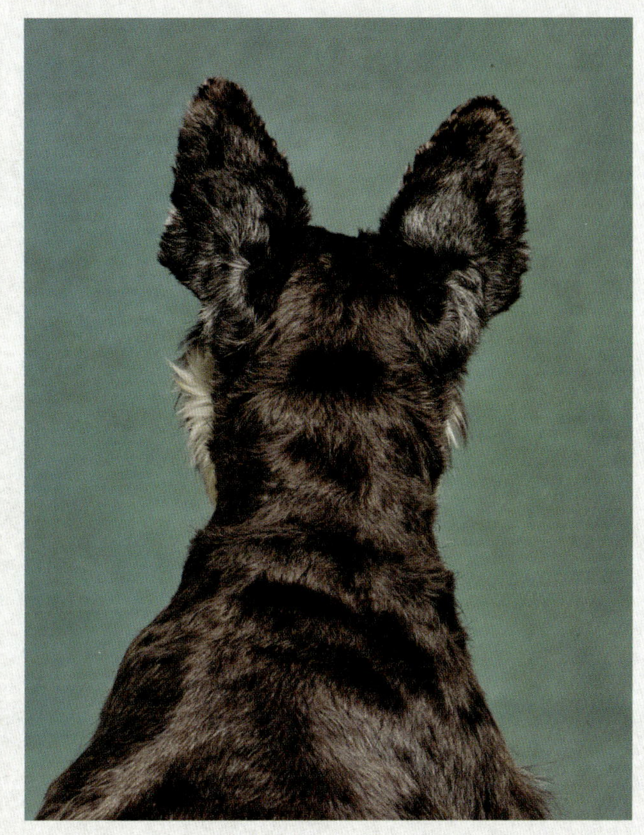

Rizzo

ALIASES: Rizz / Minirizz / Betty

BORN: 16/11/2015 **TRADE:** Style Queen **BREED:** Miniature Schnauzer

BUILD: On Fleek **EYES:** Brown **HEIGHT:** 44cm **HAIR:** Black / Silver / White

MARKS: White accents on key features

PECULIARITIES: How she maintains her eyebrows on fleek — it's a mystery

M.O: ETC. Really loves ducks. Has been known to become completely mesmerised by them. She never barks at them, but witnesses state she will not take her eyes off them until she has been removed from the vicinity of said ducks.

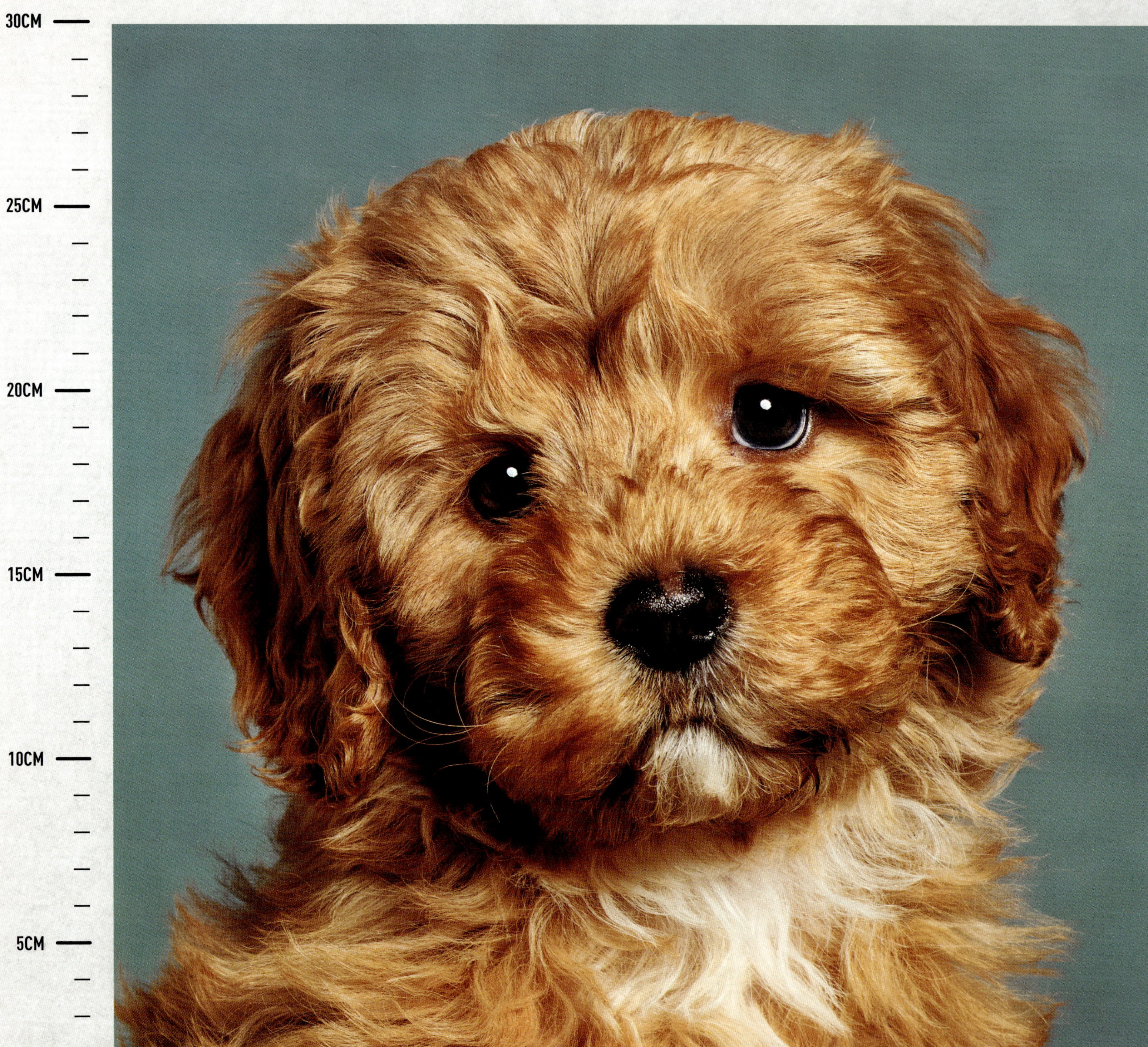

30CM
25CM
20CM
15CM
10CM
5CM

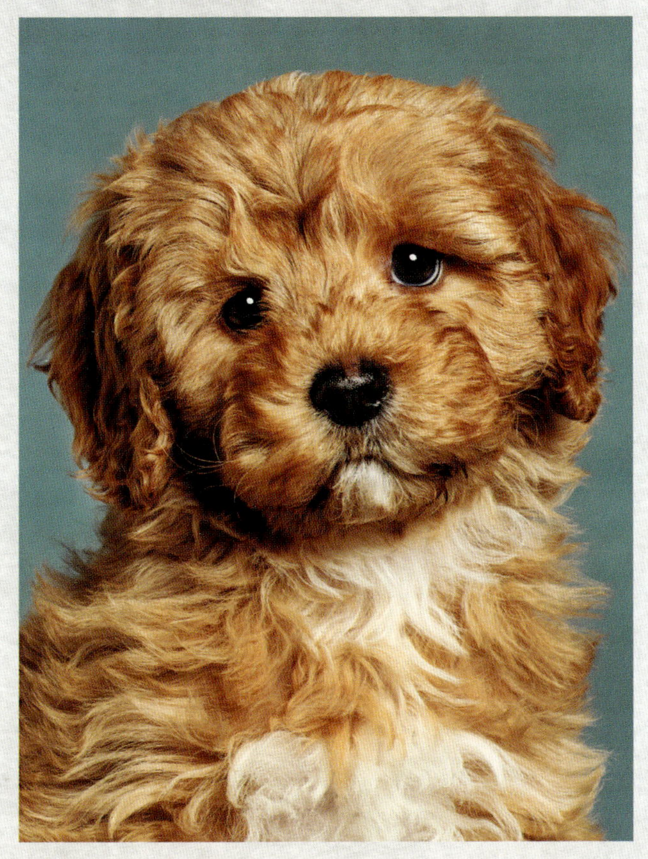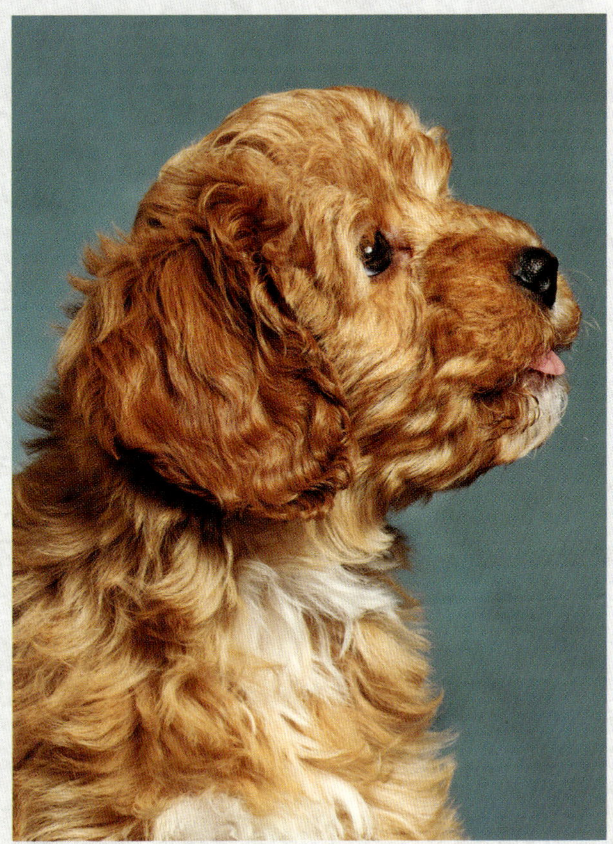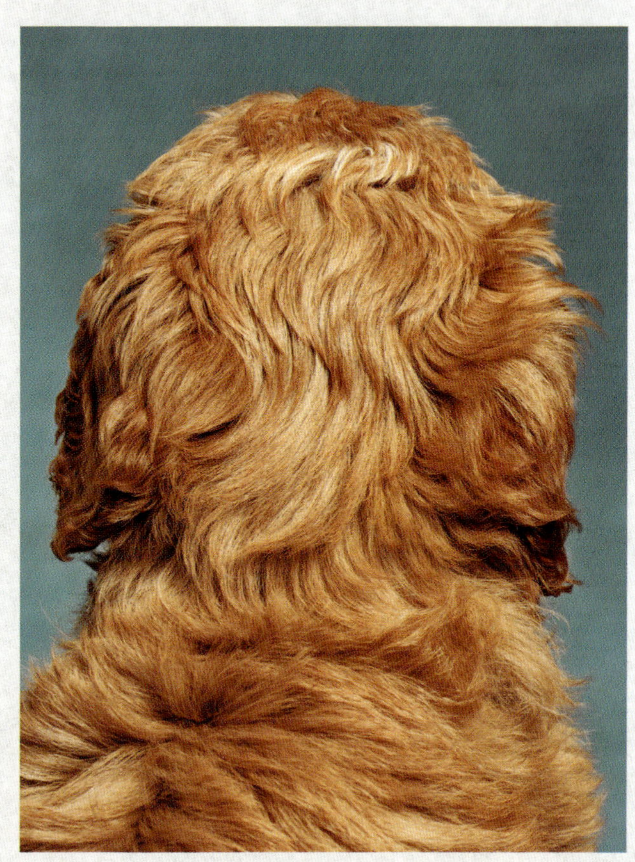

H, Mycroft

ALIASES:

BORN: 22/04/2017   TRADE: In training   BREED: Cavoodle

BUILD: Mini Floof   EYES: Brown   HEIGHT: 25cm   HAIR: Chestnut / White

MARKS: Little brown spot on nose

PECULIARITIES: Has a particularly fluffy bottom

M.O: ETC. Has been reported to take bribes in the form of bits of sausage in order to accept his sleeping quarters.

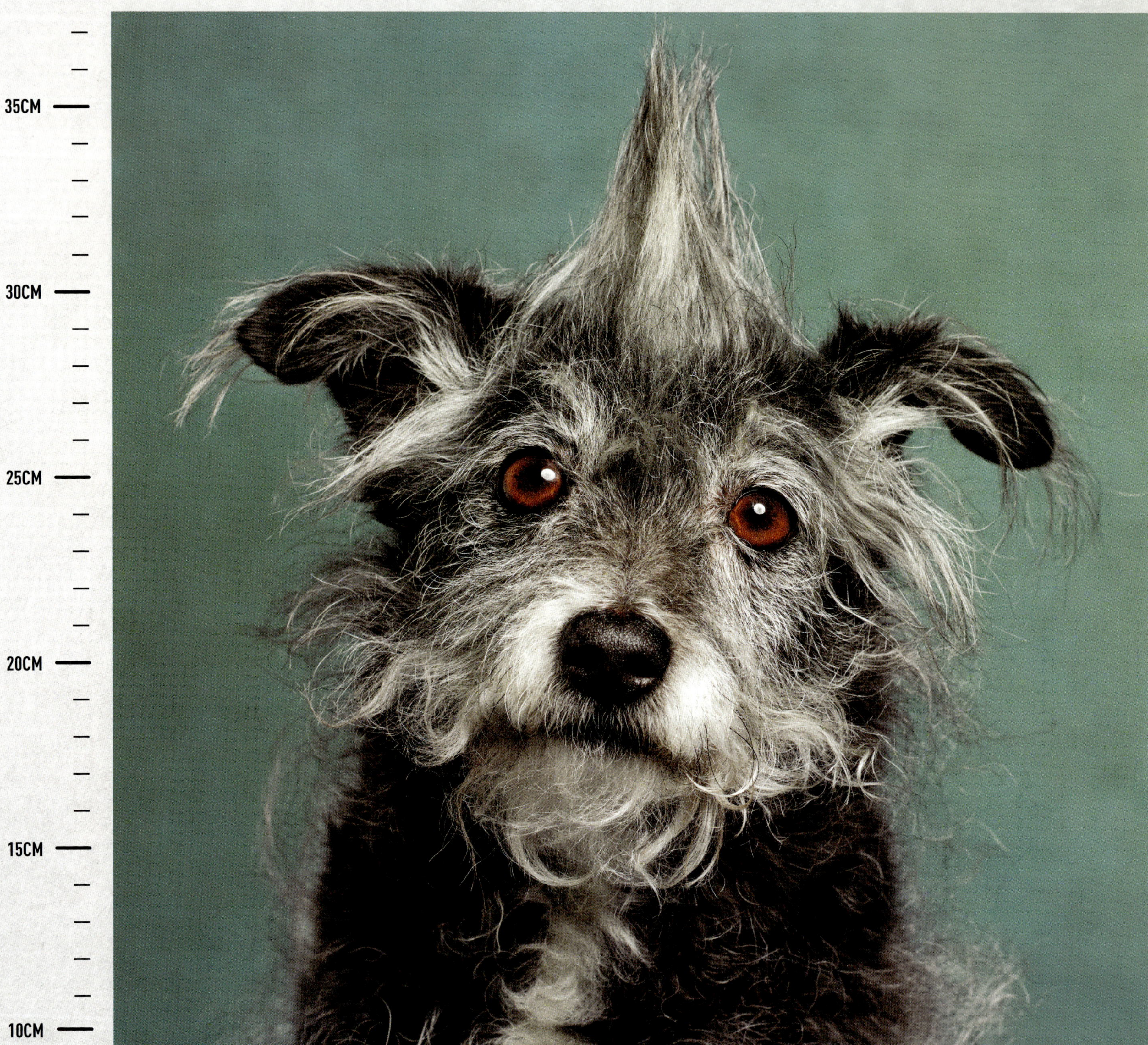

35CM
30CM
25CM
20CM
15CM
10CM

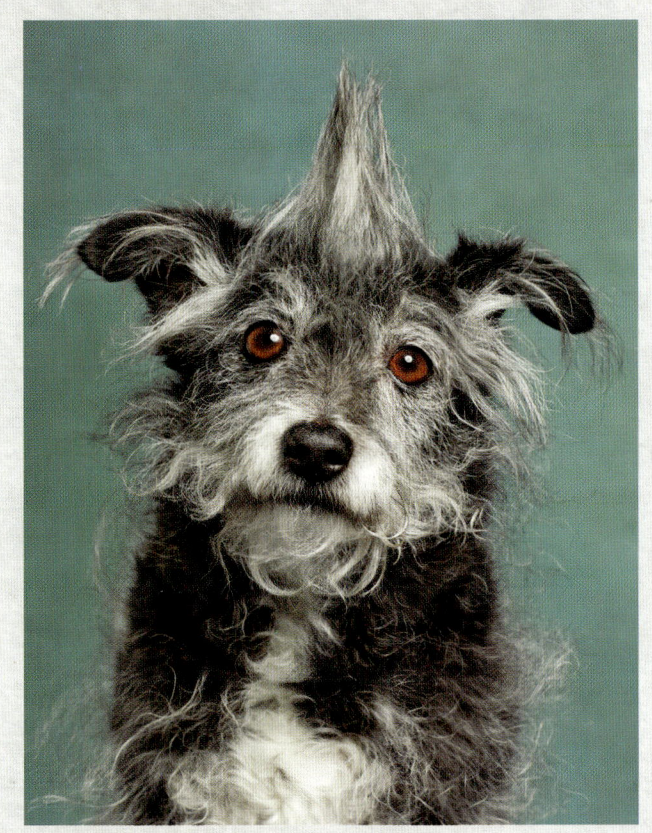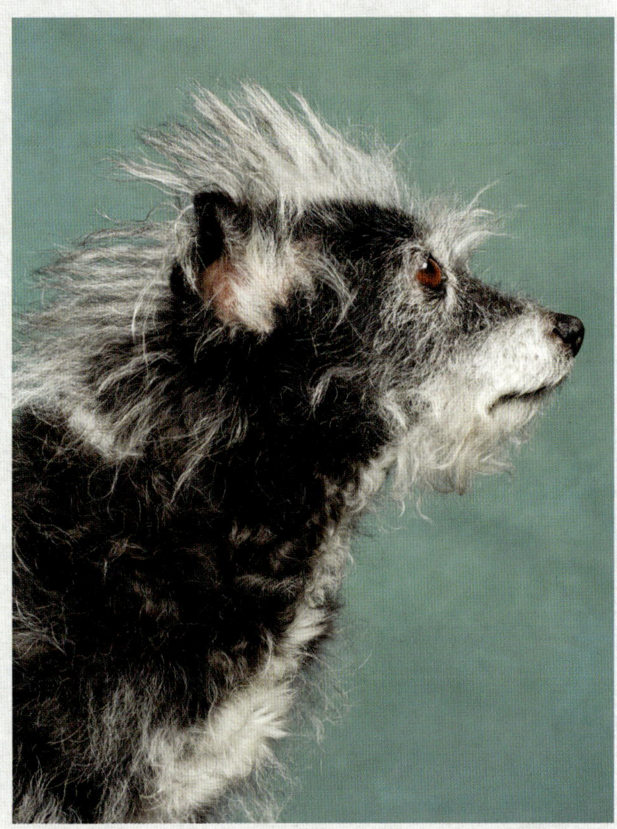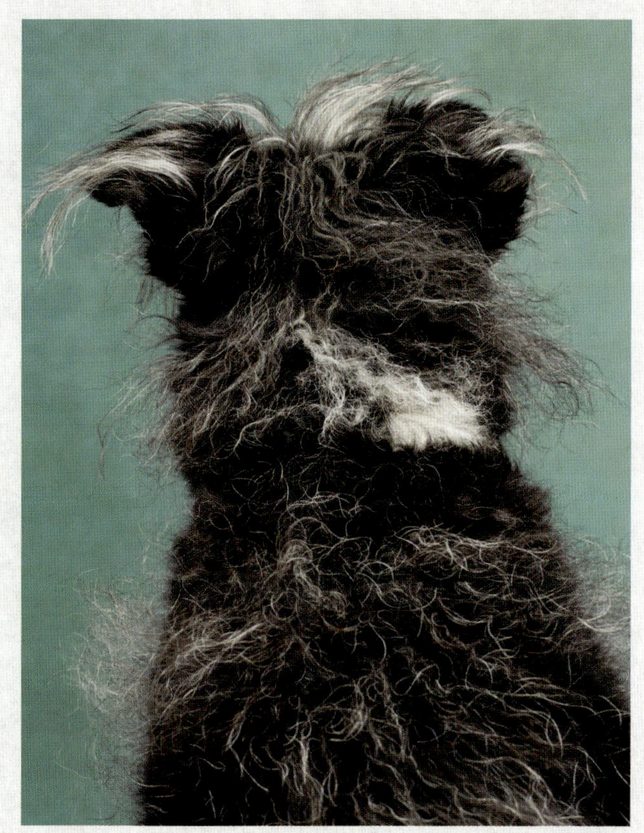

B, Rocky

ALIASES:

BORN: Unknown, 15yrs approx	**TRADE:** Kingpin	**BREED:** Mystery Mutt

BUILD: Compact   **EYES:** Brown   **HEIGHT:** 37cm   **HAIR:** Grey / White

MARKS: White highlights throughout coat

PECULIARITIES: Gravity defying hair that can hold its shape when sculpted

M.O: ETC. If loses sight of humans during a patrol — even if they are right beside him — has been known to begin running to the nearest random human for assistance.
Is not adverse to having a good roll in cow poo.

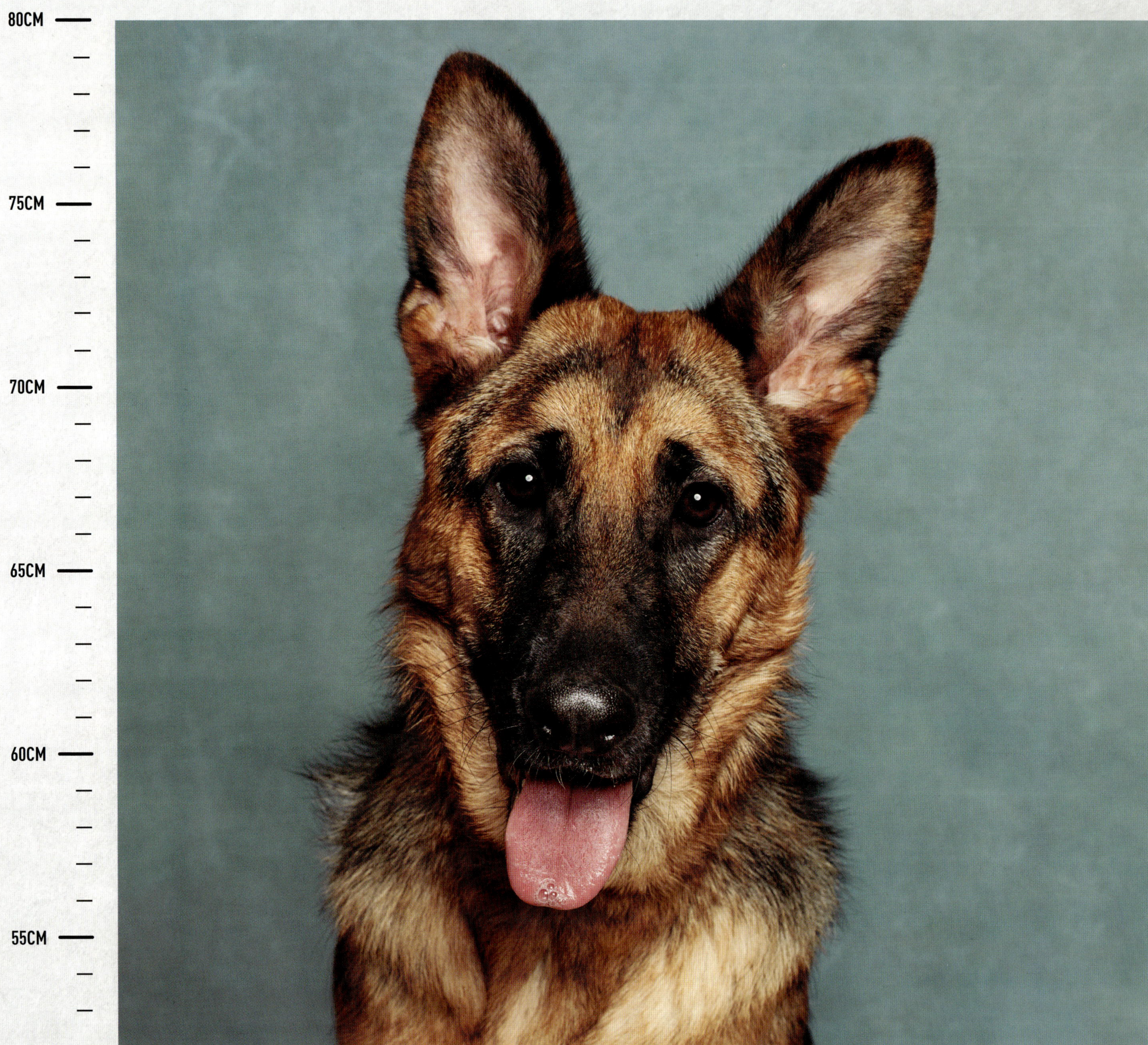

80CM
75CM
70CM
65CM
60CM
55CM

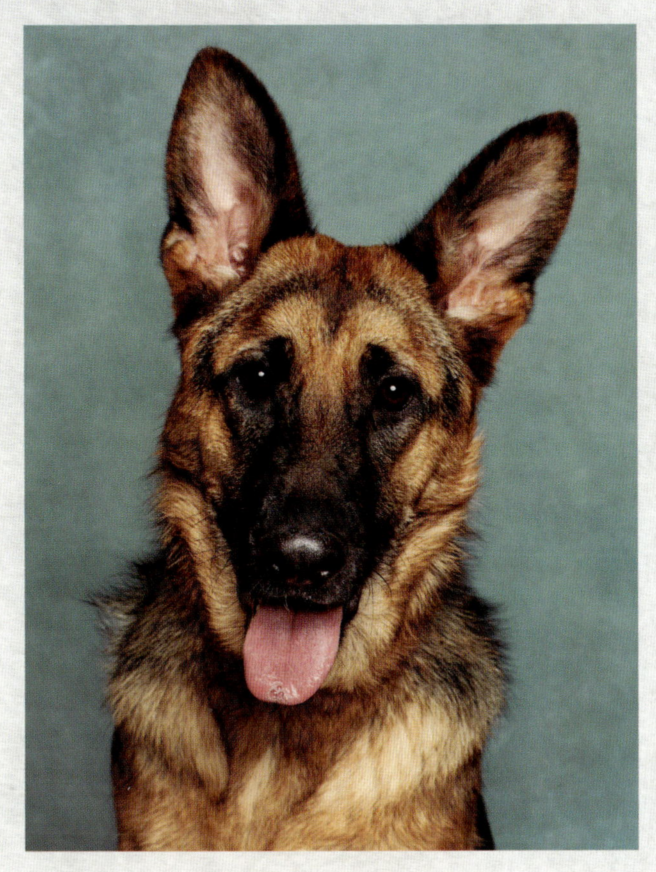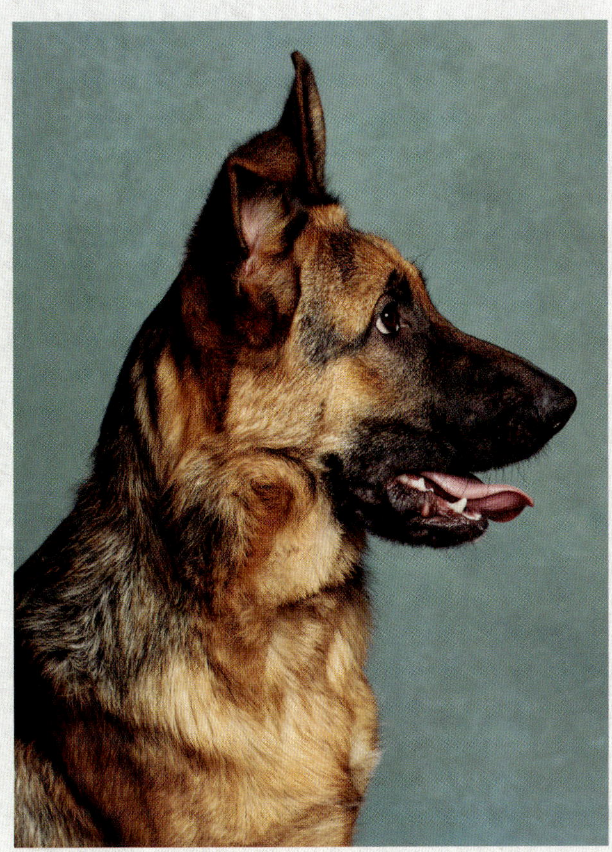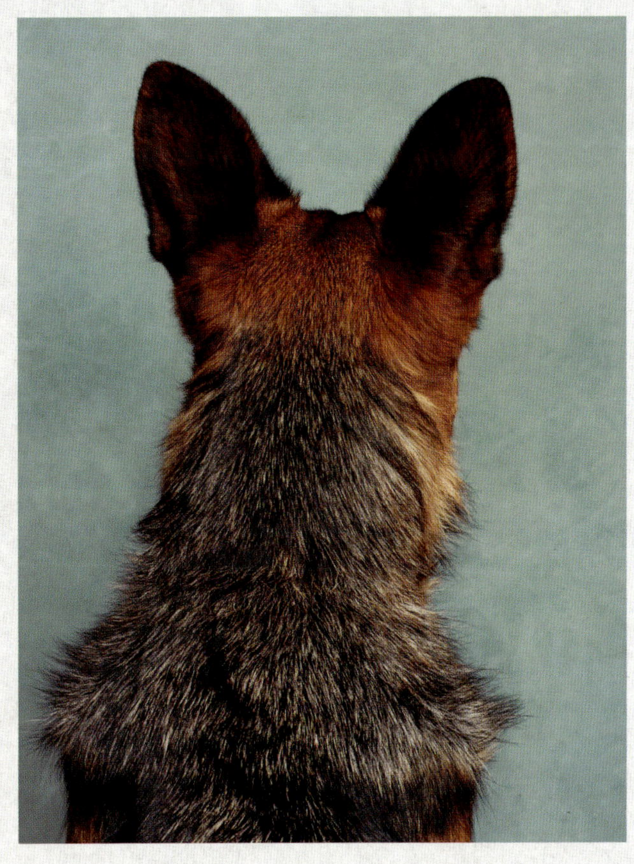

D, Lexi

ALIASES: Lex / Leki

BORN: 29/01/2017 TRADE: Loyal Sidekick BREED: German Shepherd

BUILD: Tall & Lean EYES: Brown HEIGHT: 79cm HAIR: Tan / Black

MARKS: Black mask-like markings around face

PECULIARITIES: Reported to have chewed a hole in a wall

M.O: ETC. Is obsessed with her partner in crime Ruby, will follow her everywhere.

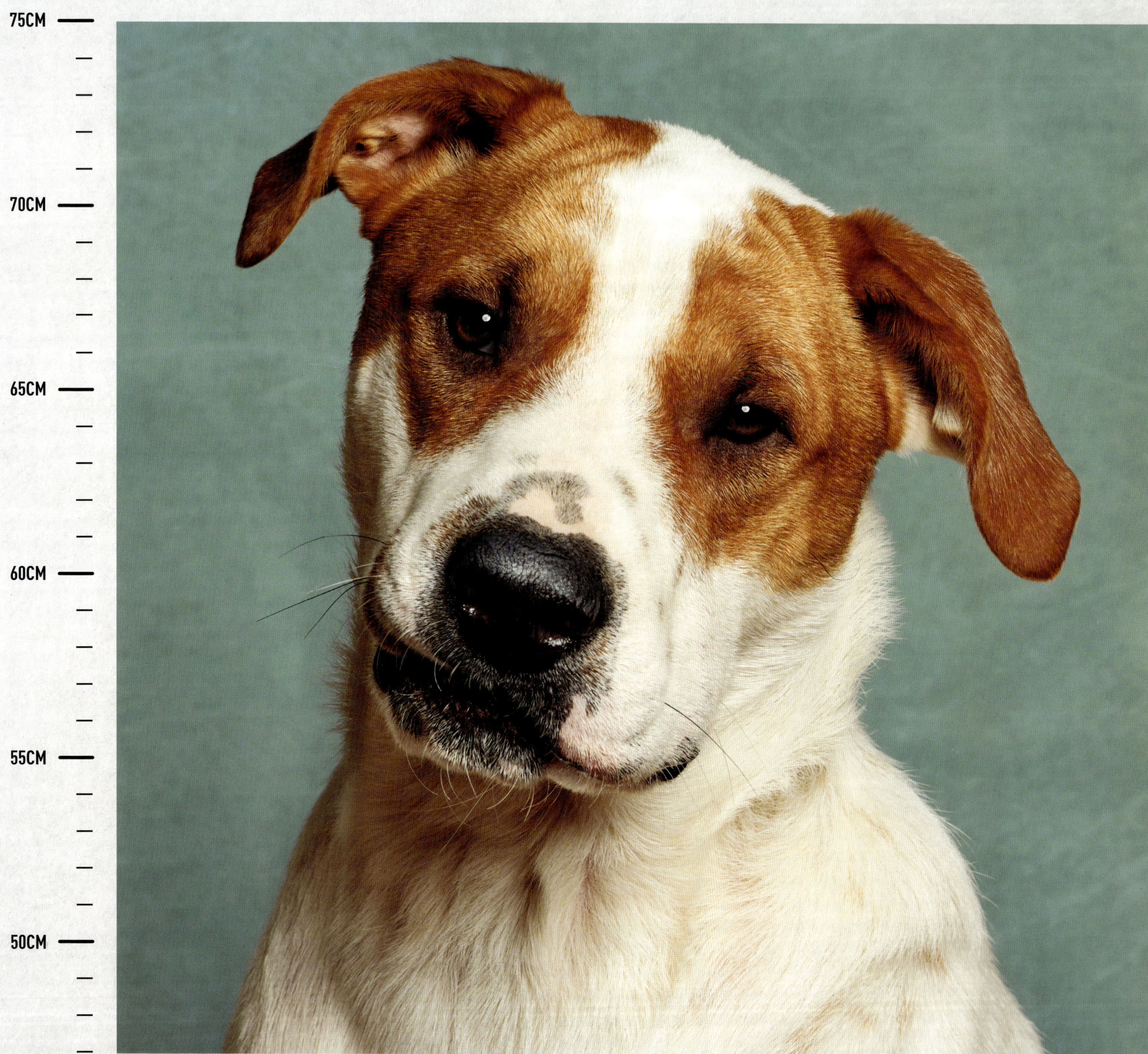
75CM
70CM
65CM
60CM
55CM
50CM

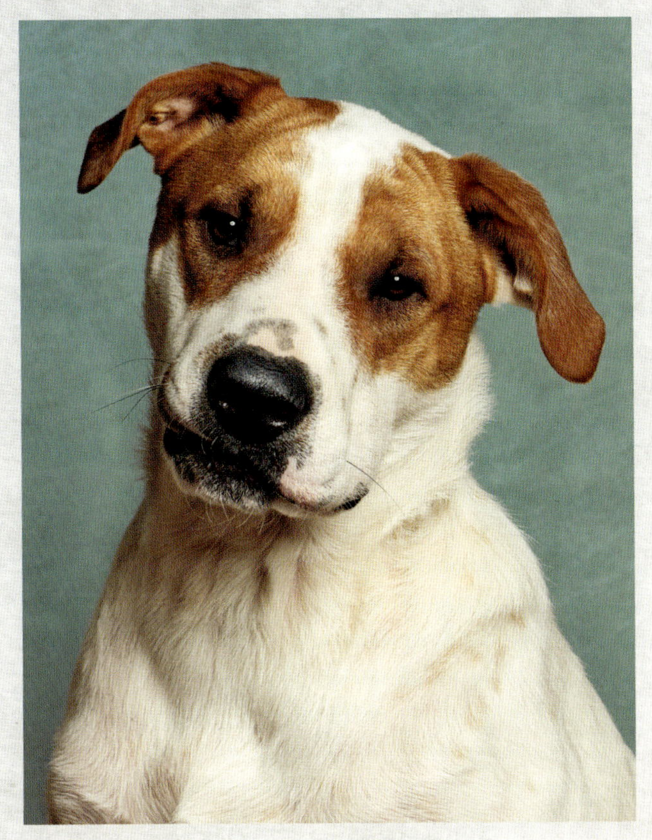 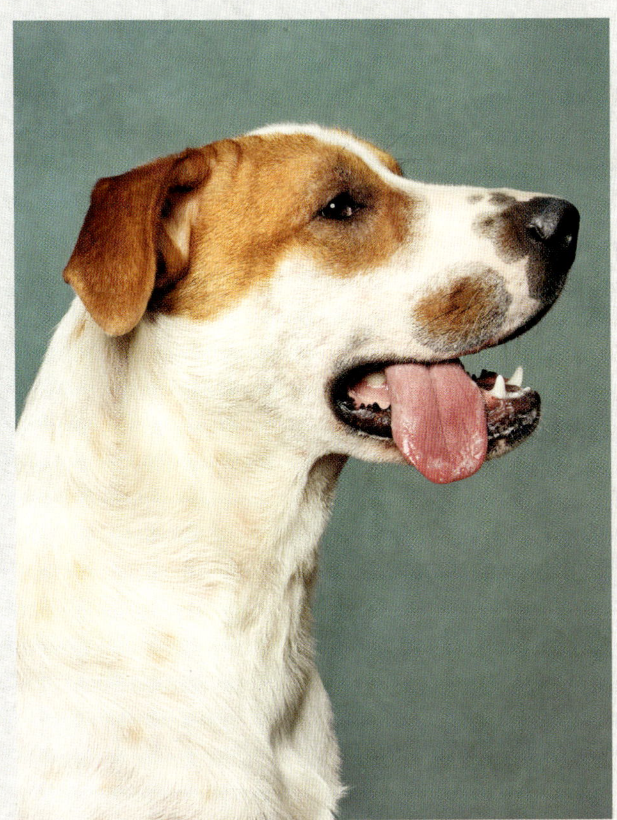 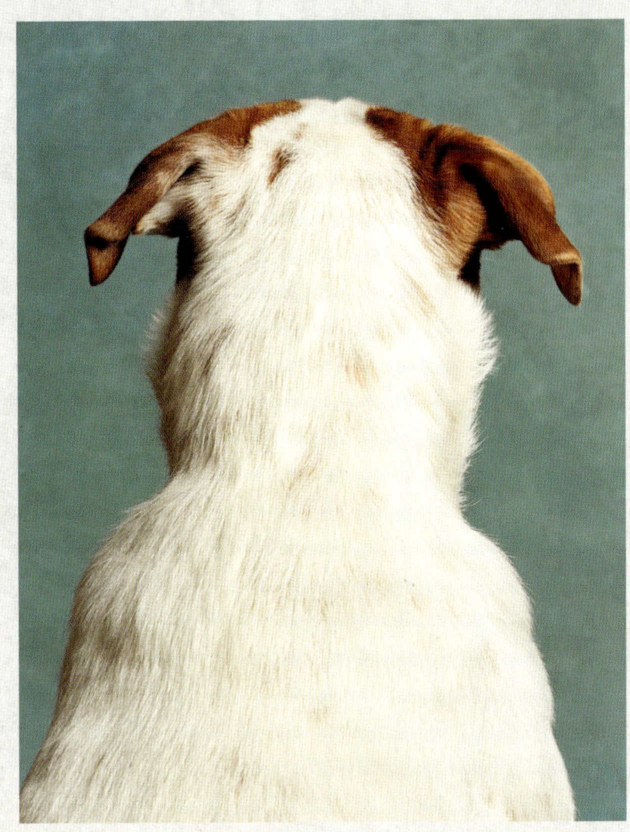

D, Ruby

ALIASES: Rubert / Rubes

BORN: 04/08/2016   TRADE: Troublemaker   BREED: Staffy x

BUILD: Solid   EYES: Brown   HEIGHT: 74cm   HAIR: Brown / White

MARKS: Black spots on nose

PECULIARITIES: Has particularly floppy lips

M.O: ETC. Enjoys sleeping in between humans with her head on the pillow —
so much so that upon receiving her very own bed, she destroyed it within
the first half hour.

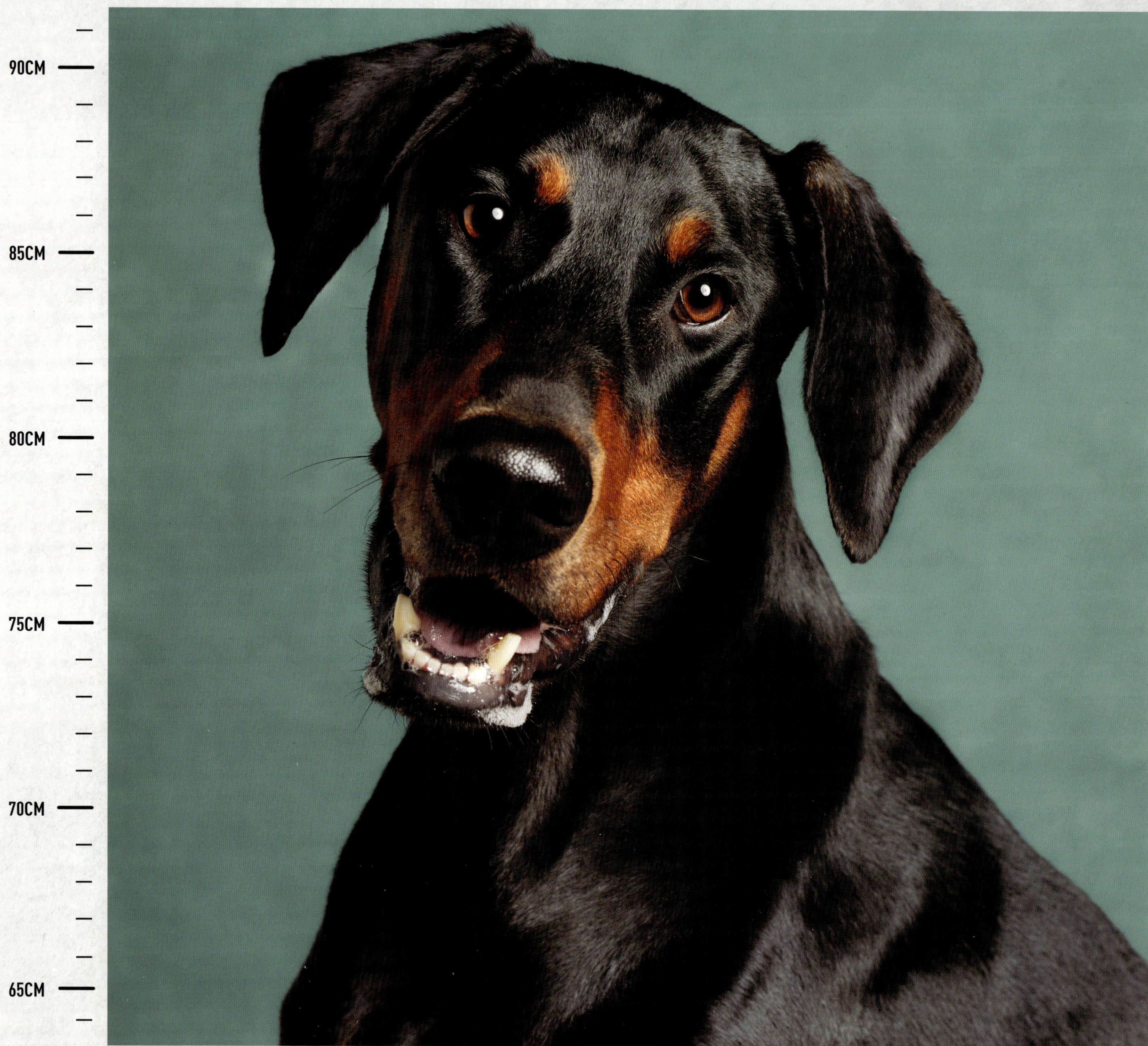

90CM
85CM
80CM
75CM
70CM
65CM

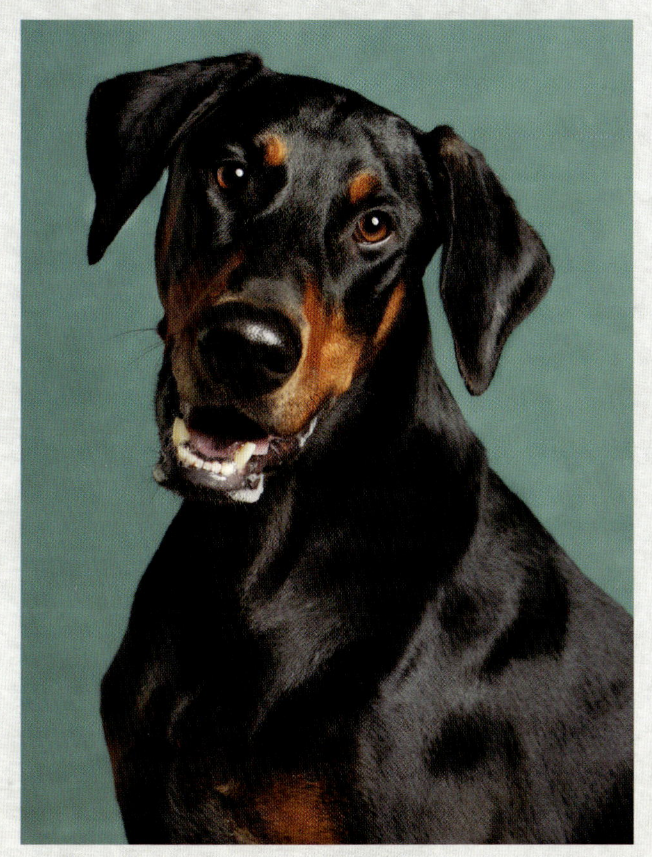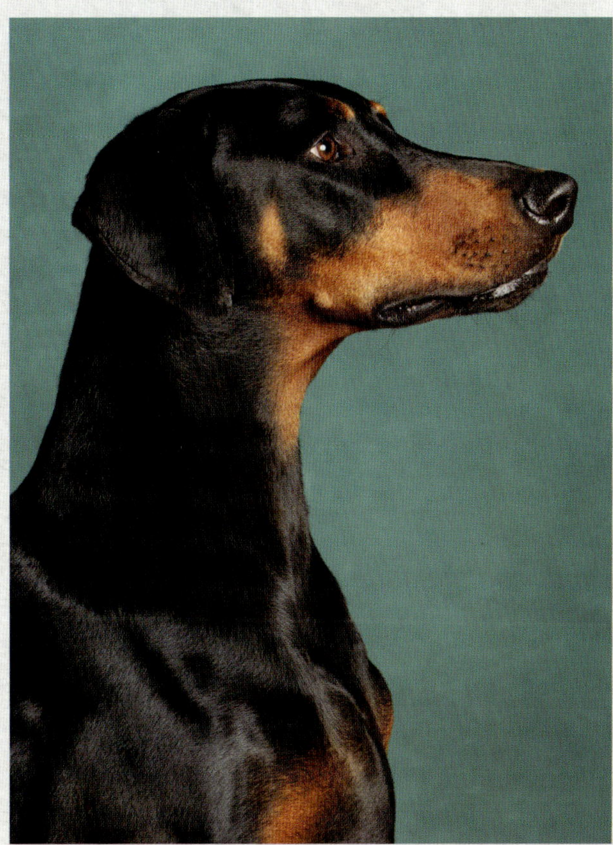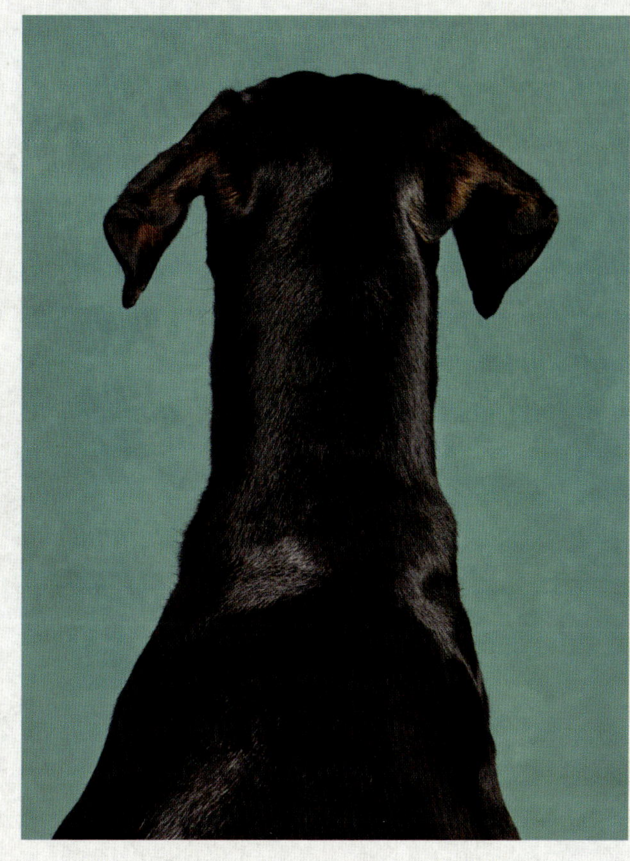

M, Duke

ALIASES: The Duke / Dooke / Boof / Old Mate / Frighty Pants

BORN: 11/09/2011   TRADE: Velcro Dog   BREED: Doberman

BUILD: Super Sleek   EYES: Brown   HEIGHT: 91cm   HAIR: Black / Rust Brown

MARKS: Little rust brown eyebrows

PECULIARITIES: OCD about balls — When a ball is around there is nothing else

M.O: ETC. Named after the great Duke Kahanamoku, who popularised the ancient Hawaiian sport of surfing — has mastered swimming like his namesake, however has not yet mastered surfing.

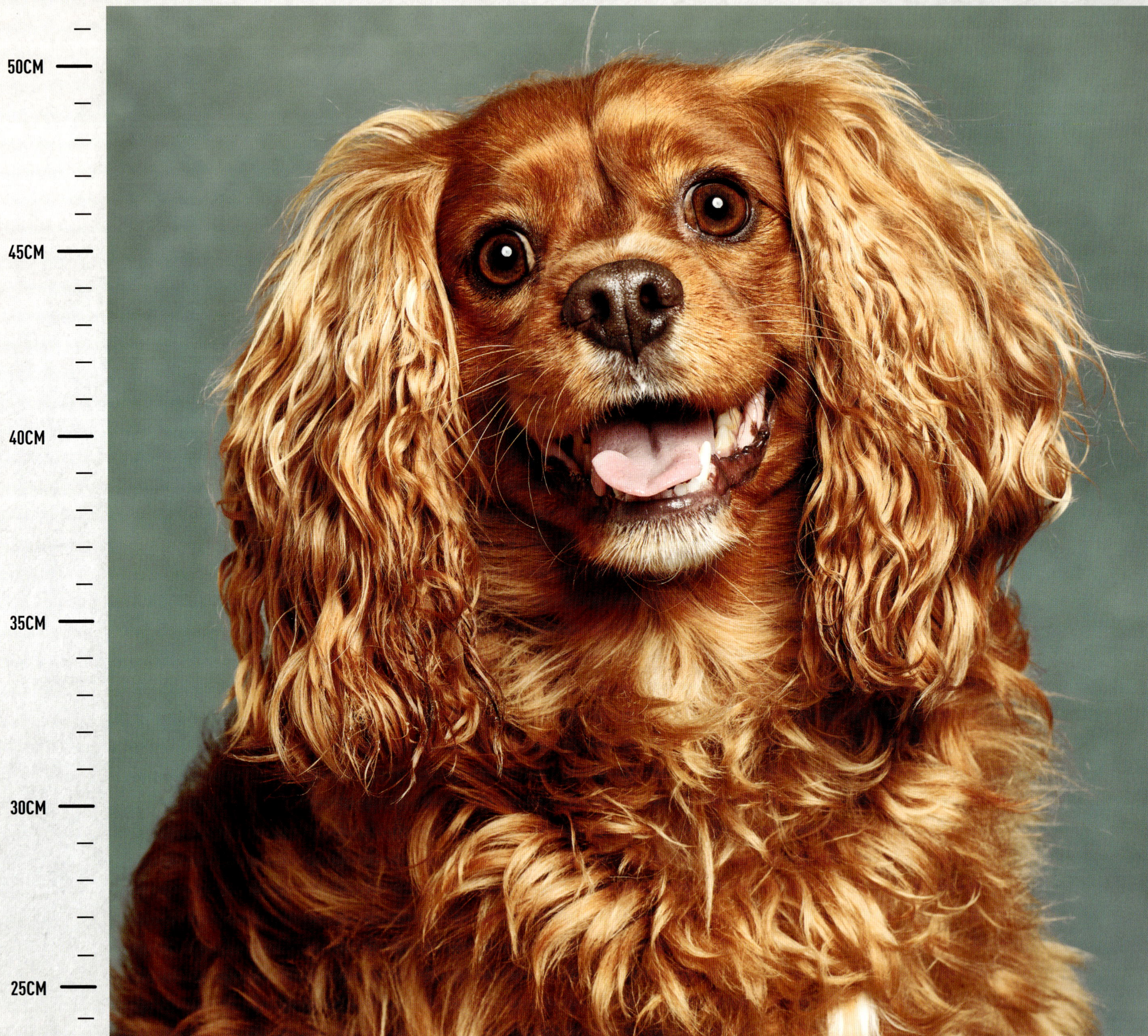

50CM
45CM
40CM
35CM
30CM
25CM

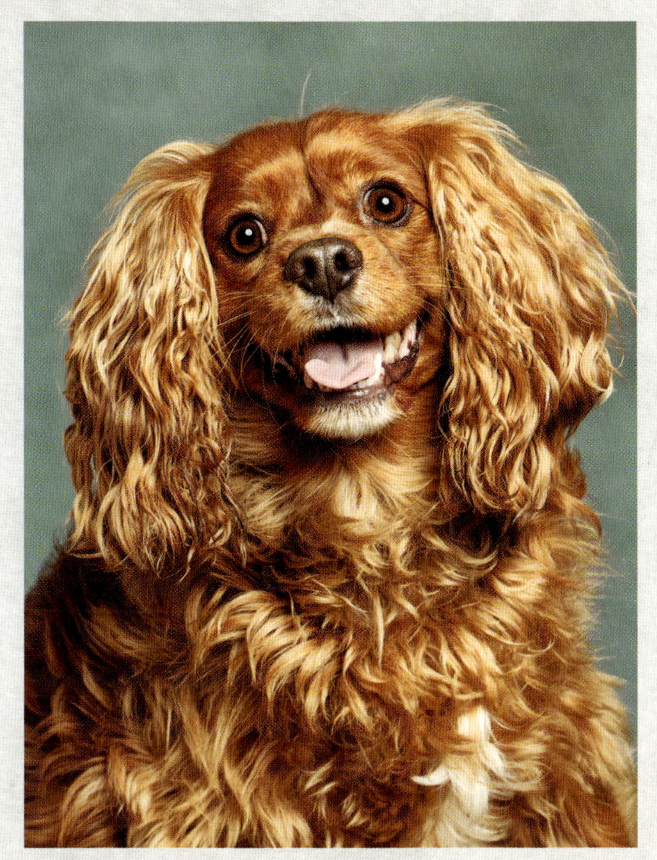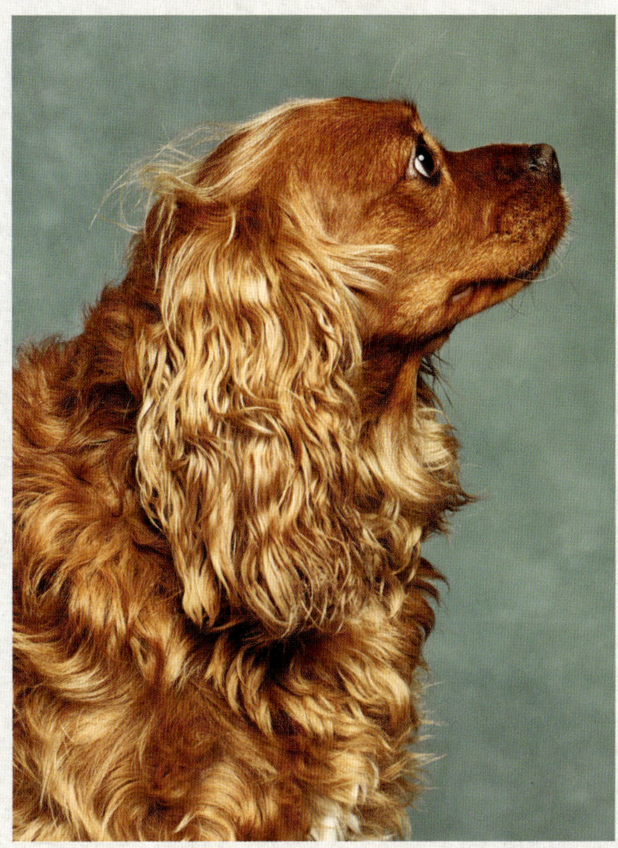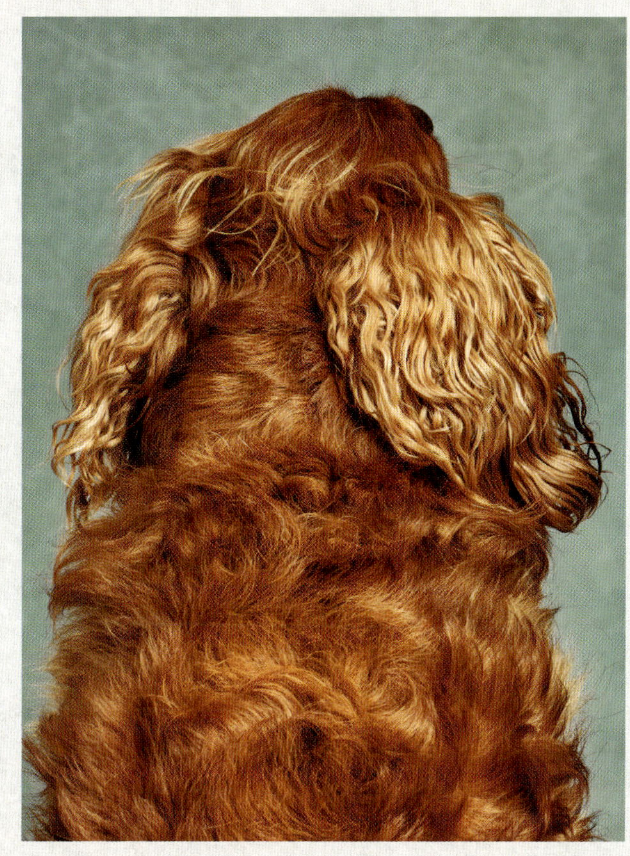

P, Ralph

ALIASES: Ralphy

BORN: 20/03/2014   TRADE: Ninja / Aspiring Model   BREED: Cavoodle

BUILD: Solid   EYES: Brown   HEIGHT: 51cm   HAIR: Chestnut / White

MARKS: Million dollar smile

PECULIARITIES: Has been seen slipping his collar while on a lead to jump into a stranger's car

M.O: ETC. Is particularly sneaky — reported to have stolen a whole steak and learnt to open sliding doors to spend the night inside — he must not be underestimated.

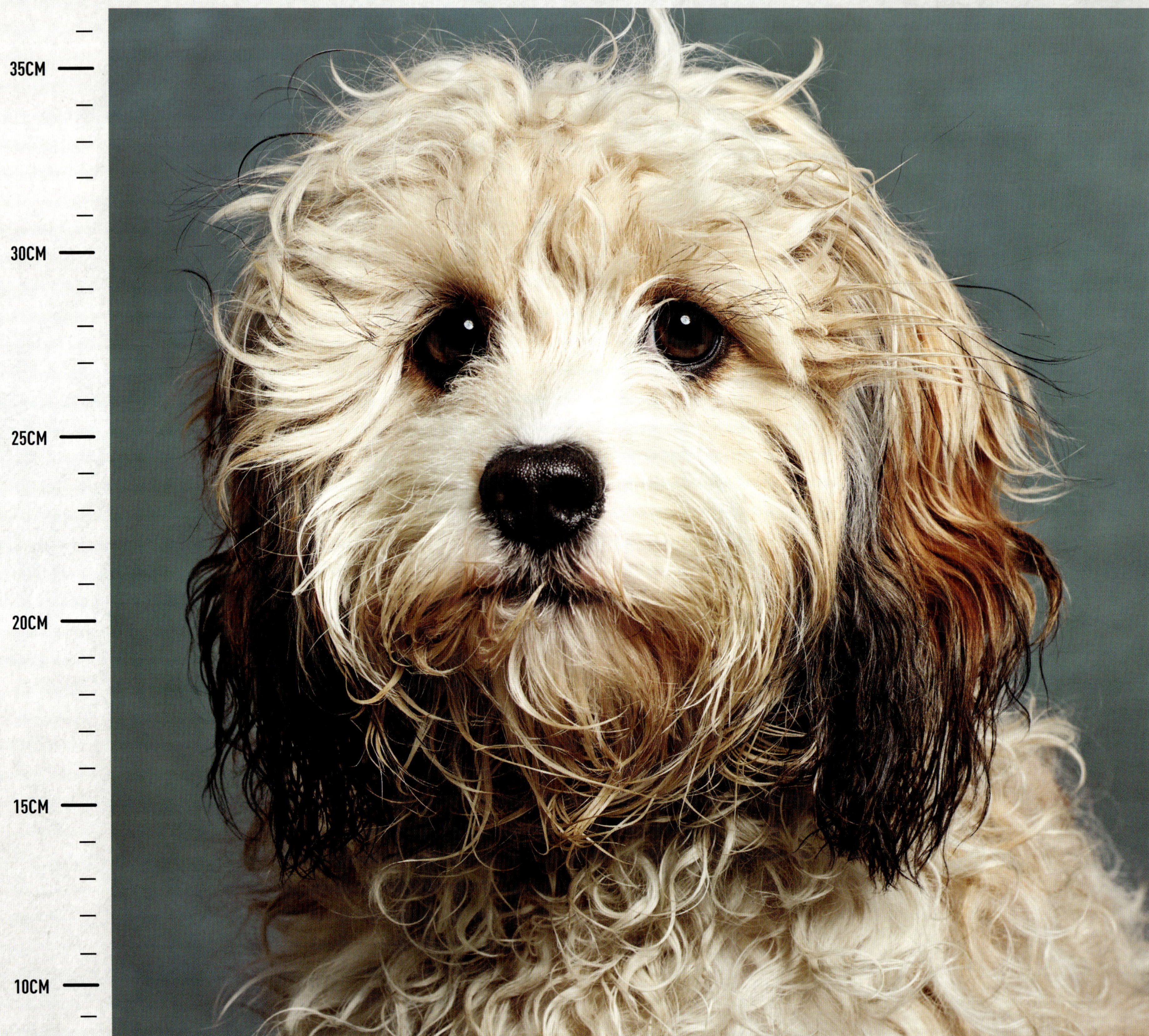

35CM
30CM
25CM
20CM
15CM
10CM

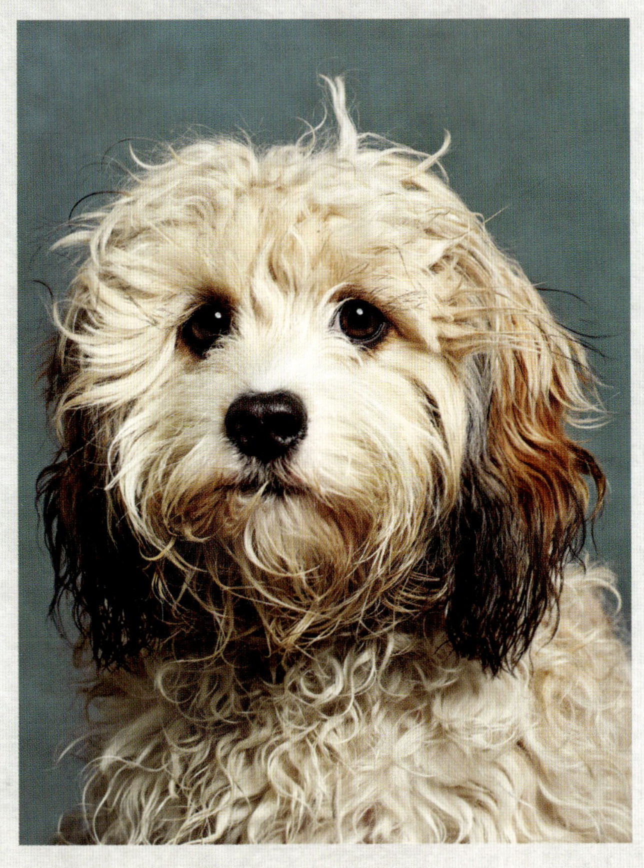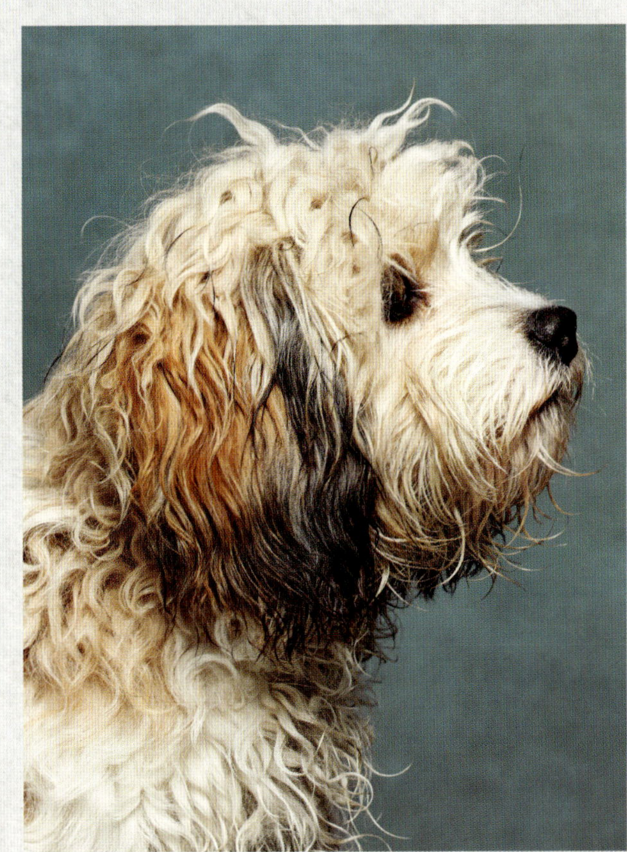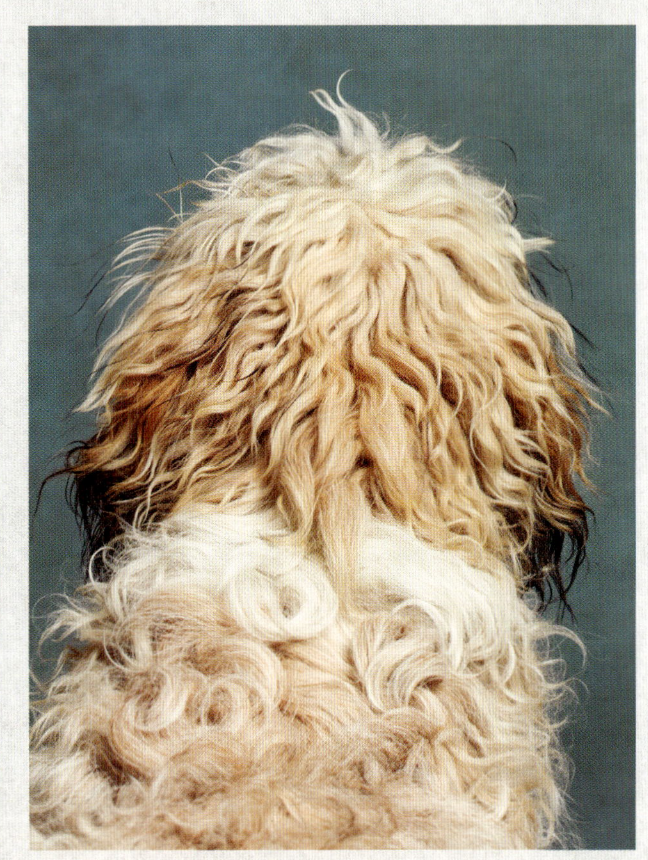

S, Winton

ALIASES: Winty Poo / Winty / Squinton

BORN: 20/09/2016   TRADE: Living Teddy Bear   BREED: Toy Cavoodle

BUILD: Floofball   EYES: Brown   HEIGHT: 35cm   HAIR: White / Brown / Grey

MARKS: Grey tipped ears

PECULIARITIES: Sleeps on back with front and back paws in different directions

M.O: ETC. Sock thief, garbage guts — will swoop in and consume anything in sight. Food and anything food related.

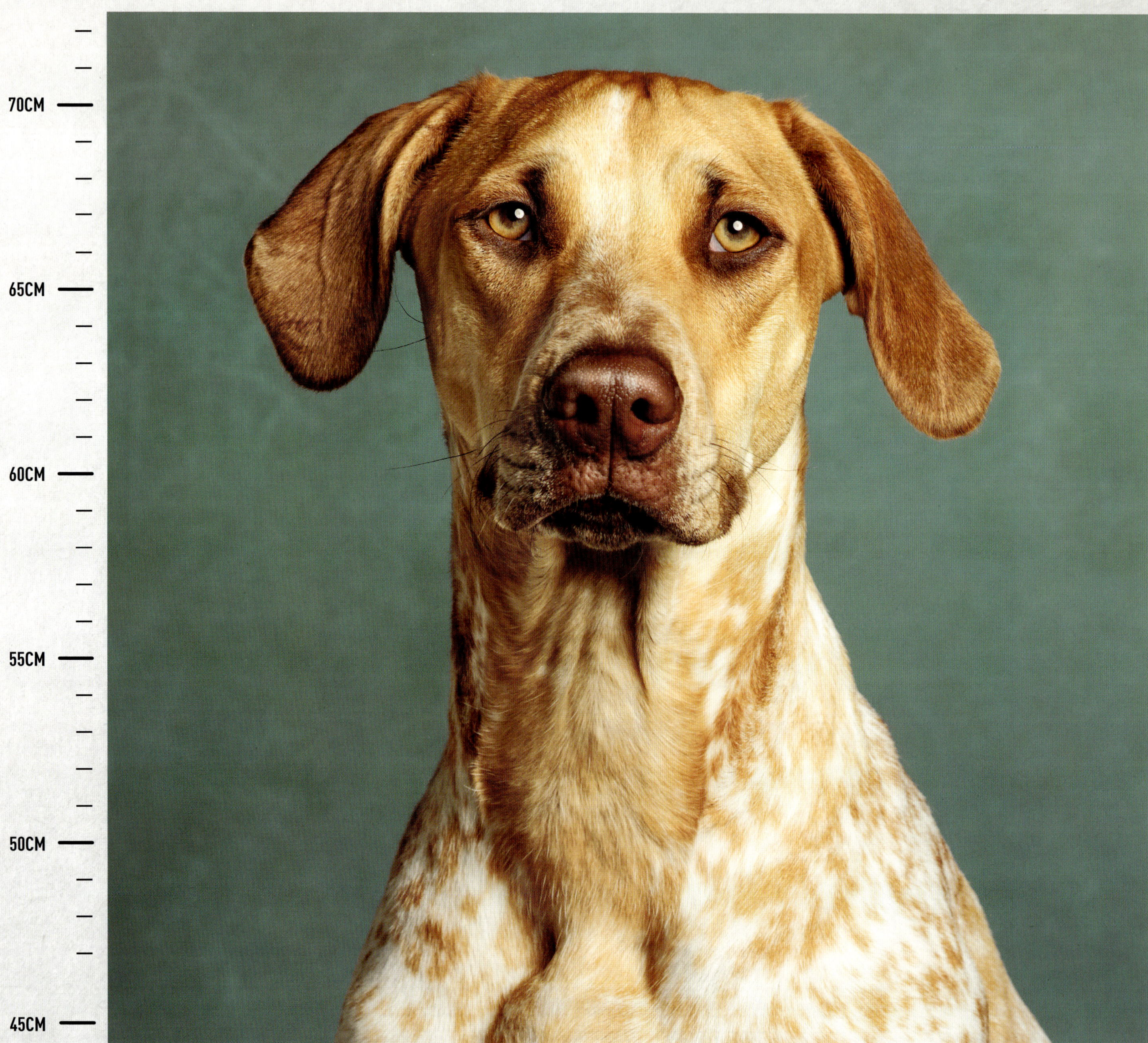

70CM
65CM
60CM
55CM
50CM
45CM

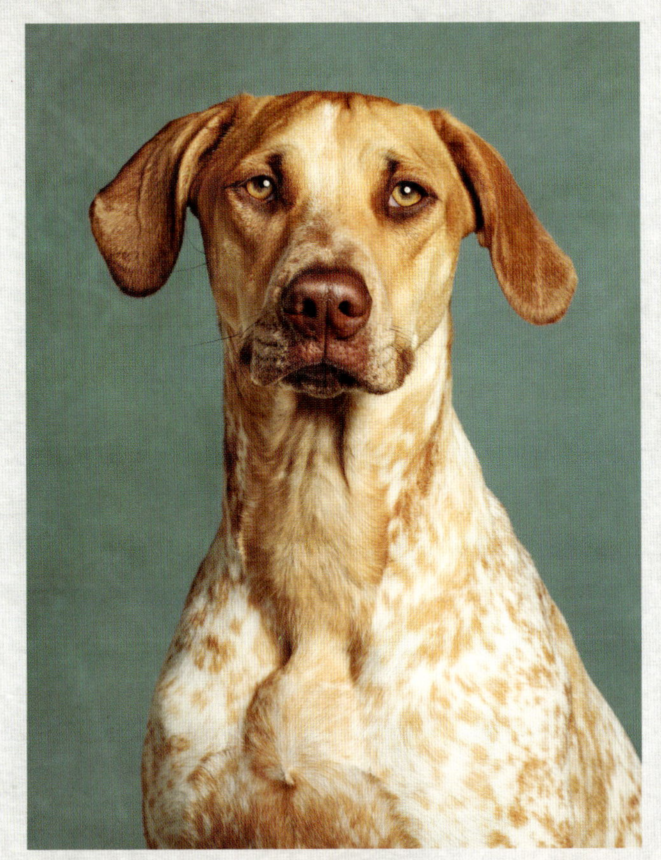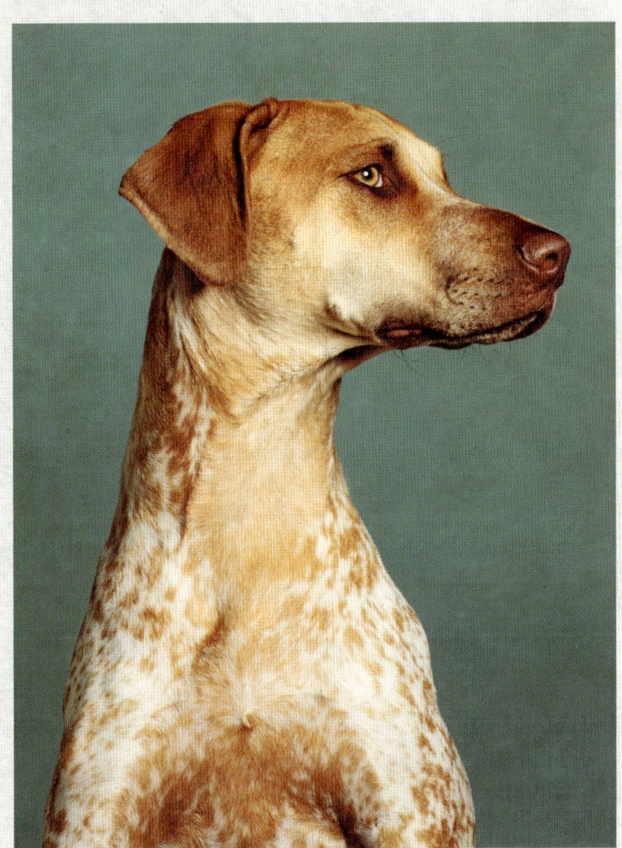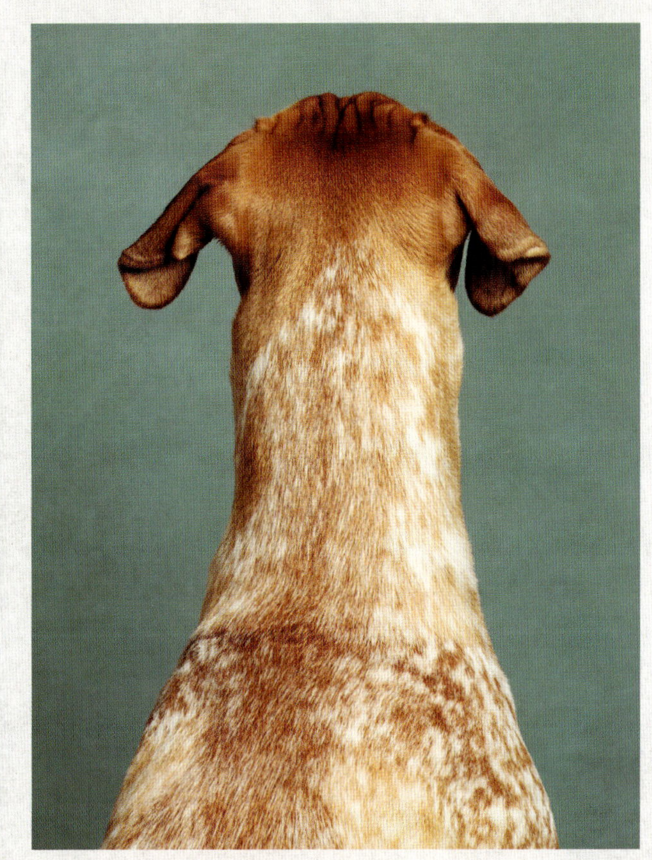

D, LUDO

ALIASES:	Ludes / Tiny Horse

BORN:	05/10/2016	**TRADE:**	Studio Dog	**BREED:**	Pointer Cross

BUILD:	Lanky	**EYES:**	Copper	**HEIGHT:**	71cm	**HAIR:**	Caramel / White

MARKS: Heart shaped patch on rear end

PECULIARITIES: Thinks he is a small dog

M.O: ETC. Is a gigantic sook and frequently vocalises his feelings. Is most commonly wearing a look of utter confusion.

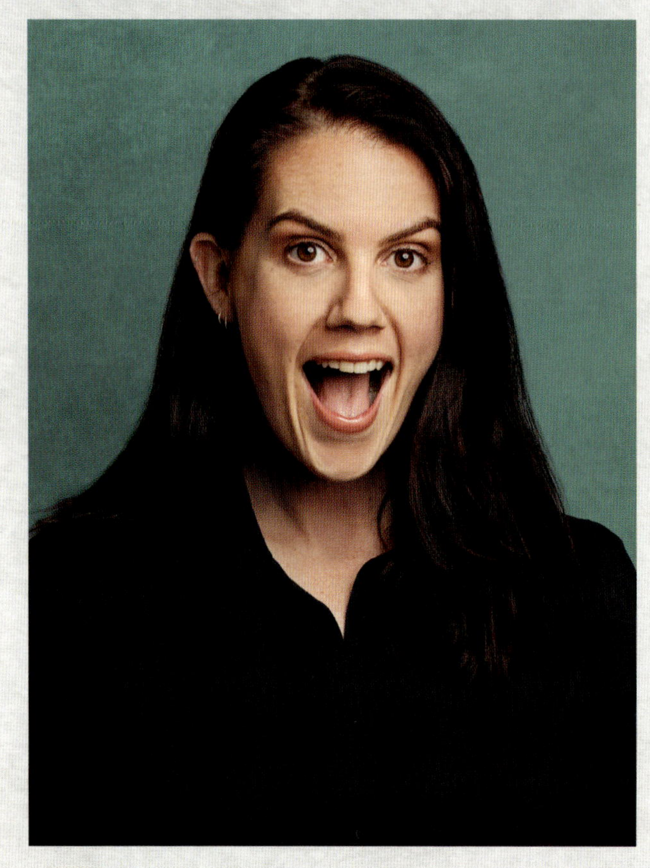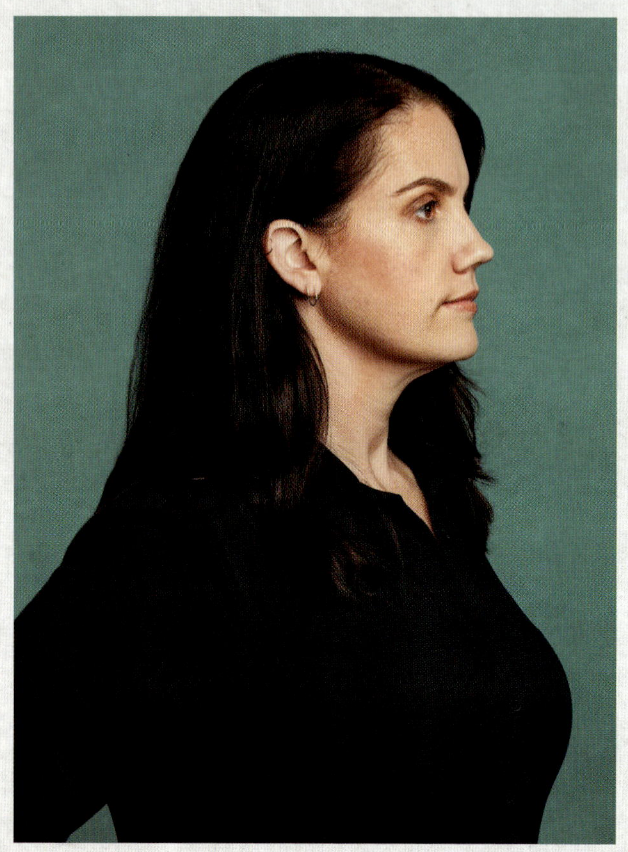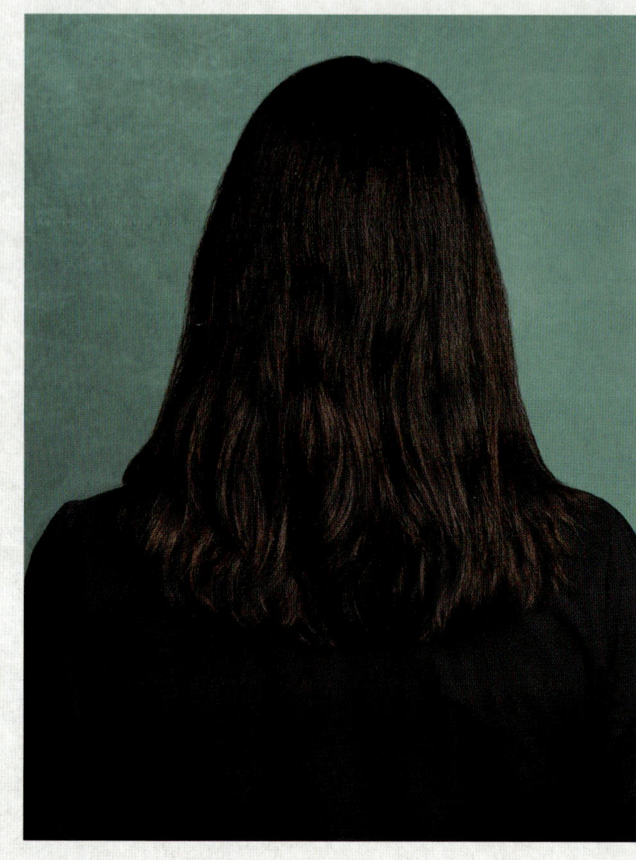

D, Lauren

ALIASES:	Loz / Lozzy / Lozzelcopter					

BORN:	04/1984	**TRADE:**	Photographer	**BREED:** Human		
BUILD:	Top Heavy	**EYES:**	Brown	**HEIGHT:** 176cm	**HAIR:**	Dark Brown

MARKS: Small scar on lower lip

PECULIARITIES: Was possibly a dog in a past life

M.O: ETC. Enjoys spending time taking photographs of animals in the studio and in the wild. Is frequently drooled on, chewed and covered in fur.

ACKNOWLEDGEMENTS

To all who graciously gave me your time and the pleasure of meeting your 'Mutts', I thank you for allowing me to capture their faces and hopefully their personalties and stories to share them with our fellow dog lovers. Without your participation and your enthusiasm this collection would not have been possible.

To my family who provided endless encouragement and excitement when I showed them new subjects.

To Jess Lomas and Michael Wilkinson at Wilkinson Publishing — thank you for taking a chance on me.

To Holly — unwavering in her support to me and my crazy ideas.

And finally to You, yes, You! You've made it all the way to the end and I do hope you enjoyed it.

Thank You.

Website: www.lozdalton.com

Instagram: @lozdphotos

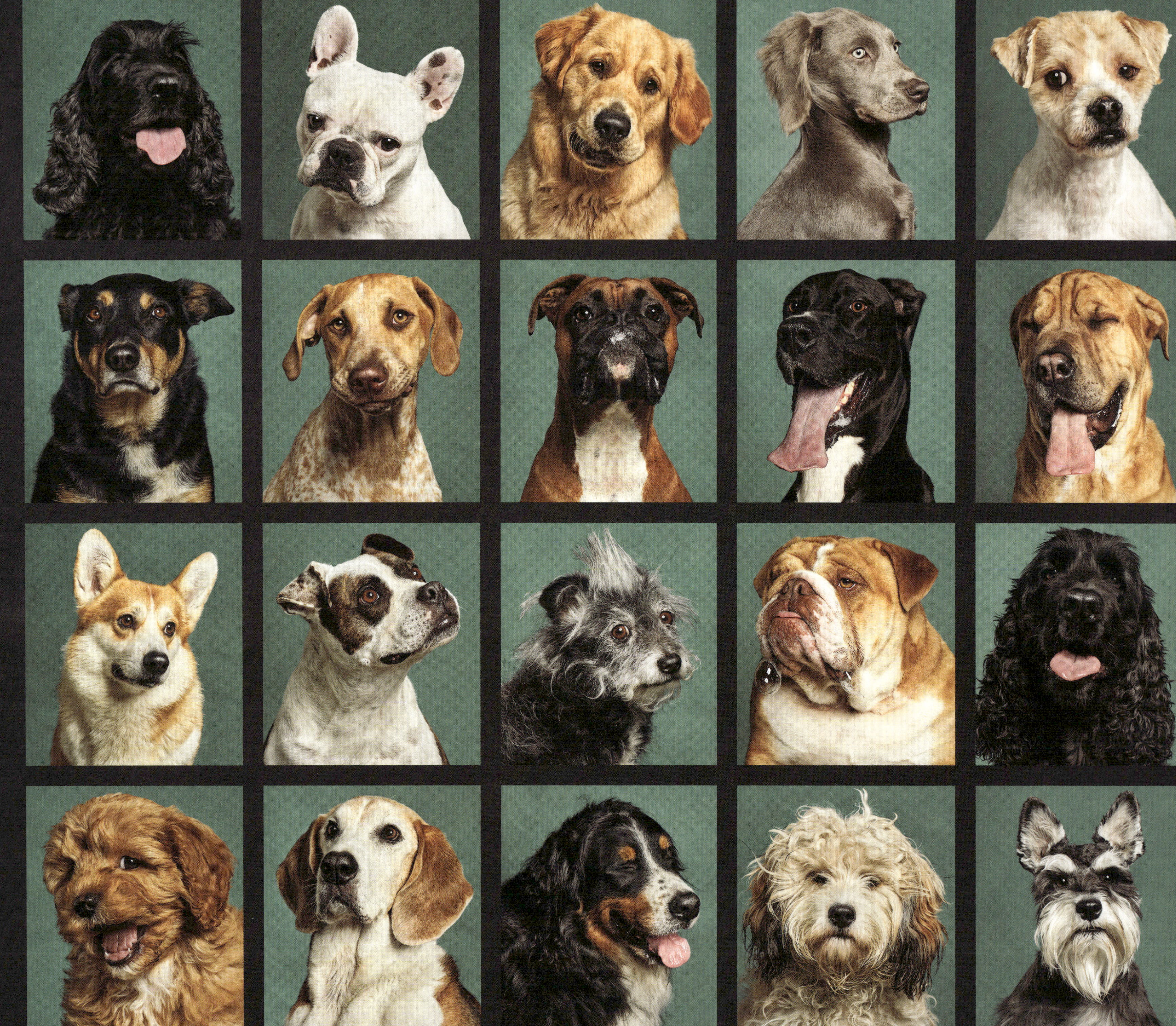